CW01208202

Of Men and Manners

Of Men and Manners

Essays Historical and Philosophical

by
ANTHONY QUINTON
edited by Anthony Kenny

OXFORD
UNIVERSITY PRESS

OXFORD
UNIVERSITY PRESS

Great Clarendon Street, Oxford OX2 6DP
Oxford University Press is a department of the University of Oxford.
It furthers the University's objective of excellence in research, scholarship,
and education by publishing worldwide in

Oxford New York

Auckland Cape Town Dar es Salaam Hong Kong Karachi
Kuala Lumpur Madrid Melbourne Mexico City Nairobi
New Delhi Shanghai Taipei Toronto

With offices in

Argentina Austria Brazil Chile Czech Republic France Greece
Guatemala Hungary Italy Japan Poland Portugal Singapore
South Korea Switzerland Thailand Turkey Ukraine Vietnam

Oxford is a registered trade mark of Oxford University Press
in the UK and in certain other countries

Published in the United States
by Oxford University Press Inc., New York

© in this volume the estate of Anthony Quinton 2011

The moral rights of the authors have been asserted
Database right Oxford University Press (maker)

First published 2011

All rights reserved. No part of this publication may be reproduced,
stored in a retrieval system, or transmitted, in any form or by any means,
without the prior permission in writing of Oxford University Press,
or as expressly permitted by law, or under terms agreed with the appropriate
reprographics rights organization. Enquiries concerning reproduction
outside the scope of the above should be sent to the Rights Department,
Oxford University Press, at the address above

You must not circulate this book in any other binding or cover
and you must impose this same condition on any acquirer

British Library Cataloguing in Publication Data
Data available

Library of Congress Cataloging in Publication Data
Data available

Typeset by SPI Publisher Services, Pondicherry, India
Printed in Great Britain
on acid-free paper by
MPG Books Group, Bodmin and King's Lynn

ISBN 978-0-19-969455-6

10 9 8 7 6 5 4 3 2 1

Foreword

During his lifetime Anthony Quinton published two volumes of collected papers, *Thoughts and Thinkers* (Duckworth 1982) and *From Wodehouse to Wittgenstein* (Carcanet 1998). The present volume offers a posthumous collection of previously unpublished or previously uncollected papers and addresses. I hope that it will illustrate, as the earlier volumes did, the enormous breadth of their author's encyclopedic knowledge, and the clarity, elegance, and urbanity of his style.

Essays 1, 9, 12, and 16 are taken from lecture scripts that so far as I can ascertain have not previously been published. Essays 2 and 22 were delivered as BBC talks. Essay 3 appeared in the *Journal of the Royal Society of Medicine*; essay 6 in the journal *Philosophy*; and essays 14, 15, and 21 in *Royal Institute of Philosophy Supplement* publications. Essays 4 and 7, on La Mettrie and Hegel, began life as book reviews in the *New York Review of Books*. Essay 8, on Richard Monckton Milnes, was a London Library lecture in 1991, published in *Founders and Followers* (1992). Essay 18 was a keynote address at an industrial forum. Essays 10 and 13 appeared in commemorative volumes on Dewey and Quine respectively. Essay 11 was the Introduction to Michael Roberts's *T. E. Hulme* (Carcanet Press, 1982). Essay 17 is an abbreviated version of a contribution to the series *Great Ideas Today*. Essays 19 and 20 were Cook Memorial Lectures at the University of St Andrews, published in Haldane (ed.), *Values, Education and the Human Word* (Imprint Academic, 2004). Essay 5, on Coleridge, is an edited version of a contribution to an Arts Council volume on *Writers' Houses*. I am grateful to the relevant authorities for permission to republish the papers already in print. I am especially grateful for the encouragement and assistance that Lady Quinton so enthusiastically offered while I was assembling this collection. I am indebted to Professor Geoffrey Sampson for compiling the index and removing numerous errors in proof.

I was greatly honoured when Tony Quinton asked me to be his literary executor. We have been lifelong friends since he supervised my Oxford graduate studies in 1959–61. But on important philosophical issues there were substantial differences between us, and for that reason I was particularly touched by the confidence he placed in me. No doubt he had in mind that throughout the fifty years we knew each other, I admired and shared his conviction that philosophy should be written in a manner that is intelligible to the non-professional reader.

A.K.

March 2011

Contents

Part I Of Men

1. Francis Bacon: How Was He Possible?	3
2. Spinoza	17
3. Dr John Radcliffe	21
4. La Mettrie	34
5. Coleridge at Home	40
6. The Trouble with Kant	49
7. Hegel Made Visible	60
8. Richard Monckton Milnes	68
9. T. H. Green	82
10. John Dewey's Theory of Knowledge	91
11. T. E. Hulme	103
12. Bergson and Whitehead: Process Philosophy	110
13. Quine on Doing Without Meaning	122
14. Ayer's Place in the History of Philosophy	137
15. The Rise, Fall, and Rise of Epistemology	153

Part II Of Manners

16. The Varieties of Value	165
17. The Human Animal	180
18. The Past and Future of Freedom	212
19. Culture, Education, and Values	219
20. A Revaluation of Values: Keeping Politics In Its Place	232
21. Morals and Politics	246
22. Words on Words	256

Select Bibliography of the Works of Anthony Quinton	265
Index	267

PART I
Of Men

1

Francis Bacon
How Was He Possible?

1. Francis Bacon in the History of Philosophy

As a figure in the history of philosophy Francis Bacon is doubly problematic. In the first place, he seems in most accounts to emerge from nowhere, to be without intellectual ancestors and intellectual debts. Secondly, although a recognized member of the general empirical tradition in British philosophy, and not without a long series of admirers for whom he fills an essentially symbolic role, he has no true followers and disciples.

The first of these problems will be my principal topic in this essay. It assumes its starkest form in histories of British philosophy considered on its own. There, two and a half centuries of almost complete inactivity seem to separate the Black Death from the publication of *The Advancement of Learning* in 1605. The Black Death is significant in the history of British philosophy for causing the deaths of William of Ockham, sheltering from papal wrath in Munich, and of Thomas Bradwardine, leader of the Mertonians and Ockham's passionate opponent. The only important British thinker in the later fourteenth century was John Wyclif. Earlier in his career he abandoned abstract philosophy for political and ecclesiastical controversy. The determination of the authorities to stamp out his subversive doctrines, continuing long after his death in 1384, had a generally repressive effect which must explain the intellectual infertility of fifteenth-century Britain.

In the early sixteenth century intellectual life in Britain revived in the circle of humanists whose chief ornament was Thomas More. These friends of Erasmus shared his indifference to philosophy strictly so called. More died for his refusal to endorse Henry VIII's decision to make himself supreme head of the English church. The religious disturbances that persisted well into the reign of Elizabeth continued to stifle original thought. The philosophy taught in the universities was conservative and Aristotelian.

Bacon exploded into this scene at the beginning of the seventeenth century in the most violent imaginable contrast to its stagnant repetition of past ways of thinking. *The Advancement of Learning* was his first properly philosophical publication. Unlike nearly all previous philosophical writing, it was written in English, in the same glittering, concretely imaginative style as his *Essays* whose first edition had come out eight years earlier. It surveyed the entire range of actual, and also possible, intellectual activity, suggesting new disciplines as well as finding a place for existing ones. On the negative side, it attacked the three prevailing styles of philosophy which he picked out as worthy of condemnation. Positively, it consisted of an unprecedentedly systematic outline of the kinds of knowledge and of the kinds of practice that could arise from that knowledge. These were all to be corrected, advanced, and, in some cases, inaugurated by the application of the method set out in detail in the *Novum Organum* fifteen years later. That method is conventionally taken to be Bacon's greatest original contribution to philosophy.

I shall suggest that this appearance of absolute originality in Bacon is an illusion. It results from confining attention to purely British sources for his ideas. But, despite his own practice, at least in his earlier years, Latin was the universal language of learning and Bacon, of course, could read and write it. If the net is cast a little wider in the sea of European thought than the small and somewhat stagnant creek occupied by Bacon's immediate British predecessors, a large array of lines of thinking can be hauled up which correspond to nearly all the main themes of Bacon's philosophy.

To do that is not, of course, to deny Bacon's very considerable originality. But his, like most other, works of human creation largely consist in the arrangement and emphatic deployment of materials fashioned by other hands. He himself insisted that, at its best, the advancement of learning, the growth of knowledge, is a cooperative undertaking. That cooperation is not exclusively synchronous. It extends also in the historical dimension. All original thinkers are engaged in intellectual commerce with their predecessors. Even in repudiating them they stage their refutations on a platform of common assumptions.

To show that it is not gratuitous to find the appearance of Bacon's absolute originality problematic, it may be helpful to follow a more or less Baconian or inductive procedure. There are several philosophers of the post-medieval period—a period in which individuality has always been valued and applauded—whose responsibility for giving a substantially new direction to the course of thought is in no way undermined by tracing the connections between their ideas and those of previous thinkers.

It would, I imagine, be a matter of common consent that the largest original contribution made to philosophy since Plato and Aristotle is that of Kant. But there is no doubt or obscurity about the nature, and the very large extent, of his philosophical affiliations. Brought up in the neatly systematized version of the philosophy of Leibniz that had been developed by Wolff, Kant was propelled in the construction of his Critical Philosophy by reading Hume. He was fully aware of this himself, describing Hume as the one who woke him from his dogmatic slumbers. To bring philosophers as disparate as Leibniz and Hume together—one for whom reason could do everything and one for whom reason could do very little indeed—was inevitably to generate an explosion of inconsistencies which could be reduced to the calm of coherence only by massive exclusions and adjustments. An entirely original conception of the powers of reason was arrived at, in between Leibniz's omnipotent penetrator of all truth and Hume's formal registrar of evident contradictions.

Kant's combination of the highest originality with dependence on previous thinkers has never been questioned. Descartes adopts a more Baconian posture, both by making little or no allusion to any sources of his thinking outside himself and by a congruously elegant and unacademic style of writing. Nevertheless his 'cogito ergo sum' is barely distinguishable from Augustine's 'si fallor sum', and Descartes's existence-proving definition of God as the possessor of all perfections is only a weaker version of Anselm's account of God as that than which nothing greater can be conceived. Descartes was right to believe that no one before him had so emphatically asserted the 'real distinction of mind and body'. The extremity of his dualism was evident in an intellectual atmosphere that was still to a large extent Aristotelian. All the same it had Platonic precedents which had been reanimated by a long line of Renaissance philosophers.

Locke—perhaps the most publicly influential thinker since Aristotle—owed a great deal of his fundamental thinking about the role of sense-impressions in knowledge to Gassendi. He owed some of it, as well as the framework of his political theory, to Hobbes, despite his embarrassed disavowals. He derived his moderate, rationalistic theology from Hooker and the Cambridge Platonists. In every history of philosophy Hegel is seen to emerge smoothly from Fichte and Schelling. Nietzsche rightly acknowledged Schopenhauer as an educator. Even the most flagrantly innovative of philosophers has an ancestry. Wittgenstein, for example, was initially inspired by Schopenhauer. His thinking acquired its characteristic initial direction from Frege and Bertrand Russell. An admiration for William James, human and literary rather than strictly philosophical, prepared him for receptiveness to the ideas of C. S. Peirce. That led on, in his later philosophy, to a conception of mind and language as essentially public and social which he shared with a legitimate intellectual descendant of Peirce, John Dewey. The convergence of their opinions, concealed under a total difference of style and, so to speak, social status, has been frequently pointed out, with gentle malice, by W. V. Quine.

The evidence of these particular examples, which could be augmented indefinitely, can be strengthened by a general argument. Wittgenstein somewhere remarked that if a lion were to speak to us we could not understand it. That is not because the lion, for geographical reasons, would speak Swahili. It is because the lion's mode of access and form of response to the world must be utterly different from our own.

Analogously a philosopher who came out with doctrines of which there had been no previous intimation would appear to be, and almost certainly would be, a charlatan. There have always been plenty of such desperately autonomous thinkers and we are right to pay them little attention. An idea will first appear in a tentative, parenthetical fashion before anyone envisages it as a serious possibility. Only when it has survived a measure of critical handling will it have established its claim to serious, systematic development. A philosopher is not a Zeus from whose head can spring a fully grown Athena of theory. Philosophy, as much as any other intellectual discipline, is a socially conducted tradition of discourse, a scene of gradual development, not a sequence of explosive novelties.

2. Bacon's Negative Criticism: False Philosophies and the Other Idols

The usual conception of Bacon's philosophy is derived from the two great works he published in his lifetime that are at once of straightforward intention and of articulate organization: *The Advancement of Learning* and the *Novum Organum*. The *De Sapientia Veterum*, a series of far-fetched, but intrinsically interesting, interpretations of classical fables, was much read in Bacon's own time but afterwards neglected. Recently Paolo Rossi has pointed out that it can be seen as a curiously, but not gratuitously, encoded way of expressing his views about a number of fundamental topics. The most important of these concern the nature of the physical world, but there are also opinions about the necessity of separating science and religion, about the need for method in the pursuit of knowledge and about realism in politics. Other smaller and equally neglected works, such as his early *Cogitationes de Natura Rerum*, written in 1607, convey the same, broadly atomistic, account of the underlying nature of the physical world. The extensive albums of purportedly factual materials, such as his *Sylva Sylvarum* and his books on the winds, on life and death, and on the dense and the rare, are only historical curiosities.

The two major works are both composed of critical and of constructive material. In the *Advancement of Learning* there is criticism of prevailing false philosophies. In the *Novum Organum* this reappears, with some adjustments, as part of his doctrine of the idols of the mind, along with causes of error in the general nature of the human mind, in individual propensities, and in language. On the constructive side the *Advancement of Learning* provides a systematic classification of the sciences; the *Novum Organum* a detailed account of the new method of eliminative induction.

The refutation of false philosophies, in each of the versions in which it is given, identifies three mistaken bodies of doctrine. That of the *Advancement of Learning* consists of the disputatious learning, in other words Aristotelian scholasticism; the delicate learning, rhetorical and dilettantish humanism, together with the kind of comprehensive scepticism to which it typically led; and the fantastic learning of cabbalists, alchemists and astrologers, students of magic and mystical correspondences. That of the *Novum Organum* associates the disputatious, or, as he now calls it, sophistic learning with two differently demarcated styles of thought. These are the empiric philosophy of Gilbert and the alchemists, and the superstitious philosophy which confuses religion and science so as to corrupt the first and to destroy the second.

In criticizing Aristotle Bacon is, of course, very far from being unique in his age. The philosophy of the Renaissance can be taken to begin with Gemistus Pletho. His comparison of Plato and Aristotle, very much to the advantage of the former, prepared the way for the Florentine Academy. More to the present point is the criticism of Aristotelian logic. That had been inaugurated by Laurentius Valla, continued by Nizolius, and had culminated in the work of Ramus. Ramus's dissertation for the degree of master of arts had defended the thesis that everything written by Aristotle is false. He went on, in writings of a less ritualized nature, to maintain that the logic of Aristotle is unnatural and pointlessly complicated.

In the works of the less cursory historians of philosophy Bacon does not emerge absolutely *ex nihilo*. Høffding, Sorley, and Copleston, for example, all mention a controversy in Cambridge in the 1580s, not long after the time of Bacon's residence there, between William Temple, an adherent of Ramus, and the orthodox Aristotelian, Everard Digby. All trace their knowledge of this fact to an article written in 1892 by a German scholar, J. Freudenthal. Bacon could have learnt about Ramus, although from a hostile point of view, through attendance at Digby's popular lectures. He could have had a more direct contact with Temple, whose edition of Ramus's *Dialectica* was the first book published by the university press at Cambridge, and who became a fellow of his college in 1576, shortly after Bacon left Cambridge. Bacon's mature doctrine does not agree with that of either of the disputants. Ramus came from a humanist tradition which set Cicero and an ideal of gentlemanly cultivation against the crabbed professionalism of Aristotle. Digby contended, against the Ramist Temple, that knowledge required inductive ascent from the particular to the universal, so that the engines of deduction should have some raw material to work on, but his idea of induction was Aristotle's not Bacon's.

Probably the most that can be said with confidence is that the atmosphere in which Bacon grew up was propitious for the criticism of Aristotle. His own very far-reaching criticism of the disputatious learning remitted deduction to the subsidiary task of organizing knowledge for expository purposes, not for acquiring it in the first place. His reason for that conviction was, consistently enough, inductive. Centuries of Aristotelian deduction had yielded no real fruit, no usable knowledge. It had simply reared a mountain of verbal distinctions on top of a handful of common-sense truths. Congruous with this way of criticizing mere disputation is Bacon's call, in the *Advancement of Learning*, for a history of the sciences, to supply a factual record from which conclusions about the conditions of its success could be inductively derived.

In Bacon's view, the knowledge that had transformed the circumstances of human life was embodied in the inventions of craftsmen, based on the observation and handling of material things, notable among them being Cardano's familiar trio: gunpowder, printing, and the navigator's compass. The repetitious frivolities of the schools were revealed in all their emptiness by the direct physical involvement of men with the material world. For him that was all the refutation that scholasticism required. To dispute dialectically with its exponents would be to concede the central point at issue. The validity of a mode of enquiry can be established only by its success in practice, not by logical reasoning alone. Rossi observes that very much this point of view is to be found in the writings of George Agricola, the founder of metallurgy, in the early sixteenth century. Agricola argues for close observation in person, rather than reliance on often fable-bearing testimony, and for clarity of language in recording it. Against the classical tradition of contempt for manual work as suitable only for slaves and mechanics, he defends it, in the active form of experiment and technology, as essential to science.

It is the same spirit of distrust of linguistic refinement for its own sake and of the uncritical reception of striking items of testimony that underlies Bacon's rejection of the delicate learning of the humanists and the fantastic learning of the occultists. The empirical and superstitious attitudes objected to in the *Novum Organum* raise some points of interest. The empirics and alchemists are associated in Bacon's critique with Gilbert, the theorist of magnetism. That fact, along with his rejection of Copernicus and his failure to mention Harvey, discoverer of the circulation of the blood, is often mentioned to his discredit. The self-proclaimed champion of natural science, it is said, failed to appreciate the major natural scientists of his own time.

Urbach has replied convincingly to these objections. So far as Gilbert is concerned, his *De Magnete* contains in its sixth and final chapter a long and ill-considered argument for the perfectly sound conclusion that the earth has a diurnal motion. Included in it is the thesis that the earth, since it is a magnet, has therefore been equipped by God with a purpose and a soul. That is directly opposed to Bacon's materialistic account of nature and his connected repudiation of final causes as a topic for science. Like the alchemists, in Bacon's view, Gilbert has leapt too precipitately to a very large conclusion from very limited investigations. In what he says about the earth's soul and purpose he has committed the further intellectual crime of mixing science and religion. It is this again which is the main fault in his eyes of those he describes as the superstitious, those who 'have with extreme levity indulged so far (in this vanity) as to attempt to found a system of natural philosophy on the first chapter of Genesis, or the book of Job and other parts of the sacred writings' (*Nov. Org.* aphorism 1xv).

The confusion of science and religion might seem to be something inflicted on Aristotle by the incorporation of his thought in a Christian philosophy in need of a theory of nature, rather than to be something practised by him. But Aristotle's God, as the prime mover, the final cause of all motion and, indeed, all change, is a clear instance of it. Bacon may have had his opposition to Aristotle fostered by much in the prevailing intellectual atmosphere and, in particular, by being exposed to Ramus while a young student at Cambridge. His insistence that science and religion must be kept absolutely distinct from each other, however, can most plausibly be accounted for by derivation, direct or indirect, from Ockham.

Human reason, for Ockham, including its intuitive power of apprehending individual things, is competent only to explore the realm of nature. The supernatural world, the realm of grace, is impenetrable to us as active enquirers. Our knowledge of it is provided by the divine gift of revelation. That and his view that abstract entities are constructions of the mind and have no real existence outside it are Ockham's fundamental doctrines. Ockham's school of productive followers did not last long in England. Roger Holcot died in 1349, as did Ockham himself; Adam Wodham in 1358. Only William Heytesbury the logician survived to become chancellor of Oxford in 1371. Ockham's ideas were most actively influential in Paris: first in the work of those premature Humeans, Jean de Mirecourt and Nicolas d'Autrecourt, then in the natural philosophy of Buridan and Oresme.

But there is reason to suppose that his doctrines were accessible to students long after his death. Oxford college libraries contain handsome printed editions of his works of the late fifteenth century. There are also interesting relics in the writings of English philosophers later than Bacon, in particular in Locke. At the beginning of the discussion of abstract ideas in his *Essay on Human Understanding* he asserts, as if it were beyond question and in defiance of by far the greater part of tradition, 'everything that exists is particular'. Also it has always been puzzling that Locke should have denied the independent reality of relations. They are not, he says, 'contained in the real existence of things, but [are] something extraneous and superinduced'. Because of that view he tries to analyse all relations into qualities of their terms. He takes causation, for example, to reduce to an active power in the cause and a passive power, or susceptibility, in the effect. This comes directly from an argument of Ockham's that if relations were real features of the world it would absurdly follow that every time I move my little finger the infinite number of spatial relationships between that finger and everything else in the world would change and so I should bring about an infinite number of changes in reality. The persistence of Ockham's ideas is even more evident in Hobbes. So it is reasonable to suppose that Bacon was aware of a precedent for his principle of the separation of science and religion. It is not necessary to go on to suppose that Ockham's and Bacon's purposes were the same. Ockham anticipated Kant in limiting reason to make room for faith. Bacon seems to be engaged in the complementary opposite of that: sequestering faith in order to set reason free.

The other important, negatively critical part of Bacon's thought is the theory of idols. The refutation of false philosophies is the fourth and final element of the theory. Labelled the idols of the theatre, it follows the idols of the tribe, the cave, and the marketplace. His account of the idols of the tribe, of the tendency of the human mind in general to error, has some affinity to the kind of scepticism that prevailed in Bacon's age. It had been encouraged by the recovery of the works of Sextus Empiricus. Having been virtually unknown in the Middle Ages, these had been published in Latin, in part in 1562, the year after Bacon's birth, and in full seven years later.

Bacon was not a sceptic, at least in any radical sense. He regarded thoroughgoing scepticism as exaggerated and frivolous. But he thought scepticism therapeutically valuable in moderate doses. He was fully aware that the senses are unreliable. But he thought that could be remedied by cautiously attentive observation and with the assistance of instruments. Greek scepticism had been essentially objective. The senses mislead us because of unsatisfactory conditions of observation. Reason misleads us because of its need for premises it cannot itself supply and because of the inescapable circularity of deduction. Bacon's idols of the tribe are of a more emotional, subjective sort: a desire for order and regularity that leads us to suppose that there is more of it than there actually is, a parental fondness for our own theories that leads us to ignore disconfirmations and to protect them from criticism by various questionable devices. The idols of the cave, the personal biases of particular individuals, are, naturally, even more subjective.

In his account of the emotional and subjective sources of error, then, Bacon gives an original slant to the widespread scepticism of the age. His *Essays*, both in their content and their title, show his dependence on Montaigne and, at a further remove, on Erasmus's *Encomium Moriae*.

Finally, there are the idols of the marketplace. These are the errors generated by language, by the unconscious acceptance of theories that is caused by words. Some words, such as 'fortune' or 'prime mover', are simply fictional and refer to nothing real. Others, arrived at by 'unskilful abstraction', classify things on the basis of superficial and unimportant likenesses. In doing so they fail to take account of important underlying differences. A familiar example is the use of the word 'fish' to cover all creatures that mainly live in the water, which mistakenly runs together herrings and whales.

Bacon's view here falls in with a persisting English tradition. It stretches back beyond Ockham, its most distinguished member, to Bacon's namesake, Roger Bacon. He listed four 'hindrances to the understanding of truth' which have more than their number in common with Francis Bacon's idols. It continues after him through Hobbes, Locke, and Bentham to the linguistic philosophy of recent times. It may owe something to the peculiar qualities of the English language, an inextricable mixture of Teutonic and Romance ingredients and notable for its absence of inflection and its richness of idiom.

3. Bacon's Theory of Natural Knowledge

Bacon's theory of natural knowledge is his distinctive contribution to philosophy according to convention. It is not a judgement I should dispute, although I think that his theory has been too much identified with one of its parts: the formal procedure of eliminative induction by the use of his celebrated tables. I suspect that this excess of attention is due to the fact that the doctrine of the tables is much more pedagogically usable than most of Bacon's writing. It approximates to the ideal of a textbook and provides material for exercises. It is thus unlike most of his writing, which is rhetorical and suggestive, any underlying skeleton of argument being concealed by literary ornamentation.

His account of natural knowledge can be distilled into eight main theses, themselves falling into two groups. Five of them concern the intellectual core of the scientific process. The three that remain concern its social, external aspects.

1. Knowledge of nature must be based on observation by the senses.
2. The senses must be assisted and corrected by instruments and the use of experiment.

3. The laws of nature must be derived from extensive and varied records of critically sifted observation by the procedure of eliminative induction.
4. Induction must proceed by gradual ascent from the directly apparent surface of nature, to the forms.
5. Firmly separated from religion, science must search for efficient and, in the sense of the fourth thesis, formal causes, but not for final causes.

The theses about the social and external aspects of science are

6. that it must be conducted cooperatively,
7. that it is cumulative and progressive, and
8. that it is for use, for 'the relief of man's estate', and not for merely contemplative enjoyment.

The first thesis, that science must be founded on careful and extensive observation, is implicit in Ockham's theory of our knowledge of individual things. Called intuition, it must precede any reasoning about general ideas, which have to be derived from our acquaintance with individuals. But observationalism is much more explicit in the work of Telesio. Bacon was familiar with his writings, and in some respects critical of them. Nevertheless he described Telesio as 'the first of the moderns'.

Against the Aristotelian doctrine that matter is merely potential, Telesio maintained that it is a concrete actuality, although passive and inert. It can be perceived by the senses from which all knowledge must be derived. Observations are stored in the memory and allow for the anticipation by analogy of what has not yet been observed. Vives had earlier stressed the importance of observation, but principally as applied to the life of the mind. In Telesio it is observation of the physical world that is taken to be fundamental.

Despite his laudatory label for Telesio and agreement with his observationalism, Bacon criticized him forcefully. He objected to Telesio's amorphously speculative thesis that two large principles, of heat and of cold, are responsible for all that happens in nature. That is a conspicuous departure from the gradual ascent on which Bacon insisted. Also deficient, in Bacon's view, was what he described as the pastoral character of Telesio's philosophy, its indifference to the practical uses to which natural knowledge can be put. But a substantial area of agreement remains. No one before Bacon had given such a definitive form as Telesio had to Ockham's doctrine of intuitive knowledge. One feature of Telesio's philosophy Bacon would not approve is its instrumentalist conception of natural knowledge as providing, not an insight into the inner nature of physical things, but analogical anticipations of the course of future or possible experience.

Bacon's second thesis is to be found clearly expressed in George Agricola. He held that only by the close observation, actual handling, and clear description of material things can reliable knowledge of nature be secured. Bacon had read Agricola, according to Paolo Rossi. But probably the main source for Bacon's second thesis was his own induction from those investigations of his age which had actually borne fruit. Further back in time there is the influence of Roger Bacon to be taken into account. Although he put forward the idea within a hermetic framework, he took natural knowledge as something to be acquired by experiment, by operations on and interaction with natural objects, and not by merely contemplative observation alone.

The third thesis, that the laws of nature must be arrived at by eliminative induction, using the tables of presence, absence, and degrees, is often seen by those well-disposed to Bacon as having something of the same status as Aristotle's doctrine of the syllogism. In one swift movement, it appears, an array of unreflective practices was made explicit and ordered into a system. At any rate it has remained authoritative since its creation. It was given renewed life through its rather exact transcription by Mill, and has subsequently formed part of comprehensive logic textbooks of an old-fashioned kind. The common practice of calling Bacon's tables 'Mill's methods' abets Mill's historically misleading concealment of his debt to Bacon.

But if Mill is indebted to Bacon, Bacon is also an inheritor. There are the first intimations of the need for methodical comparison of instances as far back as Robert Grosseteste. In Duns Scotus there is a first, but definite, sketch of the method of agreement (Bacon's table of presence) and in Ockham a similar sketch of the method of difference (Bacon's table of absence). As British philosophers Scotus and Ockham may have been accessible and have appealed to Bacon. Both were critical of the Thomist project of incorporating the largely secular philosophy of Aristotle into Christian theology. That did not make them anti-Aristotelians in natural philosophy. But it led them to oppose the followers of Aristotle who ignored the admittedly modest attention he had accorded to induction. Aristotle himself at least affirmed some connection between the first principles of science and experience. His disciples in the High Middle Ages tended to take them on trust, either as self-evident or as items of traditional common knowledge. The formal rigour with which Scotus and Ockham had become familiar through their logical studies, applied to the inductive aspect of the search for knowledge, may well have supplied Bacon with an example.

Bacon's support of eliminative against enumerative induction was also anticipated by Grosseteste, in a particular argument about the sun's propagation of heat, and by Buridan, in an argument about the motion of a projectile. Both were aware of the distinctiveness and importance of falsification, but no one before Bacon made the 'major force of the negative instance' such a central and explicitly general principle. It is ironical that Popper should have regarded Bacon, who is close to him in many ways, as the paladin of simple enumeration.

Bacon's fourth thesis, the doctrine of gradual ascent, seems original to him. But an indirect source for it can be found in his high opinion of the achievements of craftsmen, mechanics, and inventors, as compared with cloistered and over-precipitate speculators. The doctrine of gradual ascent, like other aspects of his method, is based on an inductive generalization about the necessary conditions for the successful pursuit of natural knowledge. Its primary target is the tendency of theorists to generalize too comprehensively on too narrow a basis of evidence. It also draws strength from his realistic, or anti-instrumentalist, insistence on the insufficiency of laws that concern only the straightforwardly observable surface features of the world. These need to be supplemented by laws about the fine structure of matter, the forms, or simple natures, of the particles of which ordinary things are composed.

The study of superficial causes, material and efficient, Bacon calls physics. The corresponding practice or art that it makes possible he calls mechanics, in effect craftsmanship. Metaphysics as he understands it, distinguishing it from *philosophia prima* and, of course, from theology, makes possible what he calls natural magic. This choice of phrase has misled Bacon's interpreters into supposing him to be some kind of occultist. What he actually had in mind is the kind of technology which uses an understanding of the fine structure of physical things to bring about really radical changes in them. It was on this, and not on a surface empiricism, that he rested his hopes for a far-reaching improvement of the human condition. It was a reasonable anticipation of nineteenth-century chemistry. He arrived at it by combining his own version of the atomism of Democritus and Epicurus with his conviction of the empirical basis and technical utility of natural knowledge.

I can move on to the three social and external theses, as I have called them, since the fifth thesis about the essential distinctness of science and religion has already been considered. These are much the more original part of Bacon's contribution to the philosophy of science. But they have precedents. George Agricola and, as Rossi points out, the potter Bernard Palissy firmly agreed with his final thesis about the utility of science, as, among philosophers proper, did Cardano. His sixth thesis, that it should be cooperative, imaginatively embodied in the *New Atlantis*, had been advanced with some elaboration in the thirteenth century by Roger Bacon. His seventh thesis, that it is cumulative and progressive, not just a recycling of established truths, has no very obvious earlier exponent. It is significant that the historian of progress, J. B. Bury, begins his story with Bacon (and also, in a different dimension, Jean Bodin).

That is not surprising so far as the post-classical world is concerned. Even if only the earliest Christians seriously expected the end of the world in their own lifetime, the notion that the entire terrestrial drama will eventually be wound up by its divine impresario has always been an integral part of Christian belief. Together with the doctrine of the fall of man it is hardly encouraging to the theory of progress. Bacon's uncomplicated enthusiasm for progress, conceived in exclusively earthly terms, may throw some light on the depth of his professed commitment to the religion he was so anxious to wall off from science. It should, however, be added that the indisputably devout Pascal, writing twenty years after Bacon's death, was quite unequivocal about the cumulative and progressive nature of science, contrasting it in this respect with theology as ardently as Bacon.

The classification of the sciences, which is the main topic of the *Advancement of Learning*, and its enlarged version, the *De Augmentis*, is an important procedural supplement to the substantive account Bacon gives of natural knowledge. It falls within a long tradition which began with the example of Aristotle's encyclopedic range of writings and with his explicit distinction, and further subdivision, of theoretical, practical, and productive sciences. A remark in his *Topics*, distinguishing propositions as ethical, physical, and logical, was made the basis of a division of sciences under these heads by Stoics and Epicureans. In the Middle Ages the system of seven liberal arts and three philosophies (natural, metaphysical, and moral) prevailed. Certainly with Bacon a new era in the history of this kind of classification begins. Reflecting the enthusiasm and initiative of the liberated enquirers of his time, he devised a system incomparably more detailed and penetrating than anything that had preceded it. The particular stimulus was his lively sense of what was actually going on and his lack of respect for established intellectual authority.

4. Bacon's Theories of Nature and Mind

The conventional view of Bacon sees him as essentially a methodologist and, more generally, as a prophet or propagandist of natural science. Critics have seized on his own admission that he had established only the preliminaries of his 'Great Instauration'. Its sixth and final part, 'the new philosophy or active science', the application of his method to the data, much in need of augmentation, which he had assembled, remained to be carried out by others. The critics' position is strengthened by Bacon's apparent incomprehension of the genuine scientific progress of his own age. But Bacon's faults in this respect are, as I mentioned earlier, less culpable than they are supposed to be. In particular, I drew attention to Urbach's point that Bacon praised Gilbert's work on magnetism, and attacked only his concluding speculations about the soul and purpose with which God had endowed the world by making it into a magnet. Bacon opposed Copernicus because of the interpretation of his heliocentrism as a calculating device. And he was, chronologically, in no position to know of Harvey's work on the circulation of the blood: it was not published until after Bacon's death.

Bacon's illustrative application of his method to the example of heat shows him to have been too modest in his estimate of his own achievements. In taking heat to be a type of motion he rightly rejected the ancient theory of fire atoms which persisted long after his own time in the form of the theory of heat as caloric, a fire-constituting fluid. Bacon's conclusion was substantially correct, but it was not generally recognized to be so until some two centuries after his death.

The distinction Bacon draws between physics and metaphysics, between comparatively superficial explanations in terms of what can be directly observed and more fundamental explanations in terms of underlying structure, presupposes the truth of theoretical realism, the doctrine that there is more to nature than meets the unassisted eye. In Bacon's version theoretical realism assumed its most familiar form: atomism. To reject the idea that what ultimately constitutes nature is a continuous, relatively fluid stuff is not to embrace a particular view of the nature of the atoms: whether they are all identical or whether they differ in shape or size or other intrinsic properties. Nor is it necessarily to conclude that the atoms are, or are not, separated from each other by empty space. Bacon, always ill at ease with the vacuum, thought that the expansion and contraction of matter could be accounted for by the incorporation in or the extrusion from bodies of relatively fine atoms.

Perhaps as early as 1604, in his *Cogitationes de Natura Rerum*, Bacon had praised Democritus in general terms for his atomism. But he dissented from Democritus's view that the variety of nature is to be explained by reference to the different shapes of atoms. Always doubtful about the vacuum, late in life he came down definitely against it. Nevertheless he always remained some kind of atomist. In the examination of the myth of Cupid, in his *De Sapientia Veterum*, he reaffirms it as the hidden content of a piece of ancient wisdom.

More important than his difference with Democritus about the shape of atoms is his account of the cause of motion. Democritus left the origin of motion unexplained. Epicurus ascribed a natural downward motion to atoms, modified by his celebrated swerve. Bacon maintained that motion is intrinsic to matter. It was not imparted to the physical world either by an Aristotelian God, drawing all things towards it teleologically, or by a Newtonian God, setting the whole machine going with an initial push. That idea is so clearly expressed in Telesio as to make it exceedingly likely that Bacon got it from him. It is entirely appropriate to his doctrine of the separation of science from religion.

I suggested earlier that Bacon was influenced by Telesio in combining empiricism with materialism. Telesio had held that matter is not an Aristotelian potentiality, but an actual, even if passive, constituent of the real world. Aristotle's metaphysically extreme, quasi-atomist doctrine of minima represented them as merely potential, that is to say, as the limits of the furthest theoretically possible process of division. In Averroës atoms are conceived as actually and physically indivisible entities and it is to that kind of atomism to which Bacon subscribed. It had been affirmed earlier in Renaissance by the Averroist Agostino Nifo and, at a greater remove from Averroës, by Scaliger.

Bacon gave little attention to the philosophy of mind. It is accommodated rather perfunctorily in its place in his classification of the sciences. He distinguishes two broad natural sciences of mind, logic and ethics, both very broadly conceived. They deal with the two great fields of mental activity, the exercises of the intellect and of the will. But in addition to these faculties there is the soul itself to be considered. Bacon's view is that the soul itself is not part of nature since it is literally inspired or breathed into human beings by God. It is thus not subject to the laws of nature and not a proper object of inductive study.

That is not a very coherent position. If the soul is not part of nature then its operations must be understood to have a supernatural cause and so they too are beyond the reach of inductive enquiry. Bacon's view may be a somewhat confused relic of another doctrine of Telesio's. He had held that, as well as spirit, present in both men and animals, of a material, even if very refined, composition, and responsible for sensation and for the reasoning that it based on it, human beings have also a *forma* or *mens superaddita*, which is wholly immaterial and immortal. Spirit is motivated by the instinct of self-preservation; the higher *forma superaddita* is pointed towards God. This theory satisfies the requirements of orthodoxy while keeping science and religion apart. By turning Telesio's two souls into the soul considered in itself and the soul's operations Bacon tried to pursue the same ends, but less successfully.

In this survey of the possible sources of Bacon's leading ideas the chief contributors I have identified are William of Ockham and Bernardino Telesio. It is clear that Bacon had read Telesio. The criticisms he advances of Telesio are forceful but limited in scope, specifically to Telesio's over-speculative reliance on his principles of heat and cold. But Bacon followed Telesio closely in his empiricism and his materialism and also in his account of the soul.

The main problem with the idea that Bacon was influenced by Ockham is to trace the connection. The fact that there are some very close affinities of doctrine, and even of wording, between Ockham and Locke, who was born several years after Bacon's death, suggests that Ockham's ideas survived as part of the normal university course of instruction.

Ockham and Telesio are also very notably echoed in Hobbes, whose account of motivation is very much like Telesio's. But after Hobbes, with Locke and his successors, empiricism in Britain abandoned the materialism with which it had been originally associated for conceptions of nature which enforced the assumption that all we know directly is our own sense-impressions. That was an inheritance from the kind of radical scepticism Bacon rejected, and also from Descartes. Locke still thought that there really are material things and speculated that God might have chosen to attach the power of thinking to a material substance. But the assumption that the only certain knowledge is self-knowledge led inexorably to the subjectivist extravagances of Berkeley, Hume, and Mill and, in our own time, of Russell and Ayer. In connecting Bacon to Ockham I mean to do him honour, by affiliating him legitimately to the philosopher I suspect of being the greatest of British empiricists.

2
Spinoza

Of all the great philosophers of the Western world there is none who is more perfectly and intensely philosophical, in the ordinary understanding of that word, than Spinoza. In comparison with him, Plato, with his poetic eloquence and his worldly involvements, is rather a great imaginative writer on philosophical themes; Aristotle, with his encyclopedic range of detail and his passion for minute distinctions, is more of a scientist; while Kant, with his university post, his regular habits, and the crabbed technicality of his writing, is more the ideal of a philosophy professor than of a philosopher proper.

There are three things which people in general expect of an ideal philosopher and they are all present, and very conspicuously present, in Spinoza: an appropriate style of life, a readiness to make the largest and most comprehensive claims, and the presentation of guidance about how men should live and how they should organize society.

Spinoza lived with the utmost simplicity, supporting himself, at a very modest level of comfort, with the trade of grinding optical lenses. He was a completely private, individual person, attached to no party or institution or even organized social group, and without wife or children.

Secondly, there are two ways in which Spinoza's philosophical system exhibits to the highest degree qualities that such systems are popularly supposed to possess. It was absolutely comprehensive in its scope, covering God, Nature, Man, both as a thinker and an agent, and Society. Furthermore, it was presented, in Spinoza's phrase, 'in a geometrical manner', as a sequence of exact logical deductions from definitions and first principles that he held to be self-evident to human reason. As a result there is nothing merely persuasive, let alone suggestive, about Spinoza's writing. He puts his views forward as absolutely and demonstratively certain, as proved beyond the possibility of doubt. So, both in scope and certainty, Spinoza set himself the highest possible standards of philosophical achievement.

Thirdly, Spinoza's philosophy does not aim to provide only understanding of the nature of the world we live in, but derives directly from that understanding conclusions about how life should be lived. In this doctrine about the ideal mode of human life the philosophical understanding of the world plays an essential part, for the truly free man, according to Spinoza, is the man who has achieved a proper philosophical comprehension of the nature of the world and of man's place in it. Finally, in the conduct of his own life, Spinoza conformed fully to the principles of conduct that he had deduced for men in general. Kierkegaard once said that the builders of philosophical systems seemed to him like men who built magnificent palaces, but, once they were built, continued to live in miserable hovels somewhere outside them. To no philosophical system-builder is this rule less applicable than to Spinoza.

In everyday speech to be philosophical is to accept the hazards and injuries of fate dispassionately and without despair. Spinoza was committed both in theory and practice to being philosophical in this sense.

The impotence of man to govern or restrain the emotions I call bondage, for a man who is under their control is not his own master, but is mastered by fortune, in whose power he is, so that he is often forced to follow the worst although he sees the better before him.

Spinoza was born in 1632 in Amsterdam in a family of Jews who had come to Holland a generation or more before his birth from Portugal, where they had been forced to conform outwardly to Christianity. In the seventeenth century Holland was the great refuge for the victims of religious and political oppression in Europe, having not long before won its own independence from the authoritarian and imperial rule of Catholic Spain. Descartes, Locke, and many others in that age used it as a place to which to escape from the dangers of persecution.

Spinoza soon showed his intellectual powers in the intense but narrow studies, of the Old Testament, the Talmud, and the Jewish philosophers, on which his community laid great stress, and proficiency in which was an indispensable qualification for a leading position in that community. He laid one important foundation for intellectual independence of any particular social bond by mastering a large variety of languages, so that he could live where he chose and read what he chose.

In his early twenties he was reported to the elders of his community for the heretical views he had arrived at about the proper interpretation of the Bible. In particular he had noticed that there is no clear affirmation in the Old Testament of the doctrine of personal immortality. He concluded that the soul is not something quite distinct from the body and capable of outliving it, but, as Aristotle had held, that it is simply the life or vitality of the body. These deviations from orthodoxy caused a special degree of alarm because of Spinoza's brilliant intellectual promise and the social prominence of his family. First he was offered a sum of 1,000 florins to keep his ideas to himself. But, displaying a pattern of personal honour that was to recur several times in his short life, he refused. So, with ceremonial of terrible solemnity, he was excommunicated and made an outcast. An attempt to assassinate him was even made one night when he was leaving a theatre. By the time he was formally banished he had already left, first for a village near Leyden and then to another near the Hague where he spent the remainder of his life, which ended in 1677 when he was 44 years old.

In the twenty years that were left to him he was not wholly isolated. He had a circle of friends and of rather more distinguished correspondents with whom he could discuss his ideas. One young friend and pupil tried to leave him a substantial sum of money but Spinoza insisted on returning it to the friend's family, and, when they tried to get him to take at least a small annuity, would accept only about half of what they offered. Four years before his death he had become famous enough (although his masterpiece, the *Ethics*, could not be published until after his death) for the German prince in whose domain the university of Heidelberg lay to offer him a professorship there. But Spinoza courteously refused on the grounds that such a post would compromise his independence. Spinoza died of tuberculosis, probably aggravated by the glass-dust he inhaled in his work of lens-grinding. He met death calmly and in accordance with his own principles. As he said:

A free man thinks of nothing less than of death. His wisdom is a meditation not of death, but of life.

Spinoza's most original, fundamental, and, in the eyes of his contemporaries, most shocking idea was that God and Nature, the creator and his creation, are not distinct things, but are one and the same. This pantheist doctrine had been anticipated by some ancient Greek thinkers and it is to be found in much Oriental thought. But the all-encompassing influence of Christianity had made it unacceptable to the European mind for more than a thousand years. For Spinoza the creator and his creation were not separate things but one single thing, viewed from different sides.

He arrived at this conclusion by a chain of argument derived from the traditional philosopher's notion of substance as that which exists independently or self-sufficiently. He maintained that there could only be one single truly self-sufficient, self-explanatory thing and that is reality as a whole, to which he gave the name God or Nature. In its aspect as God this one true substance is an infinite, all-inclusive mind; in its aspect as nature it is the entire material world, extended in space. Two important conclusions about the nature of man followed immediately from this first principle. The first is that man is not an immortal, self-subsistent soul but rather a temporary conjunction of a small group of the infinitely numerous ideas that make up the infinite mind of God. Spinoza allowed for the personal survival of death only in the most attenuated way: the God of whose ideas a particular man is only a minute and temporary part, like a fold in a piece of cloth, would continue to exist when he had gone, when the cloth was straightened out.

The second conclusion is that in man, as in reality as a whole, mind and body are everywhere correlated. To every part of reality, conceived as material and in space, in other words to every physical thing, there corresponds an idea of that thing. Where the thing in question is a human body the corresponding idea is a human, self-conscious, mind. Once again it clearly follows that human individuals cannot be supposed to survive the deaths of their bodies.

Although every particular thing is only a dependent part of the whole it naturally endeavours to maintain itself in existence, and it does so to the extent that it preserves itself from the destructive influence of other things. In man this preservation of the self is essentially a matter of controlling and suppressing passion, which is an effect produced by other things on him, and exalting reason in which he is most self-determined and most like God. He wrote:

> After experience had taught me that the things which commonly take place in ordinary life are vain and futile, when I saw that all the things which cause me fear and anxiety had nothing good or bad in them save in so far as the mind was affected by them, I determined at last to inquire whether there might be anything which might be truly good. . . . The things which most often happened in life and are esteemed by men as the highest good of all, as may be gathered from their words, may be reduced to three headings: riches, fame and pleasure. As for pleasure, the mind is so engrossed in it that it remains in a state of quiescence as if it had obtained supreme good and this prevents it from thinking of anything else. But after that enjoyment follows sadness. The pursuit of fame and riches also distracts the mind . . . But the love turned on things eternal and infinite alone feeds the mind with pure joy and it is free from all sorrow, so it is much to be desired and to be sought with all our might.

What Spinoza refers to in that passage as 'love turned on things eternal and infinite' is what he also calls, in a famous phrase, 'the intellectual love of God'. In unreflective everyday life we rely on inadequate, sensory knowledge of brute fact, we are driven in action by particular passions which give only passing satisfaction and hold us in bondage to the things that inspire those passions. The truly philosophical man not only secures an understanding of the nature of the world and of his place in it but also secures the most lasting satisfaction from that understanding and, in so doing, liberates himself from enslaving subordination to the attraction of other particular things and from the hazards of fortune. A true knowledge of the world, by explaining how what is the case must necessarily be so, is the only secure source of both happiness and freedom.

By his contemporaries and successors Spinoza was regarded as an outrageous and subversive atheist. The liberal thinkers of the eighteenth century, to whom his insistence on freedom and reason might have appealed, were repelled by the scholastic complexity of his style of thought. It was the German romantics of the early nineteenth century who first accorded him real respect, one of them describing him, not at all as an atheist, but as a 'God-intoxicated man'. There is truth in both interpretations: Spinoza's God is not the distinct, personal God of ordinary Christianity, but there can be no doubt of the sincerity of the religious emotions he aroused in Spinoza. In our own age, as in the age of Voltaire, sympathy with the content of Spinoza's philosophy is overridden by scepticism about his methods of reasoning. He remains a hero for Marxists who applaud his insistence on the universal correlation of mind with matter, although they add a principle of the dependence of mind on matter which is quite foreign to him. But even those who think him mistaken do not deny the honesty and splendid ambition of his thought or the stoical nobility of his character.

3

Dr John Radcliffe

No human being is more amply commemorated in the buildings of Oxford than Dr John Radcliffe. Colleges and churches draw their names from the divinities of the Christian pantheon: from the Trinity itself and Jesus, down through St Mary, Christ's body, and St John, to such marginally supernatural individuals as St Mary Magdalen and the faithful dead of All Souls. Their names often recur, but among strictly terrestrial personages the general rule is that there should be only one major edifice each. John Balliol, Walter de Merton, Nicholas and Dorothy Wadham, the 3rd Earl of Pembroke, the Revd John Keble, and Sir Isaac Wolfson comply with it. Until the great benefactions of Lord Nuffield received physical embodiment, the solitary exception was Dr John Radcliffe.

Even now Radcliffe stands alone in the splendour and multitudinousness of his gifts. There are the Radcliffe Camera and the square rightly named after it, in view of its dominant position there; there is the Infirmary and its large offspring, John Radcliffe II in Headington; there is the Radcliffe Science Library, another result of productive fission; there is the Observatory, nucleus of Green College, the sponsor of this lecture. On a slightly smaller scale there is the Radcliffe quad in University College. Some things have gone. He paid for a large east window in the chapel of University College which fell to the reforming hand of Sir Gilbert Scott in the middle of the nineteenth century. He made a substantial contribution to the panelling of the senior common room of Lincoln College—a donation which, as will be seen, does him particular credit—which may or may not still be intact. But for the most part what he gave has persisted and prospered.

I put the Radcliffe Camera first in this list of the buildings that bear his name, despite the medical context of this lecture, because it is surely the best-known and most inescapable of them. It is the spiritual centre of gravity of the University, in view both of its position between the University Church and the main bulk of the Bodleian Library and of its status as the most readily accessible bit of the total Bodleian system. It is also visually the most distinctive and characteristic piece of Oxford architecture—well ahead in postcard sales, I should imagine, of its nearest rivals, Tom Tower and the Clarendon Building. Any illustrator, anxious to evoke the thought of Oxford, would have recourse to it before any other local sight.

Radcliffe spent only nineteen of the sixty-four years of his life in Oxford, five of them as a student at University College, seven as a fellow of Lincoln, and seven in medical practice in the city. When he left for London in 1684 he had thirty years of active and highly successful professional life ahead of him. But he always kept in touch with Oxford, and its dominant place in his will revealed the strength of his loyalty. He was a college head's ideal old member.

He was born in December 1652 or January 1653 in Wakefield in the West Riding of Yorkshire. His father was George Radcliffe, a lawyer who was, at the time of his son's birth, governor of the local prison. The father is said to have been appointed to the post for strictly political reasons and he was a strict republican. He is also said to have been incompetent, but that does not follow from the fact that he was dismissed from his position in 1661. The restoration of Charles II in 1660 left undisturbed (not least in Oxford colleges) a surprisingly large number of people who had been intruded into jobs during the Cromwellian interregnum, but known zealots were removed. Thomas Hearne, the sour-tempered antiquary, said that Radcliffe's father was 'a plebeian'. That may be a little extreme, but it serves as a corrective to the family's own claim to be related to the Radcliffe family who were Earls of Derwentwater. John Radcliffe, with typical boldness, continued to use the arms of the Derwentwater Radcliffes even when he had been specifically forbidden by the College of Arms to do so. The alleged Derwentwater connection took on a creditable form late in John Radcliffe's life. The then Earl was a Catholic (and was later executed for his involvement with the first Jacobite rising). Radcliffe offered to make him his own heir, provided that he conformed to the established Protestant church. The Earl refused in a dignified and courteous manner.

Wakefield was less overshadowed then by neighbouring Leeds than it has been in more recent times, and it had the advantage of an excellent local school. Its most distinguished student was the great classical scholar Richard Bentley, who was three years old when Radcliffe left for Oxford. Contemporary with Radcliffe were John Potter, later Archbishop of Canterbury, and the learned theologian, Joseph Bingham, who was in due course to become one of Radcliffe's numerous individual beneficiaries. Both of them, like Radcliffe, were undergraduates at University College.

In 1665, at the age of twelve, which by then had become unusually early, Radcliffe arrived at that college as an exhibitioner on the Freeston foundation, a Yorkshire charity. An important influence on him was that of Obadiah Walker, who was senior fellow in Radcliffe's time and became master in 1676. Walker was a royalist with a marked leaning towards Catholicism. He had been ejected from his fellowship after the Civil War and had gone into exile for a time. At the Restoration he was reinstated and soon became a power in the college. He was devoted to the college and was an energetic fund-raiser, the first, perhaps, of that active species whom Radcliffe can have encountered.

Radcliffe resisted Walker's attempts to convert him to Catholicism, but that led to no estrangement. During the uneasy reign of James II from 1685 to 1689, after Radcliffe had settled in London, Walker emerged openly as a Catholic and, in accordance with the king's attempts to bring the university back under Catholic control, conducted mass in the college. The king's clumsy attempts to subdue the university, which, as the next century was to show, was profoundly loyal to the Stuart house, culminated in his intrusion of a Catholic president and Catholic fellows on a resisting Magdalen College. In such heated circumstances an uninhibited supporter of the king was bound to suffer. When the king was expelled and the Protestant succession, for a time at least, secured, Walker was again deprived of his fellowship and spent the rest of his life in increasing poverty. Radcliffe, however, came to his aid. According to Hearne, he sent him 'once a year a new suit of clothes with ten broad pieces and a dozen bottles of the richest Canary to support his drooping spirits'. In 1698, finally, Walker died in refuge in Radcliffe's house.

In 1669 Radcliffe graduated as BA and became a senior scholar of University College. The two fellowships of the college open to Yorkshiremen were securely filled, so he had to look elsewhere. In the following year he was elected a fellow of Lincoln, his fellowship being tied to his Yorkshire birth. It is recorded that in the following year he was the college's lecturer in logic and in 1672, the year he became master of arts, in philosophy. Although he had a copy of Locke's *Essay on Human Understanding* among his books, it is possible to wonder about the level of professional competence he had managed to attain in these subjects. Hearne, in a particularly ungracious moment, described Radcliffe as 'an illiterate sot'. There is, it must be admitted, a grain of truth in both aspects of this judgement. Radcliffe drank heavily, while earnestly advising his even more alcoholic friends to use a measure of restraint, and was not a great reader. 'I never read Hippocrates' he declared. President Bathurst of Trinity, a keen medical amateur and a patron of Radcliffe's, once visited his room and, asking where the books were, was shown some vials, a skeleton, and a herbal with the words 'these are Radcliffe's books'.

There is an apparent incongruity between Radcliffe's indifference to books for his own use and his endowing a magnificent library for his old university. His junior colleague, Dr Mead, who seems to have inherited his practice, noticed it in a sharp comparison of Radcliffe's library bequest to the endowing of a seraglio by a eunuch. Mead once gave him the Bible to read, but he got no further than Exodus. Nevertheless, he had quite a few books of his own, 200 at the time of his death. Apart from Locke his library included classical texts, a good deal of history, travel books, general literature, a lot of theology and sermons, and a few books on medicine, but not very many. The reason for that was Radcliffe's confident and unqualified dismissal of the orthodox medical learning of his age.

In 1677 Radcliffe gave up his fellowship at Lincoln after a quarrel with the rector, Thomas Marshall, who appears to have refused Radcliffe leave to practise medicine while a fellow of the College. The sub-rector, Hickes, seems to have played a considerable part in this frustration of Radcliffe's aims. In 1685, when he himself was a candidate for the rectorship, Radcliffe got his revenge by mobilizing opposition to him. But this upset did not turn Radcliffe against Lincoln, or for that matter, its governing body in general. He was the largest single contributor to a fund for repanelling the senior common room that was set up after his departure.

Radcliffe took the degree of MB in 1675, after he had been at Lincoln for five years. In 1682, two years before his departure for London, he proceeded to the degree of MD, by which time he had been an established medical practitioner in Oxford for several years. Presumably his medical studies began after he became a fellow of Lincoln and was released from the official scholastic curriculum, except to the extent that he was required to teach it.

Medical thinking—private, unofficial, independent medical thinking—was very active and fruitful in mid-seventeenth-century Oxford. There were physicians among the members of the celebrated group convened by John Wilkins, warden of Wadham, at his college and in the lodgings of the great chemist Robert Boyle in High Street, which developed, after the Restoration and removal of its members to London, into the Royal Society. Thomas Willis was the most distinguished medical member of the group, which also included, besides Boyle and Wilkins, Christopher Wren, Robert Hooke, and the mathematician John Wallis. An investigator of the nervous system, Willis is still commemorated by the circle named after him. The even greater Sydenham had left Oxford in 1656, during the interregnum, having been twice wounded as a parliamentary cavalry officer in the Civil War. Willis was helped in his enquiries by Richard Lower, the Westminster school friend who interested Locke in medicine, and who explained the role of breathing in the purification of the blood.

Willis retained a chair in Oxford until 1675, the year of his death, but, with the richest practice in London, built up with the support of the Archbishop of Canterbury, he cannot have been much in the city. The report that Radcliffe studied with him, given by Radcliffe's most recent biographer, Bishop Hone, perhaps goes too far. The belief that Radcliffe studied the works of Sydenham is probably correct. They are not very voluminous.

Radcliffe's own medical style is, I suggest, closer to that of Sydenham than it is to that of Willis. Willis was a theorist, a pursuer of explanations, a distinguished member of the school of iatrochemists, who understood medically important underlying bodily processes to be of the general nature of fermentation. Sydenham, on the other hand, was a fairly rigid and unyielding empiricist, concerned almost entirely with the observation and description of disease, not with the experimental search for its hidden bodily causes.

Medical practice in the seventeenth century, for all the academic credentials of some of its most successful exponents, was essentially a craft to be acquired by close study of the work of an adept. Formal qualifications were an ornamental addition to, rather than a functional part of, a medical practitioner's professional equipment. Radcliffe's temperament, his bluff, commonsensical self-confidence, made him very much at home in such circumstances. His aggressive disregard for orthodox medical learning naturally exposed him to criticism. Less successful competitors claimed that he relied on guessing in the absence of scholarly qualifications. His many satisfied patients were the irresistible empirical response to these objections.

All the same, Radcliffe was not hostile to organized medical instruction. The proof of this is his direct involvement with designing the scheme of Radcliffe travelling fellowships that he endowed. These were to be for ten years, initially at the then very handsome figure of £300 a year. Rooms in University College were provided. Five of the ten years, the statute laid down, must be spent abroad. Radcliffe's young colleague and successor, Mead, had himself studied at Padua, as had Linacre at the end of the fifteenth century. Medical study of an academic kind was acceptable to Radcliffe so long as it was undertaken at the right place and in the right way.

His own practice was straightforward. His therapeutic experience supported his general presumption in favour of letting the diseased organism achieve its own recovery from its own resources. He was strongly opposed to any kind of violent treatment, in particular to bleeding and purging. Some of the successful cures attributed to him in a way that established his worldly success were of smallpox patients. Where the prevailing procedure was to keep the patient in a closed and heated room, Radcliffe prescribed fresh air, in conformity with Sydenham's cooling regimen.

After seven years of practice in Oxford, Radcliffe moved to London in 1684. J. B. Nias, one of Radcliffe's modern biographers, suggests that he may have been encouraged to do so by James II, who, as Duke of York, visited Oxford in 1683. His increasing success would have been enough reason to follow the path travelled before him by Sydenham and Willis. He settled in Bow Street and, in the fashion of the age, awaited messages from patients and dealt with apothecaries in an inn, the Bull's Head, and a coffee house, Garroway's. He soon made enemies of his professional competitors through the caustic remarks which gave unconcealed expression to his disdain for their methods. He had already annoyed Dr Gibbons by giving him the nickname 'Nurse', on account of his ladylike manner with patients, very different from Radcliffe's own military bluntness. One example of that, from his first, and perhaps not altogether reliable biographer, Pittis, conveys his particular flavour well enough. A hypochondriac complained to him of singing noises in the head and was adjured to go home and wipe his arse with a ballad.

Curing a Lady Spencer at Yarnton set him up with a reputation in the great world and prepared his way in London. He was soon making twenty guineas a day. A few years later he was able to lose £5,000 on a disastrous trading venture, which he had gone into with the actor Thomas Betterton, with equanimity. On being told the news at one of his regular places of resort, he cheerfully observed that he had 'no more to do than go up 250 pairs of stairs to be whole again'. By that time, therefore, his charge had risen from twenty guineas a day to twenty pounds a visit.

Political circumstances were favourable in 1684 to Radcliffe's rapid material exploitation of his abilities. Unlike his father he was a Tory and a High Churchman. By 1684 Charles II was declining towards his death in the following year and had secured the succession to his openly Catholic brother, the future James II. The Whigs had been crushed, their leader Shaftesbury driven into exile and death, parliament had not been summoned since its peremptory dissolution at Oxford in 1681, and the Rye House plotters had in 1683 been executed for an assassination project. The most successful London doctor when Radcliffe arrived there was Dr Thomas Short, a Catholic. He died shortly afterwards and Radcliffe filled his place.

Although a Tory and unwavering in his loyalty to the Stuart dynasty, Radcliffe always remained firmly Anglican in sentiment. He was unmoved by the possible advantages of conversion to Catholicism under an openly and resolutely Catholic king. Indeed, he resisted the attempts of James II to convert him as stolidly as he had those of his old teacher Obadiah Walker. A number of his smaller benefactions illuminate the nature of his religious commitments very clearly. He made gifts to the Society for the Propagation of the Gospel, to non-juring clergy, in need after ejection from their livings early in the reign of William III, and to the Scottish bishops, characteristically ensuring, in this case, that none of the money should go to the Archbishop of Glasgow, a sponger who made a practice of doing himself well out of charitable support intended for others.

In 1686, within two years of his arrival in London, he began a professional connection with the royal family which was to be exceedingly beneficial financially, both on its own account and by way of the other patients it drew to him, and persistently turbulent, because of his inability to keep his boldly disrespectful thoughts to himself. His first royal patient was the Princess Anne, who was to succeed as queen in 1702. The initial problem here was the inability of her numerous children to survive infancy. Three had already died by 1689 when the Duke of Gloucester was born. Radcliffe managed to keep him going for eleven years, but was not in attendance in 1700 when Dr Edward Hannes, a competitor and enemy, bled and killed the unfortunate child when he was suffering from scarlet fever. That was an event of some historical importance, since Anne had no other direct heirs at the time of her death, and the claims of her exiled half-brother, James the Old Pretender, were much stronger than those of her more distant Protestant relations in Hanover.

He was called in too late to be able to do anything for Anne's elder sister, Queen Mary, William III's wife, who died in 1695. It appears, all the same, that what he did contribute on this occasion was very imperfect. The queen in fact died of haemorrhagic smallpox, but Radcliffe insisted that it was measles from which she was suffering. She did have measles as well, but it was the smallpox that killed her, according to Nias. He was also brought in in 1708 during the last stages of the fatal illness of Anne's husband, Prince George of Denmark, who had been irreversibly mistreated.

But on the whole, Radcliffe's strictly medical relations with his royal patients, and with the highly placed patients their patronage brought to him, were good. In 1689 he successfully treated two of William III's Dutch entourage, and received £500 from the new king for doing so. In the following year he successfully treated William for an asthmatic condition. The king was most grateful for the work Radcliffe did in bringing about the recovery at Namur in 1691 of the king's sweetheart, Joost van Keppel, Earl of Albemarle. Pittis reports that on average Radcliffe received 600 guineas a year from the king.

Despite these services, Radcliffe's relations with his royal patients were rendered stormy by a habit of speech that was both literally and figuratively intemperate. On one occasion when desperate messages were brought to him from Princess Anne in 1694, urging him to come to her at once, he refused, saying that there was nothing wrong with her highness but the vapours. This greatly affronted the princess who refused to deal directly with him thereafter, although, as I have mentioned, he was in attendance on her surviving son in 1700 and on her husband in 1708. Godolphin, Anne's great finance minster, tried to get her to overlook Radcliffe's bearishness, but she would not comply, with the result that when he was called upon in the end, it was too late for his skill to serve any purpose.

Radcliffe also annoyed King William III. After examining him in 1697 he observed that he would not have the king's two legs for the king's three kingdoms. But that did not lead to a complete rupture. Even in Anne's case he is said to have been secretly consulted and to have prescribed on her behalf from 'behind the curtain'.

Radcliffe's well-founded professional self-confidence made it impossible to sustain friendly relations with his professional colleagues. He mainly associated, in the strenuously convivial manner of his age, with Jacobite noblemen and army officers, who shared his Tory sympathies. His support for the non-jurors suggests that these sympathies may have taken the form of fundamental loyalty to the exiled Catholic branch of the Stuart house, as does his coming out in defence of Dr Sacheverell, the non-juring firebrand impeached by the Whigs in 1709. Between 1689 and 1695, the years of William III's French war, Radcliffe was member of parliament for Bramber in Sussex, but made no mark. He was back in Parliament again, after a long interval, in 1713, sitting this time for Buckingham, where he was now a substantial landowner. Pittis prints two short speeches that he delivered, one supporting a bill to make Scotsmen bear some of the expenses of the Union of Scotland with England by paying a tax on malt, the other in support of a bill to 'prevent the farther growth of schism'. His concluding words convey the latter's drift well:

If schools and seminaries are suffer'd to be continu'd much longer, for the Education of Dissenter's Children; the Growth of Schism may be such, as to render this House incapable of preventing it; and then Good Night to our two famous Universities; that have made us the Envy and Glory of the Whole Universe.

There was no discernible bias in the register of Radcliffe's patients. He treated the Duke of Marlborough's son, at a distance, when that great Whig's heir and only child was dying in Cambridge. Prominent patients of his own persuasion were the young Alexander Pope, for whom he recommended fresh air and exercise, and Swift. He gave medical advice to Isaac Newton and to Thomas Sprat, historian of the Royal Society and Bishop of Rochester. He saved the Duke of Beaufort from dying of smallpox in 1712 by his usual fresh air regimen.

A heavy and persistent drinker himself, and, as we have seen, at some crucial times inconveniently the worse for it, he nevertheless earnestly encouraged some of his more alcoholic friends—among them the Duke of Beaufort just mentioned—to exercise a little self-control. He was almost lachrymose about the drink-induced death of the charming young Lord Craven. There is a pleasantly humane quality to his reaction to the low state of his friend Mr Nutley. Nutley had been cast into despair by some misfortunes and hid himself away from the world in his chambers in the Temple. According to Pittis, Radcliffe called and then

> left him, with Assurances of prescribing such a Remedy as should infallibly cure him. Accordingly, going into another Room he dispatch'd his Man to his Goldsmith for Two Hundred Guineas; which being sent to put them into a green Purse...

The purse was given to Nutley with a letter in which Radcliffe wrote:

> I have consulted other Means than the Beat of the Pulse, for a true State of your Distemper... I shall take it as a Favour, if you will make Use of the small Sum that bears this Company, for the Support of a Spirit, which, if once depress'd, will rob all that know you of their lives. These Pieces of Money have 300 more of the same Complexion at your Service.

Radcliffe was clearly a resourceful diagnostician, of the same order as the psychiatrist Alfred Adler. Once when the novelist Nigel Dennis, then in his twenties and working as Adler's secretary, arrived at a party of Adler's, depressed about his being too poor to retain the affections of a fashionable woman he was involved with, Adler remarked: 'Look, here is Nigel, he is depressed, I know what he needs, he needs a cheque', and wrote him out one there and then.

Radcliffe was not insusceptible to the attraction of women. In 1693 he was on his way to getting married to the 24-year-old daughter of a 'wealthy citizen', with a dowry of £15,000 and the promise of the rest of the father's estate to come, since the girl was his only child. His medically qualified eye discerned, however, that his fiancée was already pregnant—as it turned out, by her father's bookkeeper. Radcliffe extricated himself with an elegant letter and set himself against the idea of marriage. But after a time he conceived a strong passion for the beautiful Duchess of Bolton. In 1709 another of his occasional amorous outbreaks was brought to public notice by Richard Steele in the pages of *The Tatler*.

> You are not so ignorant as to be a stranger to the character of Aesculapius, as the patron and most successful of all who profess the art of medicine. But as most of his operations are owing to a natural sagacity or impulse, he has very little troubled himself with the doctrine of drugs, but has always given nature more room to help herself, than any of her learned assistants; and, consequently, has done greater wonders than is in the power of art to perform: for which reason he is half deified by the people; and has ever been justly courted by all the world, as if he were a seventh son.
>
> It happened, that the charming Hebe was reduced, by a long and violent fever, to the most extreme danger of death and when all skill failed, they sent for Aesculapius. The renowned artist was touched with the deepest compassion to see the faded charms and faint bloom of Hebe; and had a generous concern in beholding a struggle, not between life but rather between youth and

death. All his skill and his passion tended to the recovery of Hebe, beautiful even in sickness: but alas! the unhappy physician knew not that in all his care he was only sharpening darts for his own destruction, in a word, his fortune was the same with that of the statuary, who fell in love with the image of his own making; and the unfortunate Aesculapius is become the patient of her whom he lately recovered. Long before this disaster, Aesculapius was far gone in the unnecessary and superfluous amusements of old age, in increasing unwieldy stores, and providing, in the midst of an incapacity of enjoyment of what he had, for a supply of more wants than he had calls for in youth itself. But these low considerations are now no more, and love has taken place of avarice, or rather is become an avarice of another kind, which still urges him to pursue what he does not want. But, behold the metamorphosis; the anxious, mean cares of an usurer are turned into the languishments and complaints of a lover.

His considered view about marriage was given in his reply to someone who asked him why he did not pull himself together and marry a young gentlewoman. He replied that he already had an old one to take care of. He was referring to University College, for whose advantage at Radcliffe's expense the importunate mendicancy of the master, Dr Charlett, collaborated with Radcliffe's own affection for the place.

Radcliffe became a governor of St Bartholomew's Hospital in 1690 and, characteristically, served it with vigour and generosity. In his will he left the hospital £500 a year for 'mending the diet' and £100 a year for the purchase of linen. In 1704 he moved from Bow Street to grander premises in Bloomsbury, in keeping with the fact that by then he was making £7,000 a year and was worth some £80,000 altogether. Around 1710 he acquired a riverside property at Carshalton and for the four remaining years of his life spent a good deal of his time there. His practice was largely taken over by the Dr Richard Mead already mentioned as being somewhat mocking on the subject of Radcliffe's endowment of a library.

The habit of benefaction, which took on its full magnificence only at his death, was already well established. Apart from Mr Nutley, there were other private beneficiaries. He helped a Jacobite who had slandered him. He responded to the appeal of a man condemned to be hanged: by getting the sentence commuted to transportation to Virginia he set the repentant malefactor on the first steps of a successful career. He was a friend of Dr Aldrich, logician, architect, and Dean of Christ Church, and made an anonymous contribution to Aldrich's new Peckwater quad there. Another anonymous gift was made to All Saints church in Oxford, with whose reconstruction into its present noble form Aldrich was involved in 1707 and 1708. (In recent years it has been admirably converted into a library for Lincoln College, and the Radcliffe Trust contributed to the expense, 300 years after Radcliffe ceased to be a fellow.)

I referred earlier to a Wakefield man, Joseph Bingham, who was at Radcliffe's school some years after him. He was an undergraduate at University College and became a fellow there in 1689. In 1695 he delivered a scholarly sermon on the views of the fathers of the church about some central ideas in the doctrine of the Trinity from the pulpit of St Mary's. For this he was censured by the university authorities. The *DNB* account of Bingham claims that what he had said was entirely orthodox as well as correct from a scholarly point of view and, in view of that conviction of his complete innocence, indignantly reproves the university for its failure to make amends for its injustice. In fact, Bingham was following the line of William Sherlock whose ideas about the Trinity were, from an orthodox point of view, insufficiently emphatic about the unity of the three persons. At any rate, Radcliffe came to Bingham's rescue by purchasing the living of Headbourne Worthy in Hampshire and presenting it to University College for Bingham to occupy, which he did for the rest of his very hardworking life. Not far from the cathedral library of Winchester, Bingham was able to assemble the ten volumes of his great, and still unsuperseded, book on the antiquities of the early church. It is noteworthy that Bingham's theological tendency was in the opposite direction to Radcliffe's. But Radcliffe did not let that interfere with his sense of duty to an ill-treated man who shared his birthplace, school, and college.

The period of semi-retirement at Carshalton from 1710 onwards was disturbed by the illness and death of Queen Anne. Described by Dewhurst as 'obese, toothless, constantly pregnant and prone to alcoholism', she was, although only 49, not a promising case for treatment. Nevertheless, the approach of her expected death provoked an intense political crisis. The Act of Settlement, passed in 1701, a year before she came to the throne, had fixed the succession to the throne of England on the Protestant descendants of James I, in particular, after Anne, on Sophia, Electress of Hanover. She, more fitted for that throne than her lumpish son, the future George I, died in May 1714, three months before the onset of Anne's last illness. The Act of Settlement had been reinforced by the union with Scotland in 1707 which had extended the principle of Protestant succession to the new joint kingdom of Great Britain.

But the Whigs who had dominated the queen's government from her accession in 1702 were eased out of power in 1710. For some years the Duchess of Marlborough had been replaced in the affections of the queen by the Tory Lady Masham, and political control had been exercised by the uncomfortable alliance of the comparatively moderate Harley, Lord Oxford, and the comparatively immoderate and opportunistic Bolingbroke. The opposition Whigs suspected that the Tories intended to go back on the Act of Settlement. The idea had certainly crossed many important minds and had taken full possession of others.

As the queen, after a sudden deterioration in her condition, rapidly declined, intense political anxiety was aroused and there was a turmoil of furtive manoeuvring. Mead and the queen's other doctors could see that there was no chance of recovery. Even so, shortly before the queen died, Lady Masham sent an urgent message to Radcliffe adjuring him to come. Old and suffering seriously from gout, he was unwilling to bestir himself for what was plainly a lost cause. In writing to refuse he said, reasonably enough, that in his circumstances, and in view of the queen's old and settled antipathy to him, he did not think it proper to come without an authoritative command to do so, either from the queen herself or from the privy council.

When the news of this reluctance to serve became common knowledge, as it very soon did, a storm broke about Radcliffe's head. Within two days he received threats of assassination for his disloyalty, and for safety's sake remained at Carshalton. Three months later, on 1 November, he died himself, at the age of 62.

Whatever the public may have thought of him, Oxford, no doubt actuated by a lively sense of favours to come, gave him a magnificent send-off. On 3 December a large and dignified procession made its way to St Mary's, where he was buried with all the considerable pomp the university could bring to the business. There was even an officially commissioned set of memorial verses for the occasion, of which Thomas Hearne soon remarked 'they lie as a drug on the booksellers' hands'.

The university's expectations were not ill-founded. Within the next sixty years all Radcliffe's main beneficent intentions were fully realized. He died worth some £140,000. Some of his main projects were deferred until the life interests in part of his property which he had bequeathed to his sisters were extinguished. But enough was available to set the scheme of Radcliffe travelling fellowships in operation with remarkable speed. The first such fellow was elected in July 1715, eight months after Radcliffe's death. J. B. Nias, the most thorough historian of these fellowships, says that they were of more advantage to London than to Oxford, but perhaps Radcliffe's aim was rather that Oxford should produce properly qualified medical men than that it should retain them.

One early fellow became physician-general to the army; another was the first physician at Bethlehem Hospital. In 1755 the son of the materialist philosopher David Hartley, so much admired by Coleridge, was elected, but did not stay the course, although he led a sociable, dilettante life until he was 81. Colwell, a Trinity man, I am sorry to say, retired rapidly to Bodmin and did little there. There was the father of Dean Henry Hart Milman, historian of Latin Christianity, who, after various ups and downs, became physician to the mad George III and subsequently baronet and president of the Royal College of Physicians. There was Sibthorp, commemorated in the title of Oxford's chair of rural economy, who, before dying at 38, produced his wonderful book on the flowers of Greece. The handsome Sir Charles Vaughan visited the Middle East, turned into a diplomat, and is to be seen on the walls of the hall at All Souls. After the Napoleonic era Paris became the European centre of medicine. The mid-Victorian fellows had a sad tendency to die young. One of them went to Australia and, at that respectful distance, became a homoeopath. After 1850 the term of the fellowship was reduced to three years. A fellow under the new rules was Sir Ray Lankester, who helped H. G. Wells with the early, biological parts of his *Outline of History* and was, I have always believed, the original of Conan Doyle's Professor Challenger.

The grandest of Radcliffe's benefactions got under way when the foundation stone of the Camera was laid in 1737. With the life interests in his estate now ended, £40,000 was assigned to the work, James Gibbs being preferred to Hawksmoor as the architect. The building was ready in 1747 and was opened with great ceremony in 1749. The event was rendered colourful by the delivery of a Jacobite speech by the vice-chancellor Dr King which, four years after the second Jacobite rising, caused some outrage. Radcliffe would probably have liked it.

The first librarian was Francis Wise, squire of Elsfield and friend of Dr Johnson. None of Radcliffe's own books was included in the collection. In 1811 its content was confined to science and medicine. That great Oxford medical figure, Acland, was the sixth librarian, and under his influence the Radcliffe science collection was moved to the new university museum in Parks Road. It soon overflowed the space available and was moved to a building of its own, round the corner in South Parks Road. The Camera was lent to the university, which finally acquired the freehold in 1927.

The Observatory was not part of Radcliffe's specific intentions. It owes its existence to the energy and ambition of Thomas Hornsby, who became Savilian professor of astronomy in 1768. He borrowed a sum of money from the trustees of the will of Lord Clarendon to set the project going. The foundation stone was laid in 1772 and the work was finally completed in 1795. As well as being the first Radcliffe Observer, he was also, from 1783 to 1810, Radcliffe librarian. The trustees of Radcliffe's will were persuaded to provide £30,000 for the undertaking, and were once again rewarded with a distinguished piece of architecture. In 1839 the posts of Savilian professor and of Radcliffe Observer were separated.

For reasons it is not necessary to particularize, Oxford is not an ideal place in which to carry on observational astronomy. Eventually the observatory was moved to the clearer air of South Africa. The institution was taken over by the British government; the building and site, only a few years ago, were compulsorily purchased by the state government of Transvaal at a valuation which gave the trustees no cause for complaint. It is possible to feel that after a long, not undistinguished, but surely un-Radcliffian detour into the heavens, it is right that the Observatory site should now be secured for purposes of an unquestionably Radcliffian nature.

Fourth in order of time, but by no means in importance, of Radcliffe's major benefactions was the Infirmary. Around the 1730s there was a lively development of hospital building in the towns of England. A convivial and open-handed citizen of Oxford, who lived in what was recently the Judge's Lodgings in St Giles, Thomas Rowney, gave a five acre site in 1758. The new hospital was opened for business in 1770. The Radcliffe trustees supplied the money for the building, but not for the running costs. It was a gracious gesture of those who set up the Infirmary's successor to name it as they did.

The Radcliffe trust is still a going concern, even if the university, the Bodleian library system, Green College, and the National Health Service have taken over the main products of Radcliffe's beneficence. It still owns farms which were once Radcliffe's property. Some of these were bought some years ago to form part of the new town of Milton Keynes. From this and the proceeds of the Observatory site in the Transvaal a decent holding of investments has been built. The trustees are always sympathetic to good causes in Oxford, mindful of the source of the moneys they distribute. The emphasis of their benefactions is cultural and educational. Cathedrals are provided with apprentices in stonemasonry and stained-glass work; the Allegri string quartet is sent on one-week visits to the remoter universities to give concerts and master classes; Oxford tutors in philosophy and history are supplied with teaching deputies so that they can get on with some substantial piece of writing.

Radcliffe was a product of Locke's Oxford, which was also the Oxford of Boyle and Christopher Wren, of Sydenham and Willis. The official intellectual life of the place was ossified. In Oxford, as everywhere else, the Protestant Reformation, where it succeeded in displacing the Catholic Church, failed to supplant the philosophico-scientific system of knowledge associated with it. Locke was at one with Bacon and Hobbes and all the enquiring minds of the age in rejecting the despotic rule of Aristotelian scholasticism.

In his own, comparatively inarticulate fashion, Radcliffe was part of this general movement away from a tradition of intellectual authority. In religion and politics he was hostile to innovation. Like the other Anglican Tories of the late seventeenth century, he had to face the problem of reconciling his loyalty to the Church of England, as by Henry VIII established and by Queen Elizabeth settled, with his loyalty to the Stuart house, whose male, and more properly entitled, members were obstinately Catholic. For common-sensical Englishmen in his epoch, Catholicism was associated with treason, a betrayal in the interests of France under the later Stuarts as it had been betrayal in the interests of Spain under Elizabeth. Patriotic common-sense adjusted his political loyalties to prevent collision with his religious commitments.

The same self-confident, straightforward common-sensicality that enabled Radcliffe to accommodate in his mind loyalty both to the established church and to the hereditary sovereignty of England, despite the unsettling tendency of those who had the best title to the latter to subvert the former, had the opposite effect on his conduct as a professional. It turned him into something of a revolutionary, although, mercifully, into a comparatively inarticulate one. The inadequacy of Galenian orthodoxy stared him in the face. On the other hand, he did not rush to the opposite extreme of precipitate application of new theory. One sees him through the two and a half centuries that separate him from us as a not unfamiliar kind of medical man, impatient of hypochondria, aware that very often the best thing to do is to let the body get on with the business of healing itself by providing the most helpful conditions for it to do so. The large generosity of his spirit still stands around us in the noble buildings that bear his name.

4
La Mettrie

Quite a number of notable philosophers have been doctors. Four that come to mind are Locke, Hartley, Lotze, and William James. Locke's medical services to Lord Shaftesbury got him started on his public career as ideologist-in-chief to the Whigs who wanted to exclude James II from succeeding his brother, Charles II, on the throne of England. Hartley was the associationist thinker who was such an object of veneration to Coleridge that the poet named his first son after him. Hermann Lotze was much respected by the British Hegelians of the late nineteenth century, who had all his writings translated. William James needs no introduction. Aristotle was, like Helvétius and Humphrey Bogart, the son of a fashionable doctor, but not a medical man himself. He was, however, biologically minded, believing that to understand the real nature of anything one must grasp what it is striving to become and asserting the continuity of all varieties of life: vegetable, animal, and human. All of these philosophers, with the exception of Lotze, but including Aristotle, were naturalistic, rather than spiritualistic, Hartley to the point of materialism and Locke approaching it.

Julien Offray de la Mettrie (1709–51) was the most intensely medical and the most materialistic of all doctor-philosophers. He was trained in Paris and Rheims, studied under the great Boerhaave in Leiden, served as surgeon to the royal guard, and contributed to the study of smallpox, dysentery, and vertigo. He was not all that progressive in some of the details of his practice. He was in favour of bleeding, and opposed inoculation for smallpox. In the history of medicine proper he has left only the faintest trace. His name does not appear, for example, in the gigantically comprehensive history of the subject by Arturo Castiglioni or in the well-known shorter history of Charles Singer.

According to La Mettrie's most recent biographer Kathleen Wellman, in her *La Mettrie: Medicine, Philosophy and Enlightenment* (Duke University Press), the materialistic and unedifyingly hedonistic philosophy for which La Mettrie is best known—a scandal to his contemporaries and an embarrassment to the *philosophes* among them—was a direct continuation and fulfilment of his medical interests. These were expressed in the first instance at an institutional level, in the form of a series of vigorous satires directed at the leaders of the medical profession in France. At the time his career began, physicians, who were only a fifth as numerous as the surgeons, were tightly organized to make the most of the benefits of their monopoly position in the medical world. Surgeons—the 'physicians of the poor'—combined their medical undertakings with the practice of barbering. With wigs becoming fashionable, the two trades drifted apart from each other, leaving surgeons proper free for upward social movement.

La Mettrie's case against the physicians was not just that they exploited the sick by restricting entry into the profession. His main point was that the theoretical training they received in the ancient classics of medicine and which they saw as the basis of their pre-eminence was, in fact, useless and very often harmful. The surgeons learnt by experience, on the job, where the physicians applied themselves to their patients equipped only with traditional and ill-founded lore about humours and the like. Surgeons, taking their cue from Harvey's discovery of the circulation of the blood, studied anatomy; physicians studied Latin texts. Physicians disparaged surgeons as ignorant of Latin and incapable of reasoning. To La Mettrie the inherited theory on which they prided themselves was no more than vacuous metaphysical speculation. In its place he called for a Baconian medical science, founded on experience, not abstract first principles, and with a definite practical aim.

La Mettrie's first philosophical book, *L'Histoire naturelle de l'âme*, came out in 1745. It is a more conventionally presented treatise than any of his later writings, but not a model of rational organization. It is principally directed against Descartes's doctrine of the substantial soul, the inscrutable something or other which ties our individual mental states together and the possession of which differentiates human beings from everything else in the universe. In the same way as Locke, La Mettrie holds that the soul is no more knowable in its essence than the body. What we actually know about both is what we can observe them to be or do. He invokes Aristotle against Descartes, the Aristotle who held that the soul is the principle of vital movement and activity of plants, animals, and men and not something capable of existing independently of them. He claims that motion is intrinsic to matter, not imposed from outside by some kind of miraculous divine push. Following Locke again in seeing all the contents of the human mind as derived from sensation, he is more emphatic than Locke about the fundamentally material nature of sensation, which is the effect of physical causes, which excite physical responses in the brain and nervous system by way of physical sense organs. Descartes's extraordinary doctrine that animals have no feelings, are machines in the sense of being wholly devoid of sensations, he rejects as absurd. We have as much reason to think that animals have feelings as that other human beings do. In the first place there are the likenesses between their behaviour in similar circumstances. Then there are the considerable anatomical correspondences between humans and animals to be taken into account.

L'Homme machine (1748) carries on the materialist programme of showing the mind to be part of nature by accumulating instances of mind–body connection. La Mettrie's title can easily be misinterpreted. He is not saying, under the influence of some prophetic inspiration, that the brain is a computer. Spread about his writings are allusions to such facts as the effects on memory of injuries to the brain, the likeness of our basic motives of hunger and love to those of animals, the mental aspects of sleep, eating and drinking, bodily illnesses.

In the later book he is concerned to tackle the last defensive redoubt of dualism: the conception of reason, the peculiarly human part of the soul, as entirely non-material, whatever may be true of the 'lower' mental functions, sensation, emotion, desire, memory, imagination, and so forth. He identifies reason, supposedly distinctive of the human species, with the power of speech. It is not all that distinctive since animals can communicate. He conjectures, reaching out to Washoe, that it might be possible to teach an ape to speak. A stronger argument is that human beings cannot always have spoken and must have developed their linguistic competence in the course of evolution. The use of language, he maintains, is rooted in the imagination. That, understood in the style of Hobbes and Locke as 'decaying sense', is evidently bound up with the body. Generally his tactic is to draw the boundary around the supposedly non-material element as tightly as possible and then to argue that even this is inextricably tied to what is without question bodily.

After *L'Histoire naturelle de l'âme* La Mettrie retired to Holland, but even that comparatively liberal community found *L'Homme machine* too much to bear. So he moved to the court of Frederick the Great at that hospitable monarch's invitation, a year before the arrival of Voltaire. Unlike Voltaire, he did not quarrel with his host. In the year of his hedonistic *Art de jouir*, 1751, he died at the age of forty-two, after eating some *pâté*, or, perhaps, a *pâté aux truffes*, which had gone off. Enemies put it about that, in accordance with the voluptuary principles of conduct he proclaimed, he had died of over-eating. A number of medieval English kings used to be said to have died of 'surfeit'. But, in an age without refrigerators, salmonella is more likely than bulimia.

One of the best accounts of La Mettrie is the chapter devoted to him by F. A. Lange in his great *History of Materialism* (1866). Lange says of La Mettrie that he is 'one of the most abused, but one of the least read, authors in the history of literature'. He only just makes his way into the history of philosophy.

Those historians who do pay attention to him make the point that, active in the first stages of the French Enlightenment and dying in the year of publication of the first volume of the *Encyclopédie*, he had a number of important ideas before anyone else. He was the first categorical materialist among the *philosophes*, preceding, and probably influencing, d'Holbach, whose *Système de la nature* came out nearly twenty years after La Mettrie's death, and Diderot, whose avowal of materialism in his *Entretien entre d'Alembert et Diderot*, written in 1769, and his *Rêve de d'Alembert*, were not published until after *his* death in 1784. Lange says that La Mettrie asserted the unity of all organic life before Buffon. He was one of the first modern evolutionists, although he had no explanatory mechanism to suggest, no hint of Darwin's great idea of natural selection winnowing out random variations. He anticipated the modern theory of primeval soup as the source of life in remarkably similar language, in his case it was elemental mud. He thought criminals were sick and ought to be treated, rather than punished.

La Mettrie's obscure place in the history of thought must be due in part to the uncomfortable, even scandalous, nature of his ideas. He was an atheist at a time when his intellectually progressive contemporaries were calling a halt at deism. He was an outright materialist at a time when Locke's mildly materialist followers in England—Hartley and Priestley, for example—were tentatively tracing out the consequences of his parenthetical supposition that 'it might have pleased God to attach the power of thinking to material substance', while remaining, in the spirit of that remark and Locke's own example, believers in God. Atheism and materialism were bad enough. La Mettrie's hedonism was really too much.

People beginning the study of philosophy are often a little disappointed to find that thinkers of the past who are described as hedonists turn out to be thoroughly tame and respectable. Epicurus, for example, did not recommend the riotous flinging of roses. His ideal of life was to sit about in a garden with some friends having an intellectual discussion and drinking a prudently watered glass of wine. The earlier Aristippus of Cyrene was bolder. What was of highest value for him was positive pleasure, not the defeatist *summum bonum* of later antiquity: the absence of pain. He stressed, in particular, the supreme value of present, bodily satisfaction, although he qualified this first principle by saying that the wise pleasure seeker will take account of the possible painful consequences in the future of his actions.

La Mettrie's moral philosophy is much like that of Aristippus. In opposition to the deeply rooted Platonic–Christian conviction of the unimportance or valuelessness of straightforward bodily pleasure, he applauded it. It is often intense and it is available to everyone. It is much more solid than phantoms like honour. The happiness of intoxication is as real as any other. What is more, the much trumpeted sources of higher pleasure—knowledge and culture—are more peripheral to the nature of man than the fundamental impulses of hunger and love which he shares with other animals, and they are often harmful. Reason has a place in the organization of one's pursuit of pleasure. He draws a distinction between *volupté*, pleasure pure and simple, and *débauche*, the kind of pleasure that brings suffering in its train, whether bodily pain or social disapproval. For there is a social dimension to La Mettrie's moral theory. We have to live with one another and virtue consists in conduct which society—the state and public opinion—endorses.

La Mettrie's medically based conception of human nature, as Kathleen Wellman points out, does not take it to be very greatly, let alone completely, malleable. For him *l'éducation peut peu* where for Helvétius *elle peut tout*, an expansion of Locke's view of the mind as a tabula rasa. Diderot drew on La Mettrie to resist the extremity of Helvétius's environmentalism, but, like d'Holbach, made as little as possible of this debt to him. In a proto-Freudian spirit La Mettrie contends that society asks too much of individuals, in whom it inspires unnecessary and irrational remorse. At one point, indeed, he argues that remorse is altogether irrational, on the ground that it is wholly backward-looking, unlike that other great force for virtue, fear of the law. He ignores the consideration that remorse, to be genuine, must embody an intention to behave better in future. His medically nourished awareness of the persistence of individual human constitutions and of the differences between them leads him to an attractively breezy kind of tolerance, a realism about human nature that is untainted by edifying theory.

Should La Mettrie be more highly regarded as a philosopher than he has been? His writings lack the elegant logical articulation of those of the main target of his criticism, Descartes. They lack the massiveness of the works in which d'Holbach, twenty years after La Mettrie's death, was to present a similar view of the nature of things, in an altogether less sprightly manner. La Mettrie's philosophical writings all fit into one dumpy little eighteenth-century volume of 700 pages and make agreeable reading.

For one piece of reasoning, at any rate, he ought to be honoured: his refutation of Descartes's ludicrous thesis that non-human animals are automata. Arnauld had raised the matter in his objections to Descartes's *Meditations* and had been put off with a footling answer. Descartes was led to his view about animals by his radical distinction of the contents of the universe into two, and only two, utterly different kinds of thing: the mental or conscious and the material or extended. It follows from this that the non-rational or sub-rational parts of the mind—feelings, emotions, desires, and so on—are, since they are items of consciousness, non-physical. (Most types of mental content, except perhaps sensations and images, are rational to the extent of being thought-impregnated, although they do not involve reasoning. Anger, for instance, involves the belief that its object has harmed one.)

Descartes held that living bodies, animal or human, are pieces of purely physical machinery. In the case of human beings a spiritual substance or soul is inserted, temporarily, into one of these mechanisms. Why could he not have allowed animals to have a soul, of an inferior, non-rational kind? The problem would then arise that, since this inferior conscious entity is still a substance, it would be indestructible, except by God, and so immortal. An alternative to the unpalatable implication of animal immortality would be to drop the questionable assumption that all substances are (naturally) indestructible. But that would undermine the best that Descartes has to offer in the way of an argument for the immortality of the human soul. Or again, he could have held that only the rational part of the soul is immortal, but immortality without memory, emotion, and desire seems hardly worth having. There is also the difficulty of showing animals to be non-rational, in the light of the large and inescapable evidence for their being intelligent.

All that is a problem for Descartes. What is not in doubt is that his conclusion that animals are unfeeling automata is absurd. When animals are hit they cry out and do not just withdraw like sensitive plants. Watering mouths and wide-opened eyes reveal desire and emotion in them as in us. We and they have eyes to see with, noses beneath them to breathe and smell with, mouths a bit further down to take in food and drink. Within their and our mouths are teeth to grind food into a form in which it can be swallowed and digested, and tongues with which to taste it. And so anatomically on.

La Mettrie, arguing for the continuity of humans with animals, suggests that animals have a moral capacity since they suffer from remorse. Here he may have confused a reaction he disapproved of with one he favoured; remorse with fear of punishment.

Animals are certainly given to behaviour that is in the interest of other sentient beings, but not their own, and are capable of self-sacrifice. If that is attributed to kin selection or imprinting, the same may true of our own moral achievements.

What La Mettrie does not, I think, explicitly conclude from his ideas about the continuity between humans and animals is that animals, like human beings, are proper objects of moral concern. Susceptible to suffering as we are, they are part of the overall moral constituency. A recognition of the moral significance of animal suffering is, at the very least, wholly consistent both with La Mettrie's philosophy and with his humane disposition. Materialism, which denies the superhumanity of the human race, is an impediment to inhumanity.

5

Coleridge at Home

If you drive west from Bridgwater in the direction of Watchet, Minehead, and the west Somerset coast the first place of any size that you come to—it is about eight miles along the road—is Nether Stowey. It is a little way off the main road to the left, a rather accidental-looking place, in a fairly flat region, but with rising ground behind it to the south: the northern edge of the Quantock hills.

The main street of the village winds in an agreeably casual way beside the course of a small stream. Near the top end of the village is Coleridge's cottage, a building of no great intrinsic claim to attention, which one could easily miss if it were not for the National Trust notice that stands outside it. Although tidied up and in good repair it is clearly much older than the new bungalows beyond it at the furthest extremity of the village. It must have been the last house in that direction when Coleridge came to live there in 1796. At that time he described it, cheerfully but no doubt accurately, as a hovel. But he grew to love it, being anyway none too fussy about his surroundings. At the time it was delightful to him as a refuge from all sorts of pressures: financial insecurity, and the collapse of his sympathies for the ideals of the French Revolution, in particular.

It is a simple two-up two-down affair, with four smallish windows looking out on to the street from a good deal of blank wall. There is a decent front door with an attractive little canopy over it. In Coleridge's time it was thatched, but it is now covered with severe dark red ridged tiles. It was none too well equipped in 1796. It had no oven, so Coleridge's wife, Sara, had to take things to be baked or roasted to the nearby baker's shop. Behind it there was—and to some extent still is—a patch of land on which Coleridge proposed to keep a pig and some ducks and to grow vegetables. There is reason to think that—like a great many of Coleridge's schemes—after an initial burst of enthusiasm, this did not come to anything very much.

The place had been found for Coleridge by his friend, Thomas Poole, who had not long before inherited his father's prosperous tanning business. Because of its dilapidated condition Poole was attacked by doubts, shortly before Coleridge moved in with Sara and their three-month-old child, Hartley, as to whether it was not too primitive for the young family. Coleridge overrode these doubts with characteristically tumultuous enthusiasm. He was to remain there from December 1796 to September 1798. That is less than two out of the sixty-four years of his life, but they were by far his most productive as a poet. All his best-known poems—except, perhaps, for *Dejection: an Ode*—were written there, in particular: *Kubla Khan* and *The Ancient Mariner*. In any reasonable selection from his complete poetic output the work of his twenty-one months at Nether Stowey is likely to take up half the space.

Thomas Poole, the friend who brought him there, had educated himself in defiance of his father's contempt for book-learning. He was an ardent and politically active Whig, of the democratic if not quite Jacobinical kind. His public spirit led him, in a way that is not all that usual among political extremists, to be a constant and substantial benefactor to his local community. His memorial stone is to be seen in Nether Stowey church.

Coleridge had first come to Nether Stowey in the late summer of 1796, soon after the collapse, with its tenth issue, of his periodical *The Watchman*. At the time, in the cold December of 1796, when he moved in to the cottage he was oppressed not only by that failure, but by intense eye-pain and facial swelling which drove him to opium for relief, with dire long-term consequences of addiction. He was suffering also from sympathetic distress on behalf of his friend Charles Lamb, whose sister, Mary, in a fit of madness, had recently murdered her mother.

Another mentally unbalanced person impinged more directly on Coleridge. Shortly before the move to Nether Stowey he had taken into his house in Bristol as a pupil a well-off young admirer called Charles Lloyd. He was, unfortunately, an epileptic, and a series of fits had made it necessary for him to go home to his father just before the family's departure. In February 1797 he was back with the Coleridges, but he had more fits and had to go again in March. In a manner which was not uncommon among Coleridge's younger admirers, initial enthusiasm and devotion came to be replaced by disappointment and hostility. The first entrancing impact of Coleridge's personality did not endure. In Lloyd's case the most depressing result was a novel he published in the early part of 1798 called *Edmund Oliver*, which contained an unflattering and all too recognizable portrait of Coleridge.

Soon after Lloyd's departure an altogether more important and rewarding relationship developed, his friendship with Wordsworth and his sister Dorothy. They had first met in the autumn of 1795, around the time of Coleridge's marriage to Sara Fricker and their honeymoon period of living at Clevedon on the Bristol Channel. In April 1797 Wordsworth called in on Coleridge in Nether Stowey while walking back from Bristol to Racedown in Dorset. In the same ardently pedestrian mode Coleridge returned the visit two months later. Racedown is some forty miles from Nether Stowey and Coleridge's walk there is evidence, of which there is a great deal in this period, that he was just as strenuous a walker as Wordsworth, although less renowned as such. Indeed he seems to have been a more adventurous and scrambling kind of walker than the more measured and deliberate Wordsworth.

Coleridge's first volume of poems had come out in April 1796 and went into a second edition, with poems by Charles Lamb and by Charles Lloyd added to the text in the following year. A much more significant collaboration was soon to take place. The idea of Wordsworth and Coleridge combining the new kind of poems they were writing in a joint volume as a kind of manifesto came to them in the course of one of their many walks in the Quantocks. The result, *Lyrical Ballads*, was published in September 1798, just as Coleridge was leaving Nether Stowey for good, at the outset of his trip to Germany. The famous introduction in which Wordsworth sets out their principles about poetic diction (that poetry should be written 'in the language generally used by men') and about the nature of poetry ('the spontaneous overflow of powerful feelings') was not added until the second edition of 1800. But these ideas were illustrated by example in the poems themselves.

Coleridge's most important contribution was *The Ancient Mariner*. For all its supernatural incidents and the atmosphere of magical glamour in which it is bathed, it is composed in ballad form, the simplest and most rustically unsophisticated of English poetic patterns, and its language is of the most straightforward character. Very few of the words in it are of more than two syllables: 'mariner', 'glittering', 'merrily', 'minstrelsy', 'tyrannous', and 'o'ertaking' are the only ones to be found in the first fifty lines. Some stanzas are as humble and rudimentary as *John Gilpin*.

> The ship was cheered, the harbour cleared,
> Merrily did we drop
> Below the kirk, below the hill,
> Below the lighthouse top.

The stanza that follows is composed almost entirely of monosyllables, like a song by Shakespeare.

> The Sun came up upon the left,
> Out of the sea came he!
> And he shone bright, and on the right
> Went down into the sea.

Wordsworth's finest contribution to the joint effort is surely *Tintern Abbey*. More in conformity with his requirement of the language generally used by men is *The Idiot Boy*. The topic and its treatment gave great offence to many contemporary readers.

The relationship between Coleridge on the one hand and Wordsworth and his sister on the other was one of rapturous mutual enchantment. Coleridge was not in love with Dorothy (as he was to be later with Wordsworth's sister-in-law), but he admired the combination of intelligence and sensitivity which made her such a marvellous companion for her brother. By comparison his own uninteresting, and understandably resentful, wife had little to offer but congested domesticity. The matrimonial breakdown to come is prefigured in the circumstances surrounding the writing of Coleridge's beautiful poem *This Lime-Tree Bower My Prison*.

During the first summer at Nether Stowey Charles Lamb, with William and Dorothy Wordsworth, came on a visit. Sara spilt a pan of boiling milk over Coleridge's foot, so that he was unable to go out walking with them. In the remarks with which he introduces the poem he says only, in the most gentlemanly fashion, that the author 'met with an accident, which disabled him from walking during the whole time of (his friends') stay'.

> Well they are gone, and here must I remain,
> This lime-tree bower my prison! I have lost
> Beauties and feelings, such as would have been
> Most sweet to my remembrance even when age
> Had dimm'd mine eyes to blindness...

It is clear, I think, that he was distinctly annoyed and not merely regretful. That first line is unquestionably nettled.

Soon after this mishap the invaluable Thomas Poole had found a fine place nearby for the Wordsworths to rent. Alfoxden is a spacious country house (now some kind of hotel) only four or five miles on foot from Coleridge's much more modest establishment. The Wordsworths took it for a year at the amazingly low rent of £23, and for such walkers as they and Coleridge it was almost as if they were next door. For the rest of their time there they were constantly in and out of each other's houses.

What ensured that the Wordsworths' stay would not be longer was the communication to their landlord of suspicions about the political reliability, indeed of the patriotic loyalty, of their circle. Coleridge had arrived in Nether Stowey with the reputation of being a dangerous Jacobin radical. He had never really deserved it, for his concern for the oppressed was essentially humanitarian and only political in an accidental and transitory way. His local patron Poole was a radical as well, and he and Coleridge invited into their midst the radical agitator, 'Citizen' John Thelwall, who had been remanded to the Tower of London for a spell in 1794 on a charge of high treason. When their walks, by night as well as by day, and their habit of sketching are taken into account, it is not surprising that Coleridge and the Wordsworths should have been suspected of some kind of complicity with the expected French invaders. An agent was set to spy on them. The incident is a parallel to that inspired by the presence of D. H. Lawrence and his unapologetically German wife in Cornwall in 1917.

The need of a regular income to support his literary career was always present to Coleridge's mind at this time. One possibility was to become a Unitarian minister, and now and again he went to preach in Taunton and Bristol. In January 1798 he was offered the post of minister at Shrewsbury and went there to deliver a specimen sermon. Among those in the congregation was the young William Hazlitt who has left a brilliant account of this and later encounters with Coleridge in his essay 'On My First Acquaintance with Poets'. Just as Coleridge had agreed to accept, he received the strikingly generous offer of £150 a year for life from the Wedgwood family and quickly disentangled himself.

Hazlitt came to stay at Nether Stowey in the summer of 1798 for three weeks. Already Coleridge was planning a change of scenery. He and Wordsworth proposed to pay for a tour in Germany with the proceeds of *Lyrical Ballads*, sent to their publisher Cottle in June. On 14 September he embarked in 'a spectacular greatcoat' (naturally with gigantic book-pockets) from Great Yarmouth on his first trip abroad. The

Wordsworths were seasick, but he was not. By the time he got back from his German expedition, considerably extended from the three months originally intended to as long as ten, much had happened. His second child, Berkeley, who had been born four months before Coleridge's departure, died in February, but he did not hurry home. He was not to visit Nether Stowey again until around Christmas 1801 when he stayed for three weeks with Poole.

There are three main ways in which a poet can concern himself with nature. The first is by particular description, by the accurate recording of the detail of nature, of specific natural objects such as animals, birds, trees, flowers, rocks, and streams. Secondly, there is the evocation of landscape, the recording of a general impression of the natural environment. Finally, there is the response to nature as a whole, an intimation of the place of man within it, an apprehension of the moral or spiritual significance of nature, seen as something much more than a field for industrial exploitation. Coleridge and Wordsworth were both poets of nature in the third sense, seeking to express in poetry a sense of man's connection to nature as the condition of his truest happiness and fulfilment. But they differed in the kind of description of nature from which they derived their general reflections about it. Coleridge, for all his reputation as an abstract metaphysician, is a poet of the first kind, a master of particular description. Wordsworth, commonly thought of as the paradigm of a nature poet, is, by comparison, an impressionist.

These lines from *This Lime-Tree Bower My Prison* are characteristic of Coleridge's exactness in the description of detail:

> Pale beneath the blaze
> Hung the transparent foliage; and I watch'd
> Some broad and sunny leaf, and lov'd to see
> The shadow of the leaf and stem above
> Dappling its sunshine! And that walnut-tree
> Was richly ting'd, and a deep radiance lay
> Full on the ancient ivy, which usurps
> Those fronting elms, and now, with blackest mass
> Makes their dark branches gleam a lighter hue
> Through the late twilight...

That is the product of closely attentive observation. By comparison Wordsworth on the daffodils is vague and sketchy:

> When all at once I saw a crowd,
> A host, of golden daffodils;
> Beside the lake, beneath the trees,
> Fluttering and dancing in the breeze...
> Ten thousand saw I at a glance,
> Tossing their heads in sprightly dance.

That is what happens if you wander lonely as a cloud and look at things only from a distance. Wordsworth's eye here is like Monet's; Coleridge's more like Dürer's.

Where Wordsworth appears to advantage is in his account of the leading features of a landscape. To take a homely example:

> The day is come when I again repose
> Here, under this dark sycamore, and view
> These plots of cottage-ground, these orchard-tufts,
> Which, at this season, with their unripe fruits,
> Are clad in one green hue, and lose themselves
> 'Mid groves and copses. Once again I see
> These hedge-rows, hardly hedge-rows, little lines
> Of sportive wood run wild: these pastoral farms,
> Green to the very door; and wreaths of smoke
> Sent up, in silence, from among the trees!

More glorious still is Wordworth's handling of the grander scenery of the Lake District, as in the famous passage in Book I of *The Prelude* about taking a boat out on the lake at night:

> I dipped my oars into the silent lake,
> And, as I rose upon the stroke, my boat
> Went heaving through the water like a swan;
> When, from behind that craggy steep till then
> The horizon's bound, a huge peak, black and huge,
> As if with voluntary power instinct
> Upreared its head. I struck and struck again,
> And growing still in stature the grim shape
> Towered up between me and the stars, and still,
> For so it seemed, with purpose of its own
> And measured motion like a living thing,
> Strode after me...

A. N. Whitehead has suggested that Wordsworth's descriptive bias can be attributed to the typically unchanging character of his home region: mountains, waterfalls, hilly pastures, all varying little with the passage of the seasons. Coleridge's west country is altogether more mutable.

Coleridge did not become a nature poet—or, one might add, a natural poet—in one bound. His first writings are for the most part rhetorical, verbose, and conventional. A few years before *The Ancient Mariner* and *Kubla Khan* he could write, with every evidence of seriousness:

> O meek attendant of Sol's setting blaze,
> I hail, sweet star, thy chaste effulgent glow:
> On thee full oft with fixéd eye I gaze
> Till I, methinks, all spirit seem to grow.

Only two years before his most creative period he wrote a widely noticed group of sonnets 'on eminent characters' of which this passage of fustian is representative:

> Stanhope! I hail, with ardent Hymn, thy name!
> Thou shalt be bless'd and lov'd, when in the dust
> Thy corse shall moulder—Patriot pure and just!
> And o'er thy tomb the grateful hand of FAME...

But in the same year the first clear signs of a new, more natural poetic manner, freed from Zephyrs and Muses and capitalized abstractions like Pity and Solitude and Mirth, were shown by his *To A Young Ass*:

> Poor little Foal of an oppressèd race!
> I love the languid patience of thy face:
> And oft with gentle hand I give thee bread,
> And clap thy ragged coat, and pat thy head.

His descriptive exactness appears in some lines about the ass's tied-up mother:

> Or is thy sad heart thrill'd with filial pain
> To see thy wretched mother's shorten'd chain?
> And truly, very piteous is her lot—
> Chain'd to a log within a narrow spot,
> Where the close-eaten grass is scarcely seen,
> While sweet around her waves the tempting green!

By the time he came to Stowey he had essentially liberated himself from the kind of decayed Augustan formalism which he had at first supposed to be the proper vehicle for poetry. But, being a nature poet of my first, minutely descriptive type, rather than a poet of landscape like Wordsworth, his work of the Nether Stowey period does not contain all that much in the way of direct evocation of the surrounding scenery. But there are suggestive passages.

In *This Lime-Tree Bower My Prison* he thinks of his friends 'on springy heath, along the hill-top edge' and of their getting a view of

> The many-steepled tract magnificent
> Of hilly fields and meadows, and the sea,
> With some fair bark, perhaps, whose sails light up
> The slip of smooth clear blue betwixt two Isles
> Of purple shadow!

No doubt he is thinking of them as looking towards Watchet, which is presumably the port of the Ancient Mariner's departure.

Christabel is full of standard Gothic romance material: a castle at night with owls, a thick forest, a moat, a massive gate, a toothless mastiff. All that has nothing whatever to do with the Quantocks and Nether Stowey. But in *Kubla Khan*, for all its exotic theme and furnishings, there are touches of Somerset. The 'deep romantic chasm' might well have been inspired by a stream hurling itself into the Bristol Channel between narrow banks and down a steep cliff somewhere between Porlock and Lynton. It was in that region that the poem was written. Coleridge, feeling ill in the course of making his long way home from Lynton on foot in October 1797, put up at a lonely farm near Culbone, probably Ash Farm, half-way between Lynton and Porlock. In Culbone Combe the neighbourhood is equipped with an appropriate romantic chasm. Here the poem was written. The 'person from Porlock' on whose interruption Coleridge blames its incomplete state would have had to come for only about five miles, if, indeed, there was such a person.

The cottage at Nether Stowey is alluded to in one of the first poems to be written there: the dedicatory lines to his eldest brother George that were sent to him with some poems.

> Or when, as now, on some delicious eve,
> We in our sweet sequester'd orchard-plot
> Sit on the tree crook'd earthward; whose old boughs,
> That hang above us in an arborous roof,
> Stirr'd by the faint gale of departing May,
> Send their loose blossoms slanting o'er our heads!

In *Frost At Midnight* the opening movement describes the poet sitting at night by his son's cradle in the cottage 'with all the numberless goings-on of life inaudible as dreams'. He thinks back to his childhood in rural Ottery St Mary, his exile at school in London, and promises his son a country upbringing: 'all seasons shall be sweet to thee'. In *France: an Ode* of February 1798 there are obvious references to the Somerset coast:

> ... on that sea-cliff's verge,
> Whose pines, scarce travell'd by the breeze above
> Had made one murmur with the distant surge!

That poem registers his deliverance from the French Revolution and its way of realizing the ideal of human freedom. Like the English Stalinists who swallowed the Russian invasion of Hungary in 1956 but could not tolerate the invasion of Czechoslovakia in 1968, Coleridge, who had managed to digest the Terror without any sign of distress, boggled at the invasion of Switzerland.

Possibly the best evocation of the scenery of the Quantocks in Coleridge is contained in the opening passage of his *Fears in Solitude* of April 1798 and even more its closing lines in which Stowey is mentioned by name.

> And now beloved Stowey! I behold
> Thy church-tower, and, methinks, the four huge elms
> Clustering, which mark the mansion of my friend;
> And close behind them, hidden from my view,
> Is my own lowly cottage, where my babe
> And my babe's mother dwell in peace!

The presence of the natural surroundings in which all Coleridge's great, and much of his good, poetry was written is not obtrusive in what came into existence in his short stay there. But there is enough evidence of the effect of the place upon him to invest it with an attraction over and above that exercised by its visible beauties.

6

The Trouble with Kant

In setting out to discuss *the* trouble with Kant I may seem to be suggesting that there is only one. I do think that there is one fundamental one, which is that he is a wild and intellectually irresponsible arguer. An innate leaning that must have been enhanced by the intellectual isolation of Königsberg, which preserved him from serious criticism. I shall be sticking to one particular example of this failing. It is the account he gives of the way in which the common world of experience is constructed or synthesized by applying some piece of mental apparatus—the forms of intuition and the categories—to what he calls the manifold of sensation. The rather elementary question I want to raise about this theory is that of how the claim can be made good that the outcome of this process is just one, single world; for all of us, for each of us at different times, even for any one of us at a particular time.

The question can be put in another way. Is the order of the common world wholly imposed on it by the mind or is it determined by intrinsic features of the manifold of sensation? Kant seems firmly committed to the first option: that the order of the common world—spatial, temporal, substantial, and causal—is wholly due to 'pure intuition' and the understanding. But if that is what he thinks then how can there be anything objective about the synthesized product? Could the unordered sensory material involved not be arranged in indefinitely numerous ways, each just as orderly, and so just as good, as the others?

Before getting caught up in the detailed complexities of the subject, a simple analogy may be helpful. For reasons that will appear it will not be a very close analogy, but even so it may be illuminating. Suppose you are given a bag full of variously coloured squares, with sides an inch long, and a table, and you are told to arrange the little coloured squares on the tip of the table in an orderly way. You lay the squares out in a random fashion and are at once confronted by a mass of alternative possibilities. You can arrange the squares more or less concentrically with blues on the outside, the reds around the edge of this hollow square, the greens inside them, and a block of yellows in the middle. Or you can arrange the colours in four quadrants. Or in four parallel strips, running from left to right. Or in alternating sequence—a blue, a red, a green, a yellow, starting at the top left hand corner. And so on, indefinitely. The arranging mind of the square-orderer has at its disposal an enormous number of possible ways of putting its random collection of squares together in an orderly fashion. None of them can sensibly be described as more orderly than any of the others. But it would not matter much if some such discriminations could be made. The orders discriminated would still, after all, be orders.

For an operation of this general character to get started the raw materials, in this example the little squares, have to have some intrinsic qualities of their own, in this case colour. If they were all of the same colour there would be no way of arranging them at all, other than setting them out in some regular shape: square or rectangle or diamond or triangle. This feature of the analogy corresponds to Kant's requirement that the manifold of sensation is not wholly undifferentiated. But the raw material of an arrangement can be differentiated without dictating that any one of the numerous possibilities of arrangement it leaves open is to be preferred to any of the others.

Is it an objection to the analogy I have been considering that it makes a spatial arrangement out of elements that are themselves spatial, whereas Kant appears to maintain that spatiality is conferred on non-spatial raw material by the application of the appropriate form of intuition to it? It could be replied, in the first place, that it is not easy to see how one could make a spatial arrangement out of items that are themselves non-spatial. All conceivable spatial arrangement is spatial rearrangement. It is perfectly possible to make a diagram of non-spatial items, abstract ones, for example, like philosophical doctrines or sciences. The spatial relations in the diagram do not represent spatial relations between the elements mentioned in it, which will be those of genus and species, perhaps. Nor will making the diagram confer or impose spatial relations on the distinct items involved.

Further, can it plausibly be maintained that the manifold of sensation, whatever precisely it may be, is wholly non-spatial in itself and until the spatial form of intuition is applied to it? Kant seems to know something about it and I imagine that most of the rest of us think we do too. In the *Critique of Pure Reason* he says that no judgements can be made about it, but he says the opposite in the *Prolegomena*. Its most insistent aspect, with which philosophers have, no doubt, too exclusively occupied themselves, is the visual field and its contents. We can obviously make judgements about it, to the extent, at least, of describing it, even if, as many would hold, we can do so only in terms derived from and dependant on the language with which we describe the common world. The visual field, at any moment, is an extended spatial array, whose contents are arranged on the axes up-and-down and left-and-right. The same is true of the tactical field, if one can talk of such a thing in the singular, given the multiplicity of our tactually sensitive surfaces. Its elements present themselves as above and below, to the left or the right, in front of or behind each other.

Kant, then, in holding that spatiality is imposed on the manifold of sensation by applying a spatial form of intuition to it is saying something apparently unintelligible, since what is non-spatial cannot be arranged spatially. The implication that the manifold is non-spatial is merely false, since the immediate deliverances of the two epistemically primary sense-modalities—sight and touch—are more or less momentary spatial arrays. In any case, if the spatial character of these arrays were arbitrarily imposed on them, they would be useless for his project of accounting for our experience of a common objective world.

In such a situation one is naturally inclined to wonder if one has not missed the point. Perhaps Kant is not denying that the manifold is a spatial array, that its contents stand in spatial relations to one another. What he must be saying is that the little momentary space of a given manifold is not presented as part of a single all-inclusive space (a claim no one would dispute, I imagine) and that it is that comprehensive unity which is imposed by the mind. I have argued elsewhere, in an exploratory way, that it is not inconceivable that we should have empirical grounds for acknowledging two distinct real spaces. But I do not deny that the supposition involved in that fantasy is wildly contrary to fact. My claim was only that it was an internally consistent supposition, in a way that the supposition of a multiplicity of real times is not. I agree entirely that we make it a criterion of the real existence of a physical entity that it is located in a single space, along with every other real physical thing, that all of them, and only they, stand in spatial relations to everything else.

The principle of the unity of space does not entail that space is Euclidean or that the propositions of Euclidean geometry are both synthetic and *a priori*. It is, however, an important principle and one that deserves investigation. It is a necessary truth that all real, objective physical things are in a single space. But it is not a necessary truth that we can accommodate, as we in fact can, the greater part of what we encounter in sense-experience in a single space. It is a contingent truth, even if one of the most fundamental importance, that we can critically sift what is presented to us so that the greater part of it can be located in a single all-inclusive space. If that were not so we should have no conception of an objective world. It is comparable, in a way, to the equally important fact of the more or less universal visual characteristics with particular tactual ones.

What is presented to us at one moment of perception is a spatial array of items that exist at that moment. It is limited in time to a specious present rather than a mathematical instant and it is spatially limited as well, although, in the visual case at any rate, it has no definite boundary. We naturally take it to be connected to previous momentary spaces that we can recall. We take it that it is identical with them or overlaps them, where they contain closely similar contents in closely similar spatial relations to each other. That will be the case in situations where in fact we do not move our eyes or fingers or move them only slowly. If we move them more quickly we take it that the momentary spaces are adjoining. If we happen to close our eyes while looking out of the window of a high speed train we take it, at least, that the presented spaces are spatially related.

There are perceived spatial arrays which we do not, at any rate for very long, connect with others, most obviously those present to us in dreams. These are ruled out not so much because there are no items in them corresponding to identifiable real things, since dreamed-of scenes are often familiar, but because they are causally incoherent. They may, for example, place us as observers at positions we causally could not have been at, given the positions where we fall asleep and wake up. Events in a dream, furthermore, are causally incoherent with events occurring before and after it.

How are these spatial connections established and justified? We do not perceive space itself, only spatially related things. In the elementary cases of identity and overlap the required connection is provided by the identification of items in different momentary spaces as momentary phases or stages of things which persist from one such moment of perception to another. That is made easier by the fact that our sense-experience is not, in Bergson's term, cinematographic, the presentation of a series of still-life snapshots. It is a continuum, usually with little change, sometimes no change at all, from one moment to the next. There are sudden large interruptions of continuity after which, in order to tie down spatially what is now presented, we have to hunt around for the continuants which we have hitherto used as landmarks. If I pass out at a party and come to in a strange hospital bed I may have no idea where I am. But I shall be confident that I can connect the space in which I now find myself to the space to which I am accustomed: to my house, the bus station, the cathedral, and so on. In practice I shall rely on the testimony of nurses and visitors. But in principle, and if distrustful of my witnesses, I can settle the matter directly by going out and looking around.

The best sort of things to serve as landmarks are these collections of qualities, compresent at any one time in a particular place, among which being of a definite shape, marked off in a hard-edged way from the environment, is the most important. Such things are sharply different in colour and texture from their surroundings and are solid in the everyday sense of resisting pressure of the sort that leads to deformation, a serious lasting change of shape, whether that pressure is applied to them by one's own body or by other solid things of the same general sort that come into contact with them. These are substances, in the ordinary sense of the word.

As it happens we come across a good many things of this general kind. Quite a number of them, like large natural features of the scenery or substantial buildings, retain the same spatial relations to other things of the same sort more or less permanently, as long, at any rate, as we have any epistemic use for them. They provide a stable background, against which the movements and changes of moving and changing things take place, a stage for the drama of history to be played out on.

Matters would be very different if we inhabited a continuum of intermingling fluids, having ourselves, perhaps, the bodily form of a persisting oil slick, somewhat resistant to absorption in these surroundings. Such a world, if it deserved the name, would be a phantasmagoria, the sort of condition that might prevail in a delirium.

The things that constitute the one enduring real space, then, are collections of qualities that are spatially coincident at any one moment, that continue either unchanged in qualities and relative position from one moment to the next or change in either of these ways very little between neighbouring moments and include as a dominant feature a characteristic and persisting shape, evident to sight as a marked difference of quality, specifically colour, between the outer edge of the thing and its environment, and to touch in the same sort of difference of texture.

These enduring solids are involved with space in three important ways. In the first place, they are collections of qualities existing at any given time in the *very same place*. Secondly, among these qualities the dominant one, that of having a characteristic (and persistent) *shape* is an irreducibly spatial determination. Finally, these things serve as the persisting landmarks by reference to which different momentary spaces (apart from occasional causally incoherent oddities) can be connected together in a single all-inclusive space.

I have been sketching a way in which the conception of a unitary space might be applied to our experience. It is one in which the conception is, indeed, a criterion of real physical existence, a necessary condition of our experience of a common, objective world. But it is not a necessary truth. It requires our manifolds of sensation to exhibit a number of contingent, if very deep-seated, features: that they should contain collections of qualities at the same place, that among such collections definite shape must be included, and that these shapes—including collections—should recur or persist and, for the most part, in recurrent or persistent spatial relations to each other.

I used my analogy of the bag full of squares to argue that Kant's apparent account of the workings of the space as a form of intuition made the spatial arrangement of what is presented in sense-experience a matter of arbitrary choice from an unlimited field of possibilities. The *spatial coincidence* of presented qualities and their organization into *shapes*, it seems, has no basis in the manifold of sensation for Kant but is an arbitrary contribution by the perceiving mind. I mentioned as a possible interpretation of Kant that all he meant was that only the unity of space was imposed on what is sensibly presented. And I have sketched a way in which, provided that the manifold does include the spatial coincidence of qualities, with shape among them, that imposition could be successfully brought off, although, as against Kant, I argued that success cannot be guaranteed. It could be guaranteed only if the more lavish theory that all spatial characteristics are imposed by the mind is adopted.

That Kant actually held this more lavish theory has irresistible warrant from his text. Here are two quotations from the opening paragraphs of the *Transcendental Aesthetic*, in both editions of the *Critique*. First, 'that which in appearance corresponds to the sensation I call its *matter*; but that which effects that the manifold of appearance can be arranged under certain relations, I call its *form*. But that in which our sensations are merely arranged, and by which they are susceptible of assuming a certain form, cannot be itself sensation' (*CPR* A20, B34). Secondly, a little later, in terms explicitly relevant to the doctrine of space as a form of intuition: 'if I take away from our representation of a body, all that the understanding thinks as belonging to it, as substance, force, divisibility etc., and also whatever belongs to sensation, as impenetrability, hardness, colour etc.; yet there is still something left us from this empirical intuition, namely, extension and shape. These belong to pure intuition, which exists, *a priori*, in the mind, as a mere form of sensibility, and without any real object of the senses or any sensation' (*CPR* A21, B35). He could hardly have made his adherence to what I have called the lavish theory clearer.

By it the contents of the mind in perception are allocated, exclusively and without remainder, to three classes: first, sensation (impenetrability, hardness, colour); secondly, pure, that is to say non-sensory, intuition (extension and shape); thirdly, the understanding (substance, force, divisibility). That is to say, quite unequivocally, that spatiality, i.e. extension, the occupancy of space, and shape, the occupancy of a definite region in space, are not sensory, nor part of the manifold of sensation.

What might have brought Kant up short is the converse of Berkeley's objection to Locke's account of secondary qualities. Berkeley said that it is impossible to conceive extension without colour. It is, of course, entirely possible since one can conceive it as invisible, but as having a texture, accessible to the sense of touch. But Berkeley was on to something. Extension requires some sort of filling and, of course, usually has both visual and tactual content. The converse argument which applies to Kant is stronger. Can one really conceive colour without extension? Even if it were allowed, which is at least questionable, that a coloured speck in the sky is an unextended point, it will stand in spatial relations to other such spots or to more amply formed celestial objects. The same considerations apply to hardness. As for impenetrability, to the extent that it is distinct from hardness, it consists in the exclusive occupancy of a bit of space. To penetrate that space a thing would have to get inside the original occupant. An unextended point is therefore logically impenetrable since there is no extension to be penetrated. Something else, however, another point, could *take* its place and cause it to go somewhere else. But, a point, even if at once unextended and sensible, is still spatially related to things of its own or other kinds, will possess, as one might put it, external if not internal spatial characteristics.

Why did Kant suppose that the spatial form of the world of experience is imposed on it by the mind? Part of the explanation may be that he was influenced by a long tradition of ontological contempt for relations, a tradition that was a favourite object of criticism for the early Bertrand Russell. It goes back to Locke, who said that relations 'are not contained in the real existence of things, but (are) something extraneous and superinduced' (*Essay*, bk. II, ch. XXV, para. 8) and to Leibniz to hold that they are not real but only '*phenomena bene fundata*'. But they did not go as far as Kant in extruding relations from the world and seeing them as the work of the mind, as T. H. Green supposed. Locke said they all 'terminate in simple ideas', in other words, are reducible to qualities, the indefinitely multiplicable results of acts of comparison, rooted in the intrinsic or positive natures of the things compared. For Leibniz, if they were phenomena they were still well-founded ones.

I suspect that the denial of reality to relations, whether partial, as with Locke and Leibniz, or total, as with Kant, is not, as Russell seems to have thought, traceable simply to the preference of philosophers for substantives and adjectives over verbs and prepositions. That is only the grammatical expression of an underlying ontological prejudice. Its source is the point, noted by Ockham, that if I move my little finger I bring about a huge, perhaps infinite, number of changes, since by doing so I have changed the spatial relations of everything else to my little finger. Could such a modest action really bring about such a vast set of changes? We may perhaps distinguish relational changes that involve a qualitative change in one or more of the things related and those that do not. When Bob leaves the room I become the tallest man in it without any qualitative change in me or Bob or the other men in the room. It is not a real change like my suddenly, miraculously growing taller than Bob, while he, retaining his height, is still there.

I conclude that Kant really did think that all the spatial features of the world of experience are imposed on it by the mind, without any influence or constraint on the operation being present in the given, the manifold of sensation. The endowing of what is itself non-spatial with spatial characteristics is hardly intelligible. In particular the qualities Kant does acknowledge as found in sensation are themselves, for the most part, intrinsically spatial. Worst of all, if the spatial arrangement of the contents of the world of experience were imposed on it in the way Kant describes, that order would be arbitrary. At any given time one perceiver could carry it out in any of an indefinite number of ways; he could do it in different ways at different times; there is no reason why any of the ways he chooses should agree with the ways chosen by anyone else and no reason why their ways should agree with each other.

Throughout the discussion so far I have taken for granted an ordinary, naively realistic conception of time. By that I mean that our manifolds of sensation, our momentary tracts of sense-experience, are in reality arranged in a single linear order and that they are presented as being so, in our direct perceptions of movement and other change, remembered, with more or less accuracy, as being so, and that this personal experience of time-relations is the basis for inferences about time-relations of events outside our experience, to each other and to events within it. The alternative is really too dreadful to contemplate. Is anything more irresistibly imposed on, rather than by, us than the passage of time, the beforeness and afterness of experience?

We are often ignorant or mistaken about the time-relations of past events in our own lives and in the public world. We find out about mistakes and counter our ignorance by consulting diaries, old letters, and newspaper files. If we lacked such aids to memory, like our primitive forefathers, our memories might be better than they are. Causal knowledge can help us correct our beliefs based on memories of direct experience of time-relations, but only in a secondary, dependent way. After all the knowledge of the causal relations involved rests on the assumption that the temporal relations implied by our causal beliefs are, on the whole, correctly grasped.

The continuants which, I have been arguing, are the foundations of the spatial unity of the world, are, in the everyday, more or less Aristotelian, sense of the word, substances. They have three noteworthy general characteristics which distinguish them from what Kant appears to regard as substances. They may, and many, perhaps all, do, come into and go out of existence. None of them has to be eternal. Still, there are some which were in existence before there was any experience, human or other, and will almost certainly still exist after it is all over: the stars, the sun, the moon, Mount Everest, the Rock of Gibraltar.

Secondly, they do not make up the whole material content of the world. There is also a lot of stuff about, most of it in fluid form, as liquid or gas, but some more solid, such as snow and coal and dust. The crucial point about stuff is that it has no characteristic shape, but comes in loosely and unstably bound tracts. For that reason it is only weakly individuated. It is not countable. There is *some* snow outside the front door, and a policeman.

Thirdly, everyday substances, straightforward material things, are perceptible; among them are the chairs and tables which have always been the paradigm objects of perception.

None of these three characteristics is possessed by what Kant regards as substance. According to him substance is that whose schema is 'the permanence of the real in time', that which is conserved or remains the same through all change. It is, first of all, eternal, in existence at all times at which anything exists. Secondly, it makes up the entire material content of the world, since it is the basic raw material of all fluids and other stuffs as well as of common, persistently shaped, solid material things. It follows from this second feature, and, perhaps more circuitously, from the first, that it is not perceptible. If it is too small to be broken up, it is too small to be perceived. Perhaps it can be perceived in an attenuated way in exceptional circumstances, as when a beta particle's track is seen in a cloud chamber. For the most part, atoms or fundamental particles are not perceived.

Kant's highly theoretical notion of substance is not needed to bring order into our experience; it is, rather, a glorious simplifying assumption for physical science. It might be thought that eternal objects are required for the unification of the totality of momentary spaces into a single, all-inclusive space. But that is not the case. Unification can be achieved by a reasonable number of mortal continuants, lasting long enough to overlap some of the lifetime of a reasonable number of others, handing on the torch of unification to the latter, in the style of a relay race, before they themselves fall out of it.

Kant's philosophical atoms have no part to play in the solution of what is ostensibly his main problem: that of accounting for the emergence of a common, objective world from the deliverances of sensation. What that requires, in the first instance, is only that some of what is physically real should persist for some time in an identifiable, countable manner. The main further requirement, which I shall come to shortly, is that experience should, for the most part, display enough causal regularity for the minority of wild or discordant experiences to be expelled from the objective world made up of the docile, orderly majority.

A principle of conservation like Kant's has no role, then, in the ordering of experience, As far as our ordinary conception of the real world is concerned it is quite all right for things to go out of existence, by wearing out or erosion, and to come into existence out of nothing, usually in slow stages, like an apple on a tree. People living today know, or take themselves to know, that that is not what really happens, but the knowledge contributes nothing much to their everyday commerce with the world, the ordinary management of life. The theory of conservation is suggested by facts we learn in ordinary perception: the dust on the table, proves, on closer inspection, perhaps with a magnifying glass, to be a mass of tiny particles, there turn out to be small fragments of the worn-out eraser on or near the desk. The ash left by a large log burnt in a fireplace, however, is hardly up to the job, even if the smoke is added in, and needs theoretical support.

Kant's substance, then, is a theoretical refinement of everyday perceptual substance. The latter is, indeed, an indispensable feature of our common world of objective experience. But it is not imposed on what is given in sensation in an arbitrary fashion from outside. It is prompted by the given facts of spatial compresence of qualities, including a definite shape, persisting in identical or closely similar partial relations to other such sets of qualities.

The same considerations apply to Kant's account of the category of cause. The schema of causation, he says, is 'the real in time which is always followed by something else' or 'the succession of the manifold insofar as that succession is subject to a rule'. That amounts to saying that causation is regular sequence. Causes and effects are events: changes of quality or position in one object that are followed, or even accompanied, by changes in quality or position in another. The possibility of such a connection between two such changes strikes us when the two events occur at closely neighbouring, or even, to all intents and purposes, simultaneous, times in the histories of two spatially distinct, but closely juxtaposed objects, particularly when nothing else is perceptibly happening in the neighbourhood, nearby objects all being qualitatively and positionally unchanging.

If such an association frequently occurs and neither of the two associates is ever found to occur when the other is found not to occur, we then confidently take it that there is a causal connection, through which we can infer either from perceiving the occurrence of the other. (That is a needlessly strong requirement; it is usually enough that we can infer one from another, but not in the other direction as well; we can make do with a sufficient or a necessary condition and not insist on both.)

It is surely absurd to suppose that we, or our understandings, pick about in our manifolds of sensation to find similar items and then impose places on them, near to places imposed on the members of another set of items similar to one another, so as to constitute a causal partnership. They are presented to us as spatio-temporally juxtaposed; nearness is not thrust upon them. If that were not so no counter-example to a causal claim need ever be admitted. We could always rearrange the manifold of sensation so as to produce an instance of the alleged cause near to an instance of the alleged effect.

Spatial and temporal juxtaposition are just as much part of the manifold of sensation, of what is presented to the perceiver, as colour or hardness, to take two of his examples of what it contains. In practice, of course, we are not confined to recognizing causal connection only between events that are near each other in space and time. One can shoot a bird a hundred yards away or talk to a friend on the telephone. One can put a heavy sack on a rickety table which then collapses a few minutes later. But in some cases of this sort we usually suppose, and usually find, some intervening mechanism linking cause and effect, spatially or temporally as the case requires, a speeding bullet, telephone wires, stresses and strains in the structure of the table.

We rely on everyday convictions about cause and effect to sift out items in our experience that do not fit in with the rest: dreams, hallucinations, illusions, or simple mistakes. In dreams one often appears to be in a familiar environment, full of familiar persisting things in their usual causal relations to each other. Such dream experiences, Kant would surely have to admit, involve the application of the categories. But that does not make them objectively real. In other, more chaotic dreams the persisting things are unfamiliar and behave strangely, a fact that can serve, at least afterwards, as a weak, internal, criterion of dreamhood. In either case there is a failure of causal connection between the dreamed events and events on either temporal side of the dream, the more conclusive, external criterion. People I know recall nothing of what I seem to have been doing and show no effects of what I seem to have said or done to them. My car is still in the drive, not the refrigerator it turned into in the dream. My children are still in their thirties and not twelve and ten as they seemed to be just now.

Causal knowledge about the circumstances in which ordinary things go out of existence corrects my inclination to suppose that something I failed to notice in its usual place for a moment has not suddenly gone out of existence for that moment and then come back into existence when I do see it again. The usual correlation between the chair that I touch and feel and the chair that I see sustains my belief that the chair I am sitting on, and feel with my behind, and which I take to prevent my falling to the floor, is also the currently unseen chair that I have seen and expect to see again.

In general, my freedom to determine causal connections between events is constrained by the spatial and temporal character of what is presented to me; it is not a constructive fabrication. Causality is not given, although it is as good as presented to perceivers by elementary experiences of pushing and pulling, of moving one's limbs and manipulating one's environment. In any case, its ingredients, juxtaposition and exceptionless recurrence, are features of recurrent and remembered experience.

I would agree with Kant that in order to acquire or possess a conception of an objective, real world one has to recognize causal connections. They are the instrument we use to cast out wild items or tracts of experience. Derived from the great bulk of our experience as a whole, they set the standard which the comparatively small residue of non-objective experience fails to come up to. Causality, as Kant would say, is a presupposition of the objectivity of experience.

But that does not entail either that every event has a cause or that, whatever it was like, our experience would be susceptible of objective ordering. As to the first there are many things we do not know the cause of and many of which we have no idea what sort of thing the cause might be, if there is one. Why do ordinary material things persist, in the epistemically valuable way that they do? It is enough that we have some fairly good ideas about the sort of events which could cause them to cease doing so: bombs, fires, powerful hammers, axes, boiling. and so forth. But it is not really to explain their persistence to say it is the result of the failure of such mishaps to take place. There is the physical theory of solids which explains the persistence of that which most obviously does persist in terms of its densely packed molecular structure, held together by powerful intermolecular forces. Helpfully explanatory as that may be in its way, it really does no more than shift the burden of explanation from common solids to the molecules of which they are composed and their evident reluctance, arranged as they are, to fly or wander off in all directions. Mankind formed the conception of an objective world of persisting things long before it had any notion of the molecular structure that they actually have or of their having a molecular structure of a dense and glued-together nature at all. It is enough to accept that some things persist sufficiently to get the objective world going, even if many do not: puffs of smoke, card houses, zabaglione, and so forth. We need some causal order as well, to rule out epistemic outlaws of various kinds. We do not need the belief or the fact that every event has a cause.

Secondly, the amenability of our experience to causal ordering is a matter of contingent fact, not of necessity. That experience could have been, or be going to turn into, a delirious phantasmagoria, in which the conditions of rational belief and rational agency would not obtain. If there had been a thinking being on duty during the first three seconds after the Big Bang, with new elements being formed in explosive atomic transformations and everything rushing about at vast speeds in all directions, he could have made nothing of it until it had settled down a bit.

The trouble with Kant, as I see it, is that he takes our conception of the world as an array of persisting things, causally related, in a single space and time to be the result of an imposition of the notions of space, time, substance, and cause on a wholly passive sensory raw material and thus to be entirely arbitrary. His account of the matter allows for an indefinitely large number of orders in which our successive manifolds of sensation could be arranged. None of these ways of distinguishing what there is and occurs from what I merely think is and occurs has any priority or superiority to any of the others.

It worries me that none of the many commentators I have studied draws attention to this radical weakness in Kant. Am I making a complete fool of myself? Have I fundamentally misinterpreted his meaning? I draw some comfort from the fact that no philosopher seems to be a Kantian, for all the profound respect he is usually accorded. The whole Kantian apparatus of categories and schemata and the transcendental unity of apperception survives only as a subject for study, not for use. But it is not my intention to deny that he is a great philosopher. He raised a lot of fascinating questions, and much is to be learnt from working out what went wrong with the answers he gave to them.

7

Hegel Made Visible

Until recently the only substantial biography of Hegel was the one brought out by his follower Karl Rosenkranz in 1844, thirteen years after Hegel's death. The book has not been translated and it is perhaps significant that it is merely mentioned, with no comment on its uniqueness, in Frederick Copleston's *History of Philosophy* and in the article on Hegel in the latest (last?) printed *Britannica*.

There are several reasons for this neglect. The first is trivial, but symptomatic of the difficulty of describing Hegel's life and character. It is his name, which strikes one not as that of a person but of a thing: an asteroid perhaps. Associated with that is the fact that he does not seem to have had a functioning first name. He was indeed baptized Georg Wilhelm Friedrich. But, in adult life at least, nobody seems to have called him by any of them. His devoted and affectionate wife, who was some twenty years his junior, always referred to him as Hegel. But that may have been the custom of the epoch. The mother of the heroine of *Pride and Prejudice* always addresses her husband as Mr Bennet, at roughly the time Hegel was serving as rector of a Gymnasium and toiling away at the most intractable of his works, the *Science of Logic*.

Next there is the matter of his appearance. One picture is nearly always used when occasion arises to produce one. It shows him as pale and rather flabby, with some thin hair tumbling over his forehead, his eyes looking suspiciously to his left, giving very much the impression of a bankrupt undertaker confronted by his creditors.

What principally endows Hegel with his singularly abstract transcendence of ordinary humanity is his writing. There is a lot of concrete illustrative material in the large works on applied philosophy—aesthetics, religion, the history of philosophy, and the philosophy of history—reconstructed after his death from notes of his lectures by students. But his own writings are for the most part carried on at a stratospheric intellectual altitude, with vague technicalities being moved bewilderingly about in puzzling appositions and compounds ('in-itself and for-itself' and the like). In the crowning elements of his system—the *Science of Logic* and the *Encyclopedia of the Philosophical Sciences*—this is most oppressively evident. The words do not sound like those of a person but of something altogether more diaphanous—the Absolute, it would seem.

It might be argued that there is no real need for biographies of philosophers. But as the perpetual wranglings of philosophers suggest, personality enters strongly into philosophy. Mathematicians have lives too, often quite interesting ones. Galois died in a maliciously provoked duel; Archimedes contributed to the defence of Syracuse against the Romans; Newton slaved away at deciphering the prophecies of the Book of Daniel. Knowing these things about them is no help in trying to understand their mathematical work. But Hume's grimly Calvinist upbringing helps to explain the peculiarly acid character of his hostility towards religion. T. H. Green's having had an alcoholic brother may account for the unusually moralistic tone he gave to his Hegelian philosophical commitment. Bertrand Russell's solitary upbringing as an orphan in the house of an authoritarian grandmother throws some light on the weird inhumanity of his moral thinking. The more fundamental question of why one should be interested in the works of philosophers hardly invites a rapid answer. It may be enough to say that even if their problems do not seem of intense interest, the ingenuity of their answers may be. Furthermore, throughout its history—apart from intervals of scholastic introversion, as in the fourteenth century, or in much of Anglo-Saxon philosophy today—philosophy has influentially penetrated most other varieties of human thinking. And it is proof of barbarism not to be interested in the history of the human mind.

Hegel was born in 1770 in the city of Stuttgart, capital of Württemberg, a Protestant enclave in generally Catholic southern Germany. He was the son of a middle-ranking official of the state's finance department, a man with the conscientious stolidity and respectable conventional opinions and behaviour proper to his station. He was distinguished by his concern for the education of his intellectually promising elder son. Hegel's mother is a shadowy figure who died in 1783 when he was thirteen. Hegel had a younger brother who became a soldier and died fighting in Napoleon's army in Russia in 1812. (Of the original Württemberg contingent of 16,000, only 1,500 survived.) Hegel's sister, Christiane, was nearer to him in age and much closer to him emotionally; indeed she was somewhat obsessed by him. An intelligent but unstable woman, who proved a difficult member of the household when she lived with Hegel and his wife, she eventually committed suicide.

Hegel went to school at the local, classically oriented Gymnasium and not the more socially elevated, almost business school-like Karlsschule, in accordance with his father's intention that he should become a Protestant clergyman. In pursuit of that plan he went on in 1788, on the eve of the French Revolution, to the University of Tübingen, which was in a decayed state and amounted to little more than a small and undistinguished theological seminary. (Its days of glory as the home of the Tübingen school of biblical criticism under F. C. Baur lay half a century ahead.) Hegel made up for the weaknesses of the place by neglecting his official studies and immersing himself in the currents of thought of the Enlightenment and their apparent actualization in the French Revolution; he studied the philosophy of Kant, which he took to fairly slowly, and that of Kant's immediate critics, and above all, his radical follower Fichte.

These unofficial studies were carried on in intense collaboration with the philosopher Friedrich Schelling and the poet Friedrich Hölderlin. Tübingen at least attracted some interesting students. They engaged in some of the usual student activities: cardplaying, of which Hegel remained fond, beer-drinking in the countryside, some tentative romantic episodes, the planting of a 'freedom tree' to celebrate the French Revolution. Hegel was known by his intimates as 'the Old Man'. On graduating, without distinction, in order to earn a living and to escape the threat of a clerical career, he became a tutor in a reactionary, patrician family in Berne and followed that with another less disagreeable two-year stint of tutoring in Frankfurt. In this melancholy period, his isolation was relieved only by correspondence with his Tübingen friends. One of them, Schelling, was doing disagreeably well. In 1798 he was appointed to a chair at Jena; by the time Hegel left Frankfurt, Schelling had published a number of widely noticed books. It was during this time that Hegel wrote what came out only in 1905 as *Early Theological Writings*.

In 1801, supported by a legacy from his father, who had died two years before, Hegel took an unpaid post at Jena. Before Hegel's arrival there, it had been a very lively intellectual centre, the main site of Kant studies. Fichte had been there and it was the birthplace of German Romanticism with Schiller, and then the Schlegel brothers. By the time Hegel arrived, the glory had faded. Fichte had been sacked for atheism. Not long after Hegel's arrival Schelling appropriated August Schlegel's wife and left for Würzburg, as did several other of the brighter stars. Hegel struggled on and set to work on his first major work, the *Phenomenology of Mind*, which was published in 1807. In the aftermath of the Battle of Jena the university closed down and Hegel, his legacy used up and with no job, was in a desperate position.

During his Jena period his landlady (or possibly cleaning woman) Frau Burkhardt presented him with an illegitimate son, known as Ludwig Fischer. This put Hegel in distinguished philosophical company, alongside Descartes, Hume, Marx, and A. J. Ayer. Ludwig's story is sad. Farmed out at first, he was eventually accepted into Hegel's family, with a painfully marginal status. He naturally resented this, left home as soon as he could, and joined the Dutch army, dying of fever in the Dutch East Indies in the year of Hegel's own death.

Following his difficulties over Ludwig and the collapse of his university, Hegel as usual landed on his feet, shaking off Jena and Frau Burkhardt to edit the local paper in the small town of Bamberg for a year and a half. From there he went to be rector of the Gymnasium in the altogether more significant city of Nuremberg, a considerable step up in the world. In his eight-year period of 'Nuremberg respectability' Hegel settled down into his maturity. At the age of forty-one he married into a good local family, his wife being just under half his age. Her father soon died, her mother thought the world of Hegel, and he became the *de facto* head of the von Tucher family, despite having no *von* of his own. There were evening parties and sightseeing trips into the countryside. But these comforts did not reduce Hegel's resolve to secure a chair in philosophy. In a great many letters to his kindly patron, Niethammer, he reiterated this desire as well as soliciting loans. Hegel was very good at extracting 'travel grants' to supplement his salary. Two sons were born, and Frau Hegel endured a long series of miscarriages in the ultimately successful pursuit of a daughter.

In 1816, at the age of forty-six, Hegel finally secured a chair, at Heidelberg. A year later he brought out the summary of his whole system, his *Encyclopedia of the Philosophical Sciences*, and in 1818 achieved his ideal job, a chair at the University of Berlin, founded by Alexander von Humboldt in 1809 to be a centre of *Bildung* and for the spiritual reconstruction of Germany after its catastrophic disruption by Napoleon. Two years later Hegel published his *Philosophy of Right*, which is probably the most widely read of his works today. It was the last substantial work he wrote, although the multivolume treatises compiled from lecture notes by him and his students came out after his death.

In Berlin the social life begun in Nuremberg was enlarged and became more splendid. He joined and attended various clubs but was kept out of the Prussian Academy of Sciences for the rest of his life by the unrelenting animosity of Friedrich Schleiermacher, the other leading luminary in Berlin. There was a meeting, but hardly a reconciliation, with his one-time friend Schelling, from whom he had been for many years estranged. The trips into the countryside of his Nuremberg years now gave way to travel: to Belgium, Vienna, and, finally, Paris. He met and befriended the eclectic philosopher Victor Cousin (whose mistress Louise Colet was taken over by Flaubert) and came to his aid when he was in trouble with the authorities. He enjoyed the celebrity he had achieved and especially being chosen as rector of the university. But increasing attacks on his ideas were vexatious. The inevitable dwindling of his lecture audiences was very painful to him. He stammered and was a bad lecturer, starting every bit of his exposition with the word *Also*, 'therefore'.

Most reference books say that Hegel died of cholera. There was an epidemic of it and Hegel was worried about being infected. But Hegel's most recent biographer Terry Pinkard argues conclusively that it was not cholera that killed Hegel. He had no diarrhoea and no swelling. It was probably, Pinkard says, 'some kind of upper gastro-intestinal disease'. It is somehow typical of Hegel that the cause of his death should be so vague and ambiguous.

This detail is characteristic of the immense thoroughness and pertinacity of Pinkard's *Hegel, a Biography* (C.U.P., 2001). His seventy-eight pages of reference notes, in which Hegel's letters are the preponderant element, testify to the enormous amount of work he has done. But he has not simply ferreted away at material directly relevant to the detail of Hegel's everyday life. He is particularly enlightening about the religious and political circumstances of Hegel's time. He knows a great deal about the history of Hegel's epoch and conveys it with clarity and authority. He gives an illuminating account of the political divisions within the states composing Germany in the Revolutionary and Napoleonic period.

We may assume that the purpose of Pinkard's dedicated retrieval of the factual detail, however minute and unphilosophical, of Hegel's life was not undertaken for its own sake, but in order to throw some light on his philosophical writings, which are frequently obscure and badly in need of illumination.

Like most people who have worked hard and long on a subject about which a lot of very flimsily based opinions are repeatedly expressed, Pinkard is anxious to demonstrate their falsity. He begins his preface with a list of these falsehoods. Hegel was not, he contends, the idealist forerunner of Marx; he did not argue dialectically from thesis, by way of antithesis, to a reconciling synthesis; he did not glorify the Prussian state as the ideal culmination of history or call on its citizens to obey it unconditionally. Something similar is to be found at the beginning of G. R. G. Mure's brief and elegant *The Philosophy of Hegel* of 1965, the best short book on Hegel since Edward Caird's suave and brilliant *Hegel* of 1883.

I do not quite see the point of denying that Hegel was the idealist predecessor of the materialist Marx. Marx certainly thought he was and made his own large, if highly selective, indebtedness clear. Contradiction as a moving agent in history and alienation as a recurrent feature of the human condition are obvious instances of Marx's borrowing. But what is wrong with being Marx's predecessor? It does not make Hegel responsible for him. As for the dialectic, Hegel did not use the terms thesis/antithesis/ synthesis (nor did Kant, in whose own dialectic their germs can just be detected). Fichte, on the other hand, put them firmly to work, and Fichte had a more profound influence on Hegel than is usually recognized. In any case, the exposition of Hegel's system lends itself very readily to the triadic structure imposed on it by commentators and mapmakers. Taken as a whole the system sees (1) the Idea 'passing over' to (2) Nature and then 'returning to itself' as (3) Mind. The Idea subdivides into Being, Essence, and the Notion; Nature into Mechanics, Physics, and the Organism; Mind into subjective, objective, and absolute mind. And so on, but not rigidly; there are some quartets and duets further down the family tree.

Pinkard's correction of errors about Hegel's politics are much more persuasive. He pulverizes the account of the political views of the mature Hegel given by Bertrand Russell and Karl Popper, who saw him as an abject advocate of authoritarianism and his system as a charlatan's fraud, designed to glorify the Prussian status quo. Hegel started like his contemporary Wordsworth as an enthusiast for the French Revolution, but he did not follow him all the way to docile conservativism. He favoured constitutional monarchy with a strong representative element. His ideal monarch was far from absolute, almost symbolic. On the other hand, he was opposed to democracy, at least in the radical, unmediated form proposed in the discussions of the British Reform Bill going on towards the end of his life.

Whatever his elevated conception of the ideal state, he certainly did not bow down before the Prussian state of his own day. He received (very late, he thought) the Order of the Red Eagle, third class, at the same time as his enemy Schleiermacher. But he was often badly viewed by the authorities. Although von Kamptz, the chief of police, came to a great surprise birthday party for Hegel in 1826, he was also infuriated by a number of Hegel's political activities. After the murder of the reactionary playwright Kotzebue in 1819 a persecution of 'demagogues' was instituted. Friends and students of Hegel's were in trouble and he went out of his way to help them. Pinkard's corrections of the record invalidate Bertrand Russell's joke: for Hegel, liberty is the right to obey the police.

Pinkard's five chapters on Hegel's philosophy do not do much to diminish the obscurity of his writings, although they do not—always supposing that that is possible—augment it. They stick pretty closely to the text in a broadly uncritical spirit. He glosses over the ghastly confusions of Hegel's notion of 'passage' from the Idea to Nature; we get no clear analysis of the problem of how pure thought somehow gives rise to solid, heaving, earthy nature.

Still, there are some helpful interpretative hints in the biographical chapters. Hegel's philosophy really divides into two parts: one cosmic, comprising his logic and his philosophy of nature, the other social-historical, dealing with the human mind, social institutions and their history, and the higher domains of art, religion, and philosophy. This second part was first explored in the wild, fascinating carnival of the *Phenomenology*. Hegel's original intention was that that book should be the introduction to his system. But over the following six years more grandiose ideas prevailed and he decided to develop the 'science of consciousness' (his phrase for the subject matter of the *Phenomenology*) from an altogether more comprehensive starting point: what he idiosyncratically described as logic. It was, in fact, a theory of the universe and led on to a highly speculative cosmology, his philosophy of nature.

Hegel's 'logic' was, I believe, a fairly deeply encoded theology. That interest is found in his first, theological, writing. The problem of God was the chief piece of unsettled business bequeathed by Kant to his German successors. They were not interested, as Kant was, in authenticating the credentials of natural science in the face of Hume's scepticism. Instead of consigning belief in God to faith, as Kant had, they transformed the concept of God to make it accessible to the requirements of reason. The result was a kind of pantheism in which God is Everything, Spinoza's Substance, the completed totality of things; God is not supernatural in the style of the God of Christianity or the world of Kant's things-in-themselves.

Here Pinkard's account of Hegel's early theological reflections and the intellectual circumstances in which they were carried on is particularly helpful. Concretely he was, in an Enlightenment spirit, impatient with the supernatural (his early life of Christ ignores miracles and the Resurrection). At a more abstract level he absorbed Fichte's idea that mind is the creator of everything, giving rise to it by a kind of artistic self-expression. For Fichte this is a major dramatic event in which the 'I' (which is not, of course, you or me but the 'Absolute I') 'posits' the world. By 'posits' Fichte really means 'creates', but it sounds like the much less audacious 'assumes the existence of'. For Hegel the idealistic first principle that mind creates nature is arrived at by a process, a dialectical development that starts from the bare concept of being.

If the dialectical idea was put to work in Hegel's full-blown system to prove the existence of God, or a rarefied philosopher's version of God, his idea of a sequential, cumulative process of unfolding, penetrable by reason, was derived from his studies of the human world: human nature, social life, the higher elements of culture.

His presentation of the successive forms of human consciousness, social organization, of art, religion, and philosophy, and of history itself are persuasive and illustrated with a wealth of knowledge, even if they are always contestable. All of them are essentially temporal or historical, cases of literal sequence in time. Among other examples is his explicit philosophy of history (in effect, the history of the state) in which Hegel distinguishes the pre-classical (Oriental despotism), the classical (slave-based aristocratic rule), and the post-classical, the 'German world' (i.e. Europe since the barbarian invasions). This historical triad reappears in Hegel's philosophy of art (the symbolic, represented by architecture, the classical, represented by sculpture, and the romantic, represented by painting, music, and poetry). The same pattern recurs in his philosophy of religion. First there is 'the religion of nature', including magic and the great Eastern religions, then the religion of 'spiritual individuality' (i.e. personal gods), and finally Christianity, the 'absolute religion'.

By contrast, the application of the dialectical frame to logic is simply unintelligible. But its application to nature, however weird it may be in detail, has turned out to be brilliantly prophetic of the comprehensive evolutionary development of natural science in cosmology and biology since his time. That the dialectical idea in Hegel has its source in the history of mankind explains why his 'human philosophy', the subject matter of his philosophy of mind, is so much more interesting than his logic.

Pinkard's account of Hegel's continuing concern with religion and politics, from his earliest days, supplies an enlightening context for the late Gothic extravagance of his thinking. His system is presented in uncompromising abstraction as a process of pure thought contemplating itself. In fact, it is something much better than that. It is, in its more digestible parts, a series of highly imaginative pattern-finding speculations about human society, history, and culture.

The blanket condemnation of his work by Anglo-Saxon empiricism is undiscriminating. It is true that espousing his logic would be like buying tsarist government bonds, and his philosophy of nature is a wild gamble. But to take his human and social philosophy seriously is a moderately sound investment. His importance is not merely negative, as being the provoker of Schopenhauer, Kierkegaard, Marx, and Nietzsche, but as being the main exponent, after the ignored Vico, of a historical conception of the works of the human mind. This is subliminally recognized by the fact that most of what is of interest that is written about Hegel deals with his human, not his strictly metaphysical, philosophy.

Pinkard adds a great deal to the usual conception of Hegel derived from the brief biographical notes that precede the main content of books about him or are to be found in the histories of philosophy in which he figures. The struggle to establish himself was long and painful. He did not get a paid university post until he was forty-six. His early adult years were impoverished and lonely, although he was materially comfortable after he came to Nuremberg as a school principal when he was thirty-eight. After leaving Tübingen he was not a member of any sort of philosophical community until his insecure years at Jena between 1801 and 1807; and Jena's decay as a philosophical centre was already well advanced when he got there. Everything came out of his own head and the reading he had stored in it. There is a certain heroism about Hegel's solitary endurance on the long road to the final, almost bureaucratic, dignity of his position in the 1820s in Berlin as Germany's leading philosopher.

8

Richard Monckton Milnes

The town of Crewe, in the north-west of England, is not, I understand, a place of very marked intrinsic charm or beauty. The Michelin Guide refers, rather furtively, to a Market Hall. Murray's Blue Guide speaks only of its role in modern industrial history as the home of a railway carriage works and as a major railway junction, connecting lines from Liverpool, Manchester, Chester, and other more interesting spots. I speak largely on authority in this matter since although, like many others, I have passed through it and even changed trains at it, I have not left the station to have a look around.

What connects it to Richard Monckton Milnes is, in the first place, the fact of his marriage to the Hon. Annabelle Crewe. Her brother, the absurdly named, and absurd, Hungerford Crewe, who lived at Crewe Hall, had no children. His title passed to Robert, the only son of Annabelle and Richard Monckton Milnes who raised himself to the rank of Marquess of Crewe by various forms of conspicuous public service. So the genealogical identity of Richard Monckton Milnes came to be obliterated in the ancient glory of his wife's background, as elevated to greater prominence by the efforts of his son.

But there is a certain appropriateness in the absorption of Monckton Milnes into Crewe. Like the town he is less important in himself than in his connections. He knew everybody: Tennyson, Gladstone, Peel, Palmerston, Thackeray, King Louis Philippe, the Emperor Napoleon III, Guizot, Thiers, Tocqueville, Lamennais, Montalembert, Emerson, Whitman, Henry Adams, and Henry James—to take at random a few of the people whom he had not simply met and talked to, but got to know well. He was held in deep affection by two notoriously difficult men: Landor and Carlyle. He helped to rescue Keats from the abyss of neglect and remote disapproval into which he had fallen soon after his death. He did much to assist and generally bring on Swinburne, although in the course of doing so he helped to fuel Swinburne's obsession with the Marquis de Sade by supplying the poet with Sade's works from his large pornographic collection. He took a great deal of trouble to get Coventry Patmore a job when Patmore was in a very distressed state. He was also like Crewe in being nothing much to look at.

So far as history is concerned he lives only through the others whom he helped, entertained at his breakfasts or in the country, charmed and amused. But his direct achievements have altogether faded from view. He represented Pontefract in the House of Commons from 1837, entering parliament at the age of twenty-eight in the election following the new Queen's accession to the throne, to 1863, when Palmerston had him made Lord Houghton as a modest aspect of the celebrations attending the marriage of the Prince of Wales to Alexandra of Denmark. Despite creditably regular attendance in Parliament, given his love of travel and the enormous inroads of his social calendar, and his persistent appeals to the succession of prime ministers to whom he attached himself—Peel and Palmerston in particular—he never achieved office. He thought himself qualified, by the unparalleled width of his acquaintances in and his knowledge of the capitals of Europe, to be foreign secretary. But the thought of such an appointment does not seem to have entered the heads of those who were in a position to bring it about. He was seen, surely with justice, as altogether too lightweight a figure. Disraeli, one of the very few people who actively disliked him, said that he was unique, not merely in the badness of his first speech in parliament (something Disraeli knew about from personal experience), but the fact that his subsequent speeches got progressively worse.

Nor did he do better in literature, his other favourite field. In early life he wrote about his travels, especially in Greece and further east. But *Memorials of a Tour in some parts of Greece: Chiefly Poetical* was wholly extinguished by the *Eothen* of his friend Kinglake and the almost equally successful *The Crescent and the Cross* of his friend Warburton. He published a number of volumes of verse: *Poems of Many Years* (which came out when he was twenty-nine), *Poems Legendary and Historical,* and *Poetry for the People.* But they did not amount to much. He is represented by only one poem in Quiller-Couch's *Oxford Book of English Verse*, a collection notorious for its piety towards the more boneless kind of nineteenth-century composition. From later, similarly standard collections he has been altogether excluded.

His special gifts as an unusual social being developed soon after he established himself at the age of twenty-eight in London in rooms above 26 Pall Mall. These were, until his marriage, fourteen years later, the scene of his famous breakfast parties, where every kind of lion, actual or potential, political or literary, friendly or hostile, was brought together. It was soon after his inauguration in London as a new MP and all-encompassing host that he first met Thomas Carlyle. So when, a few years later, Carlyle was casting about for help with the London Library he was projecting, it was natural enough that he should rope in his new young friend, the breadth of whose acquaintance was already unrivalled and who was blessed with a willingness to follow through in practice the missions he had undertaken. The idea of a really serious subscription library in London would no more have occurred to him than any other idea. But once it had been formulated no one was better equipped to help in its realization.

Richard Monckton Milnes's origins were comparatively modest on his father's side. His grandfather was a well-off manufacturer from Wakefield, a Whig, and a Nonconformist MP for York. For fourteen years after 1784 he helped Fox with financial support. It was he who bought Fryston Hall which Richard Monckton Milnes eventually inherited. The latter's handsome father, a true horseman and lover of rural pleasures, came into possession of Fryston at the age of twenty-one on *his* father's death. Soon afterwards he entered the House of Commons for Pontefract, the seat his son Richard was eventually to take over from him. In 1808 he married the daughter of Lord Galway and, in the following year, his only son Richard was born. A daughter, Harriet, who turned out to be taller and better-looking than her brother, followed in due course. Richard was brought up in the fairly modest house near Doncaster his father had rented and was taught at home by a tutor because of his delicate health. Richard's father was in somewhat reduced circumstances because of the debts of his brother. This was to have an important and not disagreeable effect on Richard. If it meant that he was brought up in a less grand house than he might have been, it also introduced him early in life to the charms of European travel when his parents moved to Milan in 1828. They stayed out of England until Robert Milnes's finances had been brought back into a sufficient state of repair in 1835, after nearly eight years away.

Richard arrived in Cambridge, as an undergraduate at Trinity, at the age of eighteen in 1827, shortly before his family's emigration. It was an auspicious moment for anyone with his taste for interesting company. He soon became friendly with Arthur Hallam and with the members of his circle: Tennyson above all, but also Kinglake, of *Eothen*, Spedding, the industrious editor of Bacon, and Dean Merivale. Thackeray and Edward Fitzgerald were at Cambridge at the time but he did not get to know them until later. He was to go to a public execution in 1840 with Thackeray, which he seems to have found a good deal less upsetting than Thackeray did.

The appearance in Milnes's story of Hallam and Tennyson provides an opportunity for a brief inspection of his poetical gifts. Like Tennyson he was much upset by Hallam's death, although not quite so much. Certainly his own lines on the matter are in fairly stark contrast to *In Memoriam*.

> I'm not where I was yesterday
> Though my home be still the same,
> For I have lost the veriest friend
> Whom ever a friend could name;
> I'm not where I was yesterday,
> Though change there be little to see,
> For a part of myself has lapsed away
> From Time to Eternity.

Various defects conspire to mar this expression of entirely sincere regret: its inappropriately cheerful cantering *John Gilpin*-like metre; the clumsy departures from it (though *change* there be *little* to *see*); the faded, conventional vocabulary ('veriest', 'lapsed away'). He was active in both the Union and the Apostles, which had been founded as the Conversazione Society a few years before in 1820. It was as a representative of the Union that he travelled to Oxford in 1829, with Hallam, to defend the claims of Shelley against Byron at the corresponding institution there. The main importance of the occasion for Milnes was his first meeting with Gladstone, whom he described, without irony, as 'a very superior person'. Unlike many debaters, Hallam and Milnes were sincerely attached to the poet they were defending. In Hallam's circle there was a general reaction against Byron in favour of the unfashionable Wordsworth and the still unestablished Shelley and Keats. In retreat from Byronism and, indeed, the haughty, cold-hearted forum of masculinity of the Regency period, Milnes's Cambridge friends were warmly affectionate, decorated their conversation and correspondence with endearments, and often broke into tears. It is possible to speculate on how far this all went. They do not seem to have had anything much of an amorous nature to do with women, on the commercial terms which was all that was available to them, in the manner of their eighteenth-century predecessors.

Milnes had fled in nervous despair from some examinations in Cambridge at the end of his second year and in April 1830 he left the place altogether. For a while he attended lectures at the newly opened University College, London. Later that year he joined the rest of his family in Milan, passing through Germany on the way and trying out his recently acquired grasp of the language. He developed a marked affection for Germany and things German which was not to be seriously diminished until Bismarck crushed France with what Milnes saw as exorbitant brutality forty-five years later. He acknowledged a considerable affinity to the place: 'the thing I was intended for by nature', he said, 'is a German woman'. A little later he experienced a comparable enchantment on visiting Venice. The European exile of the Milneses was not total. Milnes was soon home for a visit to his great-aunt in London and then made a tour of grand houses in Ireland, observing, without any evident striving for effect, that Dublin was not up to Venice. Visiting Rome he met a host of notables, among them Wiseman, head of the English College and in time to return to England as cardinal. This meeting may have helped, along with Milnes's generally very liberal and religiously unenthusiastic attitude, to produce the calming good sense of his pamphlet *One Tract More* on the Oxford Movement a decade later. Wiseman does not reappear in Milnes's life, but others met in Rome do: Baron Bunsen, who was rather too austere fully to perceive the kind heart under Milnes's levity, and the French Catholic reformers Lammenais and Montalembert,

He soon went further afield, to Naples and Pompeii and then to Greece, which was still in a chaotic state after its newly achieved independence. Despite his anti-Byronism he sought gossip about Byron and felt indignant at what he described in his *Memorial* as the spoliation of the Parthenon by Lord Elgin. In 1837 he went down with malaria, which he had contracted in Florence, and made the first of his major conquests of difficult literary heroes. (His enduring friendship with Tennyson was established too early in the lives of both of them to count here, although its uninterrupted continuation is to the credit of both of them.)

Landor was living outside Florence in Fiesole at the time, keeping relatively quiet after a long series of explosive collisions. The reciprocal affection between the ancient, haughty, pugnacious, classically minded master of style in prose and poetry and the young, short, plump, curly-haired, paradox-emitting chatterbox is agreeable to contemplate. A few years later Landor was even heard to proclaim that 'Milnes is the greatest poet now living in England'.

In a pleasant essay of Milnes's on Landor in his *Monographs Personal and Social* of 1873, two years before his own death, he wrote of him: 'under the most fortunate circumstances it is difficult to imagine Landor a comfortable Country Gentleman. For field sports, in which the unoccupied upper classes of this country expend harmlessly so much of the superfluous energy and occasional savagery of their dispositions, he had no taste. In his youth he had shot a partridge one winter afternoon, and found the bird alive the next morning, after a night of exceptional bitterness. "What that bird must have suffered", he exclaimed, "I often think of its look"—and he never took gun in hand again.' The more Boythorn-like side of Landor is recalled in the story of Landor throwing an Italian cook, whose dish had failed to please, out of the window and crying as the man crashed into the garden bed, 'Good God, I forgot the violets.'

Important for the future was Milnes's meeting, during his weeks as Landor's guest, with Charles Brown, who had collected all the papers of and relating to Keats he could get hold of. Unable to publish a biography of Keats himself, he eventually handed them over to Milnes and his confidence was well placed. In 1848 Brown's memoir and other papers were the nucleus of Milnes's effective rescue of Keats from obscurity and disparagement in his *Life, Letters and Literary Remains of John Keats*, the most significant by far of his publications.

In 1835 the Milnes family returned to England. Fryston Hall, which Milnes did not like—it was in an ugly, industrially polluted neighbourhood and chaotically constructed—now became their headquarters. Milnes inherited it in the late 1850s. Turning his back on its surroundings and the unappealing activities that went on there of hunting and shooting, Milnes filled it with books—including his large collection of pornography—and with colourfully assorted assemblages of friends for long, talkative visits, filled with readings and play actings and indoor games, fuelled by heavy eating and drinking.

But for the time being Milnes's effective home was to be London, where he moved into his rooms at 26 Pall Mall in 1827, the year in which he was returned to parliament for Pontefract. At that point he was a conservative, an adherent of Peel. He was not regarded as a serious political figure by Peel or anyone else in politics. His speeches were pompous and grandiloquent. But he was generally liked. Disraeli, another politician with one foot in the world of literature, was, as I have said, an exception. He made a very disobliging remark about Milnes as a host, in the guise of Mr Vavasour in *Tancred*: 'Whatever your creed, class or country, one might almost add your character, you were a welcome guest at his matutinal meal, provided you were celebrated. That qualification, however, was rigidly enforced.' That was unfair, dogs of various degrees of lameness were frequently to be seen. But a major point of Milnes's breakfasts was the presence of *some* lions for everyone else to admire.

Milnes did have one unrelenting and determined enemy in a creature of Disraeli's, George Smythe, later Lord Strangford. In 1849 Milnes was provoked into challenging Smythe to a duel. Perhaps luckily for Milnes the event never came off, although it remains obscure how the matter was settled. Even those who were not attracted by

Milnes's gaiety, amusingness, and good nature and solemn souls who disapproved of his levity seem seldom to have thought him worse than comical.

The surface of Milnes's political career is certainly unimpressive. He stuck to Peel until Peel fell in 1846 and then transferred his loyalty to Palmerston and the Whigs. But there is more consistency in his politics than that suggests. He was always in favour of reform, improvement, and the alleviation of suffering. In this Tory period he supported the repeal of the Corn Laws, he was critical of the royal family and turned into something like a republican, he wanted more democracy, supported the North in the American Civil War when most powerful people in England were enthusiasts for the South, wanted the destruction of Napoleon III but deplored the way in which Bismarck brought him down.

Once he was installed in London, Milnes gathered a large circle of friendly ladies around him. Among them were 'unfortunates' like Lady Blessington at Gore House with the Count d'Orsay in attendance and Caroline Norton, one of the three beautiful Sheridan sisters who had been edged out of respectable society by the suit brought by her husband against Melbourne. Not of the demi-monde but not of the beau monde either was the wife of George Grote, utilitarian and historian of Greece, a most entertaining and intelligent woman, who was devoted to Milnes.

Milnes married, although only at the age of forty-two, his wife being a comfortably mature thirty-seven, and they had three children. There is no evidence of previous attachments, unless the emotionally vigorous friendships with his Cambridge contemporaries can be so described. Travelling in Turkey he had been to see dancing girls and that may not have been a purely spectatorial form of entertainment. Then there is the matter of his large accumulation of erotica. That does not seem to have started in earnest until the late 1850s, when Milnes had been married for a number of years and was getting near fifty years of age. It is, after all, an old man's vice.

The crucial event for him—and in a way for us—of the first years finding his feet in London was his meeting with Carlyle, which took place soon after Milnes's installation in that city. Carlyle was a combative person with a temper rendered uncertain by dyspepsia. He preached and practised a doctrine of work. Yet he was and remained deeply fond of the apparently unemployed and frivolous Milnes. There are two explanations for this—one kinder than the other—and there is probably truth in both of them.

First, on a crudely practical basis, Milnes was useful to Carlyle in introducing him to grand and fashionable people. Carlyle, to the acute displeasure of his wife, enjoyed the company of aristocratic women, in particular that of Lady Harriet Baring, later Lady Ashburton. In 1838 Milnes's old Trinity friend Spedding helped Carlyle to recruit Milnes into their campaign to create the London Library. He had, as they did not, the knowledge and influence to get some noble and famous names involved so that they would attract others of their kind onto the subscription list. As we now realize, it was quite a close shave and Carlyle at times seemed to despair of it. But it was not for lack of effort on Milnes's part that the scheme seemed to hang for a time in the balance.

In 1840 he started a long connection with the Hotel Meurice in Paris, his home there on many subsequent visits. Montalembert, made friends with in Rome, took him to visit the salons of Lamartine, preparing himself for brief greatness in 1848, and Thiers. He met George Sand and began a long, communicative friendship with de Tocqueville. In England he heard Liszt play at Lady Blessington's and stayed with Sydney Smith at Combe Florey.

Milnes, for all his liberal, democratic, broadly republican sympathy, loved grand parades and ceremonies. He attended the fairly catastrophic Eglinton Tournament in Scotland. It was the first of a series of such outings. Republican or not, in 1842 he went dressed up as Chaucer, a good choice in respect of shape and size, to the State Fancy Ball devised by Prince Albert in aid of the distressed Spitalfields weavers. Later on he took a conspicuous part in the Paris Exhibition of 1867 and was present at the opening of the Suez Canal in 1869.

In 1842 on a visit to Egypt he met Mehemet Ali, who was running the country independently of its nominal Turkish overlord. In *Palm Leaves*, a poetic record of his travels at this time, he condemned westernization as an unmixed evil. Greece, revisited after eleven years, disappointed him in the way de Valera's republic of shopkeepers disappointed the partisans of Irish freedom. The boat he took up the Nile was called *Zuleika*, a quite appropriate bit of prospective fancy. On the way back home he called in, characteristically, on King Louis Philippe. Still a Tory by normal allegiance, he supported the social reform legislation of Ashley (later Shaftesbury).

His father, as a result of a nasty riding accident in 1840, became less mobile and more eccentric for the considerable remainder of his life. He was not so confused, however, as to fail to secure £100,000 from railway companies needing bits of his land. His son, getting nowhere in politics, managed to bear the success of his friend Gladstone, who gravely discouraged him from trying to get a post in the British embassy in Paris as being negatively motivated by the desire to get out of British politics. Disraeli's parallel success, both in politics and literature, was harder to endure.

Travel as usual assuaged his disappointments. In Berlin he met the aged Alexander von Humboldt, was kept away from the king as a suspicious character, made friends with Varnhagen von Ense, who encouraged his hobby of autograph collecting, and Bettina von Arnim. He was able to indulge in Goethe worship. On his return he wrote a sound article on the political state of Prussia for the *Edinburgh Review*, correctly predicting revolution. Late in the decade he was in Spain and Portugal.

Another way of forgetting himself was to look after the welfare of others. As Henry Adams, a severe critic of the human race, observed in praise of Milnes, 'He made it his business to be kind.' He procured a civil list pension for Tennyson, who was in financial difficulties, but, all the same, not pleased. He got a job for the desperate Coventry Patmore in the British Museum. He came to the assistance of Thomas Hood and, when he died, of his family. Although he said he preferred individual to collective philanthropy, he supported the bill for the improvement for the college at Maynooth for the training of Roman Catholic priests in Ireland and wrote a pamphlet calling for the subsidization of the Catholic Church in Ireland. Visiting Ireland to see the famine at first hand, he was sharply observant of the continuing luxury in the great houses of the ascendancy.

His turn to Palmerston and the Whigs, when Peel fell in 1846, meant he had to resign from the Carlton Club. However, the gates of Woburn were now open to him as a compensation. His constant visits to the mansions of the nobility did not prevent him from describing the aristocrats of England as stupid and helpless. And his increasing fondness for democracy did not extend to embracing any kind of socialism. In favouring a wider franchise, he was going against his own interests for he hated the often narrowly run elections he had to undergo in the comparatively rotten borough of Pontefract. His support of Corn Law repeal was also a work of self-denial for one who depended for the lavish comforts he found indispensable on rents from agricultural land.

The events of 1848, which he had correctly predicted in his article on Prussia a few years before, drew him to France to see his friend Lamartine in full, if brief, oratorical frenzy. His attitude as a jovial spectator of the revolution caused some annoyance. It is no surprise to find him, once back in England, calling on the exiled Metternich. He wrote a pamphlet criticizing the failure of the British government to assist the revolutionary movements in continental Europe. It was George Smythe's cruel review of this that led to their unconsummated duel. Milnes was oppressed by the violent reaction to the uprisings of 1848 and gave aid to the refugees who fled to England from it.

Of more lasting significance, however, was the publication of his *Life* of Keats to which I shall return later. He was now forty but seemed older. People remarked how he seemed to have no upper teeth. He was certainly getting rather fat and embarked around this time on a long series of visits to spas to counteract this tendency and the gout by which he was increasingly afflicted. His physical state impaired neither a newly arisen idea of getting married nor considerable success with an improbable fiancée, Florence Nightingale. There is no doubt at all that she returned his affection; probably she felt it more strongly than he did. She spoke with feeling, if in a rather cumbrous way, of 'his genius of friendship in philanthropy'. It was surely better for both of them that the proposal was in the end declined.

Instead, in 1851 he married Annabelle Crewe who had been largely brought up in the country by an aunt. It was hardly ideal training for the hectic social life at Fryston and in London, and the frequent travel that lay ahead of her. In fact she seems to have coped pretty well, although she became sickly, bowed, and rather melancholic in later life. Milnes's long immersion in an intensely bachelor existence in no way made him an inconsiderate husband. His established mode of life continued. As a married man he moved from his rooms in Pall Mall to a house in Upper Brook Street. His friends commented on his constant solicitousness for Annabelle's well-being. His old tutor, Thirlwall, now a bishop, slightly regretted the move from Pall Mall. 'It is very likely—nay certain—that you will still collect agreeable people about your wife's breakfast table; but can I ever sit down there without the certainty that I shall meet with none but respectable persons?' By and large the marriage, held together by solid and continuing affection rather than passion, seems to have been happy. Annabelle adjusted herself to the constant social activity of Upper Brook Street and Fryston (ominously labelled 'Freezetown' by Tennyson), but she did rather draw the line at Swinburne. She accompanied Milnes on many of his travels. She gave birth to daughters in 1852 and 1855 and a son, Robert, in 1858, the later Marquess of Crewe. She died in 1874, eleven years before her husband.

In the years of their marriage, Napoleon III became emperor. 'My old breakfaster', as Milnes called him, had often visited him in the 1840s. Disraeli recalled private conversations with him in a conveniently private bow-window in the Pall Mall room in that period. On one occasion he, Disraeli, Cobden, Kinglake, Suleiman Pasha, and Count d'Orsay were in the wildly assorted group of guests. Cobden described d'Orsay as 'a fleshy, animal-like creature'. Napoleon's seizure of power aroused fears of an invasion in England. Milnes rose to the occasion, discharging his commission with the 2nd West Riding Regiment of Militia in drilling the locals who had been called to the colours. There was a sartorial benefit from this public duty, an ornate red uniform, even unembellished as it was by anything in the way of decorations, which was to serve him well in various ceremonial events later on.

During the 1850s the arrival of several notable Americans in England gave Milnes the opportunity to display his interest in and good feelings towards the United States. This attitude was directly opposed to the generally mocking and contemptuous view of America and the Americans that then prevailed in England. It had been memorably expressed in the 1840s in Dickens's *American Notes* and *Martin Chuzzlewit*. As long before as 1838 Milnes had written in the *London and Westminster Review* a long article about Emerson, in which he explained the distinguishing peculiarities of American English, which then, as now, excited ridicule in England, as being due to persistence of uneliminated residues of Elizabethan idiom.

Ten years later Emerson, travelling in England, met Milnes for the first time and wrote warmly about him: 'Milnes is everywhere and knows everything. . . . His good humour is infinite . . . He is very liberal of his money and sincerely kind and useful to young people of merit.' Hawthorne, extremely sensitive to English slights, found Milnes 'pleasant and sensible', but, he went on, 'an intellectual and refined American is a higher man than he—a higher and a finer one'. In an agreeable comment on Milnes's physical appearance, Hawthorne said Milnes resembled Longfellow 'though of a thicker build'. That calls to mind the fine observation of William James's son who, called on to describe what an acquaintance looked like, replied 'like Jesus Christ, but thicker set'. Milnes certainly laid on a good selection of lions at one breakfast to which Hawthorne came: Lord Lansdowne, Robert and Elizabeth Barrett Browning, Macaulay, Florence Nightingale's mother, and, perhaps for reassurance, his countryman, George Ticknor.

Milnes was one of the first people in England to recognize the merits of Walt Whitman and eventually called on him when, in 1875 after his wife's death, he visited the US. During that trip Milnes also called on General Sherman in St Louis and renewed his acquaintance with Emerson, who by then, although 'easy to talk to', was no longer able to write. Milnes, as I have mentioned earlier, was something of a rarity for his support of the northern side in the Civil War. Recollection of the fact may have augmented the general enthusiasm with which he was received over there years afterwards.

During the early years of the Civil War the young Henry Adams, then twenty-three, was serving with the American embassy in London as secretary to his father, the minister. Depressed by the Whig government's recognition of the sovereign status of the Confederacy, he went to stay at fog-bound Fryston where Milnes had as guests only his friend Stirling, Laurence Oliphant, and an extraordinary-looking child who turned out in fact to be Swinburne and who put on an enthralling performance after dinner. Henry Adams never forgot Milnes's protective kindness and wrote of it in his autobiography many years later.

The friendship of the two men had another interesting literary consequence. When Henry James arrived in London in 1827 he had a letter of introduction for Milnes from Henry Adams in his pocket. Milnes got ahead of him by inviting him to a breakfast party before he had managed to present it. Milnes took him to a club where he met Trollope and then had him to stay at Fryston, where Tennyson, Gladstone, and Schliemann were also staying. James did something to return this abundant hospitality by giving Milnes, in his turn, a letter of introduction to Flaubert and Turgenev. Goodwill manages to prevail over superciliousness in James's description of Milnes:

a battered and world-wrinkled old mortal, with a restless and fidgety vanity, but with an immense fund of real kindness and humane feeling. He is not personally fascinating, though as a general thing he talks very well, but I like his sociable, democratic, sympathetic, inquisitive old temperament. Half the human race, certainly everyone that one has ever heard of, appears sooner or later to have stayed at Fryston Hall.

Milnes soon followed up the introduction to Flaubert and Turgenev and on the same visit to Paris added Zola and Daudet to his list of acquaintances.

In 1853 he was one of the three founders of the Philobiblion Society, a serious and energetic group of book-lovers, thirty-five in number: noblemen with great inherited libraries, scholars, writers, even publishers. In the season in London it met once or twice a month and Milnes was active in the production of its *Miscellanies* of which fifteen were published in the thirty-one years of the society's existence. It died in 1884 a year before Milnes did.

He was an incessant book collector but the part of his collection that has most caught public attention is its pornographic element. For the rest it was by no means confined to expensive rarities. Leigh Hunt praised it for its democratic hospitableness, describing it as 'the concentration of infinite bookstalls'. Nor was his library for show. Milnes was constantly reading and was always up-to-date on the most recently published books. When Fryston was burnt down in 1875 Milnes was away in Ireland. Most of the books were got out but many of them, as is commonly the case, had been drenched by the firemen's hoses. Returning to find many sets incomplete and many books damaged, he said 'my Dante and Froissart have turned up but Charles I's Spenser is still missing'.

Reflecting Milne's love of the famous, there were many items of an association interest—among them a piece of Voltaire's dressing gown, a presentation cup from Goethe, Richard Burton's passport to Mecca, and the visitors' book from Burns's cottage at Alloway. A large place in the collection was taken up by books on the French Revolution, books of nineteenth-century poetry, works on theology, books on music, witchcraft, and crime. With its group of works on school punishment we approach the pornographic area.

His pornographic library was, in what we must, I suppose, regard as a characteristically English style, very strong on flagellation. Milnes's taste for this was presumably not founded on experience. Unlike Swinburne he had not revelled in being on the receiving end of beatings at school. There was a lot of French eighteenth-century material. To acquire it he relied on the services of an intriguingly shadowy figure: Fred Hanley. The only son of a general who had served with distinction in Malta, he had settled in Paris towards the end of the 1840s, with a mistress whose constant presence inhibited his social movements in England. The Goncourt brothers had met him and been delightedly shocked by the depth of his sadistic obsession.

Milnes's relations with him were more businesslike. A constant flow of beautifully produced erotic rubbish was conveyed to him in England, by means of elaborate stratagems designed to evade the attentions of the customs officers. Some came across with a Queen's Messenger en route to Palmerston, others in the diplomatic bag from the embassy in Paris to the Foreign Office; others again by the helpful hand of the manager of Covent Garden. Milnes brought another new friend with an interest in the obscene, Richard Burton, into touch with Hanley and the intrepid traveller undertook to get him a flayed human skin from Dahomey.

Milnes's more virtuous impulses continued to operate. After the death by drowning of his friend Warburton, he came to the assistance of his widow and two young sons. Carlyle, who had been somewhat estranged by Milne's championing of Keats, soon warmed to him again and recruited him in the attempt to do something for the widow of Leigh Hunt. He came to the support of J. A. Froude, first at the time of the storm and expulsion from his Oxford fellowship which followed the publication of his *Nemesis of Faith* and again when he applied, unsuccessfully in 1857, for a history professorship in Oxford, and once again when his biography of Carlyle excited wide displeasure. He played some part in getting the increase in stipend for the Revd Arthur Nicholls which made it possible for him to marry Charlotte Brontë. He was busy on behalf of more generalized humanitarian purposes—such as stopping the cruel punishments to which sailors were subjected at sea (a fact that suggests that his interest in flagellation did not extend to approving of it in practice), the relief of fallen women, and the repeal of the Contagious Diseases Act.

In 1856 Palmerston offered Milnes's father a peerage which Robert Milnes refused, to the intense regret of his son. Two years later he died, still true in his old Tory loyalty, now attached to Disraeli and Derby, and cheerfully disagreeing with his son. He had received a wider education than Milnes and was given to pointing out grammatical slips and misuses of words in the writings that Milnes sent him. At last in 1863 Milnes was made a peer on his own account, taking the title of Lord Houghton. Palmerston had offered him a minor Treasury post some time before, and in the most courteous way, but Milnes realized he would look foolish, in the light of his known political ambitions, to accept it. Even so Disraeli said of him that he was too ridiculous to be made a peer.

He kept up his progressive interests in the House of Lords. As well as the humanitarian issues I mentioned earlier which belong to this period of his career, he supported the resolution for enlarging the franchise in the middle 1860s which culminated in the Reform Act of 1867.

Travel and sociability continued to the end of his life, which appropriately took place in a spa. After the age of fifty his gout became progressively worse and he was accidently dragged off his horse in Hyde Park in 1877 and was laid up for a week. In 1872 he reviewed *Middlemarch* at length in the *Edinburgh Review*. He led the movement after Dickens's death in 1870 to have him buried in Westminster Abbey. His poetic muse made a final, desperate emergence from retirement in 1873 on the occasion of Livingstone's death:

> The swarthy followers stood aloof,
> Unled—unfathered;
> He lay beneath that grassy roof,
> Fresh-gathered.
> He bade them, as they pass the hut
> To give no warning
> Of their still faithful presence, but
> 'Good Morning'.
> . . .
> Morning of sympathy and trust
> For such as bore
> Their master's spirit's sacred crust
> To England's shore.

Eating and drinking excessively to the last, he managed to live to the age of seventy-six without any catastrophic loss of powers. After the opening of the Suez Canal in 1869 he was in Paris in 1872 to see what the Germans and the Communard had done to it. He was in Italy in 1874 and, as has been mentioned, in the United States (by way of Canada) in 1875 and in Ireland when his home burnt down two years later. Early in the 1880s he made a final trip to Germany and, naturally, met von Moltke and the Austrian crown prince who was to die at Mayerling. He was in Cairo and Athens (where he had a heart attack) in 1882 and in Rome in 1883 and 1885, the year of his death. Busy to the end he had just unveiled busts to Coleridge in Westminster Abbey and to Thomas Gray at Pembroke College, Cambridge.

It had been a full and active life, a somewhat superficial one, perhaps, but carried on all over the world, in all sorts of company, often for humane and decent public purposes and unremittingly for the pursuit of the pleasure of individuals and, through it, of his own. Milnes did no harm, a lot of good, and was the cause of a great deal of fun. Three lasting achievements stand to his credit.

The first, and most important, is his reclamation of Keats from oblivion and disapproval. For people born in the twentieth century, although they are aware of Keat's misfortunes with critics in his lifetime, the idea that there could ever have been a time, after his death, when he was not recognized to be one of England's major poets must come as a surprise. His poems had been republished in two volumes in 1841, twenty years after his death, but had attracted no notice except from the young Rossetti and Holman Hunt. Where there was not simple ignorance there was intense reprobation: the sensual richness of Keat's verse was seen as the expression of a weak, unhealthy, and, worst of all, pagan character.

Milnes did not deny the paganism. For the most part he let Keats speak for himself through his poems and letters, supplemented by the recollections Milnes had assembled of the people who had known him. The conception of Keats as a brilliantly gifted poet and a courageous and dignified man came steadily to be established as a result of Milnes's work, so that it is hard to imagine the derelict state of his reputation at the time Milnes set himself to putting matters right.

Sensuality and paganism were also features of the other important poet well served by Milnes. In this case the service needed to be direct and personal since Swinburne without some managerial or avuncular figure in charge of him was bound to go off the rails. Milnes set him going in the right direction poetically. It has been suggested that he encouraged Swinburne to try his hand at Greek tragedy rather than boisterous imitation—thus giving rise to *Atalanta in Calydon*. He brought Swinburne into the world, away from his feverish and drunken isolation, among other things arranging a meeting with an early hero of Swinburne's, Landor, which turned out to be almost ecstatically rewarding. He helped him get his poetry and reviews published. In the six years in which they were close, before Swinburne turned away from his mentor, fired by an infatuation with the revolutionary ideals of Mazzini, the best of Swinburne's early poetry was composed.

Swinburne was intemperate with his pen as well as the bottle. In his huge novel *Lesbia Brandon* there is a morally unwholesome character, Mr Linley, who has much in common, at least in some of his opinions, tastes, and manners of speech, with Milnes. Could John Buchan, in his Yellow Book period, have got a look at the manuscript of the book or its unpublished proofs? That would allow for the resurrection of Mr Linley as Mr Andrew Lumley of *The Power-House*, the evil, magnetic, soft-spoken tycoon and collector from whom the thin fabric of civilization is at risk.

Milnes's final service is, of course, something which this essay is designed to commemorate: his work for the London Library. Not only did he assist Carlyle at the outset by drawing in some high-ranking personages so as to attract the attention of others of their kind. He continued to be involved in its affairs for the rest of his life. In 1857, for example, he was under pressure from a Miss Agnes Strickland to secure the appointment as librarian of the very minor poet, Alaric Watts.

I like to think that there is really more of his spirit about the place than there is of grim old Carlyle's. We all know that the gospel of work is honoured in it, not least from the enormous array of tributes to the place in the acknowledgements pages of books that have been written in it or based on its resources. It is very much a library for enjoyment as well as use, like Milnes's own, though I should not want to press that comparison too far. If Richard Monckton Milnes cannot quite claim to be the emblem of the library he can at least be the genial reverse of the medal whose obverse is the stern, commanding visage of his loving friend Carlyle.

9

T. H. Green

T. H. Green was not only the first significant English idealist, in the more or less Germanic sense of the term. He was also one of the first English professional philosophers since the Cambridge Platonists. And he was also the first significant philosopher to have taught at Oxford for five hundred years, which is the gap between his death and Wyclif's, with one exception: the redoubtable Hamiltonian H. L. Mansel, who flourished and published in the 1850s. Between Wyclif and Mansel the only philosopher of the smallest note to have taught the subject at Oxford was Robert Sanderson, who left Oxford when a little over thirty in 1619 and died as Bishop of Lincoln in 1663. (He is the subject of one of Izaak Walton's 'Lives'.) Hobbes, Locke, and Bentham, of course, were all students at Oxford, but deplored the scholastic philosophical teaching to which they were subjected there. Even Locke, who taught in Oxford for some years, did not take up philosophy seriously until long after he had been expelled from the place.

There had been rumblings of Germanic idealism before Green came into view, in Coleridge and J. H. Stirling, but they were more of a kind to excite interest than to reward close study. Green was the true originator of the school and was clearly so regarded by his contemporaries, as is made clear by the devotional tone of the *Essays in Philosophical Criticism* that came out just after his death. The fact that Bradley did not contribute, perhaps did not choose to contribute, is worth noticing.

In this essay I propose to subject the 'metaphysics of knowledge' presented in the first eighty or so pages of the *Prolegomena to Ethics* to critical examination. Its main theses are that mind cannot be part of nature since it makes nature. The mind involved here is, in the first instance, at any rate, the finite individual mind. Since mind is the acquirer or possessor of knowledge it is to that extent not susceptible of scientific explanation, whatever may be true of its more non-cognitive or physically qualified aspects. But the nature that the individual mind constructs in experience is not wholly that mind's construction. It intimates the existence of an eternal consciousness adequate to support the system of nature as a whole. The eternal consciousness is neither a theistic God, as in Berkeley, distinct from the finite minds it creates, nor is it simply the pooled totality of finite minds. It 'reproduces' itself in individual minds and they 'participate in it'. Neither individual minds nor the eternal consciousness are in time. Temporality is a relational matter and, therefore, contributed by mind to nature. The force of the word 'eternal' in the phrase 'eternal consciousness' is thus a little obscure. 'Comprehensive' might have been a better word.

The fundamental principle of Green's philosophy, as of idealists generally, is that the mind makes nature. His argument for this conclusion is of the utmost simplicity. Nature is a system or tissue of relations. In the language Green's idealist contemporaries liked to employ, it is 'through and through' relational. There is a problem about what, if anything, the ultimate terms of these relations are, but that will be considered later. Relations, Green affirms, are the work of the mind. Therefore nature, at least as regards an essential aspect of it, is the work of the mind.

Now no one, I imagine, would wish to dispute the thesis that nature is relational. Even Bradley, the most dedicated enemy of relations, would admit that while going on to say that that is just what is wrong with it. For him it is just because nature is a system of relations, which are self-contradictory, that nature is an incoherent abstraction of the discursive intellect. Many philosophers have held that relations are not part of the ultimate furniture of the world. They have seen them as ontologically dispensable, eliminable from the final analysis or inventory of the world's contents. But that does not entail that relational facts are not objective facts at all, only that they consist in or are constituted by the qualitative facts on which they are founded.

Nature is the total system of what exists in space and time. Each of its constituents has relations to each of its other constituents. It does not matter for that contention whether space and time are absolute or relative. If space and time are absolute concrete things are variously related, spatially or temporally, to them, by being at particular absolute places and times within them. If they are not, spatial and temporal positions are defined in terms of spatial and temporal relations to some conventional reference-point. But to defend the idea that nature is relational is, no doubt, to push at an open door.

Green's questionable premise is his claim that relations are the work of the mind. The most curious thing about this crucial and indispensable premise is that Green barely argues for it. For the most part he is content to rely on the frequently invoked authority of Locke. The magic formula in Locke is that relation is 'not contained in the real existence of things but (is) something extraneous and superinduced' (cf. p. 54 above). It might seem strange that one of traditional empiricism's most insistent and unrelenting critics should attribute so much authority to a most conspicuous empiricist. It may be that Green's thought is that if even so notable an empiricist as Locke admits that relations are the work of the mind then it must be as good as self-evident.

The next curious thing about Green's view of relations is that, even if Locke, from near the other end of the philosophical spectrum, appears to share it, Hume certainly does not. And Hume was of all philosophers the subject of Green's most thorough and penetrating investigation, in his introduction to his and Grose's edition of Hume's works. Hume's view of relations is sufficiently shown in what he says about the idea of necessary connection. If we examine two things we suppose to be necessarily connected, we find we have no impression of that necessary connection. What we do find are the relations of contiguity and succession which Hume takes to be just as much items of raw experience as colours and sounds.

A final curious feature, this time an extraneous one, of Green's view of relations is that it seems to have passed almost uncriticized. Critics of his metaphysics of knowledge have generally fastened on the relations between the eternal consciousness and the individual consciousnesses which participate in it. The only notable exception is Balfour in an article in *Mind* written in 1884, a year after *Prolegomena to Ethics* was published and two years after Green's death.

There is a long tradition of leaving relations out of account, ontologically speaking. It begins with Aristotle's observation that 'relations are the least of things that are'. This fairly parenthetical remark was seized on by William of Ockham. He says 'some hold that relation is not something outside the mind really and completely distinct from one or more absolute things. I think that Aristotle and the philosophers following him held this view' (*Summa Logicae*, part I, ch. 49). Locke's view may be an echo, a somewhat remote one, of the ideas of Aristotle and Ockham on the subject.

There does seem to be a tension between a philosophy which takes substance seriously and the idea that relations are part of the real constitution of the world. A substance's qualities are *in* it and in no way detract from its self-sufficiency. The qualities of a thing, at least so far as they are manifested in it, are, so to speak, appropriated by it. McTaggart exhibited some anxiety on this score. The relation between two things is not in either of them, but it is not somewhere between them like a connecting wire, for that would be another thing, generating a Bradleyan regress.

Locke's view that relations are 'extraneous and superinduced' may well owe something to his not very energetically pursued classification of ideas of relation, along with ideas of modes and substances, as complex. A complex idea is one that is either, or both, homogeneous (like a monotone patch of colour or a sustained note) or unanalysable. Since complex ideas are analysable they are also constructible. But that does not imply that they are often, or even more than very rarely, constructed, that is to say fabricated by a mind out of its stock of simple ideas, before any corresponding object is encountered. Very few kinds of substance are envisaged before they are perceived: dragons and other fabulous beasts, fairies, angels, ghosts, usually by fairly modest switches of character between kinds of substance that have been met with in experience. In the case of substance, then, complexity does not entail fabrication.

Locke says of complex ideas that they are the result of mental acts of compounding, which would indeed be how the very marginal class of constructed ideas of substance was put together. Ideas of relation are held to derive from a parallel act of comparing. Often our ideas (which here means beliefs) about the relations of objects to each other arise from a sufficiently purposive piece of mental activity to deserve the title 'comparison'. But very often they do not. I just see that cat is on the mat, hear the creaking of the door following the sound of the doorbell. These are no more the results of comparison than my seeing that a flag in front of me is red is the result of a purposive activity of inspecting. Of course an observation of relatedness requires one to hold two (or more) things in one's mind at once. But that is not always as hard as it is made out to be. Where juxtaposed duality is the ordinary case—as with eyes, nostrils, breasts—it is the solitary existence of one member of what is ordinarily a pair that occasions surprise, attention, mental activity in pursuit of an answer to the question 'where's the other one got to?'

Complexity entails analysability and, therefore, constructibility. It does not entail constructedness or fabrication, whether well-judged, like Tennyson's aerial navies grappling in the central blue, or merely fantastical, in Locke's words, like the hippogryph and the centaur. Few ideas of substance are in fact constructed and not all that many ideas of relation are. Take the relation of *being the father of*, for example. There can be no such thing as direct or immediate experience of the fact of A's being the father of B. What is involved in it is A's impregnating a woman and that woman's going on to bear B. As Hume observed, while the second of these constituents of fatherhood is a matter of reasonable assurance and, at the moment of birth, straightforwardly perceivable, the first is conjectural. It can be inferred from obvious inheritable characteristics and, more effectively, from DNA tests in recent times.

Directly perceived, given, or presented relationships are the more humdrum spatial and temporal ones, such as *being in front of* or *coming just after*, as contrasted with *being 182 miles from* or *lasting for 237 years*. The latter, more sophisticated relations are, in effect, simply conjunctions of relations of the more elementary sort and so, to that tenuous extent, complex. Comparably direct are *lighter in colour than, louder than*, and relations between simple sense-qualities generally. These considerations show that ideas of relation are not in general constructions or fabrications, but as soundly empirical as our ideas of colour or sound.

Although Green's crucial thesis that relations are the work of the mind is most insistently defended by appeals to authority, most explicitly that of Locke, but also, a bit more nebulously, that of Kant, he does approach the issue more directly and on his own account. He argues that a manifold of atomic, isolated, unrelated sensations is not a possible object of experience. He claims that this is the position of the British empiricists, from Locke, say, to Mill. That is simply false. The data of experience, as they conceive them, are spatially related to, and thus differentiated from, each other in extended sense-fields. Having broken up what is given or presented to the perceiver as differentiated and related elements of a field into undifferentiated, unrelated bits, he then asks how they can be brought together into unity and order. The question simply does not arise about experience as it occurs to the perceiver. It can be asked only in connection with a barely intelligible and gratuitous conception of Green's own manufacture.

In laying such stress on the relational character of the object of knowledge Green needs to give some account of the nature of the terms between which the relations hold. He most creditably raises the question himself. 'We cannot reduce the world of experience to a web of relations in which nothing is related, as it would be if everything were erased from it which we cannot refer to the action of a combining intelligence' (*Prolegomena to Ethics*, §42). But having raised the question he goes on to argue that it does not really arise, because it presupposes an untenable 'abstraction of the "matter" from the "form" of experience'. If we press the enquiry into what it is that mind-imposed relations relate, we shall come in the end to mere 'feeling', raw sensation that is inarticulable, not thinkable, not a possible object of knowledge. That is rather like saying that things cannot have borders or outlines because a line of zero thickness is inconceivable. Such a line on its own, so to speak, is nothing, but it is a genuine and, indeed, indispensable ingredient in anything which has a border or spatial limit. We can abstract it from the thing whose border it is, but we cannot separate it as if it were a belt. Relatedness, it could be said to Green, is present in the most elementary or thinkable, articulable experiences, but there must also be something for the relations to relate. Relations without terms are bad enough, but the notion of the mind creating *all* of its contents turns Green from a follower of Kant into a follower of Fichte.

I have argued that Green does not really make much of a case for his fundamental proposition that relations are the work of the mind. To some extent he does not really try to but is content to rely on the authority of Locke, whom I think he misinterprets. Locke, I suggest, did not think that the mind made relations up out of the whole cloth, only that they were founded in or determined by the qualities of their bearers. This, if true of comparative relations, seems certainly false of spatial and temporal ones. In any event the idea, which I have attributed to Locke, that relations are founded in the qualities of the things they relate, to the extent that it is true, does not entail that they are the work of the mind, in the sense which Green attaches to that phrase. They are not, on account of their foundedness, dependent on the mind, incapable of obtaining without it.

The belief that they are so dependent is not unlike the quaint affirmation of some recent intellectual fashion-victim that the Pacific Ocean is a 'social construction'. It is, of course, nothing of the sort; it is a vast, if none too precisely delimited, body of water, which existed long before there was any human society and which we have every reason to believe will continue to exist long after human society has come to an end. What the theorist of its social construction was trying to say is that human beings, or some of the more geographically sophisticated among them, have chosen to distinguish the vast body of water in question with a name of its own. That is a sensible thing to do since the tracts of water that compose the Pacific Ocean so defined are less tenuously connected to each other than they are to neighbouring bodies of water which are not included in it. It is less thing-like, less sharply marked off from its surroundings than, say, Australia, so that we should think of it as mass or tract of stuff, rather than a thing proper. But it is still really there, with all its contents and the relations between them, and would still be, whether or not anybody had introduced a single name for it.

Let me turn now from the topic of relations to something which Green addresses much less directly and thoroughly: the mind's knowledge of itself. He distinguishes, in a Kantian way, between the relating, knowing, transcendental mind and the empirical self, The latter is, presumably, a relational construction of the former, it has a history in time, and the terms of the relations involved are feelings and emotions, conceived in a somewhat exaggeratedly atomic way. Here again Green chooses to base his doctrine on the findings, or perhaps one should say doubts in this case, of a prominent empiricist. John Stuart Mill had famously enquired 'how can a series be aware of itself as a series'. A process might be a better description but there is no need to press the point. At any stage in the series or process, so long as it contains recollections of earlier stages, it is *ipso facto* aware of itself as a series or process. One would ordinarily suppose that what is present to self-awareness is not a lot of isolated granules of experience; we recall them as temporally and causally related. But for Green, of course, these relations are the work of the mind, specifically of the transcendental, knowing mind. As the creator of time, the knowing mind cannot be itself in time.

Is it possible to make any sense of this view? In the first place, how can what is not in time create or make anything? To create something is to bring it about that something that did not exist begins to exist at a certain time and goes on doing so. Knowledge, as contrasted with such body-related items as feelings and emotions, is the exclusive possession of the knowing mind, and must share its timelessness. Therefore there can be no literal growth of knowledge. But it is from the acquisition of knowledge of what he calls 'unalterable' relations that Green's argument for the existence of an eternal consciousness is derived. Knowledge, in fact, is inextricably involved in the passing show of feeling and emotion. I feel angry with John because I know he has betrayed a secret. I am amused by James and so pay close attention to what he is saying and learn that he is not such a fool as he looks. That is to say, knowledge produces emotion, emotion, without producing knowledge of anything but itself, is a common condition for the acquisition of knowledge. What sort of knowledge, finally, do I have of my transcendental, knowing self? Only knowledge of a philosophical, and highly inferential kind, that it is the presupposition of my having any knowledge of ordered, related objects. In that case, since even the idea of such a thing is confined to very few, it cannot be what most people are referring to when they use the word 'I'.

So far I have been following Green over ground that is familiar in general outline from its resemblance to elements in the philosophy of Kant. Kant laid stress on the relational character of knowledge, on its being in his terms a 'synthesis'. The 'forms of intuition' and 'categories', with which this synthesis is, in his view, carried out, are not of empirical origin but are brought to the task of articulating experience by the mind. Kant does not maintain that all relations are the work of the mind. He holds that that is true only of spatio-temporal relations and of such comparatively abstract, or theoretical, relations as substance and cause. Causality is plainly relational in nature; substance is not obviously so. The substance-making relation that is most relevant to Kant's purposes is, no doubt, continued identity through time. Substance and cause are, at any rate, not straightforwardly empirical conceptions and Kant had Hume's warrant for supposing them to be some sort of mental construction. In following Hume here, he was acting on Hume's central explicit doctrine, not, as Green does with Locke, on a fairly casual assertion.

The second main part of Green's metaphysics of knowledge is his theory of the eternal consciousness. Nature is an inclusive system of relations of which the nature which is the constructed object of an individual's knowledge is only at best a part. It will be a part in so far as the individual's knowledge really is knowledge. To the extent that the individual's conception of nature is not merely incomplete but also erroneous it will contain only some of what the individual supposes himself to know. Green does not spell this out but it seems to be implied by what he does say.

Now this all-inclusive system of relations which constitutes nature, in what must be the normal sense of the word, presupposes an all-sustaining mind. It is a unity and, therefore, must be held together by a single mind, the eternal consciousness. We are all, Green contends, parts or participators in this eternal consciousness.

The question that this development of his thought inescapably prompts is by what right does he suppose that there is an all-inclusive nature beyond, but including, the nature as created by the relating activity of the individual mind? Everybody, of course, believes that there is more to nature than what he knows of it. But how, on Green's principles, is he to know that? Nature, for him, must be the totality of what an individual consciousness has brought into a relational order. How can an individual consciousness know that there is more to nature than he knows there is?

In practice, of course, we all know perfectly well that nature transcends what we currently know of it. We know that we have got to know more and more with the passage of time and can reasonably infer that this process of enlargement will continue in the future. But that does not entail on Green's view of the nature of knowledge that nature beyond our present knowledge of it is, so to speak, already there. Nature is made, not found, in his view. And unbaked bread does not consist of actual rolls.

What has happened is that Green has drawn on a deep-seated common-sense belief, that there is more to nature than I know of it, which is in fact incompatible with his theory of the nature of knowledge, to mitigate the highly subjectivistic implications of that theory. There are other criticisms that could be made. In practice our belief in an all-inclusive nature going for beyond the limits of our personal knowledge is, of course, largely a product of the pooling of knowledge brought about by human communication. Most of what I, in fact, suppose myself to know is acquired from the testimony of others. But Green has nothing to say about the social character of knowledge. And that is not surprising since he has nothing to say about our knowledge of consciousnesses other than our own. What is more he would be hard put to provide one even superficially consistent with his general account of knowledge. I know other people, in the first instance, as parts of nature, as animated bodies, acting and talking. They are, therefore, the product of my mind's creative activity.

Once he has established to his own satisfaction that there is a comprehensive nature that transcends the nature that is constructed by the individual consciousness, the step of inference to an all-inclusive ordering mind adequate to bring the elements of this comprehensive nature together is easy. There are no relations without a relating mind. There is an all-inclusive system of relations that transcends nature as I know it, present to my mind and ordered by my mind. Only a universal mind is adequate to bring it into a system.

For Green the idea of an indefinitely extensive mass of nature lying, as an epistemologically unravished bride, beyond any individual consciousness is surely, then, incoherent. Of course we all believe that there is more to nature than we know of it. We suppose, on the inductive grounds I mentioned earlier, that more of it will be progressively revealed with the passage of time. We may regard this progress as indefinitely extendable, may even attempt to form, if only for purposes of refutation, the idea of complete or perfect knowledge. But on Green's view of knowledge how can we suppose that this transcending, larger nature exists already? The nature that is currently unknown by me is, on his theory, purely hypothetical. Since it is obviously not, except for the most ontologically resolute of phenomenalists, he uses it, an assumption to which he is not entitled, to supply a platform for the eternal consciousness.

There is one feature of his account which might be seen as an effort to dig himself out of the solipsistic hole he has dug himself into. There is repeated and emphatic reference, from the beginning of his exposition, to the *unalterable* character of the relations which articulate or order nature. That idea has some affinity with a very simple view about the distinction between the real and the unreal. It underlies Hume's distinction between impressions and ideas. Impressions just happen, whether I like it or not: ideas can be summoned and dismissed at will. Another more promising distinction is between what appears to be an x and goes on appearing to be an x and what appears to be an x for a moment and from then on persistently appears to be a y.

Green's word 'unalterable' cannot be taken literally. What is real is not everywhere unalterable by me. I cannot do much about the nebula in Andromeda, but I can move the furniture in my room about, paint it, break it up for firewood, and so forth. Nor, a fortiori, is what is real unalterable by anything else. It would seem that the word is some sort of metaphorical way of expressing the idea of the solidity, the achieved immunity to criticism, of a belief. The real is what I, or, more realistically, we, come to realize, and in the case of us, agree about, in the end or long run, a Peircian conception.

The most appropriate interpretation of Green's use of 'unalterable' would seem to be 'independent of the will'. In that case Green's eternal consciousness comes to resemble Berkeley's God. Berkeley found some of his ideas were independent of his will. Since the only cause of ideas he knew of was a mind or spirit, namely his own, he inferred that some other spirit caused the ideas that were uncaused by him. The familiar objection is that the analogy fails. What he knows about the causation of ideas is that minds can cause ideas to arise in themselves. What he is ascribing to God is the quite different capacity of causing ideas to arise in another mind. We can make sense of this. We understand what telepathy is, well enough, at any rate, to disbelieve in it. But there does not seem to be all that much of it about and the supposition that one is receiving messages from God is a primary symptom of schizophrenia.

Now Green is not exposed to this criticism. The individual consciousness is not distinct from the eternal consciousness, but is a part of it, participates in it. The unalterable relations in my experience are presumably those elements in God's constitution of nature which I manage to get hold of, which fall, so to speak, in my limited region of the eternal consciousness.

Neverthless there at least a serious tension between the doctrine that relations are the work of my mind and the contention that some of them are unalterable. The original thesis was that relations are the work of the mind in whose consciousness they figure. But he goes on to hold that some of them, the unalterable ones, are the work of a larger mind of which the individual is a part, a very small one, no doubt. That partial identification of the individual mind with the eternal consciousness may serve slightly to blunt the edge of this criticism, but does not turn it aside altogether.

So, even if relations were, as I have argued that they are in general not, created by the mind rather than found by it, the theory of the eternal consciousness would still be in difficulties. An unalterable relation is one that is present to, but not created by, my mind. But that is a falsifying exception to the principle that relations are the work or product of the mind to which they are present in consciousness. It cannot, in that case, be inferentially extended to show that there is a universal mind whose work is the comprehensive nature that lies beyond the present reach of an individual consciousness. Green claims to know, sensibly enough, that there is a nature that transcends the limited, imperfect individual consciousness. That fact cannot be used to prove that there is an eternal consciousness since it undermines the principle, required for that proof, that relations are the work of my mind.

Green's philosophy combines elements of the views of Kant and Hegel in an interesting and idiosyncratic way. From Kant he derives the theory that the mind makes nature, but pushing it to an extreme in maintaining that all the relations which give order to nature are mind-dependent and not, as in Kant, only some basic structural relations. This enables him to minimize acknowledgement of the need of relations for terms. What Kant saw as a distinguishable element of sensation in ordered experience, Green endeavours to write off as a 'meaningless abstraction'. His aim is plainly to avoid admitting the independent reality of anything not dependent on the mind which might entangle him with the thing-in-itself. But by laying such stress on relations he cannot escape the ineliminable terms which they entail.

He derives from Hegel the theory that the individual mind is a part of the eternal consciousness, which is, of course, the Absolute Mind in English clothing. His difficulty here is that the unalterable relations which lead him from the part to the whole are incompatible with the principle that relations are the work of the individual mind.

Green's combination of Kantian foundations with a Hegelian metaphysical superstructure is the main singularity of his doctrine. The Kantian part of it, the theory of relations, was not taken up by subsequent idealists. For Bradley, the most important of them, relations are the work of the discursive intellect or understanding. Just on that account they are, as inherently contradictory, not a feature of what is real. Reality, as he puts it, is 'above relations', a seamless, undivided whole. Green's system of relations is demoted to the status of a practically useful illusion.

10

John Dewey's Theory of Knowledge

1. Introduction

Pragmatism began as a theory of meaning. It is often dated from the publication in 1878 of Peirce's article 'How to make our ideas clear', in which the meaning of an idea is identified with its 'practical bearings', that is to say the difference its being true would make in terms of experienceable consequences in the future. It is perhaps most familiar as a theory of truth, especially in the form given to it by William James for whom the true is what it is good, expedient, or satisfactory to believe.

But pragmatism is also a theory of knowledge and was so from the beginning. In two articles that appeared in W. T. Harris's *Journal of Speculative Philosophy* as early as 1868, its second year ('Questions Concerning Certain Faculties Claimed for Man' and 'Some Consequences of Four Incapacities'), Peirce argues elaborately and ingeniously against what he calls Cartesianism, the idea that knowledge should be constructed from intuitively self-evident beliefs in minds that have been cleared of all habitual assumptions by a process of universal doubt.

As Peirce himself says, 'most modern philosophers have been, in effect, Cartesians', and this is true of British philosophers in particular. Locke's view that all knowledge must be derived from the intuitive deliverances of sensation and reflection, if empirical, and from intuitive awareness of conceptual connections, if it is not, has been the common conviction of the central tradition in British epistemology that stems from him, through Berkeley and Hume and then John Stuart Mill to Russell and such Russellian theorists of knowledge of more recent times as Price and Ayer. What is more, the varying accounts the members of this tradition have given, on their shared Cartesian basis, of our knowledge of the material world, the minds of ourselves and others, of the past and of the laws of nature, have remained, until comparatively recently, the centre of constructive philosophical interest and were long the initial core of philosophical teaching.

Yet until the publication of W. B. Gallie's *Peirce and Pragmatism* in 1952 there was no British discussion of Peirce's anti-Cartesianism, and even now such currency as its conclusions have is perhaps more attributable to the influence of the rather similar account of the 'basis-problem' in Popper's *Logic of Scientific Discovery* than to Peirce's presentation of it.

James's epistemological ideas are, indeed, familiar in the developed form of his radical empiricism through the fact that Russell was converted to them. In his essay on 'The Nature of Acquaintance' in 1914, Russell criticized James's neutral monism from the point of view of his conviction that in perception a mental subject is related to a physical object that is totally different in nature from it. By 1918 with 'The Philosophy of Logical Atomism' and, even more, by 1922 with the *Analysis of Mind*, Russell's conversion to James's way of thinking was complete. But this was hardly a conversion to pragmatism, even to pragmatist epistemology, from which James's doctrine, with its close affinities to the ideas of Mach and, on a natural reading, Hume, is really a deviation.

The chief continuator of Peirce's anti-Cartesianism was John Dewey. He combined it with James's emphasis on the acquisition of knowledge as an active and exploratory process, rather than a kind of passive contemplation, with the view, present in much pragmatism, but particularly emphasized by Schiller, that the conceptual instruments of thought are human constructions not independent Platonic existences, and, third, with an insistence on the social character of knowledge that is to be found in Peirce, to produce a distinctive theory of knowledge that has a remarkable coherence of tone despite the breadth of its scope and, it must be admitted, the frequent turgidity and amorphousness of its expression.

It is this theory of knowledge of Dewey's that I shall be discussing. I find all of its main contentions at least suggestive even if, in the form in which Dewey presents them, they are open to much criticism. In general, those constituents of the whole for which Dewey is himself chiefly responsible are, I shall argue, more acceptable as regards what they deny than as regards what they positively affirm. It is still odd that a body of extensive critical discussion that addresses itself to such fundamental aspects of the traditional British theory of knowledge should have secured so little attention here.

2. The Four Themes of Anti-Intellectualism

A term is needed to pick out Dewey's theory of knowledge from pragmatism in general. His own preferred designation, instrumentalism, is not altogether satisfactory since it concentrates too much on one part of the whole. It is perhaps best characterized in negative terms as anti-intellectualism. It can be set out by listing its four main points of conflict and disagreement with the familiar Cartesian tradition.

> 1. Where the Cartesian seeks to base all knowledge on absolutely certain beliefs, on somehow self-evident items of intuitive knowledge, the anti-intellectualist contends that all our beliefs are fallible and corrigible. In consequence the task of epistemology is not to give an account of secure and certified knowledge but rather of rational and warranted belief. In general, the beliefs on which we act are

not established certainties. The demand for established certainty is exaggerated and utopian. We must be content with warranted assertibility which falls short of absolute and ideal truth. It is in the spirit of this conviction that Dewey puts himself forward as a theorist of *enquiry* rather than a theorist of *knowledge*.
2. The anti-intellectualist sees the knower or enquirer, the pursuer of rational and warranted belief, as an active being, an experimenter, not as a contemplative theorist. It is in this connection that Dewey launches his polemics against the 'spectator theory of knowledge'. Our rational beliefs about the world in which we live and act are not the result of a kind of Augustinian illumination, passively received, and then privately worked up and systematized in the recesses of our own minds. They are, rather, the outcome of deliberate, experimental interaction with our environment. Furthermore the intellectual apparatus which we bring to this cognitive encounter with the world is not something imposed on us by the pervading structure of the world outside. Our conceptual equipment is a body of instruments that we have devised and constructed ourselves, under the pressure of our own needs and purposes.
3. The subject or possessor of knowledge or warranted belief is not, in the manner of intellectualism, a pure mind or consciousness, a Cartesian *res cogitans*. It is, in Dewey's view, an intelligent organism, an embodied thing, animated by primarily bodily purposes, and forming its beliefs about the world around it through bodily, physical interaction with it. Manipulation is at least as crucial to the formation of rational beliefs as more or less detached inspection.
4. Finally, the anti-intellectualist sees the pursuit of rational belief as an essentially social undertaking, in contrast to the subjective isolation of the Cartesian knower, exposed as he is to various kinds of sceptical desperation. Knowledge or rational belief is a social product, an accumulation of common intellectual property, made up of what Dewey likes to call 'funded experience' and on which all may draw.

In short, the intellectualist sees knowledge as something absolutely certain, which is contemplatively seen, by a mind that is at most contingently embodied, working on its own. For Dewey's anti-intellectualism what is sought is rational and corrigibly fallible belief, actively achieved, even made or constructed, and with the aid of conceptual instruments of human design, by an intelligent but embodied organism that is a natural part of the world it seeks to know, engaged on this undertaking as a collaborating member of a society of intelligent organisms of the same kind.

3. Fallibilism

Let us consider the first theme, that of fallibilism. Intellectualism, particularly in its Cartesian and intuitionist form, defines knowledge as conclusively justified true belief and maintains that all rational belief must rest on knowledge thus defined. The anti-intellectualist is opposed to the suggested definition of knowledge as utopian and even superstitious but does not so much attack it by direct argument as simply replace it by a conception of knowledge held to be more realistic and useful.

In effect, that is to say that we should not bother ourselves with absolute certainties since they are not to be had and, fortunately, are not needed. What, he asks, is knowledge for? Primarily, persistingly, and essentially for the sake of action. What we require is rational belief about the consequences of various alternative actions it is within our power to take. In being essentially practical, it is also essentially forward-looking and predictive and all such prediction is fallible.

In a way there is nothing here with which Cartesians generally, and Cartesians of an empiricist variety in particular, need quarrel. If absolute certainty is insisted on as a defining condition of knowledge then it will turn out that very little is known. Specifically what is truly known is whatever is intuitively necessary, whatever is in some way empirically self-evident and incorrigible, in other words the immediate deliverances of sensation and introspective self-consciousness, and whatever can be deduced from premises of either of these sorts by means of rules of inference corresponding to intuitive or demonstrated necessary truths. On this view most of what is of practical interest for man as an active being will not be known. Cartesian empiricists will agree that with regard to the material world, the past, the minds of others, and the laws of nature, we can have at best rational belief, for all propositions about these are neither intuitive nor demonstrable. For the most part they will be the conclusions of non-deductive inference which are at best confirmed and never certified by the evidence on which they rest. (Knowledge of the past by memory is not inferential, of course, but it is as fallible as if it were, and thus as little entitled to description as knowledge proper.) No one could be more emphatic that the beliefs of science and common sense are not truly knowledge than Russell, unless it were Hume.

But, if the Cartesian tends to admit that very little of what we believe, and, in particular, practically none of the beliefs which directly guide our actions, are truly known in his sense of the word, he still insists that the little that is truly known is of the utmost importance. This is because of his second thesis that there can be no rational belief that is not derived from knowledge proper.

Dewey does not, so far as I know, attack this thesis directly but I believe it to be mistaken. It is commonly presented as the only alternative to a coherence theory of knowledge in which every belief owes its justification to its inferential relation to other beliefs (a position something very like that to which Peirce was driven by his rejection of intuitionism). This view leads to an infinite regress which presents every appearance of being vicious. Beliefs cannot simply pass justification from one to another without, so to speak, their having some initial stock of justification from another source.

But such a coherence theory is not the only alternative to intuitionism. The fact that all beliefs that derive whatever justification they have to non-deductive inference from other beliefs are less than absolutely certain does not entail that all beliefs that are less than certain are inferential in the way described. In other words it is not clear that all rational, but less than absolutely certain, belief must be derived from beliefs that are absolutely certain and incorrigible.

It is possible to hold that there are foundations to knowledge, or, more precisely, relative foundations, which, while not absolutely certain, are nevertheless rationally believed, not on the strength of other beliefs that inferentially support them but on the strength of experiences that do not certify them but simply render them more worthy of acceptance than rejection. Just this is true, I believe, of the propositions about perceived material things and the remembered past that are the apparent, rather than theoretically alleged, foundations of our empirical beliefs about matters of fact.

If this view is accepted it is not necessary to suppose that our beliefs about the material world as we commonly take ourselves to perceive it are really inferences from antecedent beliefs about our sense-experiences or again that our beliefs about the recollected past are inferred from antecedent beliefs about memory-data.

Although these basic empirical beliefs about the perceived material world and the recollected past are not initiated or wholly dependent for their justification on inference from other, more certain beliefs, they are, nevertheless, subject to inference, in so far as they can be further confirmed by other beliefs of the same corrigible but credible status, in the light of equally corrigible general beliefs about the way in which the constituents of the material world behave and hang together. Equally, of course, they may, despite their initial credibility, be undermined by inference from a preponderating body of comparable beliefs.

This brings us back to the definition of knowledge in terms of absolute certainty. What this defining condition in fact comes to is that a proposition can be known only if it would be an evident or demonstrable contradiction to deny it or if it follows from the fact that it is believed that it is true. In either of those circumstances there would be some kind of logical absurdity in the supposition that the belief in question might be false. But without going to the length of blithely redefining knowledge as well-confirmed belief, it might be felt that that is altogether too stringent an account of certainty.

The certain, it could be suggested, is not that which it is somehow logically absurd to doubt, but that which there is no reason to doubt; that which rationally ought not to be doubted, not that which logically cannot be. Now in these terms although no basic empirical proposition may be certain as prompted by experience alone, it may acquire certainty from the addition to that confirmation of the support of other equally fallible beliefs. Certainty, on such a view, is something ascertained, not something initially given. But it could be what we ordinarily understand by the word.

I conclude, then, that the Cartesian does define knowledge too restrictively and that he is mistaken in thinking that its uninferred empirical basis must be incorrigibly certain. But such ideal certainty is not really essential to knowledge and ordinary certainty is attainable for basic empirical beliefs even if they are not endowed with it by the experiences that directly prompt them. In rejecting the Cartesian's definition of knowledge Dewey goes too far in the opposite direction and, in his emphasis on the fallibility of most practically important beliefs, says nothing that an empirically minded

Cartesian could not accept, while failing to engage with their real mistake: the assumption that the foundations of knowledge must be logically immune from error.

4. Instrumentalism

The focus of Dewey's epistemology is his attack on the spectator theory of knowledge on behalf of instrumentalism or experimentalism. At a certain level of generality the idea that knowledge is actively and purposively sought, not just passively received, is likely to secure acceptance without much difficulty. It might indeed be said that our acquisition of knowledge or rational belief is neither wholly active nor wholly passive. Surely a certain amount of what we know or reasonably believe just gets borne in on us and does not take the form of answers methodically secured to antecedently formulated questions. The process by which I have come to know that I do not like the taste of liquorice, that my colleague is in a rather irritable state today, or that a friend's wife has put on a good deal of weight, does not deserve to be dignified with the description 'enquiry'.

In very general terms like these there is plainly much to be said on behalf of an active attitude in the knowledge-gathering operation. In the tone of an epistemological Polonius one could urge that if knowledge is actively sought it will be both better founded and a great deal more copious than if it is merely allowed to accumulate in a passive manner. It is this active attitude, after all, that is the most fundamental mark of distinction between science and common sense; for whatever else it may be, science is at least a deliberate and methodical effort to answer questions about the nature and connection of things. If beliefs are just allowed to form by a kind of natural accretion they are perhaps peculiarly likely to be incorrect. To produce a final bromide: one generally does something better if one attends to what one is doing.

At the same level of rather bland generality is Dewey's insistence that the process of enquiry is prompted and set in motion by men's practical needs, that knowledge is for the sake of action. Here again, one may readily admit that a great deal of knowledge is of this kind, perhaps most of the knowledge that most people have. But there is such a thing as pure curiosity, as distinct from the curiosity which arises from a suspicion that something may have hitherto unknown properties that call for action, perhaps of a pre-emptive kind, and, one has to add, from the impure curiosity of the enquirer who has to find something out in order to pass an examination or retain a job, however practically indifferent he may be to the content of what he is seeking to find out. Polonius is waiting in the wings once again at this point, bursting with the information that many things that people have been motivated to discover by the love of knowledge for its own sake have later turned out to be of the highest significance for practical human purposes. One may sympathize with Dewey's anxiety to make philosophy serviceable to men in general in the concerns of everyday life, without feeling obliged to make out its credentials in this respect in all its aspects.

Instrumentalism takes on a more concrete and definite character in the form of the thesis that the materials of belief, the concepts in which beliefs are formulated, are human constructions and not imposed on men by the nature of things. This thesis is directed against intellectualism of a Platonic kind which takes the conceptual materials of our thought to be somehow imposed on us by the nature of things. Our conceptual apparatus, on this view, reflects, to the extent that it is adequate for its task, the structure of an objective and timeless realm of essence. Dewey was always hostile to Platonism on more or less democratic or egalitarian grounds. He took it to be the attitude to knowledge appropriate to a slave-owning society in which true rational men or citizens did not soil their hands with the work of the world but sequestered themselves for purposes of abstract, theoretical contemplation. But there is a certain vulgarity about this opinion. Mathematics and metaphysics are not dirty work, except in the marginal forms of computer engineering and sorcery, but that does not mean that they are not work, that they are not fields of active, answer-seeking effort, typically, I should suppose, more so than the routine discharge of practical tasks.

The active, imaginative invention or construction of concepts is most evident at the level of scientific theorizing. The theorist's intellectual fertility does not show itself only in bringing familiar concepts together in previously unformulated beliefs. It is also present in the devising of new concepts that are not part of the common stock of thought and discourse: elasticity of demand, deep grammatical structure, the quantum of energy, the correlation coefficient.

Concepts of this kind differ from more familiar ones like red or square or tree or dog in that they have a history, a known history, that is to say, providing a date at which they were first introduced and the name of their first introducer. But two points need to be made here. The fact that a new concept was introduced into discourse at a particular time by a particular person does not mean that it is strictly an invention. The conceptual innovator may be just as well described as having brought off a feat of discovery. The actual or possible property or relationship that he succeeds in bringing to human consciousness may well have already been exemplified in the world, even if no one before him was aware of the fact. Indeed, if the new concept is to be of any use in the formulation of true beliefs, what the concept expresses must, in most cases, have been, or be going to be, actually exemplified. (The point of the qualification is to allow for concepts of ideal or limiting cases: the perfectly elastic fluid, the ideal gas, the economy in perfect equilibrium.) The conceptual innovator, in other words, must have one foot on the earth.

Second, although the fact of historic innovation may show some concepts to be the outcome of acts of imaginative creation, those concepts will be theoretical and sophisticated ones like the examples I gave. The ordinary notions with which they are contrasted, the everyday descriptive apparatus, would seem to be a piece of common human property of unhistoric antiquity and unhistoric immunity to reform and change. One rather obvious piece of evidence for this view is the translatability of ancient or geographically remote languages into the language we speak ourselves.

It is, of course, true that there are limits to translation. I am thinking here not of the problems raised by Quine but of the problem posed by Homer's 'wine-dark sea'. Even the most elementary and familiar concepts have a sort of history and we may reasonably suppose them to have emerged as part of the natural evolutionary development of mankind. That point of view undermines the old idea of a universal and identical human reason to be found in Aristotle and the Stoics and defended by Kant on the ground of the universal validity of logic. It seems reasonable to suppose that our conceptual apparatus is not a direct reflection of the nature and structure of the world but the result of an interaction, worked out in an evolutionary way, between the world and two things located in us: our perceptual equipment, on the one hand, and our needs and interests on the other.

The view of Platonic intellectualism, that our conceptual apparatus directly reflects the structure of the world, does not have as its only alternative the idea that our conceptual apparatus is a wholly free construction, imposed by us on the indefinitely plastic tissue of our environment. Between biscuits and clear homogeneous soup is minestrone. We can allow ourselves, that is to say, our perceptual equipment and our needs and interests, an important measure of free initiative in the formation of concepts without supposing ourselves to be absolutely free in this matter. The initiative in question is to select, from all the possibilities of comparison or similarity-finding that are present in the world, those that our perceptual equipment enables us to register, those which present themselves to the close attention that is excited by need and interest and those, finally, which while not thrusting themselves on perception nor directly ministering to an interest, allow for the conveniently brief formulation of laws or are, as one might say, explanatorily fertile.

The mind or knower, then, can be admitted to be conceptually creative without denying that the conceptual outfit it creates is some kind of reflection of the world; for surely, if it did not in some way reflect the similarities and differences to be found in the world it would be descriptively useless. If our thinking is to be communicable from one person to another the words in which they express it must, where the same, apply to much the same things. We must share dispositions to classify things together and to distinguish them. If that is to happen things classified together must strike us each in much the same way and things distinguished must strike us differently, and for that to happen the things in question must actually be, respectively, alike and different. I conclude that the valid part of Dewey's instrumentalist theory that concepts are human constructions is that facts about human beings determine the selection of those features of reality that are conceptually registered but that it is genuine features of reality that the selection is made from.

Dewey's critique of the spectator theory of knowledge does not confine itself to the passively intellectualist account that theory gives of concept-formation. The formation of beliefs, Dewey maintains, as well as that of the material of belief, is a species of human action, not just the passive absorption of what he calls 'antecedent reality'. One slightly puzzling way in which this position is expressed is in the statement that a belief is a 'plan of action'. It is clear enough that beliefs are frequently *parts* of plans of action, in the ordinary sense of the phrase; indeed, it is hard to think of anything that could be called a plan of action that does not at least imply or presuppose some belief or beliefs.

But a belief can plainly be held without being part of any actually formulated plan of action in the mind of the believer, such as my belief that Sirius is a very large star.

Dewey generally sees enquiry as the result of some obstacle to action and no doubt it often is. In this situation the enquiry succeeds in removing the obstacle to action by arriving at a belief which makes the formation of an effective plan of action possible. The door is locked and I cannot get in. I look enquiringly for the key under the mat, find it there, and, in a twinkling, I form and put into effect the plan of picking it up, putting it in the keyhole, and opening the door.

The process of enquiry that terminates, if successful, in the formation of a belief will typically be itself a form of action. In the minimal case the action is that of just looking attentively. But commonly that is not enough. I see something that looks like a key in the shadows above the lintel. I think to myself 'if that is a key it will feel hard and cool to the touch' and put into operation the verificatory manoeuvre of reaching out to touch it. The confirmation of initially insecure beliefs is an exploratory, experimental process of action, so the belief-forming process of enquiry is itself a kind of action. But it is not, so to speak, all action. The hypothetical statements that set out potential confirmations of what we are inclined to believe suggest experimental lines of action that we can follow. But once the action suggested has been performed we just have to wait and see (or feel) to exercise our negative capabilities of sentience. My reaching out and touching the key is something I do; the hardness and coolness I then feel it to have is something the world (or the key, if that is what it is) does to me.

It is through an extreme of nebulosity at this point in his account of the nature of enquiry that Dewey arrives at his most surprising conclusion: 'inquiry is the controlled or directed transformation', he writes, 'of an indeterminate situation into one that is so determinate in its constituent distinctions and relations as to convert the elements of the original situation into a unified whole'. Or again: 'the outcome of the directed activity [sc. of enquiry] is the construction of a new empirical situation in which objects are differently related to one another and such that the consequences of directed operations form the objects that have the property of being known'.

In any situation of enquiry three sorts of change may be brought about. To start with there is change simply on the side of the enquirer. He was in a state of ignorance ('I don't know where the key is'); he arrives at a state of knowledge or well-founded belief ('Here is the key'). Second, there may be some change introduced by the experimental activity of the enquirer which affects the object of his enquiry. He picks the key-like thing up, has a good look at it, and concludes that it is a key. Here the key is no longer where it was, but in his hand and near his eyes, but it is still a key. Finally, he may bring about a change in the object which, as it were, frustrates the original purpose of the enquiry: 'Where is the key?' 'Well, it's in my hand now.' Or, more catastrophically, 'Where is the egg?' 'It was in my hand but now it's all over the place.'

The third kind of change is not the essence of effective, practical enquiry; it is its nemesis. It is something to be carefully guarded against, not welcomed. 'We murder to dissect' is not a metaphysical truth, but it is a methodological caution.

Beliefs are, then, often for action and they figure essentially in plans of action. In seeking to arrive at well-founded beliefs we commonly engage in experimental activity which is intended to produce a change in us and is ordinarily going to produce some change, even if not a very central or intrinsic one, in the object experimentally acted upon, its relative position, for example, its condition of illumination, and so on. But if it centrally alters the object itself the experimental aspect of enquiry defeats its own purpose. At some stage in enquiry the enquirer must be a spectator, however questioning and actively experimental or manipulative he may be at other stages. The object must be left room to do its part. If we put it to the question, it still has to give the answer. Dewey seems to represent the enquirer as a kind of inefficient torturer who does not discover the crucial thing his victim knows but rather what his victim thinks he would like to hear. Dewey is right to stress that enquiry, the acquisition of knowledge or rational belief, is an interaction between the object and its investigator. But it is an interaction, not just the converse of the one-way process presented by the spectator theory of knowledge.

5. Naturalism

Dewey's emphasis on the active nature of enquiry rather strongly implies that the enquirer should be conceived as an intelligent organism, physically interacting with the objects he investigates, and not just as a contemplating mind. It does not strictly entail that conclusion, since a disembodied Cartesian mind could be thought of as being in a way active in his contemplative operations, if only by the directing and focusing of his attention. But Dewey would rightly insist that in fact the confirmation of our beliefs involves bodily manipulation of their objects.

Many philosophers have pointed out the close connection between the spectator theory of knowledge and the tendency of theorists of knowledge to identify perception with sight. In visual perception, for the most part, the action of the body is minimal: sometimes it is just a matter of focusing the eyes; on many occasions no more bodily action is required than moving the head.

But touch, after all, is as important to our perception of the external world as sight. As Geoffrey Warnock has said, although sight is very informative and detailed in its deliverances, we rely on touch in the end for a final check on what sight prompts us to believe.

No one, in fact, would deny that the perceiver is, at least in part, a physical thing causally interacting with the rest of the physical world, or that causal influence exercised on the physical mechanism of perception by its objects is a necessary condition of anything being perceived at all. But what Cartesian theorists of knowledge would maintain is that these propositions, although true, do not affect the epistemology of perception. The knowledge they express, although it is perfectly genuine knowledge, for which any adequate theory of knowledge must find a place, is still knowledge of a secondary, derivative, theoretical kind. They can invoke the same arguments they have used to show that in visual perception all that we really or directly perceive is private entities in our own streams of consciousness to domesticate or subjectivize the deliverances of touch and organic sensation. There are, after all, touch-illusions, such as the effect of rubbing one's hands up and down together with a wire mesh between them, which makes the wire feel like cloth or silk, and once these are admitted there is an entering wedge through which the distinction between the touch-data we directly perceive and the actual tactile properties of things can enter.

In a thorough discussion of these neglected areas of touch and organic sensation H. H. Price interestingly traces the conception of causation as some kind of active efficacy, and not just the kind of regularity which is all that vision finds in it, to the experience of forceful resistance we have, by way of muscular sensation, when objects impinge on us or we press against them. At one point he says that the resistance we experience is essentially relational in nature and so no inference is required to establish an external resistor. But he is equally emphatic that we must not fail to distinguish the sense of embodiment which is the constant background to all our sensory experience from the fact of being embodied which that sense no doubt encourages us to accept as a fact but is not entailed by it.

To insist that we are, as perceivers, embodied organisms in physical interaction with the external world we perceive does not really undermine the sceptically Cartesian account of the indubitable foundations of empirical knowledge. It only highlights in a forceful way the oddity of the Cartesian account of the knower. That oddity is not enough on its own to refute the Cartesian position. After all, the Cartesian is usually going to find a place for these facts in his overall view of the structure of knowledge. To refute his basic subjectivism it is necessary to confront it more directly, as is done by the defence of fallibilism that I expounded earlier. But once we free ourselves of the ultimate Cartesian principle that all our knowledge begins and owes its ultimate confirmation to facts we perceive immediately about the contents of our own minds, the fact that we are, as perceivers, embodied organisms, physically interacting in perception with the world that we perceive can be placed at the logical and psychological beginnings of our acquisition of knowledge about matters of empirical fact and not be represented, as in Cartesian subjectivism, as a matter of more or less sophisticated and precarious theory.

6. The Social Nature of Knowledge

Every theorist of knowledge would admit that most of what we actually know or rationally believe we owe in some way to others. In recognition of this fact they usually append to their lists of the sources of knowledge some reference to testimony or authority. It will be tacked on in a rather undignified way at the tail end of a sequence that begins with perception and runs through self-consciousness or introspection and memory to inference. Quite often, indeed, testimony is regarded as a special case of inference, deriving its conclusions from premises of the form 'A says p' and 'most of what A says is true'. The first of these is established by perception, the second by induction from observed correspondence between what A has been heard to say in the past and what we have found out to be true on our own.

There is an interesting problem about testimony. Plainly we believe a lot of it when we are not in a position to affirm the generalizations about reliability which would be needed for such beliefs to be rationally accepted. What is more, when we do come to check on the reliability of external informants, we do so with critical instruments with which we have been externally supplied. I have argued elsewhere that this problem can be solved, that the tests we use on testimony are not, as the problem suggests, potentially corrupted at the source. The nerve of the argument is that other people could not mislead us about logic and perception, which are all the testing instruments required. They could perhaps prevent us from learning to speak at all, by energetically random utterance in our presence, but if they are to teach us to speak at all they cannot help teaching us more or less correctly, that is to say in accordance with the rules with which their observable practice has conformed.

Cartesian minds are isolated things, epistemological Adams or Crusoes, making their way in the world on their own. Dewey's intelligent organisms pursue warranted beliefs in a society of other enquirers like themselves and in communication with them. This, once again, is something we all know, but it occupies a very small and marginal place in Cartesian theories of knowledge. To draw attention to it is not, as it stands, an *argument* against such theories, except to the extent that it brings out the extent to which their assumptions about the foundations of knowledge lead them largely to ignore the actual character of knowledge in a world of social beings. Dewey's pursuit of a theory of knowledge that will be concerned with the actual problems of men here once again opens up a range of problems about knowledge which the tradition to which he is opposed has largely neglected.

11
T. E. Hulme

At the beginning of the twentieth century British traditionalism found expression in the writings of W. H. Mallock (of *The New Republic*) and Lord Hugh Cecil (of *Conservatism*). Cecil's was the conservatism of the country house, Mallock's of the suburban villa. But both were somewhat conventional prolongations of existing styles of thought. Before 1914, however, the first stirrings can be discerned of a harsher and more militant style of right-wing social theory. In terms of practical politics British Fascism never became more than a comparatively minor problem of public hygiene, an eruption of anti-Semitic hooliganism by means of which an upper class outcast fed his wounded vanity. But its literary effects have been considerable. In different ways many of the leading imaginative writers of the period between the wars inclined towards Fascism or at least to a considerably more ruthless and unmitigated kind of authoritarianism than anything envisaged by traditional conservatives. Ezra Pound lauded Mussolini and Wyndham Lewis wrote in praise of Hitler. T. S. Eliot, in a more defeated and melancholy way, upbraided his juniors for their animus against the Fascist dictators of Europe whom he saw, with many conservatives, as the first line of defence against Bolshevism. Yeats had a militant predilection for aristocracy in its most hierarchical form.

This whole style of thought has one of its main sources in that still insufficiently appreciated figure T. E. Hulme, who was killed in action in 1916 and whose ideas had been fully formed and expressed by the outbreak of war. Hulme's influence, which was very large considering the small scale and fragmentary form of his writings, would appear to rest on three factors: his extremely forceful personality, impressed on the circle of his acquaintances by such things as the knuckleduster made for him by the sculptor Gaudier-Brzeska, by the irresistible lucidity of his style, and by the fact that, for all their fragmentariness, his ideas did form a system with a broadly philosophical basis and with a host of significant applications to literature and art as well as in the field of social and political theory.

The firmness and clarity of Hulme's style does not conceal the fact that his ideas are often the result of incongruous borrowings. Bergson's scepticism about the intellect and Sorel's mythology of violence consort uneasily with a conviction derived from Moore and Husserl about the absolute and objective character of value. But Hulme's fundamental principle is clear enough. As a matter of principle he seeks to base all his views on a broadly philosophical foundation, a *Weltanschauung* or view of the world.

which he calls the religious attitude and whose opponent is humanism. Humanism, he holds, is so widely taken for granted that most of its adherents are unaware of it. For them it is an underlying necessity of thought which functions in their thinking much as the laws of logic do in the thinking of rational people. It is strategically essential for the sake of effective controversy that the prevailing humanist assumptions should be dug out of their asylum of unthinking acceptance. At times Hulme says that his, 'religious', view of the world is 'demonstrably true', but that seems to be simply rhetorical excess, for he nowhere seeks to demonstrate it. More often he takes the obvious implications of the word 'ultimate', in the description of views of the world as sets or systems of ultimate assumptions, seriously. One cannot, he says, directly prove to the holder of an opposed view of the world that his view is mistaken. All one can do is to drag it into the light and show carefully what follows from it, in the expectation that its unreflective adherent will then find that he is no longer attracted to it.

Humanism is, above all, a theory of human nature which maintains that human beings are naturally good, that they are both perfectible and, by and large, on the way to becoming perfect. In politics this assumption implies democratic liberalism, the idea that all should participate in the work of government, where this is seen as a matter of freeing people from the customary and institutional fetters which have obstructed their natural impulse toward self-perfection. In ethics it implies that value is relative to human desires and feelings, more specifically such doctrines as that value is derived from the contribution something makes to human pleasure or, more farsightedly, to the survival of the human race. The literary expression of the humanist principle is romanticism, which irrelevantly emphasizes the importance of the subject matter of poetry, seeks to express the infinite and to minister to the emotions. In painting and sculpture humanism leads to the glorification of the essentially inglorious human being, most notably the human body.

The religious attitude derives opposed conclusions from its assumption of human limitation and of the general fixity of human nature, an assumption whose symbol is the doctrine of original sin. The political consequence is that men need discipline and order, that the traditions of the past should be respected, that there should be authority and hierarchy, that it is desirable that nations, historically actual human groupings, should exist. Literature in general and poetry in particular should adhere to traditional forms, should seek a 'dry hardness', strive for accuracy and precision in the rendering of a freshly perceived world. In the visual arts representational enslavement to the human form should give way to a geometric art of the kind prefigured in Egyptian and Byzantine art in which that which is capable of perfection, the ideal order of abstraction, is the theme and not the essentially imperfectible topic of mankind.

The logical articulation of Hulme's opinions is dramatically characterized by human imperfection, but they have a kind of emotional affinity, if only as adding up to the comprehensive repudiation of a stuffy, *bien pensant* system of convictions about art, society, and the universe. They are fresh, bold, agreeably immodest. It is not surprising that they were extremely influential. Commentators on Hulme fall over themselves in their eagerness to insist that his position was not original. His admirer Michael Roberts says 'he was not an original thinker'. No doubt most of the large ideas Hulme brought together have some sort of family likeness to ideas available at the time he was writing. But bringing them together in at least a rhetorically persuasive way was an original achievement. None of those he drew his ideas from could have brought it off because none of them, not even Sorel, had anything like his effective range. (Bergson wrote about everything, but often in a rather second-hand way.) Nearly all good ideas turn out to have been thought up by someone other than the person conventionally supposed to have first hit on them. But the anticipator did not know how to make the best use of his discovery.

Hulme's most direct influence was on art and poetry. He was the first theorist of abstract art in this country, fruitfully enthusiastic about Epstein at the crucial early stage of the latter's career, supplying a measure of stiffening for Wyndham Lewis, whose frequently unconvincing bluster showed a need for support. At much the same time he was the leading theorist of imagism, in this case reinforcing his aesthetic precepts with some practice. It now appears that the five short poems printed at the end of Herbert Read's edition of Hulme's *Speculations* as the 'complete poetical works' were seriously worked at and not just thrown off for instructional purposes. There are three more in Roberts's biography of Hulme and a total of twenty-eight pages of poems in Alun Jones's *The Life and Opinions of T. E. Hulme* (1960).

His political views are the least concrete and developed part of his corpus of convictions. In his introduction to Sorel's *Reflections on Violence*, seeking, apparently, to dissociate Sorel from the thinkers of the Action Française with whom he was for a while in sympathy, Hulme puts in an uncharacteristically pious footnote which states that 'no theory that is not fully moved by the conception of justice asserting the equality of men, and which cannot offer something to all men, deserves or is likely to have any future'. That is far removed in sentiment from the contentions of his lecture 'A Tory Philosophy', exhumed by Alun Jones from the pages of an obscure paper and republished in *Life and Opinions,* where Hierarchy, presented as the opposite of Equality, is associated as a political good with Constancy, Order and Authority, and Nationalism.

The most important single recipient of Hulme's influence is undoubtedly T. S. Eliot. It is clearly enough acknowledged in Eliot's famous self-classification of himself as 'classicist in literature, royalist in politics, Anglo-Catholic in religion'. Eliot takes over directly from Hulme both the rejection of humanism, understood in Hulme's way as liberal-romantic optimism, and the connected idea that the tenacity of its assumptions is much increased by the way in which they saturate the language we use, from which they can be squeezed out only by the most unrelenting vigilance and effort. In Hulme's spirit too is Eliot's early endorsement of poetic impersonality. And although Eliot does not seem to have become directly aware of Hulme's ideas before the publication of *Speculations*, in 1924 seven years after Hulme's death, his own poetry in the pre-*Waste Land, J. Alfred Prufrock* period has marked affinities with the imagism

Hulme was both defending and practising. That practice received an almost hyperbolical approbation from Eliot who wrote of Hulme as 'the author of two or three of the most beautiful short poems in the language'.

There is, for all Eliot's loyal acknowledgement of indebtedness, a good deal of difference between the two. Hulme's pessimism is breezy and vigorous; Eliot's gloomy and listless. The central difference between them, in thought rather than temperament, is in what they understand by *religion*. For Eliot religion is straightforward Anglican Christianity, as defined by the creeds of the Church, taken in a pretty literal sense. It is, to the uninvolved, a religion of self-abasement and self-denial. Hulme had little perceptible tendency to either of these. When he talks of human imperfection it is the limitations of others that he has principally before his mind. There is nothing to indicate any pangs of self-disgust.

Furthermore, the absolute values on which Hulme insists are, to the extent that they are ethical, very far from being Christian. His ideal of human excellence is close to that of Sorel who was an uncompromising affirmer of the claims of heroic virtue, an exponent of the morality of honour, a less fetid and sickly Nietzsche. Hulme was conspicuously devoid of the prime Christian virtue of humility and his evident lack of qualms about the fact suggests that he did not think much of it. For one who saw all the debilitating spiritual weaknesses of the age as stemming from the thinkers of the Renaissance, he was curiously committed to the Renaissance ideal of heroic *virtù*.

I have discovered no reference to Christ in Hulme's writings nor does any characteristically Christian sentiment appear in them. Indeed in his frequent references to the rightness and spiritually hygienic necessity of the 'religious attitude' he has very little to say about God. In his essay on romanticism and classicism he says that 'part of the fixed nature of man is the belief in the Deity' but even here God is mentioned in the most abstract possible way. The real meat of Hulme's religious view of the world is the doctrine of original sin. But the belief that human beings are unalterably limited and imperfect is not associated in Hulme with any doctrine of redemption. His actual position comes out with genially ferocious clarity in the last section, 'The Religious Attitude', of the long chapter, 'Humanism and the Religious Attitude', with which *Speculations* begins. There he says that 'few since the Renaissance have really understood the dogma [viz. of original sin], certainly very few inside the Churches of recent years ... no humanist could understand the dogma. They all chatter about matters which are in comparison with this, quite secondary notions—God, Freedom, and Immortality.'

Hulme's religion, in short, is really half a religion, the bleak, negative part. In that it resembles Hobbes's religion. In both, an absolute ideal, or, one could just as well say, an idealized Absolute, is set up with no definite positive characteristics, only the abstract, honorific ones of infinity and perfection, as a way to show up as sharply as possible the finitude and imperfection of mankind. Hulme is quite a bit like Hobbes in other ways. Both are unmitigatedly English. Both are impatient thinkers, with some mathematics in their mental constitution. They are writers of forceful knockdown prose, full of concrete imagery, ideal for use as an instrument of cheerful vituperation. (Wyndham Lewis, who seems never to have got over being held upside down over the railings in Soho Square by Hulme, described his writings as 'incredibly badly written'. This silly judgement comes as no surprise from the worst writer of English prose in the twentieth century, although Hulme is very often a *careless* writer.) Hobbes and Hulme agreed on the desirability of strong government, but for undisguisedly hard-headed, practical reasons. There is no Burkean nostalgia about them. Both took the whole life of the mind for their province. Both could make dreadful mistakes; Hobbes, most conspicuously, in his attempts to prove that the circle could be squared.

This inevitably raises the question of Hulme's status as a philosopher. By and large he has been completely ignored by exponents of that discipline. *Speculations* was reviewed in *Mind* not by a philosopher but by I. A. Richards. Hulme does not figure, as far as I can tell, in any history of recent philosophy, not even J. A. Passmore's highly detailed *A Hundred Years of Philosophy*, or in any encyclopedia of philosophy. That might be put down to his explicit attachment of himself to the hopelessly unfashionable Bergson. The fact is, however, that he was a complete philosophical amateur, not without shrewdness, but displaying no aptitude for sustained philosophical argument, perhaps, even, no awareness that such a thing existed or could be of some interest or value. The articles on some philosophers of his age that begin *Further Speculations*, brought together by Samuel Hynes in 1955, are wholly non-argumentative, being no more than the immediate emotional reactions to the works in question of a sensibility reasonably familiar with philosophical literature.

The shrewdness I mentioned comes out in the distinction he draws between the technical, more or less analytic philosophy practised by Russell, Moore, and Husserl in the first decade of this century, and *Weltanschauung*, the putting forward of general views of the world, attitudes towards human nature. The former, an 'investigation into the relations between certain very abstract categories', is a science; the latter is not. Sometimes he describes it as an art; at others, more compellingly, as autobiography or personal statement. Philosophy as a whole is, he asserts 'a mixed subject', half science, half ideology. In the past philosophers have generally pursued the science because of the use they believed they could make of it to underwrite the ideology.

Something like this distinction has been very widely accepted by philosophers, in the English-speaking world at any rate, in the twentieth century. It is clearly drawn in the closing paragraphs of Russell's *History of Western Philosophy*. The type of analytic philosophy he himself practises is, he writes,

able, in regard to certain problems, to achieve definite answers, which have the quality of science rather than of philosophy ... Its methods ... resemble those of science. I have no doubt that, in so far as philosophical knowledge is possible, it is by such methods that it must be sought ... There remains, however, a vast field, traditionally included in philosophy, where scientific methods are inadequate. This field includes ultimate questions of value ... (p. 834)

Most philosophers of Russell's kind have regarded questions about ultimate values as not being susceptible of rational demonstration. One who did not was G. E. Moore, about whom Hulme made some admiring remarks and whom he may have encountered in either of his two periods at Cambridge. Moore held that goodness is a simple quality, as simple as yellow, whose incidence must just be perceived, in some non-sensory fashion. Its presence in 'states of consciousness', where alone it is to be found, is a matter of brute, objective fact. Such a theory makes values objective, but at the cost of leaving disagreement about them barely intelligible.

Moore supposed his theory about value to be part of technical philosophy, a matter of discriminating the relations between certain very abstract categories. Like other philosophers he went on in his last chapter (in *Principia Ethica*) to set out his results; that is, to reveal the findings of that power of ethical intuition which his technical enquiries had shown to be valid, to his satisfaction, at any rate. Those findings were not very Hulmean, being the morality of the Bloomsbury group, elevating the contemplation of beauty and affectionate personal relations above everything else. It would have been objectionable to Hulme for its 'humanist' assumption that nothing could be of value but states of human consciousness and for the sedentary, unheroic nature of the states ennobled. But at least he would have preferred it to the 'compassionate' or 'caring' moral outlook of modern social Christianity.

Hulme's real concern in this area is that one's *Weltanschauung* or ultimate system of values should be *absolute*, not subordinated to human desires and feelings, rather than that it should be *objective*. It is perfectly consistent to take certain things to have value independently of their capacity to minister to human desires and feelings without believing that their value is objectively demonstrable or a matter of truth or falsity at all. Such a voluntarist kind of scepticism about value is congruous both with Hulme's temperament and his endorsement in principle of tension and struggle.

The conversational informality of Hulme's writing on philosophy leaves it open to a good deal of technical criticism and objection. Is his theory of three levels or orders of reality—inorganic, organic, and ideal—part of scientific philosophy, as it certainly seems to be? (It is very close to the Trinitarian ontologies of Bolzano and Frege, the two greatest scientific philosophers of the nineteenth century, neither of whom had any perceptible ideology whatever.) If it is, what is it doing as the foundation of the religious attitude, in opposition to the 'principle of continuity' adhered to by humanists? For in that case it is being used to prop up a system of values in defiance of Hulme's belief in the absolute distinction of scientific philosophy from ideology.

The point can be made in another way by considering Hulme's notion of a critique of satisfaction. Attitudes to the world or ultimate value-systems, he says, owe much of their power to their latency. What is needed is to bring them out into the open and then to ask what particular human desire or partiality they serve. They need to be subjected to a 'critique of satisfaction' which he seems to conceive as an objective way of adjudicating between basic emotional biases. But no way of going about the adjudication is suggested. In the end it seems that, once a system of values is brought fully into the open, with its emotional roots and its ideological consequences fully traced out, its acceptance or rejection becomes a matter of personal decision.

Hulme's philosophical activities were seriously interfered with by his early involvement, at first intellectual and then personal, with Bergson. (Bergson helped him to get readmitted to Cambridge with an elegant testimonial and he translated Bergson's *Introduction to Metaphysics*.) Bergson's thought, with its depreciation of the analysing, scientific intellect, was calculated to provide relief from that nocturnal disquiet of the later nineteenth century, the 'nightmare of scientific materialism'. But Hulme soon got over the distress occasioned by that metaphysical spectre. The humanism that became his principal enemy numbers Bergson among its adherents. The fear of finding man to be a part of nature, which could be said to be the emotional source of his philosophy, is just the sort of wet, suburban state of mind which Hulme wants to bring his critique of satisfaction hard down on.

The firmness and definiteness of Hulme's own convictions and his cheeky indifference to academic pieties minimized the ill effects of his Bergsonian involvement. A good tune was played, even if on a curiously inappropriate instrument, a march-tune for quick-stepping riflemen on a leaky church organ.

12

Bergson and Whitehead
Process Philosophy

I

The dramatic assertion of Heracleitus that everything flows did not get taken up by anyone else as an account of the nature of reality. It was adopted by Plato as an account of the nature of *appearance*. But even that did not survive to oppose the psychological atomism of Locke, Hume, and many subsequent empiricists. The idea that everything is really process, fluid in nature, did not come into its own until late in the nineteenth century.

More than anything else the doctrine of evolution brought it back to the centre of philosophical attention. That doctrine implied that concepts and beliefs are not simply copies of recurrent features and of actual or possible states of affairs in the real world but are, rather, instruments contrived by human beings in the course of their struggle to survive. They came to be seen as practical devices, and not as the fruit of theoretical contemplation. More fundamentally, the world itself, or the organic part of it at least, was revealed by evolution to be a scene of continuous variation and not as a minuet-like reshuffling of antecedently fixed units. The subsequent resolution of matter into energy by physics completed the liquidation of the world.

That line of thought had a large array of manifestations in the late nineteenth century. First of all there is the philosophy of Nietzsche, where it is to be found in its utmost extremity. In Vaihinger's doctrine of fictions it takes the form of a theory of knowledge. With Bergson a comparable theory of knowledge paves the way to an ontology of process. William James acknowledged an affinity to Bergson and argued that thought is a stream, against the atomistic artificialities of the prevailing account of the character of mental life. His English associate Schiller insisted that the sharp divisions between rigid and persisting bodies to be found in the common picture of the world are a construction, at best a diagram or caricature, perhaps a complete fabrication or imposition. In Whitehead's system most of these earlier sources, scientific and philosophical, are drawn on to bring about the displacement of objects, understood as products of the fallacy of 'misplaced concreteness', by loosely bounded and thoroughly interfused events.

In the 1920s Whitehead carried on a campaign against 'Aristotelian substance', the idea that reality consists of things, that is to say of definite, demarcated, persisting *solids*. That everyday picture of the world had attained its most elaborate exposition in the classical physics of Galileo and Newton. In attacking it they were possibly influenced by their reading of Bradley, for whom the discontinuous world of common sense and science is a contradictory appearance presented by a reality, or 'absolute experience', which has the same seamless character as immediate feeling in its pure, elemental state, unmutilated by the analytic intellect.

The theory that the world of solid things is a mental construction, not a presentation of what there really is, derives, then, from a multitude of converging sources. The idea that the mind is active, not contemplative, in securing knowledge had the authority of Kant. His references to noumena or things-in-themselves, however, had very often been in the plural and, when he referred to the thing-in-itself in the singular, it was rather to the common character of a kind than to one all-embracing individual. For those, like Ward and Bradley, who took experience to be continuous and reality to be mental or experiential in nature, it inevitably followed that reality is continuous. Evolutionism applied to the activity of thinking supported, from an unexpected direction, the Hegelian view of the abstractive and thus falsifying character of the analytic intellect used in everyday life and science. The account of the organic world of which the evolutionary theory of thinking is a part, or, perhaps, by-product, suggests that at least it does not contain a fixed repertoire of natural kinds.

These considerations do not really add up to a complete case for the incorrectness of the picture of the world as a plurality of persisting solids. The intellect may be active and practically motivated but that does not entail that the conclusions at which it arrives are false. It could even be argued that the opposite is implied. Unless our concepts were applicable to the real world and our beliefs, to a considerable extent and, at any rate, in their general drift, were true we should not have survived. But when physics, the most advanced of sciences, itself came to reject the world of persisting, solid substances, for which it had hitherto provided the most distinguished intellectual support, the case for the conception of reality as continuous process may well have seemed fully made out. To conclude that is to assume something which many accept without question, that if a solid thing is composed wholly of processes it does not really exist. It is, at any rate, not an assumption to which pragmatists are entitled, given their contention that physical theories are instruments, mental contrivances for the convenient ordering of experience.

Bertrand Russell was a resolute and indefatigable opponent of Bergson and the pragmatists and, after a period of initial fascination, of Bradley. Yet he agrees with them about the things or substances of common sense and science. Perhaps there is a trace of influence here from his old tutor, James Ward, who attacked the psychological atomism of Locke and Hume in the interests of what he called the 'presentational continuum'. More obvious is the influence of Whitehead, closer to him both as teacher and collaborator. Whitehead regarded the ordinary view that the world consists fundamentally of persisting things or substances as the fallacy of 'misplaced concreteness'. Aristotelian substances, as he and Russell called them, are constructions out of events, momentary incidents of experience, which they tend to identify with events in the physical order of space-time. Thus an ordinary thing, for Russell, or an unordinary thing, such as an electron, is no more than a set of similar events at neighbouring bits of space-time.

As I mentioned earlier the influence of Kant is not hard to see at work in all this. In his view what is given is what he calls the manifold of sensation, a phrase that clearly implies its continuous nature. The intellect then brings its transcendental apparatus of categories to bear on the given and by mysteriously 'synthesizing' it produces the conception of a spatio-temporal world containing persisting substances, standing in causal relations to one another. The world thus constructed, or synthesized, is, Kant contends, empirically or phenomenally real, which is not, it would seem, to be really real. That is the privilege of the elusive order of things-in-themselves, or noumena, which look as if they are meant to serve as the causes of our sensations, despite Kant's insistence that the idea of cause applies only within the phenomenal world.

Kant thought that the common material world of everyday life and natural science was objective, the same for all enquiring minds, allowing for a bit of error in detail here and there. That was because he thought, for deeply unpersuasive reasons, that everyone set about constructing their own versions of that world with the same basic intellectual outfit. Even then only the general form of different obscure constructions of the world could correspond, not particular details. The requirements of practice, most primordially the requirements for success in the competitive struggle for existence, would not seem to guarantee any such unanimity in modes of thought. The late nineteenth-century revival of the idea that the world is a continuous flux or process, now seen as being articulated by human minds in such ways as may prove convenient or useful to them, is a result of the hold of evolutionary principles in that age.

If the mind is seen as a product of evolutionary competition it is going to be considered, along with other such products as the eye, the hand, and the digestive system, as having the nature it has because of its success in serving vital needs. From a more theistic point of view it had been taken to be either a finite copy of the divine mind or a fragment of it. That would endow it with the power to apprehend the divinely created material world as it really is. But seen as an evolved device for the solution of practical problems, it is assimilated to other makeshifts improvised by human beings, to tools and weapons that come in all shapes and sizes. Evolutionary thinking also affects conceptions of the objects of the mind. The natural world, particularly its organic part, is a scene of continuous variation. Its contents are not drawn from a limited range of natural kinds, a fixed repertoire of patterns for the divine craftsman to work from, like the passenger list of Noah's ark.

The upshot of this general line of thought is that the natural world is not in reality carved up into definite, clearly demarcated, persisting items, each of a wholly distinct kind. That is only appearance, something imposed on the world by the intellect.

Reality is a continuum or flux, not an array of distinct items. Sometimes it is suggested that the continuum or flux is completely featureless. In that case the carving of it up into distinct items must be completely arbitrary and the general agreement between different perceivers in picking out much the same items as each other becomes an unintelligible miracle. So also does the fact that this arbitrary carving up is useful and contributes to the evolutionary success of those who guide their actions by it.

A more plausible suggestion would be that there are vague and indefinite differences within the flux, of which the common conception of a world of distinct things is a kind of simplified diagram, like the map of an oil-spill or a weather chart. A simplified idealization of the facts is often a good deal more useful, because simple to take in and handle, than the exact truth in all its detail. That way of looking at the supposed continuum rules out the quite common comparison of the workings of the mind with the activity of a baker, cutting biscuits out of dough with variously shaped cutting devices. The dough is completely homogeneous—at least down to a level very much below the size of a biscuit. The baker can do whatever he likes; his raw material is completely passive under his choice.

Another—but still, broadly speaking, gastronomic—comparison is sometimes invoked which takes some account of the intrinsic character of the continuum being ordered: that of, as the saying has it, 'carving reality at the joints'. Carving in private life is, no doubt, a pretty hit or miss affair, but there really are joints in the poultry subjected to it. More appropriate would be a comparison with the different ways meat is butchered in different countries, which has the result that the words for pieces of butcher's meat in one country cannot be translated into the words with the same overall range of application in another. The nature of the beast sets some limits to the ways it can be carved up, but still leaves the butcher a good deal of freedom.

II

It is time to examine in more detail the nature of these distinct things or Aristotelian substances of which the natural world is taken to be composed by common sense in everyday life and in all but the most refined investigations in science. What I shall from now on call *things*, in a restricted, but surely recognizable, sense, and as contrasted, primarily, with stuff, occupy at any time a definite position in space. They are the exclusive occupants of this tract, indeed volume, of space, together with their parts, which do not occupy all of it, and the wholes, if any, of which they are parts, which occupy further space beside. A thing, therefore, has a definite shape or contour with sharp edges, points at which the object leaves off and its environment begins.

Most, but not all, things preserve their shapes through time; all of them perhaps if their environment remains stable. Under stress some are more or less elastic, reassuming their original shape when the stress is removed. Others are merely flexible and are deformed or reshaped by stress. For all objects there are stresses under which they will break, either into recognizable bits or, if shattered, into fragments or powder. But all things offer some resistance to stress, have a measure of rigidity. Because of that things can move without change of shape or other characteristics, let alone loss of identity.

While solid things have sharp edges, stuff tends to peter out, getting thinner and thinner in density. When things collide they repel each other or one of them breaks, or even both do. Stuffs intermix in various ways, sometimes blending peaceably like fresh milk in tea, sometimes curdling. Tracts of stuff, unlike solid things, have only a tenuous identity, like that of the river Heracleitus could not step into twice. A small puddle in a quiet cellar may be identifiable for quite a long time ('you still have not cleared up that puddle in the cellar'). But a cloud will ordinarily not be, let alone a puff of smoke from a chimney or a gust of wind.

The distinctive features of things, as contrasted with stuffs, can all be seen as modes of solidity. To have a definite shape is to be a geometrical solid. To retain that shape unless interfered with by externally applied stress is to be physically solid, to offer resistance to shape-changing pressure. That physical solidity is what the human sense of touch perceives as tangible solidity. The exclusiveness with which a thing occupies its volume of space is a kind of logical solidity, the impenetrability mentioned by Locke, but that is not peculiar to things.

A conspicuously important kind of thing is the living organism. It is sharply bounded by its skin (less neatly by its hair, if it has any). It moves both as a whole and in part and with rare, limpet-like exceptions, would be unable to survive or reproduce itself unless it could. Different kinds of organism are ordinarily distinguished by their shape, so much so that the only words we have for these distinguishing shapes are derived from those for the kind of organism in question: giraffe-shaped, frog-shaped, etc. Stuff is never distinguished by its shape, since stuff has no standard, typical shape.

Another important class of solid things is that of artefacts. These are standardized by design and by the process of their manufacture. The activity of designing and manufacturing such paradigmatic solids is difficult to interpret in the language of flux and the continuum.

What may be called dead matter—that which is neither organism nor artefact— often takes the form of solid things. Stones of various sizes, from mountains down to bits of gravel, are the most obvious example. But mountains can vary a good deal in shape, and also are somewhat indeterminate in respect of their bottom edge, while stones can be of pretty well any shape. We could view these items, which are without question geometrically, physically, and tangibly solid, as being reified stuff. Their hold on thinghood is very firm in view of their possession of definite shape and of rigidity or resistance to stress. Much ordinary stuff is often partially reified in occurring in a tract with a definite shape which is retained through a period of time, as with a snowman or a joint or slice of meat or the gas in a well-stoppered canister. *Tract*, like *piece, bit, chunk*, and others is a reifying word, but the thinghood it assigns is of an honorary, amateur, or second-class sort. What these reifying words pick out as things have only a precarious hold on shape.

It is quite a different point that a tract of stuff, itself a second-class thing, may well be made up of true things. A heap of coal, if it is of good quality, will be wholly composed of highly thing-like lumps of coal, which used, of course, to be called *coals*. A heap of sugar is perceptibly composed of individual granules, each of them a true thing. If we go beyond perception we are assured by chemistry that all fluids are composed of particles that have some thing-like characteristics, although we should, perhaps, be wary of too readily ascribing a definite shape to molecules, let alone their smaller components. But I shall argue that chemistry requires even the constituents of atoms to be thing-like enough to be counted.

In the ordinary conception of the natural world, then, there is much that takes the form of distinct and persistent things. But much too is stuff, without definite shape or identity through time. However some stuff can be perceived to be composed of things and all of it, if chemistry is to be trusted, is made up of entities that are at least thing-like. Is the prominent position of solid things in our ordinary conception of the world significant? If there really were no such solid things, as process philosophers contend, would it matter?

III

The first important casualty to follow the disappearance of solid things would be the application of mathematics to the world. Without persisting, clearly distinct things there could be no counting. Counting takes time; the first items counted need to be still identifiably there at the end of the operation; the whole set counted needs to persist identifiably if the count is to be checked. If anything is to be done with the results of the counting operation the things counted have to continue identifiably in existence after the counting.

Management and administration of all but the most rudimentary sort requires counting, as does all but the simplest face-to-face barter in trade and the most primitive, Crusoe-like productive industry. Where money is involved, even if the counting of coins is circumvented, there has to be numbering of items bought or sold and hours worked.

Solid things are also indispensable for measurement. Spatial distance is measured by measuring rods that are assumed to be rigid. Time is measured by clocks, weight and other magnitudes by measuring machines that are calibrated. To use them the coincidence of indisputably solid pointers with calibrations that are clearly demarcated and persist through time, even if they cannot move independently as most solid things do, have to be observed. Distance, time-interval, and mass, measured by rods, clocks, and weighing machines, are the three aspects of the natural world with which physics is concerned. In a world without the solidities on which physical measurement depends there could be no physical science. Nor, of course, could there be organized production or trade.

Just as the application of arithmetic requires countable units, whether for counting or for measurement, so geometry requires a world of solid, distinct, persistent things if it is to be applied. Surveying requires landmarks and stable tracts of ground picked out by them. The geography of a fluid world could at best be momentary and, given our limitations, very local. Without geography there could be no use of maps for the rational planning of journeys.

It might be argued that our notions of space and time also require solid things. A panorama of fluid processes, in which stuffs flowed about unconstrained by the temporary reifying influence of such solid things as river-banks and wine-glasses, would not provide that background of entities not moving from one moment to the next which is required to determine what is moving and what is not or, more fundamentally, to link the space of the panorama at one moment to the space of another. Perhaps spatial judgements of a topological sort could be made about above and below, in front and behind. Perhaps enough processes could be identified from one moment to another which had not changed their qualities and spatial relations to each other (however that might be determined in these circumstances) to enable them to be taken as the unmoving background of motion. Certainly temporal judgements of before and after could be reasonably made, although lapses of time could not be measured. What is clear is that the conceptions of space and time and of spatial and temporal relatedness available to an observer in a world of fluid processes would be extremely attenuated. And in fact we identify processes by reference to the solid things involved in them—riverbanks and fireplaces.

How, again, should we conceive of action and of its essential means, the intentional movement of some part of the body, in a world of fluid process?

At this point anyone who claims that the physical world is really a fluid continuum or process will protest that, by taking the solid things of the common conception of the world and interpreting them as processes, he is not to be understood to be depriving them of the amount of demarcatedness, persistence, and solidity required to let them be counted, be measured, and serve as measuring instruments, to serve as spatial landmarks, and so on. To say that the demarcated, persistent, solid thing is a fictitious construction imposed on a continuous flux undoubtedly would seem to imply the deprivation protested against. To see whether it does it is necessary to look at the reasons given for saying that the physical world does not really contain solid things. The most persuasive of these is based on the findings of science and I shall consider it first.

IV

The science to which I shall be alluding is of a popularized sort as will be evident from the three levels of increasing sophistication from which I shall consider it. The first of these is that of persistent observation, the others those of molecular and submolecular physics (largely as gleaned from expositions of the subject designed for the general reader). By persistent observation I mean observation that is close, attentive, and makes use of such subscientific observational aids as magnifying glasses.

What persistent observation shows is that ordinary solid things do not have neat, geometrical shapes. There is a kind of fuzz at their edges, insistently obvious in the case of sacks, rough tweed jackets, and leaves, but discoverable by persistent observation of wooden and metal boxes, knife edges, and other paradigms of sharpness of outline. That might be thought to show, not that such things have, ultimately, no definite or precise shape, but only a much more irregular one than we ordinarily suppose. However that irregularity makes it a little difficult to regard the precise spatial limit of a solid thing as something fixed and objective, rather than a matter of convention or decision. A wooden trellis would not be taken to occupy the space of the gaps between its wooden members, but what about a piece of woven cloth in which there are minute gaps between the fibres?

Still at the level of persistent observation, rather than physics, there are items that we do not know whether to regard as parts of solid things or as other things attached to them. A human body may have a spot of mud on one wrist, hair growing from its head (some, no doubt, loosely attached and about to come away from the scalp the next time it is combed), and a small red scab on a minor wound, hanging on by a thread. My inclination is to say that the mud is not part of the body, that the hair is until it falls out, and that so far as the scab is concerned I am a don't-know. If that is right the human body in question is, in a very minimal and practically trivial way, of course, spatially indeterminate or vague. There is a penumbra of stuff around it which is neither definitely part of it nor definitely not part of it.

Consider next a man snoozing in a comfortable armchair, an apparent emblem of inertness and inactivity. In fact, his body is the scene of a great deal of activity: he stirs in his sleep and changes his position, he breathes, changing his overall outline. Inside there are the incessant churnings of his digestive and circulatory systems. What is true of him in these respects is true of all organisms, if less spectacularly so in the case of much smaller ones than he. The crucial point is that his and their shapes, sizes, and positions are constantly changing.

At the elementary level of persistent observation, then, it would seem that what we ordinarily regard as solid things are not of an absolutely definite shape at any one time and that organisms are non-rigid, non-shape-preserving, from one moment to another.

When we turn to elementary physics and consider ordinary solid things as collections of molecules these tentative conclusions are reinforced. Even in a solid the molecules are not jammed together as an unbroken mass, but are arranged in a lattice, like eggs on layers of egg trays with the trays removed. In the lattice the molecules are not at rest, but are, so to speak, shuddering. Moving to the nature of matter beneath the molecular level the turmoil of process is inescapably present. If we think of the molecule as a planetary system, it turns out to be a nucleus with one or more electrons whirling about it at distances very great relative to the size of either of them. Pushing further on, the electron becomes a packet of energy or a vibration. At that point solidity evaporates altogether. But even in the planetary model it is in trouble. At the edge of an apparently solid, determinately shaped thing as, indeed, throughout it, is a tumult of whirling particles.

It does not really matter for the purposes of my argument that my allusions to physics may be out of date or even mistaken in detail. What the facts I have adduced show is that the shape of solid things is not *absolutely* determinate at any given moment, that they do not in general *exactly* retain their shape from one moment to another. But is that of any real importance? It might be argued that it shows the difference between solid things and fluid ones to be one of degree not of kind. However the difference of degree is so great that the virtual solidity and rigidity that common material things possess is sufficient to distinguish them from unreified, continuous stuff.

The edge of a metal box is not quite as geometrically regular and not so clearly demarcated from the surroundings of the box as we may have imagined. But the size and rapidity with which the character of what is present near its edge changes from one point to another is of an altogether different order of magnitude from that of the change of character at the edge of cloud or a fogbank or a spoonful of cream in a bowl of pea soup. It may be admitted that wherever the intensity of some characteristic varies over a tract of space it will do so continuously. At the most minute level there may be no instantaneous leap from one intensity to a wholly different one. Even so, the rates at which such variations manifest themselves differ enormously.

V

Scientific considerations of the sort I have been looking at seem to have played a large part in the rejection of the objective reality of solid things by Whitehead and, much under Whitehead's influence, by Russell. That is not at all Bergson's point of departure. For him science and common belief both follow the intellect in what he calls the 'postulation of the unorganised solid'. He started from the contrast as he saw it between the way we think about time and the way in which we actually experience it. We think about it as a succession of distinct moments; we experience it as an unbroken, undivided continuum. There is something in this but not as much as he thinks. Certainly our experience of time is better represented by something like the soliloquy of Molly Bloom than by the sort of minutely detailed diary which runs: '8.02, woke up. 8.04, had bath, shaved. 8.16, ate bowl cornflakes, boiled egg etc.' In reality these incidents run into one another: after waking one thought about the bath and ran it; while having it one looked forward to breakfast and so on.

The scientific or intellectual notion of time does not, anyway, treat it as discontinuous. Crucial scientific concepts like velocity and acceleration presuppose its continuity by being defined as the limits of velocities and of rates of change of velocity over ever smaller intervals of time which converge on the instant at which velocity or acceleration is being sought. Velocity at an instant is a logical construction of just the same kind as the average man, a mathematical abbreviation.

What Bergson is doing, in regarding time as experienced as real time is to identify the given, the immediately experienced, with what is real and concrete, all else being more or less falsifying abstraction. From the premises that the given is not thing-like, but a continuous flux, and that only what is given is real it follows inevitably that the real is continuous, not inhabited by solid things.

I believe that one or other of these premises is mistaken so long as the term *given* is interpreted in the same sense in both of them and, unless it is, the inference is not valid. The given may be interpreted as the states of consciousness of which one is immediately aware in self-consciousness or introspection. In that case the given can reasonably be held to be a continuous flux. But it is far from obviously the whole of what is real. On the other hand it may be interpreted as that which is directly perceived, in which it is known to exist without reliance on memory, inference, and testimony, ordinarily as a result of the action on the senses of what is known to exist. In that case there is something to be said for the proposition that only the given is real, provided that it is loosened to read: only what is of the same general nature as the given is real. But on that interpretation there is nothing to be said for the view that what is given, or, on this interpretation, directly perceived, is a continuous flux. Much of what is directly perceived is solid, clearly demarcated, and persistent in shape.

If the thesis that the given is continuous is taken to mean that everything that is directly perceived is continuous it is false. In the only philosophically interesting sense that can be given to the phrase, we do directly perceive visibly and tangibly solid, sharply demarcated things, whose solidity survives and persists under all but fairly exceptional stresses. Possible accounts of the nature of direct perception that I am ruling out are, first, perception of things without such intermediary aids as mirrors, microscopes, telescopes, and, perhaps, ordinary spectacles. At any rate in this connection, no one would deny that that sense of direct perception is of little philosophical interest. Most of what we can perceive with some sort of mechanical assistance we can also perceive without it, even if in less detail.

The second, and more philosophically influential, idea of direct perception takes its objects to be whatever one knows for certain or even infallibly to exist whenever one takes oneself to be perceiving something. I should contend that nothing, or as good as nothing, is directly perceived in this sense. That is a view I have argued for at length elsewhere and there is no time to repeat the argument here. The crucial point is that in calling all perception that does not come up to this impossibly exigent standard indirect, it implies that all beliefs that are in this sense cases of indirect perception must be based, if they are to be justified at all, on beliefs that are, in this hyperbolic sense, direct.

In ordinary perception we form beliefs about our material environment, without reflection, that are justified and can be raised to certainty, to the level of knowledge by further perceptual beliefs of the same kind and by background knowledge of the way things of the sort apparently perceived ordinarily behave and of the material circumstances in which they ordinarily occur.

Many objects of direct perception, in the sense in which I understand it, are solid, demarcated, persisting things. Many are not: we see soup as well as the croutons floating around in it. But states of consciousness, the items that are given in the sense of being what is present to self-consciousness or introspection—beliefs, desire, emotions, sensations, and the pleasure and pain that accompany them—these are not distinct, demarcated, countable things. That is the error of psychological atomism. They are certainly not solids, possessors of a determinate, let alone persistent, shape, since they are not presented as spatial at all, except to the extent that some of them acquire a kind of courtesy location from that of the parts of the body at which their physical causes are to be found.

They are not always, or even often, very clearly demarcated in time. Pains start sharply enough for the most part, but commonly peter out, as do bouts of anger or annoyance. A mood of depression will peter in as well as out. These states coexist in our consciousness, differing in character and duration, so far as that can be fixed, varying in intensity in a way that cannot be more than intensively measured. Arithmetic does not apply to them, as Hume and Ryle have strenuously affirmed, only comparisons of more and less.

It is reasonable to hold that nothing but states of consciousness are real only if it is supposed that nothing but states of consciousness are directly perceived. Some, like Schlick, Carnap, and Ayer, believing the latter, have resisted the inference to the former and have been prepared to concede reality to constructions out of the states of consciousness which are all, they suppose, is given. Others, like Whitehead and Russell, conclude that only the given, in their sense, is real, but mitigate the subjectivistic outrageousness of that conclusion by more or less breezily identifying the events which are states of consciousness with the process-constituting events which are all, in their view, that physics countenances as the basic furniture of the world. In that startling identification the two lines of argument I have considered for the doctrine that the world consists not of solid, substantial things, but of processes, come together.

VI

A final line of argument against the real presence in the world of solid things is based on the nature of language. Language, it is said, is at once atomic and selective. It picks out selected chunks of the continuum as topics for comment or subjects of predication and goes on to describe what has been thus more or less arbitrarily picked out in general terms which leave out most of what is there to be described.

The language that is most notably atomic or particulate in form is, of course, written language, tidily partitioned into words and sentences. Spoken language might seem to be more of a continuum. That appearance is misleading. Our language, as we learn it, is mastered by us in bits and pieces. First of all, we learn to use single words, which are in fact one-word sentences of the form 'here is a so-and-so', and then learn how to combine these and other words learnt with their assistance ('ball is blue', 'socks are blue', 'hat is on chair', 'ball is on table') into explicitly complex sentences. Most of that initial vocabulary consists of the names of solids. Some of it refers to fluids, like milk, but usually in temporarily reified shape, thanks to cups and glasses.

The language of others, when it is oddly pronounced, or, more important, is a language unfamiliar to us, will seem to be a continuous flux. But in fact it is not and to come to understand it is to see that it is not.

Language is undoubtedly selective. But there can be truth short of the whole truth and the witness's oath wisely makes provision for both. A cannonball is, to all but the most theoretically refined intents and purposes, spherical, even if to describe it as such is to leave out all mention of the curious design on its surface. A thing can be spherical without being a geometrically perfect sphere. We may reasonably suppose, with Plato, that nothing in nature definite enough in outline to have a shape is a perfect sphere. That does not turn it into a continuum blending indivisibly into its surroundings.

Some process philosophers make much of the thought that our cognitive activities are evolutionary acquisitions, built up in the struggle for survival. Some of them like Bergson and the pragmatists say that we adopt concepts and beliefs because they are useful: Nietzsche, more histrionically, because they serve our will to power. That does not entail that the concepts in question are fictitious abstractions or the beliefs false. Beliefs will be useful to the extent that they *truly* assert what will as a matter of fact lead from things we are able to do to, or from, situations we want to produce or prevent, encounter, or avoid. They will not be true unless the concepts they embody apply to what is really and as a matter of fact there. Simplicity is an advantage; the whole truth in all its encumbering detail can delay and obstruct effective action.

I have been arguing that such simplification or idealization as physics may show to be involved in the concepts of solid things which are our point of entry into cognitive mastery of the world is minimal and insignificant. Nor are solids any less directly perceptible than continua. They are not theoretical constructions reared up on the foundations of the flux of states of consciousness. That is just as well. We are active beings and most of what we want to manipulate is solid. We are, after all, solid things ourselves, with the measure of flexibility characteristic of animal organisms, at least until we cease to live, when we first become really solid and then decay into liquid form.

13

Quine on Doing Without Meaning

1. The Shock of Demythologization

It is hardly surprising that the publication of 'Two Dogmas of Empiricism' in 1951 should have come as a shock to the part of the total philosophical community that was disposed to take note of it. That group were thought of and thought of themselves as analytic philosophers. But 'Two Dogmas' and, even more, its contemporary, 'The Problem of Meaning in Linguistics' (both out in book form in 1953 in *From a Logical Point of View*), treated meaning in a sceptical, dismissive fashion, in very much the same manner as analytic philosophers themselves, at least in their inter-war heyday, had relied on the notion of meaning to dispel the pretensions of metaphysics. What, after all, did the analytic philosophers take it upon themselves to analyse but meaning?

Schlick, the doyen of the Vienna Circle, was quite explicit about this. Philosophy, properly conducted, consisted, in his view, of the analysis of meaning. Others advanced methodological slogans in which much the same thing was said in slightly different terms. Wittgenstein saw himself as engaged in *the logical clarification of thoughts*, Carnap espoused *the logical analysis of the language of science*, Ryle and other Englishmen, concerned not to jeopardize amateur status, claimed to practise *conceptual analysis*.

Meaning, for these philosophers, was the basic or primary subject matter of philosophy; a hidden ingredient, along with a lot of questionable stuff, in what had always passed for philosophy; the first thing with which a purified, rationally self-conscious philosophy should concern itself. Its task was to distinguish the meaningful from the meaningless; to distinguish one kind of meaning from another—cognitive from emotive, for example; to distinguish those statements whose truth value was determined wholly by their meaning from the empirical remainder of the statements that aspired to truth value at all.

A disquieting consideration was that all this confident and variegated application of the idea, notion, or concept of meaning, or, at any rate, use of the word 'meaning', was being carried on without anything very promising being available in the form of a theory of meaning, an analysis of the concept of meaning, or in other, presumably synonymous, words, an account of the meaning of the word 'meaning'. There was agreement that meaning was not the same as reference or denotation. The authority of Frege was ritually invoked as to the existence, if not as to the nature, of the distinction.

It was not exactly a novelty, having been categorically proclaimed by John Stuart Mill and being discernible in the thought of a long line of thinkers before him that can be traced as far back as the Stoic doctrine of *lekta*. There was some convergence to agreement on the incorrectness of the old empiricists' view that the meaning of a term is some kind of image. The most that was available in the way of a positive account was more an instructive gesture than a theory: the identification of the meaning of a linguistic expression with its use. But attempts to flesh this out in detailed behavioural terms did not secure wide assent.

Quine's programme of demythologization was thus inaugurated in circumstances in which it was calculated to cause embarrassment, by impinging on an admittedly weak spot. In 'Two Dogmas' the topic of meaning is approached indirectly, by way of criticism of the analytic/synthetic distinction, in the first instance. Analytic truths are those that can be reduced with the aid of definitions to truths of logic. What, Quine enquired, are the criteria of synonymy implied by the claim of such definitions to correctness? Secondly, he argued that since there is no single proper response to a collision between experience and our beliefs, but rather a choice as to what to drop, between singular statements, laws of nature, and even, in very theatrical circumstances, the laws of logic, there is no fixed empirical meaning associated with each empirical sentence in the form of a class of kinds of experience which would establish it and another class of kinds of experience which would refute it. For present purposes the crucial point Quine makes is that interchangeability *salva veritate* is not a criterion of synonymy and nothing comparably clear and definite seems available.

In 'Meaning in Linguistics' the thesis of 'Two Dogmas' that 'meanings themselves, as obscure intermediary entities, may well be abandoned' is developed further. We need mention meaning only in the contexts 'has meaning' and 'means the same as' and need not mention it at all if we substitute for these, respectively, 'is significant' and 'is synonymous with'. The sensitized eyebrow may quiver here slightly at the thought of how these substitutions are to be legitimized. But since their aim is pacificatory rather than explanatory, and so not a working part of the argument, the eyebrow should come to rest. Quine says 'we resolve to treat [the] whole context in the spirit of a single word, "synonymous"'. We can agree to approach this spirited manoeuvre in the same sort of indulgent spirit.

The discussion that follows of how significance is to be determined is full of the sort of ingenious subtleties we expect from our author. The grammarian's job is seen as a matter of setting out syntactically legitimate constructions and picking out the morphemes that can legitimately serve as the elements of the constructions, the minimal units of significance, single words, stems, and affixes. The possibility of an unwelcome semantic intrusion is acknowledged. The grammarian cannot just list these elements of significance. Quine says this is because it is unrealistic to expect the grammarian to exhaust the vocabulary of the language he is studying. Two other, perhaps overlapping, problems seem to be more serious. One is the extrusion from the list of heard sounds of those that provoke what Quine calls a bizarreness reaction. The other is that of winkling out 'non-linguistic noises', audible chunks of conversational filler like 'er' and 'um', I suppose. Some of these, instances of idiosyncratic speech defects, may be reacted to as bizarre. But 'er' and 'um' are universally mouthed and of the same order of frequency as 'is' and 'and' and 'the'.

It is at any rate the other context—'means the same as' or 'is synonymous with'—that has mainly preoccupied Quine since this first broad overview of linguistic science. The word 'significance' is not to be found in the index to *Word and Object* and the topic of significance is not conspicuously adverted to in its content. The two earlier essays wind up with a fairly pessimistic conclusion about the lexicographer's problem of, as Quine puts it, 'making sense of the notion of synonymy'. Truth value preserving interchangeability establishes only coextensiveness. Intuitive semantics, the tangle of everyday beliefs which sets the lexicographer's problem, holds that not all coextensive expressions are synonymous. In the concluding sections of 'Meaning in Linguistics' Quine argues that the best prospect for a criterion of genuine synonymy is to seek it as relating longer segments of discourse than single words or phrases. And it is this course he pursues in chapter 2 of *Word and Object* and again, more recently, in 'Use and its Place in Meaning'. The outcome is chastened notions of stimulus synonymy and stimulus analyticity, which fall short of good old intuitive sameness of meaning and analyticity, but which are more exclusive than, respectively, mere coextensiveness or resolutely adhered-to truth.

Quine's powerful and intricate development of these themes has elicited a lot of criticism which he has parried with characteristic resourcefulness and vigour. Some analytic philosophers have been led by his probings of their former articles of faith to admit conversion. Others have agreed that there is a great deal in what he says and that things will never be the same again. But many, like Newman in the early 1840s, remain uncomfortably unregenerate. As one of these last I have only the modest aim of raising a number of questions about details in the complex fabric of his argument, not because I am bold enough to suppose that I can show him to have gone wrong, but rather to draw attention to what seems to be unfinished business or holes that need to be stopped.

2. Are Significance and Synonymy Enough?

I begin with a matter that is fairly marginal to the main issue but not without interest if the notion of meaning in general is considered. Quine proposes that the word be used only as contained in the contexts 'has meaning' and 'has the same meaning as' or as buried in 'is significant' and 'is synonymous with'. We may ask, first, how are these two related? Does 'has meaning' or 'has a meaning' amount to 'have the same meaning as something-or-other'? Intuitive semantics suggests to me that they do not mean the same as 'has the same meaning as some other expression'. Only if it is allowed that every expression is synonymous with itself are the notions of significance and synonymy firmly bolted together. Synonymy is a relation of identity in a certain respect. Identity, in logical strictness, is a reflexive relation. So every expression is synonymous with itself. Must we conclude that 'no one is as beautiful as I am' is a logical falsehood? It would be more reasonable to say that it is a colloquial alternative to 'no one is *more* beautiful than I am' or, to keep out an identical twin, to 'no one other than I is as beautiful as I am'.

There is, however, a more serious difficulty about treating the relation of synonymy in a logically formal way. This is that two meaningless expressions, since each has no meaning, have the same meaning as each other. Do 'er' and 'um' by meaning nothing mean the same? Colloquially, to say that you and I have the same something is to suggest that we really do have the something or some of it. But 'you and I have the same balance on our current accounts' is not falsified by the fact that our respective balances are zero. It would seem consistent with the adherence to the forms of logic exemplified by taking the relation of synonymy to be reflexive to regard the having of no meaning by a pair of expressions as a way of having the same meaning. But in that case the link between significance and synonymy is snapped. Quine has always spoken explicitly of the two concepts as the residuary legatees of the notion of meaning, without the least suggestion of any connection between the two. I have paused over the matter only to introduce the thought that some other contexts ought to be acknowledged as well. In 'Use and its Place in Meaning' Quine mentions these contexts but does not discuss them.

A surely indispensable context of 'meaning' is the phrase 'knows the meaning of', in which case the problematic word can be buried in 'understands' where that verb is followed by the name or description of some linguistic expression. The interment is not very satisfactory; bits of the corpse stick out. An irate parent who enquires 'Do you understand what I am saying?' is not pursuing a semantic investigation. Such cases could perhaps be kept at bay by limiting the complements of 'understands' to the names only of linguistic expressions. There would still be trouble. 'Polish cavalrymen don't know the meaning of the word "fear"' does not owe its truth simply to the fact that they do not know English.

'Knows the meaning of' is not the same as 'attaches a meaning to'. The former implies, as the latter does not, that the meaning attached is the significance the word has in the linguistic community. That may possibly be defined as a set of speakers who all use most frequently words that they use in common (i.e. some sort of basic English). Where the meaning attached is not the public significance that one knows if one knows the meaning of the word something is adrift. Either the semantic dissenter is misusing the word, under the impression that he is using it in its public significance, or he has recruited it for some private purpose. That is part of what is involved in the thesis that language is a social art. All the same a certain priority invests 'attaches a meaning to'. Unless, roughly, a collection of people all attach a meaning, and the same meaning (a point that should, perhaps, worry Quine), to an expression it does not have a (public) significance. Only if they do does what they do amount to knowing the meaning of that expression.

Knowing the meaning of an expression is not innate, whatever else may be afoot down there in the deep structure. That proposes another context for consideration: 'giving' or 'explaining' or 'specifying the meaning', whose one-word surrogate, of course, is 'defining' in a large but familiar sense of the word. A species of this activity is, obviously enough, supplying a synonym. It needs to be carried on in an explicit sort of way, that is *as* the provision of a synonym, by saying for example, 'great-grandparent' means the same as 'grandparent's parent' or, in written form in a dictionary, by some such device as putting *definiendum* and *definiens* in different type faces.

It appears that not all words have synonyms within their own language. More to the point, they could not all have instructionally usable definitions of this lexical kind. There has to be an initial stock of significant expressions, whose meaning has not been learnt in a lexical way, for such definitions to get across that the defined term does not merely have the same meaning as the terms defining it, but what that meaning is. Lexical definition is inescapably secondary, for the same reason that not all property rights can be derived from gift or exchange. The analogue to primary appropriation is, of course, what used to be called ostensive definition and appears in Quine as conditioning a subject to readiness to utter or assent to another's utterance of an expression upon the occurrence of one of a set of patterns of sensory stimulation.

As that last remark shows, I am not suggesting that Quine has not accommodated these notions of knowing the meaning, attaching a meaning, and explaining the meaning in his reflections on the subject. I am merely saying that mention of meaning is natural in connection with all of them and is not peculiar to the two he picks out. His preferred contexts are, I have argued, not all that closely involved with each other. His first one, significance, is involved in *knowing the meaning of* rather intimately. There can be no such thing unless the expression whose meaning is known has a meaning, a shared public one. The knowledge in question is acquired; new entrants to the linguistic community have its regular linguistic practices inculcated in them. That is brought off in various ways: with perhaps deceptive simplicity by the lexical provision of synonyms, by connecting expressions with what learners observe, and, what usually gets pushed to the edge of the field of attention in philosophical accounts of the matter, by grammar. Quine, rather exceptionally, assigns enquiries carried out under the rubric of his first context to grammar, seeing that discipline as concerned to specify the laws in accordance with which elements of significance are combined in significant sequences. The question of the significance of the elements themselves is partly that of explaining how they can acquire it from association with sensory stimuli. Beyond these bricks of the process of construction is the syntactical mortar. If anything has meaning 'all' and 'and' and their kind do.

3. What is a Criterion of Synonymy?

If the notion of a criterion of synonymy is pressed a little, it reveals a mildly disconcerting self-referential character. The naive or intuitive semanticist is confident that the phrase 'is synonymous with' has a meaning, indeed that it has pretty much the same meaning as the phrase 'means the same as'. He believes, with varying degrees of assurance, in the truth of many statements of the form '*x* means the same as *y*' and finds the beliefs of others largely coincide with his own where their topics overlap, in particular those of various lexicographers as set out in their dictionaries. He approaches this mass of raw material in the hope of finding something that indeed means the same as 'means the same as' and also does so in an epistemically or evidentially illuminating way. It must, that is to say, express the content it shares with its synonym in a way that makes clear how it is to be found out that one expression means the same as another. The apparently self-referential aspect of the situation is that the criterion that emerges must satisfy the conditions laid down for itself. Well, one might say, it would be a pretty poor thing if it did not bring that off. If it laid down a condition that it did not itself satisfy it would undermine itself. But the way would be left open for other, less ill-starred efforts. In the same way a grammar book had better lay down conditions of intelligibility with which it itself complies. In that case we might succeed in understanding it because the conditions of intelligibility it lays down, but does not comply with, are mistaken. In our case a criterion of synonymy offered might still be synonymous with 'synonymy' without being epistemically helpful about how we come to be in a position to apply the term. That would be the situation if 'having the same meaning' were proposed for the role.

It does seem that it is at least a necessary condition for the adequacy of the criterion being sought that it should mean the same as 'mean the same as'. Synonymy is not an observational relation like 'above' or 'larger than' in many, and the most straightforward, of their uses. In other, old-fashioned words, the meaning of 'synonymous' or 'means the same as' cannot be explained by simply presenting or enumerating pairs of expressions to which it applies.

Quine's position here is, however, not that of the naive semanticist and an air of paradox attends it. He institutes a search for a criterion of synonymy, knocks out some plausible candidates, and concludes that no such thing can in fact be arrived at. That would be a bit disconcerting, given that 'means the same as' is not an observational term. But it would not be the end of the world, or even the end of the general public employment of 'means the same as'. He does not, I think, draw the conclusion that 'means the same as' is not significant and should be abstained from altogether, although he describes it as a will o' the wisp. I take it that his conclusion is that it is not satisfactory for use in science, specifically linguistic science. It is significant; it is non-observational. It must, therefore, be introduced to learners by words and not by association with non-verbal stimuli. But, he holds, no one fixed effectively-applicable set of necessary and sufficient conditions is forthcoming.

Thus he is not saying that there is no criterion to be found for something there is no such thing as, but only that the verbal dispositions associated with the word in question are too amorphous or wayward to satisfy the requirements for the incorporation of the word in the vocabulary of science. But is this not a common state of affairs? The everyday word 'mad' is notoriously unclear, but it is the basis from which the reasonably scientific term 'psychotic' emerged.

The crucial problem, of course, with regard to 'synonymous', and any other non-observational expression introduced verbally, is to distinguish those introducing expressions which are, in the traditional view, definitive from those that are not and which state only contingent, accidental truths about the things to which the expression being introduced applies. In other words, what is the difference between meaning the same and applying to the same things?

4. Reflections on Coextensiveness

Quine's view is that there is no difference here of the kind that amounts to a discontinuity. He sees only a continuous variation is the degree of firmness with which we hang on to a biconditional of the form 'all and only Fs are Gs' in the face of apparent counter-examples 'here is an F that is not G' and 'here is a G that is not F'.

I suggest that it may be fruitful to approach this question from a recognition of the fact that it is rather hard to find examples of coextensive F and G that are admitted to be non-synonymous by those who believe in the distinction. That old pair of stalwarts 'man' and 'featherless biped' is at risk from plucked or wind-blasted chickens or from chickens bald at birth. His own proposal of 'having a heart' (or 'cordate') and 'having kidneys' (or 'renate') is guardedly put forward with a 'perhaps'.

There is a suggestive analogy here to the problem of distinguishing genuinely law-like from merely accidental generalizations. Why, in the face of the unexceptionless regularity of their association, do we refuse to admit a law-like, causal connection between the sounding of the factory hooters at A and the immediately following emergence of workers from the factories in B, 200 miles away? Is it not because we have a better, independent explanation of the emergence of the workers at B (bells ringing inside the factories at B, for example)? This is a better explanation than the other because it does not collide with well-founded beliefs about the distance from which hooters can be heard.

The coextensiveness—to the extent that it obtains—between 'man' and 'featherless biped' is accidental, because the extension of 'man' is associated with it directly as that which makes it significant and by association with which it is taught, while that of 'featherless biped' is the result of two other direct endowments of significance, being the common part of their independently demarcated extensions. That is to say— as in the hooter analogue—we have different accounts of the way in which the terms involved come to have the extensions they do. Furthermore—in parallel to the point in the hooter case about the distances from which hooters can be heard—the nature of these accounts is such as to rule out the hypothesis that the two terms are synonymous by reason of having the same relationship to the extension they share: for one is related to that extension directly, the other indirectly.

Let us consider Quine's non-synonymous pair: *renate* and *cordate*, offered as abbreviations for 'has kidneys' and 'has a heart'. It is clear that the more familiar terms do not have the same extension, or almost certainly do not. Travellers at a wedding feast in Lapland must have compared notes in some such terms as 'I have a heart; what have you got'; 'Oh, bad luck I don't, I've got kidneys'. The same exchange could occur, or more directly to the point, be true of, two aspiring animal physiologists settling down to a bit of organ identification.

In Quine's example 'has' is doing duty for something like 'is an animal which has as a standard part of its anatomy'. But since it does the same duty in both of his pair we do not, once we have taken note of it, need to harp on it explicitly. In his pair then 'has a' in the same significance occurs in both. 'Heart' and 'kidneys' plainly have different extensions. There is thus no guarantee that the extensions of the two composite terms will be the same; it is simply an accident that they have turned out to be. The elements of the two compounds have been endowed with significance through their respective extensions. These are inevitably the same for the shared element 'has a', different, as it happens, for 'heart' and 'kidney'. No question is begged, I think, if we say that we know the meaning of 'has a heart' and 'has kidneys' long before it occurs to us that the two terms are coextensive and that the significance we attach to them would not be altered if it turned out that they were not, as perhaps they are not. But, as far as the relation between 'cordate' and 'has a heart' is concerned, coextensiveness is guaranteed by the fact that the first is introduced simply as an abbreviation for the second, as 'bachelor' is for 'unmarried man'. In the words of *Principia Mathematica* the shorter expressions are no more than 'typographical conveniences'.

The principle that coextensiveness without synonymy is exceptional, a kind of accident that can be explained away, applies only to what may be called open general terms. Singular terms—the descriptions that Quine admits to the language of science, at any rate—are plainly compounds whose somewhat marginal shared extension— either one thing or nothing—is determined by the independently fixed extensions of their elements. The principle equally does not apply to those rather fishy expressions, singular predicates, as one might call them ('Judy Garlandizes' or 'is identical with Judy Garland') which Quine fabricates for the sake of getting rid of proper names.

If the principle is true of open general terms it implies that, as far as they are concerned, coextensiveness is good evidence of synonymy. Two such terms may be synonymous because both are endowed with significance by association with the same set of observable situations, selections from which are used to convey the significance of either term to learners. Or they may be synonymous because one is introduced and taught as no more than a convenient replacement for the other. These circumstances will guarantee coextensiveness. But two terms may turn out to be coextensive by way of quite different extensional ancestries, so to speak. It is these explainable, and comparatively exceptional, cases that excite the intuitive sense of a difference between synonymy and coextensiveness.

5. Is Synonymy Inescapable?

At this point it is tempting to conclude that there could not be coextensive open general terms that were not synonymous unless there were ways of endowing and communicating the significance of some words which did not consist in associating the words with what I shall have to call representative samples of their extensions, but correlated terms as synonyms. Otherwise every pair of terms with the same extension would be synonymous. If 'featherless biped' were taught through its extension and not understood by way of a prior understanding of its parts it would mean the same as 'man'.

It is not enough to understand 'featherless' and 'biped' in order to acquire an understanding of 'featherless biped'. One has to understand also that, in this case, being FG is equivalent to being F and being G. And that is important since that equivalence does not always hold. Sometimes, as in 'French polisher' or 'moon walking', the noun hugs the adjective too closely. In others, for instance 'large molecule' or 'small galaxy', the adjective cannot do its job unless it goes hand-in-hand with the noun, amounting as it does to 'large as molecules go' or, more perspicuously, 'larger than most molecules' (or, more probably, 'most kinds of molecule').

Quine's way of resisting the temptation I spoke of to infer the existence of lexical synonymies from the existence of coextensive general terms that are not synonymous is to regard both the alleged fact and its supposed implication as no more than apparent. He agrees that words are taught by means of other antecedently understood words but sees the instructive operations as simply the statement of truths which helpfully embody the word being taught. 'Fs, Gs, and Hs are, by and large, Ks', perhaps, and 'Ks are by and large Ls, Ms, and Ns.' These sufficient and necessary conditions are for him pretty much on a par, not divisible into legitimate analytic wives and freely associated synthetic concubines.

Let us consider a particular case, the way in which most children probably come to learn the conditions for the use of the word 'mother' as a general term. First, a particular individual of a pre-eminently present character is named 'Mother'. Then it is realized that that one is the child's personal mother and that other children have mothers too. At this stage 'mother of x' amounts to 'woman who mainly looks after x', where x is a child. Eventually elementary biology rears its theoretic head so that rational cognizance may be taken of stepmothers and foster-mothers and aunts giving a hand to widowers, and then 'mother of x' becomes 'woman from whom x's body came into the world'. The fact surely is that until very recently the earlier, prebiological, account of 'mother' was no more than the conjunction of two statistical truths: that most mothers are the women who mainly look after their children and most of the women who mainly look after particular children are the mothers of those children. And children stuck at that stage do not really know the meaning of the word.

The arrival of surrogacy has created a problem for the definition of 'mother of x' as 'woman who bore x' by breaking the connection between 'woman from an egg of whom x developed' and 'woman in whose body the egg that developed into x grew'. Most of the women with respect to whom either of these is true for a given x are women for whom the other is true as well. In the few cases where they diverge we have four choices: to deny that they are mothers, since they do not satisfy both conditions; to say that only the egg-donors are mothers; to say that the embryo-harbourers alone are the mothers, and finally, to say that both are. The first is unappealing, not just because it reckons as false the generalization that everyone has a mother (or, as I should say, defines 'mother' so that the generalization expressed by those words turns out to be false). It also tends somehow to insinuate that x is not quite human, is really an artefact. The second is preferable to the third, since much more of what x is going to be is attributable to the unique genetic package of the egg x grows from than from the presumably altogether instrumental body in which the embryo x grew from developed. But, of the three, it is the third which is closest to what most people would regard as the current meaning of the word. The fourth, I think, has nothing going for it.

The sense that the phenomenon of surrogacy confronts us with a choice that has to be made confirms the assumption that bearing is a criterion of motherhood of a different status from that of being the main looker-after. For we do not just find ourselves more inclined to hang on to one of what we had hitherto taken to be truths more than to others. We are moved to decide in unison, to turn over in bed all together, for the sake of effective communication, not least in law-courts, where desperately un-Quinian views about meaning prevail. (Although it has to be admitted that there is at least a legal *theory*, namely legal realism, which has a somewhat Quinian flavour.) The child, until it knows something about the way in which children come into the world, does not know the meaning of the word 'mother', although it attaches *a* meaning to 'mother' which allows for reasonably coincident application. And just because 'bore x', taken to cover the whole process from fertilization of own egg to birth, is synonymous in the traditional way with 'is the mother of x' the separability of the parts of this defining process calls for decision and not just collective drift.

6. Evidence of Synonymy

Quine aims for scientific austerity in his account of the evidence on which the linguistic scientist must rely. He writes 'All the objective data he has to go on are the forces that he sees impinging on the native's surfaces and the observable behavior, vocal and otherwise, of the native' (*Word and Object,* p. 28). However, he does not require the linguist to be passive. He allows him to experiment, to provoke utterance from the speakers he is investigating. More specifically, he sees the linguist as uttering terms of the speaker's language in an interrogative way and looking for assent or dissent.

This enlargement of the field of admissible evidence does take what would seem to be quite substantial liberties from Quine's point of view. First, there is the matter of interrogation. The speaker studied has to recognize the linguist's utterance as a question. In our community, of course, a rising intonation will do the trick well enough. We all know that 'that is a *cat*' means the same as 'is that a cat?' But for Quine that can hardly be taken for granted.

A second, analogous problem arises about assent. In *Word and Object* some convenient, scrupulously hypothetical proposals are made for deciding which of the common reactions, 'evet' and 'yok' to questions means the same as 'yes' and which the same as 'no'. It would be disputatious to try to make too much of this. But it does seem to imply that the linguist cannot embark on the first steps of his enquiry without recourse to the notion of synonymy. The reply might be that provoking utterance is considered only as a way of speeding up the linguist's enquiries and not as indispensable. And, furthermore, despite some of the harder things said about synonymy, it turns out to be quite acceptable in the end in at least the limited form of stimulus synonymy between observation sentences, next as between expressions that are interchangeable parts of sentences that are stimulus synonymous, and, finally, by what Quine sees as a reasonable conjecture, as synonymy of those expressions as interchanged in almost any context. So at least the linguist's reliance on the notion is not part of an argument that concludes to that notion's illegitimacy.

The naive or old-fashioned semanticist is tempted to argue that while Quine may be going further than he ought from his point of view in taking some reactions of speakers to be signs of assent and dissent, once embarked on this course he could go further. Must he restrict himself to observing what speakers recurrently come up with in recurrent situations and to enriching the material he has to work with by interrogatively making some of the more intelligibly regular-looking remarks when a situation of the apparently associated kind occurs? Language is largely learnt by individuals being trained in the practices of others. It is seldom invented, and never innate (Quine points out the conventional element in cries of distress). One way in which this happens is where a learner exhibits puzzlement. He repeats some expression he has just heard in an interrogative tone and with a tincture of indignation. 'A schismatic'; perhaps with the addition of some such phrase as 'What's that?' If he is told that, well, a Protestant is a schismatic, or a Trotskyist, or a liberal Jew, etc. he will surely not be said to understand or have learnt the meaning of the word by storing away the raw disjunction, although if it is fairly long it will enable him to agree with other speakers of his language in his application of it. To understand it he has to realize that 'schismatic' means the same as 'member of a dissentient subgroup within a group professing a system of beliefs', or words to that effect, uncontroversially equivalent to that defining phrase.

To say that, I realize, is simply to deny the continuity that Quine holds to obtain between replying to 'schismatic, what, pray, is that?' with the formula about dissenting subgroups, and replying with a list of kinds of schismatic. Now if that list had tacked on to it something along the lines of 'and others who are like them in the way they are like each other' the learner might well work out for himself what one is inclined to call the general principle involved. He would grasp what it is to be a schismatic over and above learning how to apply the word in a way that will be endorsed by his fellow speakers. In the list case he is put into a position to find out, by reflection, what the word means. But the formula specifies the meaning. However I see that that contrast invites the response: you have simply represented a difference of degree as a sharp discontinuity, set up a distinction without enough difference to sustain it.

7. The Limits of Synonymy

I should like to approach the topic from a different, less head-on direction. There are at least four matters to which Quine draws attention which are, I think, matters he is right about and which undoubtedly have a bearing on previous assumptions about meaning and which show, in different ways, that sameness of meaning is neither as pervasive nor as straightforward as old-style analytic philosophy took it to be. But in showing this I do not think that they enforce such a comprehensively critical attitude to synonymy as Quine generally adopts.

The first is his factual observation that by no means all the entries in a dictionary connect synonyms to synonyms. He puts the point more strongly. 'It accounts', he says, 'for only a small minority of the entries in a dictionary.' I think this needs expansion. There are, indeed, a lot of dictionary entries that do not offer synonyms, but there are several distinguishable reasons for this. First of all, a serious, non-pocket-sized dictionary will include all sorts of odds and ends; abbreviations of one sort and another, for example, and proper names of persons and places, ships, buildings, and so forth whose bearers are identified. Next there are words whose meaning cannot be given in a verbal definition, but only more indirectly, by mention or description of what they apply to. That class includes, but goes well beyond, words for sensory qualities, Lockean simple ideas. Also in it are words for natural kinds, of animals and plants, which get some such explanation as 'any of a species of long-haired Peruvian quadrupeds, etc.' But that still leaves a great deal, among them many of the more interesting and important words we use.

An example of a definition that Quine dismisses as supplying only a synonym plus stage-directions is that of 'addled' as 'spoiled, said of an egg'. That strikes me as a perfectly good account of 'addled'. It says that in the limited range of its significance, smaller than that of 'spoiled', it means the same as 'spoiled'. What more could one ask for? Claimed synonymies are not as sparse in dictionaries as Quine suggests.

A second consideration is the falsity of the old 'second dogma' of empiricism: the thesis that the meaning of all statements of fact, or basic ones, at any rate, consists in their association with defining sets of verifying and falsifying experiences. This is true, at most, of introspective reports. It does not adequately account for 'That is a cat' or 'The top of the column of mercury is against the number 35', to head off more explicitly in the direction of science. 'That is a cat' is first learnt as the thing to say in what teachers take to be circumstances where the learner is having the sort of experiences you have when there definitely is a cat present. But such experiences, and others like enough to be mistaken for them, also occur in odd shadow conditions, when toys have been left about, in dreams, and so on. So mastery of the sentence 'That is a cat' involves being aware of various states of affairs which, if they obtain, defeat the prima facie claim that there is a cat present: such as that it cannot be picked up, that it does not move when picked up, and many others.

That can all be admitted without prejudice to the idea that words for material things, and, perhaps more to the point, for their qualities and the relations between them, can be verbally defined. The loose fit between language and experience, afflicting both *definiendum* and *definiens*, cancels out in just the same way as the vagueness of 'bachelor' and 'unmarried man' do. Is a male child of six a bachelor? Well, yes, to the extent that he is a man.

A third consideration is that it is generally not possible to set out defining necessary and sufficient conditions for common nouns in terms of the properties of the things they apply to, the error in the old theory of complex ideas. Where these nouns classify kinds of living things like horses or lemons, there is ordinarily a set of properties all of which are possessed only by a minority of ideal specimens, but most of which are possessed by nearly all, and absolutely all specimens, however unideal, are born from or grow on the same trees as reasonably good specimens. This is a sensible semantic response to nature's lack of standardization or quality control. It is called for also, to some extent, by the functionally defined products of craft—hand-made knives and chairs, for instance—but less by products of manufacture. This fact is connected to the fact that the learning of many common nouns is primarily ostensive. But by no means all. *Friend, secretary, wife*, for example, are not ostensive in this way. So although the consideration being discussed introduces a limit to verbal definability it does not do so to a great extent.

A final consideration is that the technical terms of the sciences are constantly undergoing changes of application, which are retrospective in effect, in the light of new knowledge. This may make it hard to say whether the revision of a term's extension involves a change in its meaning or the recognition of previously mistaken application. There is a lot to say here and I doubt if I am qualified to say it. What I would contend is that to the extent that it is true of the technical terms of the sciences it is not true of non-technical discourse.

8. Logic and analyticity

Quine's critique of synonymy was first introduced as part of a campaign against the analytic/synthetic distinction. But he admits two kinds of alleged analytic truths, only the second of which are vulnerable to doubts about synonymy, those, namely, which can be reduced, by replacement of synonym for synonym, to instances of logical truths. That still leaves the question open as to the analyticity of explicit instances of logical truths.

I think Quine's main argument here is the holistic one that the truths of logic are part of the total fabric of science and are up for revision, when some revision is called for, just as much, even if not to the same extent as, everything else. And he supports the liveliness of that possibility by referring to proposals that the law of excluded middle should be dropped to accommodate quantum physics.

What can, surely, be argued here is that defenders of the analytic/synthetic distinction are even keener for explicitly logical truths to be recognized as analytic than for implicit ones to be so classified. Thus it would seem polemically correct to give as much attention to them as to the notion of synonymy, by recourse to which the scope of the analytic is extended further.

I have no time to do more than sketch a countervailing line of argument. This is that unless some special status is given to at least some truths of logic, perhaps only the law of non-contradiction, it is hard to see how revision ever gets called for. All swans are white, we start off with. Oh, here is a black swan. What of it? Well, if all swans are white there are no non-white swans, and a black swan is a non-white swan, so there is a non-white swan and also there are no non-white swans. That is an explicit contradiction and is, as it were, where to stop. If we were to go on: there is a non-white swan, there are no non-white swans, it is not the case that there is a thing of a given kind and nothing of that kind, there would be no reason to call a halt anywhere. What we see as a collision, an incompatibility, requires us not just to assert logical truths but to use them inferentially. And there were other embedded, operative inferences in the chain of assertions about the colour of swans, as revealed by the occurrence of the word 'so', which covers the moves to 'There is a non-white swan' and to 'There are no non-white swans.'

I do not think it can be proved that anything other than the law of non-contradiction is indispensable, rather than is never, reflectively, dispensed with. But to regard logical truths in general as on a par with the most comprehensive laws of nature, as Quine's holism does, fails to take account of the fact that either we accord some statements in the whole a special, inferential status or no element in the whole is, so to speak, relevant to any other. The formally conceivable option of hanging on both to observation reports, however refractory, and the currently accepted array of laws of nature and adjusting the laws of logic to make them fit is too radically unappetizing to sustain the conclusion that the difference between the laws of logic and nature is only one of the degree to which we are unwilling to drop them.

This line of argument needs completion with an account of the meaning of logical terms and what is involved in our grasp of it. But I have gone on long enough.

9. Afterword

One final irreverent thought. Throughout these remarks I have followed Quine in taking 'is synonymous with' to mean the same as 'means the same as', despite his doubts about sameness of meaning. In linguistic fact there are two respects in which this particular identification might be questioned. First, and more firm, is the convention that synonyms are single words that mean the same as other single words. So, in ordinary speech, although 'unmarried man' means the same as 'bachelor' it is not a synonym, because it is a two-word phrase. Quine's 'furze' and 'gorse', to which we may add 'whin', are more proper.

Secondly, in works that are called dictionaries of synonyms words that are approximately the same or similar in meaning are brought together, not those only that are identical in meaning. Very few single words in one language mean exactly the same as any other single word in that language, for obvious, evolutionary reasons. Quine has himself written appreciatively of the *American Heritage Dictionary*. One of the many services of that excellent compilation, along with the verdicts of its usage panel, are the lists of synonyms. These are everywhere words of similar, not identical, meaning. For 'cruel' they are 'fierce, ferocious, barbarous, ruthless, pitiless'. And, consistently with that practice, the definition offered for 'synonym' in the book is 'word similar in meaning to another word'.

14

Ayer's Place in the History of Philosophy

When A. J. Ayer arrived in Oxford in the autumn of 1929 he had no thought of becoming a professional philosopher. He intended to go to the Bar, but, in the manner of an Etonian, by way of Literae Humaniores rather than the study of law. He had read a couple of philosophical books. The first of them was Russell's *Sceptical Essays*, which he bought on its first appearance in 1928. The other was Moore's *Principia Ethica* (1903), to which he had been led by a reverent aside in Clive Bell's *Art* (1914). These choices were significant. Ayer always thought of himself as Russell's successor. He modelled his thought on that of Russell, both in its content and in its unguarded expression, and also, to some extent, his manner of life, both political and amorous. What he got from Moore is less obvious, although his respect for Moore is evident, as is shown by the preface to *Language, Truth and Logic* and by his devoting a book to a close examination of his ideas, along with those of Russell. An important likeness is that both Moore and Ayer were provoked to philosophize by the assertions of other philosophers, not by problems arising outside philosophy in mathematics or the sciences, in history or everyday life.

Ayer avoided the full rigour of an Oxford training in the classics, devoting one term only to the acquisition of a minimal requirement in them. So, at the beginning of 1930, he started on the formal study of philosophy. The philosophical scene in Oxford at that moment was, for the most part, drab and wintry. Adherents of Cook Wilson, who had died in 1915, exercised a fairly oppressive intellectual authority: H. A. Prichard from the chair of moral philosophy, H. W. B. Joseph as an overwhelmingly energetic college tutor. (For what it is worth, at least as an index of their subsequent reputations, neither is honoured with an article in Edwards's *Encyclopedia of Philosophy* (1967) and Joseph does not even secure a mention.) British Hegelianism, in opposition to which the school of Cook Wilson originally defined itself, was represented by H. H. Joachim. He, like most Oxford philosophers of that time, had given himself over to the historical study of the subject. There was also the wayward and defiantly isolated R. G. Collingwood. The only notable books published by Oxford philosophers in the 1920s were Collingwood's *Speculum Mentis*, of which nobody took any notice, in 1924 and, in 1926, *Statement and Inference*, the posthumous compilation derived from the lectures of Cook Wilson and used by his followers as a kind of textbook.

By the 1920s orthodox idealism was more or less extinct outside Scotland. The Cook Wilsonians had turned their antiquated artillery on to what they saw as the even worse errors of the Cambridge philosophers, who had done so much more than they had to undermine it. Prichard had vehemently criticized Russell's theory of knowledge in an article in *Mind* in 1915 and he and Joseph were persistently hostile to Russell's logic. Moore, as an ethical consequentialist, was one of those who, in Prichard's view, had committed a fundamental mistake in moral philosophy. The only book Prichard published in his lifetime, *Kant's Theory of Knowledge,* had come out in 1909: Joseph's main work, his *Introduction to Logic,* as long ago as 1906.

There were, however, signs of renewed life. H. H. Price, Prichard's favourite pupil, in a disconcerting betrayal, had been converted to the theory of sense-data advanced by Russell and Moore. Ayer, as an undergraduate, attended the lectures that were to be published by Price in 1932 as *Perception*. The more influential of Ayer's philosophy tutors was Gilbert Ryle. After an early interest in the phenomenological movement, revealed in a respectful, if finally suspicious, review of Heidegger's *Sein und Zeit* (1929), Ryle was, by the beginning of the 1930s, showing marked Russellian tendencies. 'Are there Propositions?' of 1930 presents a reductionist account of propositions that was to be echoed in the second chapter of Ayer's *Foundations of Empirical Knowledge* ten years later and in his London inaugural of 1946: *Thinking and Meaning*. Ryle then laid out a comprehensive programme of analysis on Russellian lines in 1932 in his 'Systematically Misleading Expressions'.

Cambridge was unquestionably livelier as a philosophical centre, in spite of its comparatively minute population of philosophers. From 1922 it had Wittgenstein's *Tractatus* to discuss and, until 1927, Ramsey to discuss it with. Also in 1922, Moore's *Philosophical Studies* had brought together a number of influential essays. C. D. Broad published his *Scientific Thought* a year later and in 1925 *The Mind and its Place in Nature*. At a geographical distance, but not at a very large spiritual one, Russell brought out his *Analysis of Mind* in 1921 and *Analysis of Matter* in 1926.

Not much was going on in other British philosophy departments. The most imposing product came from Manchester: Alexander's *Space, Time and Deity* in 1920. Exported fruitfully to Australia by John Anderson, it was respectfully ignored in its country of origin. Kemp Smith's *Prolegomena to an Idealist Theory of Knowledge* (1924) and some elegantly written works by Laird were all that Scotland had to offer. The United States supplied little in the way of exact or minute philosophy in the 1920s. It was an era of massive constructions: Whitehead's *Process and Reality* (1929), Dewey's *Experience and Nature* (1929), and *The Quest for Certainty*, the first volume of Santayana's *Realms of Being* (1928).

The disparaging tone of these judgements of the philosophy of the English-speaking world in the 1920s calls for justification. The decade surely does look weak when it is compared with the effectively preceding period from 1900 to 1914. That roughly Edwardian epoch had contained the early and best works of Russell and Moore. Wittgenstein had come to Cambridge and electrified it. McTaggart's *Hegelian Cosmology*

(1901) and *Some Dogmas of Religion* (1906) had provided exemplary displays of argumentative rigour. In Oxford idealism was still quite lively with Joachim's *The Nature of Truth* in 1906 and Bradley's *Essays on Truth and Reality* in 1914. Prichard and Joseph, as has been mentioned, published their most substantial work at that time. In the United States William James was copiously productive up to his death in 1910. The early, less amorphous, Dewey was at work. Santayana's five-volume *Life of Reason* (1905) belongs to this period, as do Royce's *The World and the Individual* (1900) and the collective volume *The New Realism*.

The large and altogether more adventurous philosophical activity of the Edwardian age as compared with the 1920s is to be explained—to the extent that it can be or needs to be explained—by the general spiritual devastation of the First World War. That suggestion is confirmed if one looks further afield to continental Europe. It was in the Edwardian era that the main and characteristic works of Croce and Bergson were published, as were the earlier and better works of Husserl, Vaihinger's *Als-Ob* (1911), Cohen's *System der Philosophie* (1915), and Cassirer's *Erkenntnisproblem* (1906). By the 1920s Croce and Bergson had moved to the margins of the subject and the orthodox academic philosophers of importance were Husserl, Cassirer, and, perhaps, Nicolai Hartmann. Only near the end of the decade did Heidegger sound a new, arresting note.

From an Anglo-Saxon point of view a more promising publication than *Sein und Zeit* came a year later in 1928 with Carnap's *Logische Aufbau der Welt*. In the United States a sign of a livelier period to come was C. I. Lewis's *Mind and the World-Order* in 1929. These two books coincide approximately with the return of Wittgenstein to philosophy, and Cambridge, and the emergence of Price and Ryle in Oxford. Ayer's philosophical career, then, began after a period of comparative sterility, but at a moment when, in Britain, the United States, and Europe, the first indications of renewal are to be discerned.

It might also be said that not only had the recent philosophical past been comparatively sterile, but the immediate philosophical present was, to vary the image, a bit of a vacuum. Russell's best work was behind him and, so far as philosophy is concerned, he was a spent force. Readers of Raymond Chandler will remember Big Willie Magoon, head of the vice squad of the Bay City police. He failed to come across with something for which he had been paid and was seriously worked over by some heavies. As a result he was never much use afterwards. Something of the same kind happened to Russell when Wittgenstein demolished the ideas in his large and ambitious manuscript of 1913 on the theory of knowledge, in the course of a series of painful conversations in May and June of that year. 'I saw', Russell wrote to Ottoline Morrell three years later, 'that I could not hope ever again to do fundamental work in philosophy.' Moore had little new to say, however emphatically and persuasively he said it, as was shown by the publication in 1953 of lectures he had given as far back as 1910 and 1911. Broad confined himself to elaboration and criticism of the ideas of Russell, Moore, and, in the 1930s, McTaggart. Wittgenstein had been invisible for more than a decade. Ramsey was dead. The Vienna Circle had only just come into being. The field was wide open.

Ayer's account of his philosophical education in the first volume of his autobiography is rather sketchy. He recalls being introduced to the *Tractatus* by Ryle. He read Russell's *Our Knowledge of the External World* (1914) and *The Analysis of Mind* (1921). The origins can be discerned in these three books of his later central doctrines about necessity, perception, and the mind. He also read Ramsey and Broad, James's *Pragmatism* (1907), Poincaré and Nicod. He does not say what problems preoccupied him. Nor does he say anything much about the development of his thinking up to the point in 1936 of its first, strikingly finished and comprehensive expression.

There is little echo in his writings of any influence of the thought of Prichard and Joseph, apart from two negative reactions. The first of these is his repeated insistence that, as he puts it in *The Problem of Knowledge* (p. 15), 'from the fact that someone is convinced that something is true, however firm his conviction may be, it never follows logically that it is true'. That is hardly consistent with his conclusion in the following chapter that statements in the present tense about one's own immediate experience are incorrigible. For that is to say that, if I genuinely believe I am in pain or aware of a red patch, it follows that I am. The original thesis seems to be aimed at the Cook Wilsonian doctrine that knowledge is something unique and indefinable and such that we must know when we have it. Another echo is to be heard in Ayer's treatment of the doctrine of internal relations. In *The Foundations of Empirical Knowledge* it is examined in connection with an argument quoted from Joseph (pp. 200–2).

In November 1932 Ayer went to Vienna and was courteously invited to attend meetings of the Vienna Circle. It was what he learnt there and from the pages of *Erkenntnis*, which had started publication, under the editorship of Carnap and Reichenbach, in 1930, that he was inspired to the extraordinary *tour de force* of *Language, Truth and Logic*. A good way of bringing out the depth of Ayer's involvement is to compare the impact of a similar visit by an American contemporary at much the same time.[1] Ernest Nagel, a few years older than Ayer, spent the academic year 1934–5 in Europe, his principal stops being Cambridge, Vienna, and Warsaw. News of the existence of logical positivism had already been brought to American philosophers by an article about it in the *Journal of Philosophy* in 1931 by Albert Blumberg and Herbert Feigl. Nagel's report of his intellectual expedition is, as one might expect, thorough, serious, and reliable. He became a recognized associate of the Circle, but more as a fellow-traveller than as a fully committed zealot. He had contributed a boiled-down version of his doctoral thesis on the logic of measurement to *Erkenntnis* three years earlier and also an article on reduction in the sciences around the time of his European trip. Perhaps he was already, in his mid-thirties, too much involved with American naturalism to undergo a major conversion.

Ayer, on the other hand, completely ingested the four main doctrines subscribed to by the Vienna Circle: the identification of meaning with verifiability; the reductionism

---

[1] Ernest Nagel, 'Impressions and Appraisals of European Philosophy' (first published 1936), in Nagel, *Logic Without Metaphysics* (1956).

which that implies if subjective experience is taken to be the basis of knowledge; the theory that necessity is analytic, a matter of linguistic convention; and a radically non-cognitive account of judgements of value. In taking on these views he was not content simply to report them. He had even in his mid-twenties an established intellectual allegiance to the philosophical analysis of Russell, Moore, Wittgenstein, and Ramsey. The special achievement of *Language, Truth and Logic* was the remarkable, almost seamless unification of his initial philosophical inheritance with the whole range of the main ideas of the Vienna Circle. Where he differed with the orthodoxy of Carnap, Neurath, and Hempel, rejecting what he labelled as its 'formalism', it was with ideas developed by Schlick. Where Carnap and his allies denied that statements can be compared with extra-linguistic fact and so took basic statements to be adopted by convention, Schlick saw them as direct reports of the facts of experience.

A survey of the contents of *Language, Truth and Logic* will show how comprehensive Ayer's reliance was on the doctrines of the Vienna Circle. The title of the first chapter is 'the elimination of metaphysics'. That phrase is a translation of the first words of an article by Carnap in *Erkenntnis: Überwindung der Metaphysik durch logische Analyse der Sprache* (1932). There Carnap identifies the meaning of a sentence, first, following Wittgenstein, with its truth-conditions, and then with its method of verification or, in the case of a word, with the criteria of its application. He goes on to say 'in the domain of *metaphysics*, including all philosophy of value and normative theory, logical analysis yields the negative result that the alleged statements in this domain are entirely meaningless'.[2] That and a few other references to value in Carnap were developed, with the aid of some apparatus from Moore, into the notorious sixth chapter of *Language, Truth and Logic*: 'Critique of Ethics and Theology'.

In his *Überwindung* Carnap admits that the problem of the given, of the empirical basis of knowledge or, as he would prefer to put it, of the nature of protocol statements, is not yet solved. He soon went on to opt for the conventionalist view that they are statements about what is observed that are agreed upon by that shadowy, but quite cosy-sounding group, the 'scientists of our culture-circle'. In 1934 in 'Über das Fundament der Erkenntnis', Schlick effectively criticized that position.

Although Ayer agreed with Schlick that basic statements are to be verified by the experiences to which they demonstratively refer, he denied that they are absolutely certain and incorrigible. His reason was 'that a sentence cannot merely name a situation, it must say something about it. And in describing a situation one is not merely "registering" a sense-content: one is classifying it in some way or other, and this means going beyond what is immediately given.' He goes on to say that to apply a word such as 'white' to an element of one's experience is to say that it is similar to other contents of experience: 'those which I should call, or actually have called white' (*Language, Truth and Logic*, 126, 128–9). He did not support this view for very long. In 'Verification and Experience',

---

[2] Translated in Ayer, *Logical Positivism*, 60–1.

within a year of *Language, Truth and Logic*, he was expressing doubts about it and in the second chapter of *Foundations of Empirical Knowledge* in 1940 and in the introduction to the second edition of *Language, Truth and Logic* in 1946 he explicitly rejected it.

In claiming that all necessity is analytic Ayer depends as much on the *Tractatus* as on the Vienna Circle. But like Carnap, and unlike Wittgenstein, he took the truths of mathematics as well as those of logic to be tautologies. He wisely did not follow Carnap in defining 'tautology' in a narrowly truth-tabular way. The idea that logic and mathematics are useful because we, as finite intelligences, cannot trace all the implications of our thoughts was, as a footnote shows, derived from Hans Hahn's *Logik, Mathematik and Naturerkennen* of 1933. Ayer's refutation of Mill's account of mathematical truths as empirical generalizations of the widest possible scope was not dependent on Frege, whom, by 1936, he does not appear to have encountered. He unfortunately ascribes to Mill the view that the truths of logic, as well as those of mathematics, are empirical, fixing that mistake firmly in the heads of several generations of students. Mill, in fact, acknowledged what he called 'propositions merely verbal'; held that all essential propositions are identical propositions; and that deduction gives no new knowledge, says no more in its conclusions than is already contained in its premisses.

Ayer's fifth chapter, on truth and probability, follows Ramsey on truth. It advances the theory about the corrigibility of all empirical statements whatever which he soon came to doubt and eventually to drop altogether. In a few concluding pages he had some suggestive things to say about probability. He defines it as the degree of confidence with which it is rational to entertain a hypothesis. He does not specify criteria of rationality, but says they are conventional and vary through time. That is to embrace the kind of conventionalism he rejected in the case of basic statements. Our old friends, the scientists of our culture circle, whose practice determines for Ayer what rationality currently is, are called back from epistemological retirement. The conception of probability as an intrinsic property of a hypothesis and Keynes's view of it as an unanalysable logical relation between hypothesis and the evidence for it are dismissed without argument. The frequency theory is not mentioned.

The significance of his brisk aside about probability is that it sustains the only solution he admits to the problem of induction. It is rational, he says, to be guided by the past in forming expectations about the future because that is what rationality is, by definition. No doubt the current practice of those we should ordinarily describe as scientists is rational in that sense. But (as Ayer would surely have insisted) we can guarantee their rationality only by defining 'scientist' so that no one who deviates from being guided by the past counts as one.

His dealings with God and the immortal soul in chapter 6 derive fairly directly from Carnap's *Überwindung*. But the insistence that neither metaphysical sentences nor their negations can be asserted since both are equally devoid of sense is Ayer's own. It has, as he saw, the consequence that neither atheism nor even agnosticism is any better off than theism, a concession that was not much appreciated by its adherents.

The main business of chapter 6 is the thesis that judgements of value are expressions of feeling and not statements of fact, natural or non-natural. Ayer relies heavily on Moore to dismiss naturalism, although he rephrases Moore's argument. The intuitive non-contradictoriness of 'this is pleasant but not good' is appealed to instead of the intuitive substantiality of the question 'is this pleasant thing good?' The verification principle is invoked to deal with Moore's positive view about the nature of goodness.

Ayer's own positive account of the matter is a sharper edged version of Carnap's *Überwindung* (1932) contention that metaphysics (including value judgements) 'serves for the general expression of the attitude of a person towards life'.[3] In his *Philosophy and Logical Syntax* of 1934 Carnap interprets moral affirmations as imperatives, a more plausible view than Ayer's, as subsequent developments in moral philosophy have shown. It seems probable that the main source here was the celebrated distinction of scientific from emotive language in *The Meaning of Meaning* by Ogden and Richards of 1923. They say, in terms Ayer takes over almost word for word, '"(this) is good" serves only as an emotive sign expressing our attitude to *this* and perhaps evoking similar attitudes in other persons, or inciting them to action of one kind or another' (p. 125). Ayer's account of moral disagreement is taken from W. H. F. Barnes's 'Suggestion about Value' of 1933.

In the four chapters so far considered the main borrowings have been from the Vienna Circle. The balance tilts towards Ayer's British, predominantly Cambridge predecessors, in chapters 2 and 3, where a conception of the nature of philosophy is set out, and in the two final chapters which are about mind, matter, and the self and three 'outstanding philosophical disputes'.

The idea that philosophy should be a business of analysis was affirmed at some length in the last chapter of Russell's *Our Knowledge of the External World* (1914) and it was consistently practised as analysis, with a slightly different inflection, in the writings of Moore. In his neutral monist period from about 1918 onwards, Russell tried to analyse material objects and minds into what he called 'events'. He took material objects to be constructions out of sensations and sensibilia, these being gently reified equivalents of Mill's 'permanent possibilities of sensation'. Minds and their states were seen as constructions out of sensations and images, eked out with bodily behaviour where that seemed desirable.

Ayer drew on Price's *Perception* (1950) in his firmly phenomenalist account of our knowledge of material objects in chapter 3. But he restates Price's theory of objects as 'families' of actual and possible sense-data in linguistic form: sentences about objects are translatable into sets of sentences, categorical and hypothetical, about sense-data. No place is found for Price's 'physical occupant', that ghostly vestige of the substratum of Locke.

---

[3] Carnap in Ayer, *Logical Positivism*, 78.

He follows Russell in holding that sense-data are neither physical nor mental, these being properties of logical constructions. But for the detail of his account of mind he draws, not on Russell, but on Carnap and Hume. In his *Aufbau* Carnap had distinguished the *eigenpsychisch* from the *fremdpsychisch*, the mental states I experience directly from those I ascribe to others on the basis of their bodily behaviour. Ayer was driven to this by his belief that the argument from analogy is unacceptably metaphysical. He was to question that four years later in *Foundations of Empirical Knowledge* and abandon it altogether in 1953. The argument from analogy was rehabilitated by the consideration that, since it is only a contingent fact that I have the experiences I do, there is no logical or necessary obstacle to the possibility that the experiences of others might have been mine. The way out he followed was suggested to him by Ryle's article of 1936 'Unverifiability by me'.

Ayer's Humean view of the self as a series of experiences contained one wholly original element. Hume had been baffled in his attempt to find a relation which could connect a series of experiences into a self. Ayer's suggestion was that the experience of oneself must all 'contain organic sense-contents which are elements of the same body' (*Language, Truth and Logic*, 194). That, as he saw, rules out the possibility of the survival by the self of bodily dissolution. It also ensures that no experience can belong to more than oneself, which the resemblance and continuity which Hume was inclined to favour failed to do. It makes my identification of my body (under some other description, of course) prior to my identification of myself, which is not too bad. But it also requires that every total momentary experience of mine should contain a veridical organic sensation of my body. That is a very questionable proposal, but I shall not pursue the matter here. It may be noted that later theorists of personal identity—Bernard Williams and Sidney Shoemaker, for example—who have claimed that it entails bodily identity have not done so in Ayer's way.

A final thesis of *Language, Truth and Logic* which was soon dropped was also borrowed. From C. I. Lewis's *Mind and the World-Order* Ayer took the thesis that statements about the past are really hypotheses about future experience, on which we shall have to rely on in order to verify them. It implies, I suppose, that our memories are really thoughts about the future. It can be circumvented by the consideration that it is a contingent fact that my experiences occur at the time that they do.

Language, Truth and Logic, then, is almost wholly composed of pre-existing material. It was brilliantly presented, with astounding concision, and its content fitted very well together, despite the geographical remoteness of its two main sources. That is not surprising when one reflects that the philosophers of Cambridge and Vienna continuously interacted. Russell and Wittgenstein were, in a turbulent way, teachers and pupils of each other. The Vienna Circle studied them both and as intently as they studied anyone.

A special virtue of the book, over and above its excellences of style, its force, lucidity, and euphony, is its intellectual order. The elements may be borrowed but they are admirably arranged. After *Our Knowledge of the External World* Russell's books became increasingly loose and casual in construction. That can presumably be attributed to the loss of self-confidence caused by Wittgenstein's ruthless criticism. Moore's laborious repetitiveness and his confinement to a minute range of topics, however strategically important, was unsatisfying in a different way. The *Tractatus*, with pretty well all the argument left out, hovers about on either side of the frontier of intelligibility. Ramsey's small, brilliant *Nachlass* was, in its more philosophically interesting parts, largely rough notes. Broad and Price were admirably lucid and thorough and Price's writing had a particular kind of charm. But they were not, as Ayer unquestionably was, exciting.

Presenting the ideas of Vienna Circle in British costume he extricated them from the lavish use of symbolism, the off-putting technical terms, and the computer-like detachment of Carnap's writing. More in the manner of Schlick he conceived the philosopher to be, however doctrinally subversive, a citizen of the republic of letters. Also like Schlick, who wrote an article on the Vienna Circle and traditional philosophy, he drew attention to the many anticipations in the philosophy of the past of the ideas he was expounding. Berkeley was invoked for his phenomenalism, so long as its theistic attachments were removed. Ayer was also in sympathy with his slogan: 'Mem, To be eternally... recalling men to Common Sense' (*Life and Letters of George Berkeley*, Clarendon, 1871, p. 455). The task of philosophy is not to justify our beliefs but to analyse them. In fact, Ayer probably absorbed that idea from Moore. He saw Hume as right in what he said about meaning, the two kinds of significant proposition, causation and, broadly speaking, the self, even if his thoughts were couched in too psychologistic an idiom. But Ayer's attention to the philosophy of the past faltered when he came to consider examples of metaphysical illusion. Carnap in his *Überwindung* had illustrated his thesis with a short passage from Heidegger and a single sentence from Hegel. Ayer made do with a single sentence from Bradley.

It was the fact that Ayer's revolutionary message was expressed in the literary form of a discursive essay and not in the manner of a scientific textbook, together with its elegance and brevity, that gave it such an impact. It was addressed to intelligent readers in general, from the then radical publishing house of Gollancz, and in an attractively up-to-date physical form: dumpy in shape with wide margins and a wholly non-Victorian typeface: Aufbau by Bauhaus. (The move to Macmillan for his next book in 1940—they were to be his publishers for the next thirty-two years—was a turn towards academic respectability and exclusiveness.) Many of the intelligent readers aimed at took it up. No British philosophical book since Russell's *Problem of Philosophy* (1912) a quarter of a century earlier can have been as widely read.

Ayer's later books—*Foundations of Empirical Knowledge, Problems of Philosophy,* and *Central Questions of Philosophy*—and his five essay collections are, by and large, confined to the topics treated in *Language, Truth and Logic*. That is as much a tribute to the superb economy with which they were treated there as a criticism. The book's philosophical agenda covered a wide enough range for anyone's philosophical career. And there are new thoughts presented and new fields explored in the later works. But he did not move far from his starting point.

The main novelty of *Foundations of Empirical Knowledge*, apart from the limited changes of mind about incorrigibility and the argument from analogy already mentioned, is the contention that theories of perception are not competing substantive doctrines but, rather, proposals of 'alternative languages'. It is not very clear what that amounts to. Does someone who rejects the sense-datum language have to say that some material objects exist only for one person, or intermittently, or have different properties for different people? The arguments used to show that only sense-data are directly perceived could then be mobilized to show that all direct perception is of private material objects and that public material objects, spatiotemporally and causally interconnected in a common world, must somehow be constructed out of them. In that case the alternative offered is of the most trivial, merely typographical kind. What is clear is that nobody seems to have paid much attention to it until J. L. Austin criticized it in *Sense and Sensibilia* (1962). By that time Ayer had explicitly, if quietly, dropped the whole idea. In his essay of 1945 on the terminology of sense-data he accepts the criticism of it by H. H. Price.[4]

Thinking and Meaning, Ayer's London inaugural of 1947, is very properly dedicated to Ryle. For it is a thoroughgoing exercise in dereification, in which the thinking self, the instrument with which it thinks, the process of its thought, conceived as a sequence of mental acts, and the object of thought, its reference or meaning, are all resolved into the expression of thought in significant sentences. Particularly Rylean is the insistence that what have usually been conceived to be mental acts, such as believing and doubting, are really dispositions to come out with certain sentences or to act in certain ways. There is also a distinct echo of Ryle's 'systematically misleading expressions' in the assertion that for an expression to have a meaning there does not have to exist a thing which is its meaning.

Ayer's remarks about meaning in this lecture indicate a much closer attention on his part to philosophical logic. In his *Philosophical Essays* of 1954 it is the topic of the first three items: on individuals, the identity of indiscernibles, and negation. Then four epistemological items rehearse, with minor modifications, the familiar topics of sense-data, basic propositions, phenomenalism, and our knowledge of other minds. Finally Quine's ontology is considered, Ayer's ethical theory is presented with greater suavity but without substantial alteration, Bentham's principle of utility is sympathetically explored, and the view that freedom and determinism are compatible, affirmed in pellet form in the footnote of *Language, Truth and Logic*, is defended and modified. In its 1946 version, as reprinted in *Philosophical Essays*, freedom is defined as absence of constraint, not as having no cause at all. A group of factors is brought together as constraining causes and thus as cancelling responsibility, but no account is given of what principle links them together and distinguishes them from other, non-exculpating causes of action.

The essay on individuals tentatively puts forward arguments for the eliminability of singular terms and the possibility of a purely predicative language implied by Quine's

---

[4] A. J. Ayer, 'The Terminology of Sense-Data', in *Philosophical Essays*, 103–4.

extension of the theory of descriptions to all referring expressions. The issue is taken up again in an essay on names and descriptions in *The Concept of a Person*, but now what was earlier suggested is categorically affirmed.

Quine's use of his regimented language, in which all reference is carried out by quantifiers, to reinstate ontology in a new, logically respectable form, set Ayer thinking generally about what there is. In his study of William James (in *The Origins of Pragmatism*) and again in an essay 'What there Must Be' in his *Metaphysics and Common Sense* of 1969, Ayer turns to the question. Against Quine and Russell he concludes that reducibility does not imply some kind of inferior existential status, as 'mere constructions' or fictions, in the items to which it applies as contrasted with the unassailably real existence of the elements from which they are constructed. Analysis may eliminate singular terms. It does not fictionalize material things. Here again I think there is a distinct echo of the Vienna Circle, particularly of Carnap's *Scheinprobleme* (1928) and Schlick's 'Positivismus und Realismus' (1933).

They had maintained that the reducibility of material things to sense-experiences casts no shadow whatever on the reality of the material world. It simply makes clear what the empirical reality of material things consists in. For such things to exist the course of sense-experience must exhibit certain kinds of regularity. If it does there is no further question about the real existence of the material things defined in terms of these regularities. To infer that, as Schlick puts it, 'only the given exists' (*Es gibt nur das Gegebene*) is to fall into unacceptable metaphysics.

In his positive views about ontology Ayer takes an exactly opposite position to Russell. Sense-experiences are not ontologically prior to material things since their occurrence is absorbed into a comprehensive theory of a material world. There they occupy a very modest place, as parts of the histories of sentient organic bodies. Priority for knowledge is one thing: priority of existence another. Ayer takes ordinary material things and the theoretical entities of sciences as competing for the status of being the real components of the material world. He vacillates between the two claimants— intellect urging electrons, sentiment pressing for tables—and concludes that it is a matter for choice and not very important anyway.

The Problem of Knowledge of 1956 has an excellent chapter on memory. It dispels the influence of a radically misguided chapter of Russell's *Analysis of Mind* (1921) on the subject. Memory is having beliefs about the past that do not depend on inference or testimony. It is not images accompanied by feelings of familiarity and pastness, whatever they may be. Some interesting points are raised in the final chapter on myself and others. If a person is simply a contingently related series of experiences, why should an experience not occur on its own, unrelated in a person-constituting way to other experiences? Why, in other words, should there not be unowned experiences? Personal identity is addressed once more, in a guarded, hesitant way. Perhaps Hume's accusation of a circularity in the definition of personal identity in terms of memory can be circumvented. Survival of bodily dissolution seems conceivable. Yet purely psychological criteria of identity seem insufficient.

There are three substantial novelties in the book. First, there is the neat account of what is needed to turn true belief into knowledge as the 'right to be sure'. The question has not been pressed as to why Ayer does not take the ethics of belief to be as non-cognitive as the ethics of conduct, as he did by implication in his account of rationality in *Language, Truth and Logic*.

Secondly, there is the helpful schematization of problems in the theory of knowledge, about perception, other minds, the past, induction and so on as arising from the scepticism generated by a gap between certain kinds of belief—about material things, past events, the minds of others, the laws of nature—and the only evidence that is available for them—sense-data, memories and traces, behaviour and observed regularities. That was not new. It was present in the pre-war writings of John Wisdom and set out clearly in an article about Wisdom by Douglas Gasking in 1954. Something along the same lines had also been worked out by Friedrich Waismann. These sources make one wonder if it was not something casually let fall in conversation by Wittgenstein.

Ayer, like the other exponents of the scheme, recognized four standard ways of dealing with the gaps. First, intuition, which claimed direct access to the other side of it. Secondly, the theory of a general principle which could serve as a bridge across it. Thirdly, reductionism, which closed the gap by defining the things concluded to in terms of the evidence for them. Fourthly, the melancholy option of scepticism. Ayer conjured up a fifth contender, grandly called 'the method of descriptive analysis', which seemed to be a matter of admitting the gap and then blithely doing nothing about it.

In fact, once more confronting the question of our knowledge of material objects, he does something rather different, and offers a kind of watered down reductionism. Our beliefs about the material world are not translatable into statements about sense-data. They should be understood as a theory which draws all its support from the evidence of sense-data. There is an air here of trying to settle an overdraft with a cheque drawn on the same account. It shifts the problem to that of the relation of a theory to the evidence for it: is it like the detective's theory that the injury to the deceased was caused by a blunt instrument (later found in the shrubbery) or like Newton's theory that the fall of apples and the orbiting of the sun by the planets are manifestations of the same gravitational force? For better or worse, Ayer stuck to this position until his final treatment of the topic in *Central Questions of Philosophy* in 1973.

By carrying out the ungracious task of tracing most of Ayer's original ideas, and many of those he came to express later, to external sources, I am not suggesting that there is no more to his achievement than the communication of these borrowings. He wrote some lively pieces of philosophical polemic: defending the sense-datum theory against Austin's often captious objections, setting ferociously about Malcolm's view that dreams are stories we are disposed to tell when we wake up, and arguing against Wittgenstein's view that a private language is impossible. He expounded Peirce and James, Russell and Moore, with thoroughness and distinction. His special kind of clearheadedness proved valuable in his work on probability, a subject often liable to be swamped by fruitless technicalities.

An unstated assumption behind this excavation of Ayer's intellectual borrowings is that a thinker's place in the history of philosophy is determined by the originality of the interesting or influential things that he says. I do, indeed, believe that assumption to be broadly correct. No doubt the more one learns of the history of philosophy the more one realizes that what one had supposed to be the proprietary great thoughts of those commonly reckoned to be great philosophers had often been thought by someone else first. Descartes's *cogito ergo sum*, one learns, is an echo of Augustine's *si fallor sum*. Locke drew heavily on Descartes, Gassendi, and Boyle. Nevertheless Descartes put his *cognito* to uses of which Augustine had no conception and, although there are identifiable fragments of other men's ideas in Locke's encyclopedic *Essay* (1690), the plan and basis of the whole great undertaking were his own. The special greatness of Kant is surely for the most part due to the novelty of his ideas.

Rather than considering the question in general terms it will be better to try to fix Ayer's place in the scheme of things by comparing his achievements with those of his contemporaries who qualify for such a comparison. Broad and Price were lucid and persevering exponents of ideas put into circulation in the first years of the century by Russell and Broad. Broad had the advantage of knowing a good deal about natural science and about the history of philosophy. Price's great merit was his cautious deliberation, his extremely high standard of what the clear understanding of a problem and its proposed solutions consists in. Their main service was to domesticate the inchoate innovations of others. That is something that Ayer accomplished with greater force and comparable distinction.

Two more obviously appropriate comparisons are with Ryle, ten years his senior, and Austin, his near-contemporary. Ryle, too, was an extensive borrower. His philosophical logic derives from Russell and the *Tractatus*, his philosophy of mind from intimations that had come to him of the thinking of the later Wittgenstein. But he put his own stamp very markedly on what he took. That is in part a matter of his breezy, epigrammatic, resolutely non-technical style. That style was in tune with a mode of proceeding that relied heavily on analogy and, in general, avoided the laborious protection of these from all possible objections. Oddly, in the light of their respective ways of life—collegiate in Ryle's case, metropolitan in Ayer's—it is Ryle who is the less academically respectable and conformist. He steered clear of all the standard etiquette of philosophical writing: the identification of aims, the footnotes, the polite references to Professor This and Doctor That. In the end I think I should accord him a larger place on the philosophical map than Broad, Price, or Ayer, but I admit that it is a close-run thing.

The main reason for it is that, whether by accident or design, his own versions of late Wittgensteinian doctrine are really very different from the original. The distinction between knowing-how and knowing-that was an insight of great value, however easy it is to take it for granted once it has been pointed out. The boldness with which he dismissed Cartesian dualism, by interpreting all mental life in terms of dispositions to behaviour, has the merit of providing something definite to discuss, rather than endlessly puzzle over.

Austin was the critic who got furthest under Ayer's skin as is clear from the indignant tone of Ayer's response to his criticism of the sense-datum theory. Like Prichard and Moore he was a rigorously minute philosopher whose scrupulous pursuit of exactness gave him an extraordinary personal command over his contemporaries. He went further in that direction than his acknowledged master, Prichard, because of his greater intelligence and general mental agility. But his reputation has not survived him. A later generation finds it difficult to understand. Apart from 'speech acts' his innovations in the philosophical vocabulary are seldom heard.

The two philosophers with whom Ayer is most appropriately to be compared are Quine and Popper. Both, like Ayer, are intellectual by-products of the Vienna Circle; in Quine's case gratefully (*Word and Object* (1960), after all, is dedicated to Carnap), in Popper's with a constant determination to emphasize his differences from it. I think it is fair to say that there is no new idea in Ayer that deserves to receive or has received the kind of attention that has been given to the innovations of Quine and Popper.

Quine's multifarious assaults on the notion of meaning as the chief instrument of philosophical explanation, on the analytic–synthetic distinction, on modal and intentional discourse, on assumptions about translatability, his revival of ontology, and his naturalistic account of the theory of knowledge, add up to a major change of direction in philosophy. Not all that many have chosen to follow him very far down the path he has pointed out but his ideas have proved to be inexhaustibly discussable.

Popper's fundamental idea that science progresses by adventurous conjectures, controlled by attempts to overthrow them, is not without forerunners. Something like it is crucial in the philosophy of science of Whewell and it plays a part, if not such a commanding one as for Popper, in the brilliant chaos of the writings of Peirce. But there is no reason to suppose that Popper had the least familiarity with either of them at the time in the early 1930s when he was writing his *Logik der Forschung* (1935). Whewell had been obliterated by Mill in the English-speaking world and was quite unknown anywhere else. As for Peirce, M. R. Cohen's pioneering selection, *Chance, Love and Logic* had come out in 1923 but it did not contain any of Peirce's more Popperian pieces and was anyhow almost certainly unknown to him.

Secondly, and more to the point, Popper's very various developments of his fundamental thought go in directions altogether unexplored by Whewell and only partially by Peirce. Peirce, like Popper, adopts a comprehensively fallibilistic theory of knowledge and rejects determinism. Of Popper's own invention are his attack on the view that there are general laws of historical change, his account of probability as objective propensity, his defence of science as an account of the real nature of things against instrumentalism and essentialism, his application of evolutionary ideas to the theory of knowledge, and the connected doctrine of 'World 3', over and above the realms of matter and consciousness.

Quine and Popper arrived at their main new ideas early on: Quine by 1936 in 'Truth by Convention' and 1939 in 'Designation and Existence', Popper by the date of his first book, 1935. Holding firmly on to them ever since, they have established their fertility by the substantial and interesting body of extensions and applications they have made of them. Ayer, on the other hand, tended to circle round a number of topics, varying his attitude towards them, sometimes opting for one view or another, sometimes concluding that it is a matter for decision, sometimes simply confessing doubt as to what the right answer is. The one thing he never questioned is the primacy of sense-experience, even if, with his later replacement of sense-data by 'qualia', he tried to mitigate the subjectivity of his preferred foundations for knowledge. For all the bold iconoclasm of *Language, Truth and Logic* the abiding impression is one of doctrinal indefiniteness. (It is interesting that he never responded to Quine's rejection of analyticity except in a couple of non-combative pages of *Central Questions of Philosophy*.)

It is that, I think, that must explain the fact that his influence has been so much less than that of the two major contemporaries with whom I have been comparing him. I speak here of influence on philosophers, since Quine is unknown to the part of the general reading public which thinks it would like to know something about philosophy. As every teacher of the subject knows, Ayer has enormously influenced beginning students of philosophy. Since most of them do not go far with the subject, that influence must be, with many, a persisting one. As a paradigm of a philosopher for educated people he is surely exemplary for his unswerving dedication to argument, to explicit reasoning concisely expressed in the clearest language.

It is noticeable that his influence has been comparatively small in the United States. In the post-war years when this country was a net importer of visiting philosophers they crossed the Atlantic to learn about Wittgenstein, Ryle, and Austin. That must be partly due to the fact that, from the late 1930s on, the Americans did not need an intermediary to convey the message of the Vienna Circle, since most of its leading exponents were coming to be installed there in university posts. Furthermore Ayer's ideas about necessary truth and phenomenalism had been anticipated in the United States, seven years before *Language, Truth and Logic,* in C. I. Lewis's more substantial, if less exciting, *Mind and the World-Order.*

Another possible factor is that philosophers in the United States, as in Cambridge in its greatest days, typically know more mathematics and natural science than philosophers in Oxford. Ayer was always an enthusiast for science, but the enthusiasm was of a generalized, rather ideological kind. I believe it was essentially secondary to his animus against religion. The sensationalism to which he always remained faithful was something he shared with the great generation of late nineteenth-century unbelieving philosophers of science: Mach, W. K. Clifford, Karl Pearson. Present-day philosophers of science—Popper, J. J. C. Smart, the Reichenbach of *Experience and Prediction* (1938), even Carnap after the mid-1930s—take for granted the objectivity of the basis of empirical knowledge. Ayer's distaste for religion seems to be the central vision and object of emotional commitment which it is the office of the brilliantly deployed dialectical manoeuvres to protect, rather as a conviction of the immortality of human souls, related by spiritual love, is the soft centre in need of fascinating ingenuities of argumentative defence in the case of McTaggart.

Ayer thought of himself as the main representative in his own time of the British empirical tradition, running from Hume through John Stuart Mill to Russell. It is a natural and intelligible point of view. His interpretation of the leading ideas of that tradition, in the sharpened form given to them by the Vienna Circle, undoubtedly gave it a new lease of life. But in its most vigorous form at the present time that tradition has moved beyond the doctrinal constraints he accepted from it about necessity, perception, and the nature of science.

Although I have come to think his place in the history of philosophy is not as large as I had thought before settling down to write this essay, I think I understand why I should have thought I did. In the first post-war decades philosophy in Britain was dominated by Wittgenstein and Austin, one a genius, the other enormously gifted, but both execrable examples in many ways. Confronted by dire imitations of their respective styles of writing and reasoning Ayer stood out as a marvellous champion of the best traditions of rational discourse.

15
The Rise, Fall, and Rise of Epistemology

I began the study of philosophy in an organized fashion after I was demobilized in 1946. My first steps were firmly Lockean. Innate ideas, substance, primary and secondary qualities, and personal identity were the topics of the first term's essays, along with smaller infusions of Descartes, Berkeley, and Hume. The fundamental examination paper in those days in Oxford was General Philosophy and that meant the problems in the theory of knowledge that had exercised the great philosophers of the seventeenth and eighteenth centuries and, beyond them, Russell, Moore, Price, and Ayer. The syllabus was very clearly set out by the chapter headings of Russell's *Problems of Philosophy*.

But that all changed in the late 1950s and early 1960s. Where once phenomenalism, knowledge of other minds, knowledge of causal connections, knowledge of the past had reigned supreme they were replaced by such matters as reference, identity (in general, not just of persons), truth, meaning, conditionals (particularly counterfactual ones). A fairly reliable indicator of British philosophical fashion is supplied by the appropriate supplementary volumes of the proceedings of the Aristotelian Society in which the symposium subjects for each year's Joint Session are to be found.

Originally this new domain of primary concentration was called 'philosophical logic'. The expression seems to have fallen into comparative neglect. No important books have had it as all or part of their titles, although some useful ones have. Sir Peter Strawson's Oxford Readings volume with this title dates from 1967 when it was, perhaps, already on the turn. It has been replaced by 'philosophy of language'. That may reflect a squeamishness brought on by the indiscriminate use of the word 'logic' in the high days of post-war analytic philosophy when works about the logic of personality, of prayer, of history, and so on abounded. Another factor may have been a desire to mark it off from the much more restricted field of the philosophy *of* logic.

The epistemological tradition that ended, it may be suggested, around 1959 or 1960, with the publication in those years of Strawson's *Individuals* and Quine's *Word and Object*, was really established by Locke. Descartes had contributed indispensably to its inauguration with his radical scepticism and consequent endeavour to reinstate the human capacity for knowledge. But for all the massiveness of his influence, he was an epistemologist only *per accidens*. The entirely suitable subtitle of his *Meditations* is 'in which the existence of God and the real distinction of mind and body are demonstrated'. These are matters of ontology, not theory of knowledge, and his more local, more legitimate intellectual progeny—Spinoza and Leibniz—are builders of comprehensive metaphysical systems.

Locke, too, had a system, but it was an epistemological one, more particularly of a foundationalist variety. The basis was simple ideas of sensation and reflection. From them complex ideas, most notably that of substance, were constructed and from some of them the existence of qualities and substances in the actual, objective world were inferred (at least according to a conventional interpretation of his somewhat inchoate utterances). Of comparable importance to this distinction between the basis of human knowledge and what is inferred or constructed from it is Locke's distinction of kinds of knowledge; intuitive, demonstrative, and sensitive. His account of this distinction and of the proper objects of the kinds distinguished is somewhat rough and ready. Intuitive knowledge is not only of evidently analytic truths (the prime instance of his favourite 'agreement or disagreement of ideas') but also of the presence of ideas in our minds, whether or not any real object corresponds to them. Thus we have intuitive knowledge of both necessary and contingent truths. Demonstrative knowledge is the result of intuiting the logical consequences of intuitive premises (so must, it would seem, be confined to necessary truths). Finally, there is sensitive knowledge, the knowledge we have of things existing independently of us, which is really no more than 'Faith or Opinion'. The existence of God he holds to be demonstrative. But as derived from the non-analytic, non-trifling premise that there is intelligence in the universe, something that is intuitive in his second, weaker sense, is presumably contingent. Moral truth is also demonstrative, but he hardly explains how.

A great deal of the apparatus of contemporary theory of knowledge is to be found here. No serious attention is given to memory and testimony, although there is a glancing reference to the latter in his discussion of probability and a similar reference to the former in his chapter on 'our knowledge of the existence of other things'. And, surprisingly for a compatriot of Bacon, he nowhere explicitly refers to induction. But most of the familiar furniture is set out in a recognizable way. Furthermore, despite his belief that natural science is, at least ideally, demonstrative, he shows unprecedented cognitive modesty in admitting that all the substantial beliefs about the world that are really worth having are not matters of certain knowledge but are no more than probable.

Leibniz examined Locke's *Essay* at length. Berkeley and Hume, agreeing with Locke as to what the central problems of philosophy are, criticized him with great force but failed to undermine his authority in his own epoch. Because of the absurdity of their positive conclusions (material things are collections of ideas in God's mind, partially and fitfully downloaded into ours, and we have no reason to believe in the existence of anything but what is currently present to our senses) they were little read and not taken seriously when they were. Locke was quickly established as the principal object of study for university students in the British Isles and as essential reading for intellectually serious people everywhere (most influentially, of course, Voltaire). Aristotle's *Metaphysics* was pushed out towards the margin of the syllabus. The eighteenth-century philosophers other than Locke who were widely read in Britain were Clarke and Butler, Bolingbroke and the Deists; philosophers of religion and morality. In theory of knowledge Locke was without serious challenge.

Kant made no deep inroads into British thought until long after his death, in the 1870s and after, and then only in thick Hegelian disguise. Where Descartes was a metaphysician taken to be an epistemologist, Kant underwent the opposite experience. His German successors turned his attack on metaphysics into metaphysics of a new kind. The first principles of human knowledge which he had tried to demonstrate with the dizzying complexities of his transcendental and metaphysical deductions were more economically affirmed as principles of common sense or human belief by Thomas Reid and Dugald Stewart, who, in effect, grounded them on intuition. Mill was the chief critic of the culminating philosophers of the Scottish school, Hamilton and Mansel. But he shared their Lockean conception of what the main problems of philosophy are. Bypassing the idealist interlude of the late nineteenth century, the same conception is to be found in Russell, from *The Problems of Philosophy* to *Human Knowledge* getting on for half a century later. It is also the evident organizing formula for two comprehensive surveys, published in the Russellian age; Laird's *Knowledge, Belief and Opinion* (1930) and Hamlyn's *Theory of Knowledge* (1970).

Not only does most subsequent theory of knowledge stem from Locke, there is very little of it in his post-medieval predecessors. Bacon, living in an intensely sceptical age, made short and superficial work of scepticism of the senses and confined himself to the topic of induction, which, he took for granted, could be vindicated only if it established its conclusions with certainty. Hobbes took even less notice of scepticism. Bacon at least went to the length of arguing that if one of our senses deceived us we could apply the others to correct it. Hobbes just breezily assumed an uncritical naturalistic account of perception. Going further back, in the early middle ages an Augustinian, and so broadly neo-Platonic, view of knowledge as the result of divine illumination prevailed; after the recovery of Aristotle, his comparative indifference to epistemology set the standard.

A possible reason for this neglect of the subject in the middle ages is the fact that all but the most disreputably subversive thinkers proceeded from the unquestionable (and, indeed, unquestioned) assumption that a benevolent God would not have created us with radically defective intellectual equipment. Theory of knowledge, however, flourished in the ancient world where there were no religious obstructions to it. Plato was provoked by the Sophists into the work of refutation, in the *Protagoras*, and to that of defining knowledge in the *Theaetetus*. The problem posed by his exemplary demonstration that there is more to knowledge than true belief is, of course, still with us today. Although resistant to scepticism Plato's response to it is at least concessive, even perhaps defeatist. We can have knowledge of mathematics and morals but only opinion about matters of natural fact. The Platonic academy after his death developed the sceptical side of his thought which was a persisting philosophical tradition into Roman times. Both Cicero and Augustine wrote treaties 'against the academics', i.e. sceptics.

The sceptical philosophy of the ancient world was summed up in the writings of Sextus Empiricus (mid-third century AD). Their rediscovery in the sixteenth century and publication in the 1560s met the religious doubts of the period, excited on the one hand by the Protestant Reformation and on the other by the worldly humanism of Italy. Erasmus and Montaigne in the domain of general literature are the most conspicuous of those who received its influence. Descartes brilliantly, but insecurely, turned it on its head. But its staying-power was evinced by the dominance of Locke. That dominance, I have suggested, continued until comparatively recent times, about 1960. But one notable interruption must be acknowledged, that of absolute, or Hegelian idealism. After some small, premonitory rumblings that vast intellectual contraption burst on the British philosophical scene with the publication of T. H. Green's huge introduction to his edition (with T. H. Grose) of the works of Hume (1874) and F. H. Bradley's *Ethical Studies* (1876).

Neither Green nor Bradley was in any recognizable sense an epistemologist. This was very much in the spirit of their joint inspiration, Hegel, who had maintained, in a somewhat disputatious way, that it was an impossible undertaking. Both were, certainly, involved with epistemology from outside, as it were. Green's first major work of theoretical philosophy was his long-drawn-out critique of empiricist theories of knowledge up to and including Hume. But his critique did not attempt to revise or improve upon what it was directed on. Nowhere does Green classify the sources and objects of knowledge. Drawing on an ill-judged remark of Locke's that relations are the work of the mind, he derives from this, and the vague assertion that all judgement affirms a relation between its constituents, the conclusion that judgement is the work of the mind, and so no sort of reflection of an independent reality.

Bradley concerns himself with conceptions that figure in the theory of knowledge–substance, qualities, primary and secondary, relations, the self and so on–but only to argue that since they are all one and all 'relational' they are infected with contradiction. What passes for knowledge is the work of the discursive intellect and is only of appearances. It is a kind of intellectual makeshift useful in practical life but with no claim to truth. For knowledge of the indivisible unity of the world as a whole we must turn to speculative reason, which supplies only the pretty diaphanous assurance that the Absolute is one and a flux, like but 'higher than' the flux of immediate experience, a kind of liquefied Parmenideanism.

In 1903 fatal blows were delivered at the prevailing idealism by Moore and Russell and the Lockean tradition was restored in the next two decades. By 1920 idealism was only vestigial. The German intellectual occupation of the last years of the Victorian age turned out to be as superficial as the Roman occupation that had come to an end a millennium and a half earlier. An interesting indication of this superficiality has come to light only quite recently. In the fifth volume of Russell's *Collected Papers* are to be found the essays written by Russell as an undergraduate for his tutors James Ward and G. F. Stout. They turn out to be entirely conventional in subject matter, about themes in Locke, Berkeley, and Hume, with some attention to Descartes, at one historical end, and to Kant, at the other. They are pretty good essays, as might have been expected, and Ward's comments are sensible, to the point, and entirely within the Lockean tradition. His own 'panpsychism' was clearly a private matter, like a second family hidden away in a suburb.

Although Russell had left academic life and, on the whole, philosophy by 1920 and Moore had settled down to a steady practice of repeating himself, their way of doing the subject was carried on by Broad and Ewing in Cambridge and by Prichard and Price in Oxford. Doctrinally sympathetic epistemologies appeared in the inter-war years in Europe from Schlick (*General Theory of Knowledge*) and Reichenbach (*Experience and Prediction*), and in the United States, notably from C. I. Lewis.

Here, as elsewhere, Wittgenstein was the odd man out. The *Tractatus* is a work of philosophical logic for very much the most part, for all its *obiter dicta* about induction, solipsism, death, and morality. It was certainly taken to be so by the members of the Vienna Circle. It appears, indeed, that they for a time persuaded him to admit their Machian interpretation of his elementary propositions as reports of immediate experience. That would have the effect of moving it in the general direction of epistemology (towards something like Carnap's *Aufbau*). But the persuasion did not last. A great deal of the *Philosophical Investigations* is a response to one particular philosophical problem, that of our knowledge of other minds. But the rest are not touched on.

Some years after his death *On Certainty* was published, which is a collection of notes on Moore's defence of common sense and his proof of an external world. Moore had said he knew for certain that there existed material things, that there were minds that were conscious of them, and that people generally knew for certain that these two propositions were true. There is no question, Wittgenstein held, of our doubting these things, since they are the hard framework of all our thinking about the world and ourselves and, he concluded, there is therefore, no sense in saying, with Moore, that we know them to be true. That, one might say, is Reid, in a Viennese rather than an Aberdonian accent.

Ryle was also a non-epistemologist, even an anti-epistemologist. His only explicit comment on the subject is a rather hostile entry on it in Urmson's *Concise Encyclopædia of Western Philosophy and Philosophers* (unsigned but readily identifiable as his on stylistic grounds). His topics were meaning, reference (in his early days), the analysis of mental concepts, philosophical method, and the philosophy of Plato. He touches on perception, but in an epistemology-dampening way, in the chapter on observation in the *Concept of Mind* and there are some enlightening *aperçus* on memory and self-knowledge elsewhere in the book. His goal was conceptual exploration, not the justification of belief. It is in keeping with this that in an essay on Locke, contributed to a French encyclopedia and to be found in his *Collected Papers*, he says that Locke's main achievement is the distinction of kinds of proposition, not varieties and sources of knowledge.

Austin presents more of an epistemological appearance. *Sense and Sensibilia*, however, is not a contribution to the problem of perception (that of how belief in the existence of material objects is to be justified) but a rejection of the supposition that there is such a problem, rather than a collection of fairly loosely inter-related issues. Early in his career he advanced an account of the allegedly performative character of the verb *know* of which, rightly, nothing whatever has been heard since. Strawson abstained pretty rigidly from the theory of knowledge for a long time, breaking out only in a *Festschrift* for Ayer in which he may have been guided by courteous respect for the maxim 'when in Rome...' Ayer alone, of the major British philosophers of the middle of the century, remained faithful to the Lockean tradition. His *Problem of Knowledge* of 1956 may be seen as its last gasp.

The submersion of epistemology by the philosophy of language was associated with, and is perhaps not all that clearly distinguishable from, the Americanization of British philosophy that took place after 1960. From the end of the war until around 1960 American philosophers poured over to see what was going on in Britain. Quite soon the flow was reversed (with many of the ablest British travellers not coming back). The change was noticed and described, by, for instance, Ayer:

> Wittgenstein was very largely responsible for diverting Western philosophy from a course which it had steadily pursued from Descartes to Russell ... The dominant tradition, inaugurated by Descartes, was one that assigned a central role to the theory of knowledge. (*Wittgenstein*, 142)

But the change has not been much explained, although Dummett, who welcomes it, has propounded a justification. In an essay of 1967 on Frege's philosophy, to be found in *Truth and Other Enigmas*, he says that Frege first and, in the end, most influentially, rejected the Cartesian assumption that theory of knowledge is the fundamental philosophical discipline, looking back, beyond Descartes, to Aristotle and the Scholastics:

> For Frege as for them logic was the beginning of philosophy; if we do not get logic right, we shall get nothing else right. Epistemology, on the other hand, is not prior to any other branch of philosophy; we can get on with philosophy of mathematics, philosophy of science, metaphysics or whatever interests us without first having undertaken any epistemological inquiry at all. (p. 89)

That is pretty much of an aside and it would be unreasonable to examine it too minutely. It might just be remarked that the priority of logic to philosophy is one thing, that of *philosophical* logic, or the philosophy of language, is another. Secondly, the philosophies of mathematics and science are surely theories of mathematical and scientific knowledge for the most part, while many, perhaps most, metaphysical issues are rooted in epistemology: those, for example, of mind and body, of the reality of the past, of the existence of universals.

We must, of course, understand what the words and sentences that we hear and utter mean before we can consider claims to knowledge of the truth of the propositions they express. But we do not need to have an articulate *theory* of meaning. And that is just as well, given the absence of any sort of consensus about what kind of thing a theory of meaning ought to be.

We can, however, ask why Frege's and Wittgenstein's shift of the centre of philosophy from knowledge to meaning proved so influential. In the first place, by 1960 epistemology seemed somewhat exhausted. The project of reductively analysing all other knowledge into immediate, infallible knowledge of sense-data had collapsed and so had the sense-data into which the analysis was supposed to terminate. Today sense-data are more or less a philosophical heritage site. The realization that memory is a store, not a source of knowledge, not some kind of retrocognition, seemed to exempt it from epistemological examination, wrongly, since things can go bad in store as well as be polluted at the source. The passionately affirmed, but by no means universally persuasive, private language argument seemed to have dissolved the problem of our knowledge of other minds. A general air of fatigue and exhaustion hung over the theory of knowledge. It seemed time to move on from its over-cropped soil to some more promisingly fertile region.

The new ground proved fertile enough but not of intellectually edible material. Even if the move to new ground had been more successful, there is a practical consideration to be taken into account. A part, perhaps a very large part, of the importance of philosophy (and that it has some is clear from a look at its history and its influence on the whole universe of thought) is that it is taught to, and studied by, people the vast majority of whom are not going in the rest of their lives to be philosophers at all, in any but the most marginal way. Are they going to benefit from being lowered into the whirlpool of sophisticated controversy that makes up contemporary philosophy of language–of linguistic holism, the rejection of a substantive distinction between sense and reference, the causal theory of reference, possible world semantics, all of which, says Dummett, seem to him mistaken? (ibid. 441.) Quantum electrodynamics is in a significant way prior to, or more fundamental than, classical mechanics, but classical mechanics is the place to start.

Given the chaotic state of the philosophy of language and its own long tradition it is not surprising that the theory of knowledge should show signs of revival. Inside the circle of the old field of problems a small, bright flame was ignited in 1963 by Gettier, illuminating the long dormant problem of Plato's *Theaetetus*: what more is there to knowledge, as there must be, than truth and belief? The ingenious counter-examples with which he undermined the conventional proposal of justification as the third condition released a violent flow of more or less ad hoc repairs to the challenged definition. It soon seemed more promising to drop justification altogether and replace it, as Goldman did in 1967, with the requirement that a true belief counts as knowledge only if it is caused by the state of affairs which makes it true. Another proposal was that a true belief is knowledge only if it has been arrived at by a reliable method. These larger proposals introduce an interesting innovation in epistemology, namely *externalism*, the doctrine that there can be conditions of knowledge which the subject satisfies without being aware of the fact.

As the concept of justification was being extruded from the definition of knowledge it was still crucial for something that could well be seen as more important than knowledge strictly so called: reasonable or justifiable belief. The abandonment of sense-data cleared the way for a revised, more moderate foundationalism, one that did not require infallible foundations. Such a position goes some way to meet the claims of the supporters of coherence as the prime, or sole, provider of justification and knowledge. Haack, who set out a moderate, fallibilist compound of foundationaism and coherentism in her *Evidence and Inquiry* (1963), uses, as an image of the rapprochement, a crossword puzzle. Answers based simply on the clues are foundational, fitting in with existing letters is the element of coherence. That allows a certain priority to foundations; until they have supplied something there is nothing for coherence to work on.

Just how far coherence must be admitted to determine justification, now that old-style infallibilist foundationalism has been rejected, is perhaps the most lively area in theory of knowledge at the present time. It certainly bulks large in the best recent textbook of the subject known to me: Dancy's *Introduction to Contemporary Epistemology* (1985). I shall not attempt to explore it further here but shall turn to other innvovations—the serious study of what has hitherto been a very marginal interest of theorists of knowledge and the confrontation of a new, less playful, sceptical challenge to the possibility of knowledge.

Most studies of the subject that aim to be at all comprehensive make some reference to the role of testimony in our stock of knowledge or belief. There is something about it in Russell's *Outline of Philosophy* (1926), a longer, and more penetrating, treatment in Price's *Belief* (1964). But the first full-length philosophical study of the topic is that of Coady (*Testimony*, 1992). What is really under consideration here is the social character of knowledge, the fact that nearly everything we claim to know or reasonably believe we have acquired from other people. Popper's theory of objective knowledge puts the point dramatically, although not in an epistemologically relevant way. The most substantial contribution here has been Goldman, the proponent of the causal theory of knowledge, in his large *Knowledge in a Social World* (1999).

Old-style, Cartesian, subjectivist theory of knowledge represented the individual knower as completely self-made epistemically speaking. Relying on the usual sources—perception, memory, and inference—he identifies belief-producing organisms in his environment and, after checking their reliability against his own findings, takes over beliefs that have passed his test. No one ever said anything as weird as this explicitly but it is implied as an account of how we get knowledge and beliefs from others by the labelling of that procedure as 'testimony'. The natural habitat of testimony is in a law court. There witnesses are sworn in, their evidence is presented, it is subjected to critical scrutiny. This picture has no place for the primordial fact that it is other people who teach us how to speak, to express our beliefs, and to understand the utterances of other people in general.

The conception of the individual knower as a kind of Robinson Crusoe should be replaced by one in which he is placed from the outset in a belief-supplying community, in which vast tracts of information, good and bad, lie about, and between which he has to navigate. Conventional epistemology describes and evaluates the acquisition of first-hand knowledge. But philosophers do not reflect on the social aspect of knowledge. Nor, I suspect, do they know anything about the work that has been done—by non-philosophers—in this field. How many know the work of Patrick Wilson, a librarian, who describes his *Second-Hand Knowledge* as 'an inquiry into cognitive authority'? It is not mentioned by Goldman in his very widely based book of 1999, although it came out sixteen years earlier.

The educational value of social epistemology depends on the fact that, on the whole, people are much better at managing the beliefs whose epistemic status is investigated in ordinary theory of knowledge than they are at dealing with second-hand information: what is brought to their notice by advertisers, politicians, newspapers, radio, and TV. Belief is a little like strong drink; taking too little is not a problem, taking too much is. Credulity needs to be guarded against, primarily to sources of belief like those enumerated above, all of which are self-regardingly motivated. But we need to be critical as well about beliefs emanating, or purporting to emanate, from respectable, institutional sources, notably 'science' and 'experts', both of which embrace a multitude of levels of justified credibility.

There might be something to be said in favour of a private knowledge argument, parallel to its private language correlate. Popper argued that knowledge, particularly scientific knowledge, requires a community of investigators to keep a check on each other's reasoning. (The correctness of that view is not undermined by his own conspicuous hostility to criticism and impermeability by it.) It would probably prove quite as difficult to formulate precisely enough for it to be worth discussing as its Wittgensteinian predecessor. But just as it is quite clear that language is in fact social, whether or not it demonstrably has to be, it is equally clear that knowledge is, in a very deep-seated way, a social phenomenon.

I have welcomed the emergence of social epistemology for its educational merits, as well as its more narrowly intellectual virtues and interestingness. There is another, broadly educational task which a theory of knowledge is currently much needed to perform. That is to offer systematic and coherent resistance to the prevailing tides of irrationalism. From all directions the champions of various 'victim groups'—women, homosexuals, non-white people—proclaim that there is no such thing as objective truth. This does rather excite such responses as 'is that so?', 'do you expect me to believe that?', 'how do you know that?', 'what reason have you for believing that?'

Since generalized irrationalism is evidently self-refuting and yet is passionately affirmed, since it tries to get something across at the same time as it invites us to pay no attention to it, one should, perhaps, look around for a consistency-preserving reinterpretation, as we do with such less dramatic absurdities as 'well, he is and he isn't'. A prime source for irrationalism is the Nietzschean proposition that all belief is motivated, interested, an instrument for the exercise of power. No doubt some belief is motivated but much is not, at least discernibly, such as my belief that at the moment of writing it is Monday and that the sun is shining. But two points should be noticed. First, it must be asked what is the status of the proposition in the common-sense social psychology of belief that belief is interested? Either it is true (or nearly true or probably true) or there is no reason to pay any direct, non-diagnostic attention to it. The second is that it does not follow from the fact that a belief is strongly motivated that it is false or unreasonable. Certainly, where the connection between a belief and desire is very close and direct, suspicion may be aroused. The beliefs irrationalists use their doctrine to protect are much closer to their ideological preferences than a belief in objective truth and scientific method is to a desire to dominate the lower orders.

People in the more intellectual professions need some sort of training in resistance to irrationalism. They need to be clear that it does not follow from the fact that knowledge is a 'social construction', which indeed it is, that it is therefore some kind of imposture nor that the reality it purports to be knowledge of is some sort of fantasy.

Theory of knowledge, I have contended, has had a long and distinguished career. In Britain, at any rate, it has been the central philosophical discipline since Locke, apart from a short interruption in the late nineteenth century and from its demotion to a subordinate role since about 1960. I have argued that it does not deserve this subordination, that there are signs that it is still alive and well and that it has recently developed in a socially valuable way.

PART II

Of Manners

16

The Varieties of Value

I

My starting point is a strange and remarkable disproportion in the way in which philosophers distribute their attention between the two main parts of their subject. The two parts I have in mind are theoretical philosophy and practical philosophy: the critical study of thought as bearing on knowledge or justified belief and the critical study of thought as bearing upon action. I believe that what I am saying is definitely true, with very few exceptions, of the philosophers of the English-speaking world and I am inclined to think that it is largely correct as regards European philosophers in general.

The disproportion in question is that, while theoretical philosophy concerns itself with the whole range of thinking that is orientated towards knowledge and belief, practical philosophy concentrates almost exclusively on moral action, action, that is to say, considered from a moral point of view.

Individual theoretical philosophers may specialize, but, as a group, they attend with comparable degrees of closeness and thoroughness to perception, memory, our awareness of our own mental states, our beliefs about the mental states of others, and to inference, whether deductive or inductive, including the principles of logic, mathematics, and methodology, whose truth is implied by belief in the validity of inferences. But, while every kind of thinking that leads to belief not directly related to conduct has had, and continues to receive, serious attention from philosophers, only moral thinking, among the whole broad range of our styles of thinking about action, is positively investigated. All the other kinds of thinking that determine choice and action tend to get lumped indiscriminately together, in a kind of common grave, as if worthy of consideration only for purposes of contrast, as in service to self-interest, inclination, or desire.

Theoretical philosophy takes serious account of all the main institutionally organized interests of the intellect: natural science—physical, biological, and psychological—history, theology, linguistics, social science. Practical philosophy gives detailed, sharply focused attention only to morality.

There are, admittedly, blind spots in theoretical philosophy. But they occupy so small a part of the total possible field that the extremity of the opposite situation in practical philosophy is brought into higher relief by acknowledging them. The most important case is that of the very fitful attention given to the place of testimony or authority in the domain of knowledge or justified belief. Works of theoretical philosophy that aim to be comprehensive so as to serve as textbooks more often than not make no mention of the matter. But most of what each of us claims to believe with justification has been accepted on the authority of someone else, whether in person, as parent or teacher, or in the pages of a book.

It could be argued, however, that this is not too serious an omission, since testimony is inevitably a secondary, derivative source of knowledge. The authority, or his ultimate source, is worth believing only if he established the belief he is communicating for himself, and his clients can, and sometimes should, check his reliability.

But what is left out of the effective scope of practical philosophy, by its preoccupation with morality and its undiscriminating amalgamation of all non-moral aspects of thinking about action, is the greater part of the total field. Matthew Arnold once made the puzzling remark 'conduct is three-fourths of life'. I shall not pause to interpret it or to question its confident numerical precision, but, in something of the same spirit, I want to say: the greater part of conduct is non-moral. The great majority of everybody's practical thinking includes no moral considerations whatever. Shall I clean my teeth before or after I have my bath? Shall I choose an apple or a banana from the fruit bowl that is being passed round? Shall I wear my white shirt or the one with green stripes? Shall I work in the garden or tidy up my desk? When practical problems like these confront us we ordinarily do not consider the question from a moral point of view and that is reasonable, for there is ordinarily nothing in the situation of choice to which moral considerations apply and which they can attach themselves to.

That is not to say that such choices never have a moral aspect. Consistent neglect of personal hygiene is morally objectionable as showing a lack of consideration for others. If the choice at table had been between animal meat and a salad a vegetarian would see it as a moral issue. Somebody may just have given me a green shirt as a present and will think I do not like it if I do not wear it as soon as an opportunity arises. Perhaps the state of my desk is weighing more heavily on my wife's mind than the leaves lying about the garden. But these are special cases.

Another thing that needs to be acknowledged is that our actions are, in a way, much more systematically inter-related than our beliefs. Much of our action is carried out as part of some fairly complex programme, into which morality may enter. A man hurries to catch a train. Why? To get to work on time. What is the point of that? To avoid sour looks from his immediate superior at his place of work; to avoid prejudicing his chances of promotion; not to leave his two colleagues without help in the grim task of bringing up today's deliveries from the basement. Our beliefs on the other hand, are comparatively atomic or autonomous. Many of them are worth having even if they are not part of some organized system.

Later on I shall consider whether some explanation can be found for this asymmetry in philosophical investigation of theory and practice. But first I shall go on to illustrate it by looking at some strange views philosophers have been led to adopt; after that I shall distinguish non-moral values, together with the motives that inspire action directed towards them, and enquire what are the significant differences between them and how they are related to each other; and I shall also argue that their neglectful amalgamation has had bad consequences for the philosophical understanding of morality.

II

The basis of the ordinary, and in my view mistaken, way in which moral and non-moral values are contrasted is an ancient and, surprisingly, persistent theory about the springs of action. That is, of course, the Platonic doctrine which derives the conclusion that human beings are induced to act either by reason or by desire from the conception of human beings, in their life on earth, at least, as compounds of an immortal mental thing, a soul, and a transient physical thing, a body.

Roughly speaking, the soul is the seat of reason and the body is the seat of appetite or desire. It is the function of reason to control desire. At a kind of ascetic extremity the demands of the body are wholly transcended, that is when a human being is engaged in the ideal form of life, completely absorbed in theoretical contemplation. In Plato's version (of which what I have just presented is an exceedingly summary abridgement) this ideal of life is not conspicuously moral in any sense that we should recognize in the modern world. But the incorporation of the fundamental ideas of Platonism into Christian theology led to an identification of reason with the moral aspect of human nature, that is as a combination of intellect with the will to act in accordance with its dictates, conceived as altogether opposed in character to desire or appetite.

The most influential expression of this point of view in post-medieval philosophy is that of Kant. The human agent, according to him, is the scene of a constant battle between duty and inclination and duty is something discovered by the only kind of reason which he sees as equipped to arrive at truth, the practical reason.

A familiar difficulty for the doctrine that human action is the outcome of a persistent competition between reason and desire is that it does not account for the power which it assumes that reason has to move us to action. Kant is insistent that the moral motive, which he takes to be the will to do duty for the sake of duty, is no part of the natural, body-bound equipment of human beings. It is purely rational in character. How, then, can it move us to act any more than the knowledge that 27 is 3 to the power of 3?

Another difficulty for his kind of dualistic theory of human agency he deals with rather more persuasively. After all, reason, broadly understood as the intellectual or cognitive aspect of human nature, plays an important part in non-moral activity, and, as well, in immoral activity. A great deal of intellectual skill may be exercised in such seemingly morally indifferent activities as playing chess or proving a theorem in mathematics and also in activities that would conventionally be regarded as immoral, such as planning and executing a complex bank fraud or robbery.

For Kant such things are the work of understanding, not reason, *Verstand* not *Vernunft*. In allowing this he does at least acknowledge that the domain of desire, inclination, or appetite is internally variegated in more ways than by simply being directed onto different objects. Some desires are immediate and more or less instinctive, such as those for food, drink, and sexual partners. Others for more remote objects, like an elevated position in the world, call for a great deal of planning and calculation and require a lot of knowledge of causal relationships. Beside the imperatives of morality he recognizes that there are counsels of prudence and rules of technical skill. But he maintains an absolute distinction between these as hypothetical imperatives, leading us to act only upon the prompting of desire, from what he sees as the categorical imperatives of moral obligation. When we follow our inclinations, then, our intellects, here called understanding, are in the role of servants to desire. When we do our duty intellect, here called practical reason, is master.

An earlier eighteenth-century account of the springs of action, that of Bishop Butler, also acknowledges prudence, which with benevolence and conscience it describes as principles, as well as what Butler called particular passions. This set of distinctions makes the useful point that prudence and benevolence are of a second-order character and presuppose other desires—my own in the case of prudence, those of others in the case of benevolence—to supply them with content, since they are aimed at maximizing the satisfaction of those two classes of desire.

But Butler makes no explicit provision for the kind of action to which Kant's rules of skill would lead us. At least that is correct if the most straightforward interpretation is put on the phrase *particular passions*. It suggests a sudden, emotionally intense state of mind, demanding immediate expression in action. Much the same is true of the words *desire* and *appetite*. One desires an attractive person as a sexual partner; one has an appetite for food. But it would be absurd to speak of an appetite for good health (served by dieting, exercise, and giving up cigarettes) and it would at least be very artificial to describe good health as something one desired.

Now these facts about idiomatic correctness are trivial in themselves. But they bring to notice some questionable implications of the unidiomatic uses. In the first place it suggests that the purposes of human action are generally of a primordial, bodily kind, calling for little or no intellectual effort from those who entertain them. Secondly, their bodily character attracts a measure of moral stigma to the non-moral springs of human action in general. It serves to obscure the fact that most human desires are not what puritanical moralists call animal desires. (For that matter, many of the desires of animals are not animal desires in that sense either.)

It might be thought that these historical considerations are not relevant to current thinking about morality. But that is far from true. In the English-speaking world, at any rate, moral philosophers have been obsessed with the cognitive problem of whether and how it is possible to establish the truth of moral beliefs. Their role in guiding action has either been ignored altogether or it has been explained by interpreting moral utterances as a kind of imperative, without pausing to consider the question of the circumstances in which it is reasonable for someone who issues an order to expect that it might be obeyed. Where the motives of action have been considered in any detail it is either in the course of discussing moral responsibility and the freedom of the will or as a problem in the philosophy of mind.

I shall later come to discuss the bad effects on moral philosophy that I take the neglect of non-moral values to have had. So far, I admit, I have been concerned with the variety of non-moral springs of action or motives, rather than of non-moral values. But the two things are directly connected. To want something, to have a preference for it, to have a favourable attitude towards it, to strive to get it or bring it about, to desire it—all this is to ascribe some sort of value to it. The ascription may be mistaken. In that case the rational agent modifies his wants, attitudes, preferences, or desires and hopes to do better next time.

The practice of treating non-moral values as an undifferentiated mass (conceived sometimes as the objects of desire in general, sometimes as rationally calculated, systematic self-interest) although widespread is not universal. One large, although little remembered, exception is that of R. B. Perry, biographer of William James. His last major work, *Realms of Value* (1954), investigates a long list of different values. In building it up he follows the clue that, just as kinds of knowledge can be distinguished by looking at different intellectual or knowledge-seeking institutions, so kinds of value correspond to different institutions offering practical guidance for conduct. The main values he comes up with are moral, political, legal, economic, customary, scientific or intellectual, and aesthetic.

There is an evident bias in Perry's list of favour of the public and cooperative kinds of value. Unless the categories of the economic and the aesthetic are stretched in such a way as to detach them altogether from the institutions in relation to which they were introduced there is no provision in his list for the greater part of the objects of human striving and for the values realized by it to the extent that it is successful. In nearly 500 pages he has nothing, or next to nothing, to say about health, food and drink, sexuality, friendship, or the family.

His bias was to a great extent corrected in the other main treatise that set out to expound the plurality of values. In G. H. von Wright's *The Varieties of Goodness* (1963) the crucial clue is, in accordance with the spirit of its epoch in English-speaking philosophy, rather minutely linguistic. It starts from the modest consideration of the different prepositions that can be attached to the word *good*: a thing or person can be good *at* or good *for* or good *as* something or other.

The kinds of goodness he enumerates are instrumental (as of knives), technical (as of carpenters), medical (as of eyesight), beneficial or utilitarian (as of advice), hedonic (as of a dinner or the weather), eudaemonic (as of the circumstances of life), and moral (as of the characters and acts of human agents). He admits that his list is not exhaustive. It strikes one as also perhaps insufficiently exclusive but I shall not pursue that point here. He distinguishes, persuasively, happiness from welfare, taking the latter to be the good of man, which it is the task of moral action to preserve and promote. Happiness, he says, in a suggestive, but, as he admits, obscure and metaphorical way, is the consummation of welfare. He has nothing to say of aesthetic and intellectual value.

A third exception to the rule of neglect of the plurality of non-moral values was C. I. Lewis, particularly in his *The Ground and Nature of the Right* (1955). He correctly pointed out that, far from being simply moral words, *good*, *right*, and *ought* and their opposites apply to intellectual activities of believing and reasoning as literally and straightforwardly as they do to action. Secondly, they are far from confined to the domain of morality when they are applied to action. 'The field of judgement of right and wrong', he says, 'extends to whatever is subject to human deliberation and calls for decision' (ibid. 9).

In listing the kinds of value Lewis starts from a Kantian list of varieties of right conduct: the technical, the prudential, the moral. The end of technique is the minimally costly realization of some particular good. Prudence aims at maximizing the good of the individual in his life as a whole. Morality is directed towards maximizing the good of all. I believe that to define morality in such terms as these is a mistake, particularly when it is combined with the assumption that morality ought to prevail over prudence where their requirements conflict. For the fact is that they nearly always will. In every situation where we can choose what to do there is always something we *could* do which will augment the good of others at the expense of our own unless we are in the most dejected circumstances of anyone, so it implies that we should always sacrifice our own well-being for the sake of others. But I defer consideration of this topic for the moment.

In Lewis's conception, technique finds means for ends that are inherently valuable, means that are on that account instrumentally valuable. These elements of value contribute to, or where negative presumably detract from, well-being, the systematized good of a life as a whole, and such individual well-beings add up to the good of all.

Inspired, but not dominated, by these three conceptions of the plurality of value, I propose the following list, not as a final account of the matter, but as using each to compensate for the limitations of the others. There is the hedonic value of simple pleasure or enjoyment; the technical value of efficiency in the pursuit of any valuable end; the economic value of material benefit or advantage; the aesthetic value of what satisfies disinterested contemplation (a well-born cousin, perhaps, of hedonic value); the medical or hygienic value of health, physical and mental; the intellectual value of knowledge.

These valued things are particularly, but not necessarily or usually the objects of passions in any sense we could give the term, although any persistent desire is likely to become emotionally intense from time to time. Unless there were elemental or primary values there would be nothing for prudence or for morality to apply to. Hedonic and aesthetic value, as well as medical disvalue—pain and inability to function—are the most elemental values. Technically right action enables them, and, of course, other, secondary values, to be realized. Economically right action is, from one point of view, a form of technically right action, but of a more systematic and comprehensive kind. From another point of view it provides a simple means of getting valuable things without making them. The intellectual value of knowledge is valued for its own sake, as the object of a desire to know which is inadequately described either as curiosity or by Aristotle's term: wonder. Knowledge is also, and more fundamentally, valuable as a means, supplying the causal information needed for technical skill.

It does not matter that the list I have proposed makes no claim to completeness, so long as it is at least representative of the main kinds of value in a way that the earlier lists I have mentioned are not. It is clear what steps need to be taken to improve on it. There is a large body of literature concerned with the rational conduct of life to be consulted in which that enquiry is not only not confined to morality but may be concerned with it only to a small extent. The genre begins with the wisdom components of the scriptures of China, India, and the Jews. It is largely disentangled from religion in the post-Aristotelian philosophers of classical Greece. It reappears in the long sequence of essayists and aphorists from Erasmus, Montaigne, and Bacon, by way of the French *moralistes* and Voltaire, down to Schopenhauer.

III

For a number of reasons it is a mistake to describe these particular values as all being kinds of pleasure, even if books with such titles as *The Major Pleasures of Life* are sources it is sensible to consult in seeking inventories and accounts of them. The first is that pleasure suggests, even if it does not strictly imply, passive enjoyment. Human beings find their most intense and persisting satisfactions in activity; if they are fortunate, indeed, in their work. But work and pleasure are conventionally opposed, as when an immigration official enquires into the purpose of a traveller's visit to a foreign country.

Secondly, there is also an informal association of the same kind between pleasure and bodily enjoyment. That is not to say that the phrase 'pleasures of the flesh' is a pleonasm, but only that it is to these that the mind turns first when pleasure is mentioned. That is no doubt a distortion brought about by religious asceticism. It is a distinction of the same sort as that which leads to the identification of morality with sexual abstinence in unreflective thought and colloquial speech.

Thirdly, and still as a matter of rhetoric more than semantics, the ordinary conception of pleasure is of an enjoyment or satisfaction that is atomic or instantaneous. But most satisfactions or realizations of value are much more systematic than that. Listening to a symphony or eating a good dinner is not ordinarily a sequence of momentary delights whose total value is in the sum of the value of its parts.

Nevertheless something which could, with suitable precautions, be described as pleasure, but which is better described as enjoyment or satisfaction, is the ultimate basis of all value. It is what is crucially present in what I have called the more elemental cases of value: the hedonic, the aesthetic, and the medical. Derivative values—the technical, much of the economic, much of the intellectual—depend on their service as a means to these ends. The 'principles' of prudence and morality, to the extent that they are seen as the harmonious maximization, respectively, of individual and general good, are directed to the realization of no proprietary value of their own, but are applied, as devices of rational selection, to potential values of the elemental type or to values instrumental to them.

Beside morality, then, in human choice and direction of conduct are prudence, like it a procedure for the maximization of prior values, and a great range of specific values and disvalues, varying greatly among themselves as immediate or instrumental, as atomic or systematic, as passive or active, as bodily or mental, as momentary or enduring, and so on. This conception corrects two erroneous pictures of the objects of human wants and efforts. The worse of the two simply identifies all the non-moral values as mere inclinations or desires, aimed at pleasure conceived in the narrowest, most colloquial sense. The second opposes morality to self-interest, taking all particular desires to be self-interested. Neither view is usually affirmed explicitly. But Kant, although he knew better, usually writes as if the first mistaken picture were correct.

IV

Bishop Butler's term for the non-moral, self-related maximizing principle of conduct, *self-love*, is unfortunate. It suggests self-admiration rather than a concern with the interests of the self. Two other terms for what he has in mind are *self-interest* and *prudence*. Neither of them is altogether satisfactory.

The defect of self-interest as a term for the disposition to guide one's choices so as to have the best life possible is that it is connected too closely to the pursuit of competitive satisfactions or values. There are many objects of human desire which are competitive in that their realization or enjoyment by one person inevitably excludes their enjoyment by another. The most obvious cases of this are material possessions and money. But there is also status, since ruling political elites, Olympic teams, titles of nobility, and so forth are inevitably limited in number. Power, to some extent associated with status, is scarce as a matter of logical necessity. It is an asymmetrical relation: if A has a power over B in some respect, then B does not have power in that respect over A. Furthermore power does not amount to much unless it is power over a number of people.

We call someone self-interested if he is predominantly concerned to maximize his competitive satisfactions. But many of the values which people want to realize are non-competitive. Many more are counter-competitive in that the satisfaction of people other than the agent is an essential part of them. The desire for knowledge that leads someone to make new discoveries yields something that he wants and would not have been available to be advantageous or otherwise satisfying to other people unless he had discovered it. There are three qualifications to this thesis, but they are all contingent. The first is that what is discovered may be something that other people do not want to know, not merely in the sense that it does not interest them, but that they wish that it was not known. A prime instance of this kind of thing is scandalous information about some public figure. Perhaps in most such cases more people will want to know than will desire that the fact should not be known, although the desire of the interested majority is likely to be less intense.

A second qualification is that some discoveries confer a competitive advantage on their discoverers: money, reputation, Nobel prizes. A third is that the effort the discoverer puts into his enquiries might have been put into some form of activity even more beneficial to other people. This possibility of subtraction from benevolence is not a very serious one. The discoverer is more likely to have selected as an alternative course of action either some other line of research or else something even more remote from benevolence, although no more hostile to it, like working in his garden or sailing a small boat. But then there is also the chance that he might have chosen to do something malevolent. Work can keep people out of mischief as well as preventing them from doing straightforward public good.

It would be quite inappropriate to describe someone who labours at an engrossing intellectual or artistically creative task as self-interested on that account alone. Further conditions must be satisfied, for example, that he has taken it on only as a means to the acquisition of competitive goods—'money, fame, power and the love of women' in Freud's phrase—or that in carrying it out he has neglected some specific obligations, to his family, perhaps, or his creditors.

It is not merely inappropriate, but absolutely mistaken, to describe as self-interested the action of someone whose purpose in doing it is the satisfaction of someone else. Although universal benevolence, altruism in the fullest sense, is rare, and perhaps non-existent, everyone but a small minority of psychological monsters has a direct interest in the well-being of some people other than himself. As Hume rightly observed our generosity is somewhat confined. The theory of kin selection, by supplying the evolutionary explanation of our concern for those who share our genes, puts this limited instinctive modicum of altruism on a scientific basis. But beyond this there is in most people a measure of what Hume called sympathy. By that he meant a desire, on the whole, and other things being equal, that other people, whoever they may be, should not suffer. There is also acquired or learnt altruism which takes the form of a direct concern for the well-being of people to whom one is not related.

Concern for the welfare of others, or moral action generally, may of course be promoted by self-interest as a means to the agent's individual advantage. Most often, perhaps, that takes the negative form of acting so as not to incur their hostility and the unpleasant consequences to which it may lead. In that case the concern for others is self-interested. But, even if that motive were operative in all of an agent's altruistic conduct to some extent, it would not follow that he was entirely self-interested. Our motives are often mixed.

I am inclined to think that there is an intermediate region between calculating, self-interested altruism and an immediate desire for the well-being of others. This is where an agent forgoes an advantage he would get at their expense because of what taking it would do to his self-respect or, again, where he is driven to act in such a way by feelings of guilt. But, although these sorts of case show concern with the self, rather than others, they are not directed towards a competitive advantage and could not reasonably be called instances of self-interested conduct.

V

Prudence is a better word than self-interest for the disposition to pursue the greatest good for oneself in one's life as a whole or, as one might put it, to pursue a good life by rational means. Its fault is a certain negative, defeatist quality. It implies a strategy of minimizing losses rather than of maximizing gains, of caution and wariness, rather than adventure or enterprise. The rationality it enjoys is limited in the way that economic rationality is limited. A man may feel that his life is less good than it might have been if he had given more of his attention to listening to serious music. In criticizing his current conception of a good life for himself he is not accusing himself of imprudence. Prudence, as we ordinarily understand it, is a business of resolute avoidance of harm. It is also on the opposite side to spontaneity, presumably on the ground that more surprises are unpleasant than agreeable.

Nevertheless prudence is well-established, much less misleading than self-interest as a name for the rational pursuit of a good life by an individual, and it does apply well enough to the style of consideration an agent would give, if rational, to the major decisions of life, those on which his long-run happiness or well-being depend: of what career to follow, of whom to marry, of where to live. So I shall continue to use it and the adjective *prudential*, with the added warning that it is not to be interpreted in a purely negative sense.

The intellectual aspect of that concern with rational pursuit of a good life whose motivational aspect is prudence is wisdom, the common subject matter of the books which I suggested earlier as a source for a fuller list of the varieties of value than I had provided. More precisely it is worldly wisdom or *Lebensweisheit*. That, of course, is what most unsophisticated people mean by the word *philosophy*. The adverb *worldly*, often put in front of *wisdom*, tends to invest the wisdom referred to with a morally questionable or disreputable air, as if it were inevitably cynical. However it was probably put there in the first place to distinguish it from the sort of wisdom that is concerned with what, if anything, happens to us after death.

VI

So far I have been arguing that the non-moral ends of action cannot be treated as the objects of an undifferentiated mass of desires nor, collectively, as the objects of self-interest. Desires for specific things differ in many ways. Some of them are for competitive goods, but others are not. Desires for competitive goods are, no doubt, self-interested, but self-interest as a disposition is not simply having and acting on such desires. Every time I eat something I am taking out of circulation something someone else hungrier than I might have eaten. Self-interestedness, as a trait of character, is a relative notion, like tallness. To be self-interested is to be more than usually indifferent to the claims of others to the objects of one's competitive desires.

Other desires are for non-competitive objects; others again for counter-competitive ones. Among these last are those desires for the well-being of others which are among our motives for moral conduct. As such, along with other elemental incentives, like hunger, sexual appetite, curiosity, taste for the beauty of nature, and so on, they help to constitute the raw material on which prudence or practical wisdom operates to arrive at the largest possible system of harmonious satisfactions.

What this appears to imply is that prudence is ultimately sovereign over morality, since part of the rational conduct of life is a matter of deciding what part morality shall play in it, to what extent the various desires which impel us to moral action should be indulged. (Prudence is in addition *epistemically prior* to morality, to the extent that morality is a matter of protecting and promoting the well-being of others, since to pursue the well-being of others we have to know in what it consists, what, as the sometimes insincere saying goes, their best interests are. But that is another matter.)

In accepting the implication of the sovereignty of prudence or wisdom over morality it seems that I am in direct collision with the widespread conviction that moral reasons for conduct override all other claims, or, more extremely, that its overridingness is what makes a reason for action moral. There are obvious difficulties with the theory of overridingness. What *in fact* overrides other reasons for action in cases of conflict is quite commonly not supposed, by either the agent or anyone else, to be the moral element in the conflict. But if the overridingness of the moral is its being *right that it should* override then the question is: what sort of *should* is this? If it is a moral *should*, the thesis is empty. It must be, then, a prudential *should* and, to the extent that the thesis is defensible, it is. The question *why should I be moral?* is a question as to the place of morality in the good life rationally pursued. Self-interest and morality are calculated to come into conflict. But since prudence and self-interest are far from the same thing, prudence can enjoin abstention from self-interest, and it does.

But does it enjoin complete abstention? Many theories of morality, intentionally or not, imply what could be called moral imperialism or moral totalitarianism. By that I mean the view that in every situation of choice there is something the agent morally ought to do, from which it follows that every other choice in that situation would be morally wrong. Ordinary utilitarianism, and any unguarded consequentialist theory, has this implication when it proclaims that one ought always to do that which contributes most to the general happiness or to the good of all.

On the reasonable assumption that the most comprehensive account of the goal of moral action is the increase of the general good and the reduction of its opposite, it becomes necessary, if this excessive moralism is to be contained, to recognize distinctions within morality. I suggest that, first of all, there is a field of moral obligation proper, which requires us not to act so as to harm or cause suffering to others. Here are to be found the almost universally recognized rules which forbid killing and injuring others, stealing from them, deceiving and defaming them. It also includes the keeping of promises. The expectations and plans of others depend on our honouring our undertakings to them. If we do not harm will generally ensue to them.

Secondly, there is the field of charity, in which the aim is to reduce or prevent by our action harm to others that has not been caused by us, but by natural causes or the actions of yet other human beings. Here, as in the first field, the aim is negative, the elimination of harm or suffering. But the requirements of charity are open-ended. As far as a single human agent is concerned there is no limit to the opportunities he is presented with of charitable action. It is probably correct that no one has ever seized all the opportunities for charitable conduct that it was practically possible for him to take, themselves only a small part of those it was conceivable for him to respond to. Of course people are charitable to markedly different extents. The more charitable are more morally admirable than the less. But the non-charitable are not wicked or, at any rate, not in the way or to the extent that those who fail in their duty are.

Thirdly, there is action directed towards the positive increase of the general good, of well-being or happiness. This is morally admirable so far as it is motivated by a direct concern for human welfare. When it is, it is neither a matter of obligation, nor a form of charity; it should be called, rather, generosity or, perhaps, benevolence. The opportunities for the exercise of generosity are as boundless as those of charity. If it, as well, is included in the scope of duty or obligation, as it is by most consequentialist theories of morals, even if inadvertently, a quite unacceptable concept of morality is implied. As Popper has common-sensically observed, we surely do not feel that there is any moral claim on us to augment the happiness of those who are already reasonably content. It is more important to concentrate our concern for others on cases where we can reduce suffering.

Most positive contributions to the general well-being are probably motivated not by a general concern for the greater well-being of mankind but by impulses of personal affection for family and friends, at the smaller end of the scale, and by such factors as ambition, the love of knowledge, or the desire for artistic expression at the larger end.

I am proposing as rational a conception of morality which is both finite and negative, at least in its primary part, the domain of obligation. It is negative, but not finite, in its secondary part, the domain of charity. It is rational because it takes account of the differences both of importance and of practicability of the two kinds of requirement of conduct. An indication of the higher importance of obligation is that the legal systems of all politically organized societies include the enforcement of the rules of duty as their primary constituent.

It is a mistake to run obligation and charity together since it is to ask too much. By treating what it is reasonable to insist on with what it is reasonable only to encourage, it tends to weaken the more important claims of obligation. By setting an unreasonably high standard of conduct it is calculated to bring about inadequate performance over the whole range of morally desirable conduct.

The need for some sort of distinction along these lines has long been evident to those engaged in practical moral thinking of a reflective kind. Catholic moral theology, from an early stage of its history, accepted the idea of supererogation, the doing of morally good deeds beyond the call of duty. That admission recognized that most human beings would not adopt morality as a vocation. To absorb the full claims of charity into the domain of the obligations one recognizes is to aspire to sainthood. The first Christians, convinced that the destruction of the world was imminent, did have this aspiration. So, from time to time, have various Protestant groups. Moral utopianism, however, is hard to sustain when the millennium obstinately fails to arrive.

But a distinction between the morally essential and the morally optional is seldom to be found in philosophical treatments of morality. Views which imply that there is no distinction are embraced without awareness of what they entail.

On the other hand, the inclusive, non-finite view is ultimately a necessary consequence of the conception of human nature embodied in supernaturalist religion. If human beings are really immortal rational souls in temporary association with desiring bodies, it is the welfare of the soul that must determine the character of a good life and that will be one in which moral claims of obligation and charity prevail over all others. The acceptance of supererogation by the church is a makeshift or compromise, a reluctant accommodation to human moral weakness. It is altogether more at home in a secular ethics.

In claiming that only the primary, strictly obligatory part of morals—not harming others and keeping one's promises to them—is essential and compulsory it may seem that I have run into inconsistency. For did I not say that morality is subject to prudence, rather than the other way round? But primary morality is that part of morality as a whole, I should contend, that prudence endorses as overriding other ends of conduct and motives directed towards those ends. To follow it is to satisfy elemental impulses of our nature. It is also desired as enabling us to be the kind of person we want to be. Furthermore it is prudent, in the narrowest, calculating sense, in two ways. It preserves us from the hostility of others and it contributes to the maintenance of social peace and of practices that are indispensable for effective human cooperation.

We should not think of morality as somehow uniquely imposing obligations *ab extra* on unregenerate human nature. Exactly analogous conflicts between what we unreflectively want to do and what we realize would, on rational consideration, be best for us to do crop up in other domains of conduct. There is nothing particularly moral about our struggles to resist the temptation provided by delicious but fattening food; by the greater easiness of not bothering to fix the leaky tap; by the pleasure of spending money it would be more prudent to save.

VII

I have been arguing that morality is not the same thing as the good life, even if its primary part is an essential constituent of the good life and its secondary, charitable, part is a desirable constituent of such a life, to be fostered by moral education, but not to the extent of obliterating all other human purposes. I have represented our impulses to dutiful and charitable action as part of ordinary, earthly human nature and not tied up with some quite distinct, and, indeed, opposed, supernatural ingredient in our constitution. I have claimed, too, that most positive good is secured by action in which moral motivation plays little or no part. I have assumed that there must be non-moral goods to give morality, as a second-order mode of determining action, a content, namely the desired ends of others which it is the task of morality to promote, in its negative way.

I began from the fact that, apart from aesthetics, morality is the only major field of practical thinking which has received serious and systematic attention from philosophers. I shall finish by discussing two bad consequences which follow from this narrowness of view. It should, perhaps, be added that these are, in themselves, intellectually bad, although like other intellectual mistakes, they may indirectly have morally bad consequences as well, may lead to avoidable harm to people other than the mistaken theorists.

The first of these bad results is that a number of areas of first-order reflection about practice are insufficiently investigated. The most important of them are the technical, the economic, and the medical. There are large bodies of doctrine about the ways in which to pursue efficiency, economic advantage, and health. But the general assumption prevails that there is nothing problematic about these ends themselves. The usual assumption is that efficiency, economic benefit, health, and other non-moral values are entirely uncontroversial and objective. It is assumed that we are all agreed in our criteria of these values and that we can unquestioningly set about the discovery of rules which order actions as better or worse means of realizing them. That assumption is questionable.

Consider the case of health. It is an interesting and somewhat suspect fact that textbooks of pathology tend to define disease or illness, the lack of health, in statistical terms. They identify it as a condition of body or mind that deviates from the average to a pronounced degree. As it turns out they do not adhere to this principle. Pathologists do not regard being two metres tall or having red hair, both properties of a small minority of the human race, as forms of illness. More fundamentally, they do not answer the question: why should the medical profession strive to bring everyone into much the same bodily and mental condition as everyone else? To the extent that they are right to do so it is precisely to the extent to which being in the average condition is one that people generally want to be in or enjoy being in or that leads to persisting states of that kind.

But people's wants and satisfactions vary. One person's health could be another person's illness. There is, plainly, room for dispute. So is there in matters of efficiency and economic benefit. A precise and conclusive procedure can be imposed to settle questions about them. But, like the criterion of statistical normality in the case of health and sickness, this smothers the contestable nature of the value in question rather than eliminates it.

To make this point about health, efficiency, and so on is not to take a sceptical attitude towards medical and technical judgements. There is possibility of dispute here, but it is comparatively marginal. The range of relevant factors is sharply limited: to pain, dysfunction, and death in the medical case, to time and cost in the technical case. That consideration leads into the second bad consequence of the obsession with morality at the expense of other fields of practice.

Ethical theorists, in emphasizing the distinction between morality and the undifferentiated remainder of forms of practice, and particularly by detaching moral motivation from ordinary human nature, from desires and emotions, have exaggerated beyond reason the difference between them as matters of knowledge or justified belief. For the past half-century ethical theory in the English-speaking world has been dominated by the non-cognitivist account of moral convictions and utterances which takes them not, as they seem to be, as statements, true or false, reasonable or unreasonable, but as interjections or imperatives.

That point of view draws strength from the elevated kind of aesthetics which is regarded as philosophically serious. If the humbler aesthetics of food and clothes and furniture and scenery had been the object of comparison the result would have been different. For here there is much less disagreement than there is about art, particularly about art that has been recently created and to which people have not had time to become accustomed. And even more so if the comparison had been with seriously reflected on technical, economic, or medical value. The theorists' obsession with morality, then, both deprives other forms of practical thinking of the philosophical attention they deserve, and also leads to radical misunderstanding in moral philosophy itself.

17

The Human Animal

1. Introductory

In the century and a quarter since Darwin's *Origin of Species* came out in 1859 man's conception of the relation of his own species to others in the animal kingdom has greatly changed. The progress and effective popularization of zoology, on the one hand, particularly of work on animal intelligence and behaviour, and the decline of supernatural religion, on the other, have loosened the hold of the idea that there is an absolute and fundamental difference in kind between animals and human beings.

Human beings take an overwhelmingly large place in our conception of the world in which we live. In all sorts of ways we rely on and make use of animals, treating them in a manner that is morally open to serious question. But, for most of us, our direct relationships with animals are confined to those we make pets and companions of and, by and large, treat reasonably well. In stockyards and laboratories much less agreeable conditions prevail. A memorable account of this fearful belowstairs or engine room is given in Peter Singer's *Animal Liberation*.

Our lack of moral consideration for animals is underpinned by a variety of questionable beliefs about the nature of the differences between animals and men. It is to these that I address myself, arguing, generally, that there are really no hard and fast distinctions between the minds or reasons or wills or moral capacities or qualifications for direct moral consideration between the two. I return at the end to the moral question and finish on a doubtful note, questioning the capacity of our habitual attitudes towards the permissible treatment of animals to withstand rational investigation.

When we talk conversationally about animals, what we usually have in mind are mammals, the dramatis personae of children's stories. Throughout most of the history of philosophy the difference between men and animals has been stressed, indeed to a very great extent simply taken for granted. For most philosophers, as for most unreflective people, the great division of the concrete constituents of the world is that between persons and things.

The first element of spiritual (as distinct from technical and institutional) culture, namely religion, has, at any rate in its higher forms, been the great social enforcer of this particular dualism. Judaism, Christianity, and Mohammedanism, the great monotheistic religions, have endorsed it without qualification. In religions in which reincarnation is recognized, above all in Hinduism, change from animal to human and from human to animal at turning points in the sequence of lives is accepted, as it is also by comparatively minor mystery sects such as Pythagoreans, Orphics, and Gnostics. In Egyptian religion and Hinduism there are animal gods, or, some would say, gods in animal form.

As human history has progressed, the importance and pervasiveness of human relationships with animals have steadily diminished. The lives of hunters are completely bound up with those of animals; so, in a different—in some respects more intimate—way are the lives of pastoralists and ploughmen. On the other hand, animals have only a precarious foothold in the urban settlements in which civilized men have more and more come to congregate. But the conviction of an impermeable barrier between human and animal prevailed long before serious urbanization.

A somewhat ambiguous evidence of the hold of the distinction on the human mind is to be found in what is often now seen as the most important ingredient in the humanity of human beings: grammar. First of all, there is the distinction between personal pronouns and the impersonal 'it'. Then, associated with it, is the practice of bestowing proper names on human beings and only very fitfully and infrequently on animals. However, in uneducated speech anything whatever—a car, a spade, a cat, a snake—may be referred to as 'he' or 'she'. Only the weather remains obstinately 'it', an implicit but perfectly correct recognition of the fact that in 'it is raining' the word *it* is not used referentially, as is shown by the obvious impropriety of the response '*what* is?' Furthermore, while some animals are given proper names, people are often referred to, even addressed, in general terms: 'Boy', 'Waiter', 'Nurse'.

Anthropism, as I shall call the idea that the most fundamental distinction between the concrete contents of time and space is that between human beings and everything else, is comparable to an idea most people tend to have from time to time about themselves: that they are utterly distinct from all other human beings, who are themselves, by and large, pretty much like each other. We know that that kind of instinctive metaphysical egoism is an illusion whenever we look back over our own pasts in memory, in a home movie or photograph album, or in attending to the conceptions of us formed by others. Nevertheless, when so to speak *inside* our own lives, we find it hard to resist the notion that we are, individually, unique. Something comparable, some peculiarity of perspective seems to be at work in anthropism.

The findings of zoology and anthropology, articulated in an evolutionary manner, can be drawn on to loosen its hold upon us. The main point is that, although there are breaks in the evolutionary narrative as one species is followed by another, the overall sequence is continuous. Men are linked to other primates as the latter are to the prosimians from whom they evolved. What is more, there is no clear boundary between the men we are today and our predecessors, on the other side of which all are nonhuman. I think it is fair to say that anthropologists neither agree very precisely as to where the line between mere anthropoids or hominids and men should be drawn nor do they think it of any great importance to decide the issue. Most would say that *Homo erectus* is a man, some that only with *Homo sapiens* do we get true man. It is generally agreed that our species, the supplanter of Neanderthal man, *Homo sapiens sapiens*, appeared on the earth 50,000 years ago.

The continuity of men and animals is no doubt most pronounced and incontestable in their anatomies. In a dim light and at a distance an ape and a hairy man are easily confused. An ape is very much more like a man than it is like a lynx or a turtle or a tuna, to confine the comparison to animals of the same order of magnitude. Continuity is still present when we turn from anatomy to behaviour. Animals use tools; creatures as marginally human as *Homo habilis* seem to have made tools; *Homo erectus* certainly did. Our species is marked off by a further step forward: we began the use of tools to make tools. Most mammals are social, as are animals of many other classes. Cooperative hunting, the protective and educative mammalian family, division of labour, a hierarchy of dominance and submission, are all to be found in animal species that everyone would agree are nonhuman. What is peculiar to man is what I have called spiritual culture: religion (first seen in the burial practices of the Neanderthalers), art (the invention of our own species 20,000 or 30,000 years ago), writing (in the wake of the first development of urban living), and science.

The older varieties of reflective anthropism took man's spiritual culture to be the outward expression of his fundamental distinguishing mark: the soul. At the opposite extreme of the spectrum of beliefs, the Marxist takes technical culture, which, along with natural resources, constitutes the 'conditions of production', to be an essential factor in the socio-economic basis of human existence, indeed to be the dynamically crucial one. What I have called institutional culture is one aspect of the superstructure whose nature is determined by the socio-economic basis. The other is the realm of 'ideas and beliefs', of ideology or, in my terminology, spiritual culture. The Marxist, taking spiritual culture to be dependent and epiphenomenal, a mere by-product of the serious productive business of society, does not make it the defining characteristic of mankind. He finds that characteristic in technical culture, in the consciously designed production of the necessities of life with tools that man has himself made.

A number of distinct tendencies in contemporary thought converge on the idea that the ultimate distinguishing mark of man is his mastery of language. There are two difficulties about its application. One is that there is no agreed way of deciding what makes a method of communication into a language proper. The other is that we have no clear idea when what would generally be held to be truly linguistic communication began. Certainly no nonhuman animal now living communicates linguistically so far as we know. We have no idea how many of our extinct forebears did.

But before confronting the question directly of how definite and how important the distinction between humans and nonhuman animals is (in the light of the evident physical, psychological, and social continuities between them), it will be as well to supplement the historical account of their evolution with a survey of the very varied and often very close relations between them.

2. The Relations between Men and Animals

Animals pay very little attention to fellow animals of other species except when they hope to make a meal of them or fear that they will be a meal for them. Men watch birds, but birds largely ignore men unless they get worryingly near. Special concerns interest them in worms and cats; with birds of other species they indifferently coexist.

But man, the most curious and most omnivorous of creatures, beside the theoretical concern of zoology with absolutely all animals, has a variety of practical concerns with a great many of them. He eats far more kinds of them than the members of any animal species do: mammals, of course, as well as birds, fish, and crustaceans. He comes into possession of them by hunting and by rearing. He uses some animals—most conspicuously dogs and falcons—to help him in hunting; dogs, again, assist him in the control of his flocks of domesticated animals. Dogs and cats help him to get rid of the rats and other nuisances who make off with the crops he has ploughed for and harvested with oxen, horses, or camels.

Man does not kill animals merely to eat them (or to avoid being eaten by them) as other animals do. He uses their hides for all sorts of purposes, from clothing and containers to the making of tents, and, less lethally, drinks their milk, or turns it into butter and cheese, and clips their wool to make clothes and blankets. A particularly important aspect of the Neolithic revolution that brought in farming was the use of strong animals as energy sources: to pull loads, to draw ploughs, and, in due course, to carry men themselves about when hunting, fighting, on trading voyages, nomadically travelling to new pasture, herding stock, emigrating, or simply making social visits.

Until the domestication of dogs inaugurated the great Neolithic step forward into agriculture, man's relations with animals were distant and, although often respectful, generally hostile. Men hunted animals in order to eat them and to make themselves safe from them. Their dependence on animal flesh gave them an interest in the biological success of its suppliers, in an abundance of game. The great cave paintings of France and Spain 20,000 years ago are widely supposed to have played a part in magical ceremonies designed to ensure the fertility of the objects of the chase, and, perhaps, to express admiration for their powers, even to propitiate them for the injuries done to them.

In the long hunting period of human history—something like 99 per cent of its duration so far—men had to know a good deal about animals, about how they behave and what could be done with them. But only in the few thousand years of agriculture, which lasted until the nineteenth century in Europe and is still the dominant form of life in many places, have men and animals been intimately involved. By the time men had the skill and occasion to build permanent dwellings, there were animals trained to be welcome members of the family circle and, in the routine of milking, herding, feeding, and ploughing, men were occupied with them throughout the working day.

At this stage of human development the purely practical use of animals by men merges into a companionable one. A hunter and his dog, a falconer and his hawk, will evolve a measure of mutual trust and affection from their collaboration in a common purpose. Similarly the regularity of the relationship between a ploughman and his team, a mahout and his elephant, or a rider and his mount will take on the individualized quality of intimate human relationships. The grief at such an animal collaborator's death will be something more than the distress appropriate to a major economic misfortune; it will also be sadness at the loss of a friend. Even the less individualized members of a herd of cattle, always driven or milked as a group, and probably destined for slaughter in the end, will evoke warm feelings by their mildness and amenability.

It cannot have been long after men had settled homes and the habit of keeping animals in them that the purely companionable keeping of animals, as pets, began. It is right that the first animal to be domesticated should still be man's supreme animal companion. The dog's unrivalled combination of friendliness and intelligence, his freedom from suspicion and resentment, his sublime suggestibility, the intensely individual quality of his affection together equip him outstandingly for his familiar role in human life. The cat is too private and independent, the horse too nervous and, because of his size, too cumbrous and inconvenient, to offer serious competition. The power of men to make something out of practically nothing is shown in some of the less responsive animals they show affection to, or at least an interest in: white mice, goldfish, turtles, canaries, rabbits, gerbils, and stick insects.

The industrialization of the world has not stopped short of agriculture. In the factory farm where cows are mechanically milked or battery chickens pass their lives in small cages under artificial light, the individual, more or less personal relation that prevailed between men and animals in the agriculture of the past is extinguished. Apart from the keeping of pets and the purely spectatorial business of visiting zoos, there are few activities left in which men and animals come together: hunting for sport, riding for exercise. Man's ingenuity has created an environment for him in which he need have nothing to do with animals at all. Nutritionists warn him against animal flesh for its high content of cholesterol and calories. His clothing is increasingly the product of industrial chemistry. Bureaucratic frenzies about hygiene exclude animals from more and more places. Vegetarians and conservationists, concerned for the well-being of animals, seek to keep them out of men's meals and region of influence. For our good and theirs, it seems, we must have as little to do with one another as possible.

Men's ideas about animals, beyond the practical lore of the farmer or trainer and the scientific findings of the zoologist and the veterinarian, both of which are none too well known professional specialisms, take an imaginative form in certain religions (and in aspects of most religions), in art and literature, and in a widely spread deposit of common assumption and belief, a compound of proverbial or symbolic wisdom and illusion.

We must derive our conceptions of the earliest religions of mankind, first, from the religions of people still living on the earth who share the Upper Palaeolithic culture of the first men we have reason to suppose to have been religious and, second, from such evidences as we can exhume that are reasonably susceptible of religious interpretation. The most important social relic in still-existing primitive societies of a large place for animals in religion is totemism. A totem is usually an animal, and it serves as a symbol for a group or individual. In its group form, totemism, by clubbing people together, helps to unify society. But there is more to it than its socially functional cash value. In the light of the cave paintings of men who, 20,000 years ago, had reached a stage of development comparable to that of the totemic aborigines of Australia, we may infer that it derives from some kind of religion in which animals were worshipped.

Once we arrive at the religions of civilized mankind, we are met at the beginning with the gods of Egypt. These are notable for being exceedingly numerous and for being, for the most part, in more or less animal form, animal-headed, at least. Experts in the field are reluctant to suppose that this theriomorphism about the gods amounted to theriolatry, the worship of animals. Certainly to conceive the objects of worship in animal form is not in itself the worship of animals. But to separate the two definitely it is necessary to claim that the Egyptians thought of the gods as beings, essentially human or personal in nature, who chose to dress up or present themselves in the form of animals. It may well be doubted whether, in terms of the conceptions available to them, the ancient Egyptians were able to distinguish between seeing the gods as persons in the form of animals or as animals with the mental attributes of persons.

Osiris, the suffering god, is the most human member of the Egyptian pantheon. Horus is usually a falcon, Set a pig, Anubis a jackal, Hathor a cow, Bastet a cat. The only comparably animalistic major religion is Hinduism. Not only does it recognize a host of animal gods, its doctrine of reincarnation allows the soul, on the death of a human body it has been inhabiting, to enter into the body of an animal. However, since the passage of the soul from a human to an animal body is conceived as a punishment, there is a tension between this idea and the notion that some gods—inevitably conceived as being higher than man—are really animals.

The series of Mesopotamian religions whose high god is Marduk or Bel seem to have conceived him and his fellow deities as essentially human—from some points of view, a little all too human, perhaps. And, as was mentioned before, the religion of the Hebrews, the first of the great monotheistic religions, has always been resolutely anthropomorphic. We read in the first chapter of Genesis: 'God said, Let us make man in our image, after our likeness.' Soon after, the man thus created is adjured to set himself up as a despot over all species: 'have dominion over the fish of the sea, and over the fowl of the air, and over every living thing that moveth upon the earth'. The devil appears to Adam in the guise of a serpent.

On the whole the Old Testament displays an unrelenting hostility to animals. The dove who brought the olive branch to the ark is not unsympathetic, and the ravens who fed Elijah served an approved purpose. But the more usual tone is that of Goliath's remark to David: 'am I a dog that thou comest to me with staves?' or 'is thy servant a dog that he should do such a thing?' As for Nebuchadnezzar, on going mad, 'his dwelling shall be with the beasts of the field'. At least Balaam's ass is allowed to complain about the way in which he is treated, but he does not get an apology.

The New Testament is not much better. Its most memorable animal story is that of the Gadarene swine. It is extraordinary that in this vast compilation of the literature of a pastoral people there should be no sympathetic account of a relationship between a human being and an animal. Only in metaphor are animals presented in an agreeable light. There a literary convention serves to keep them at a distance from us, safely immured in a kind of zoo by a figure of speech. Repelled withdrawal prevails wherever animals are described as interacting with human beings.

Christianity, we may conclude, imposed anthropism on Western man. It has been assisted in the task by a leading tradition in philosophy: the exorbitant dualism of mind and body affirmed by Plato, which was reanimated in the early modern period by Descartes and is still extremely lively today in the thought of a variety of philosophers who agree that man, and man alone, is not a proper subject for science. Between Plato and Descartes there was, for five hundred years, a strong countervailing force in the scholastic articulation of Christianity in terms of the philosophy of Aristotle, who maintained the continuity between men and animals. Between Descartes and the most recent revival of dualism lies Darwin's doctrine of evolution, which sees all living things as part of one family.

Anthropism is not only an error about 'our' place in nature, as will be argued later. It is also, perhaps, in conflict with our nature. An older and better founded conception of the continuity between men and animals shows itself in all sorts of ways in which animals have been represented as persons, as beings with experiences and temperaments in many respects like our own.

The most prominent of these is literature, in many of what may be felt to be its less central manifestations. Folktales and fairy tales abound with intelligent and talking animals. These are nowadays largely read by children, apart from those whose business it is to study them professionally. Most modern books in which personified animals figure are of this comparatively undifferentiated kind: *The Wind in the Willows*, *The Just So Stories*, the stories of Beatrix Potter. In them, animals are represented in their normal surroundings, engaged to a considerable extent in activities natural to the kinds of animals involved. Mr Toad lives along a riverbank, Squirrel Nutkin in a wood. The animals, although personified, are not detached from their natural setting.

Two distinct forms of development from that kind of story move in very different directions. The first is that of the fable, begun by Aesop, at its best in La Fontaine and Krylov, where the animals are no more than symbols for certain types of human being, in which an alleged characteristic of a kind of animal is used to pass moral comments on the same characteristic as present, or over-present, in human life. The second is the novel of attempted naturalistic empathy with animals, such as Henry Williamson's *Tarka the Otter* or Richard Adams's *Watership Down*, or, to take older examples, Kipling's *Jungle Books*, *Jock of the Bushveld*, and the stories of Ernest Thompson Seton.

Unless they are sophisticated fables, serving a satirical purpose, and having no serious implication whatever about the kinds of animals that ostensibly figure in them, animal stories draw on a large submerged mass of conventional assumptions about the nature and leading traits of character of the animals they mention. In the empathetic books there is an attempt to represent animals as they in fact are. But in most nonfabulous, nonsatirical fiction about animals, the assumptions about the characteristics of animals are very often profoundly mistaken.

The wolf, in common belief and animal stories alike, is viewed as a direct danger to human life. Farley Mowat, in his *Never Cry Wolf*, tried to correct this gross misapprehension which has led to efforts at extermination entirely out of proportion to the dangers involved. Wolves can, indeed, be a nuisance by preying on animals men wish to eat themselves, but evidence of their attacking human beings is exceedingly hard to find. Man's intimate relationship with domestic animals has given him reasonably accurate notions of what they are like. About wild animals he is, for the most part, grossly misinformed.

The extent of his misinformation is entertainingly set out by Boyce Rensberger in his *The Cult of the Wild* (1977). Lions are not particularly noble. They do not kill only for food. Like lesser cats they often kill slowly. (Wild dogs kill much more quickly.) They are spongers, eager to live off the kills of others. They are lazy; females do most of the work of hunting. Cubs are often left to starve. Fights between lions do not end in the rational capitulation Konrad Lorenz observed in dogs; they often fight to the death.

Wolves are highly sociable animals who are so averse to fighting that they will go to great lengths to avoid it. With them the Lorenzian machinery of submission works and preserves peaceable social cohesion. The few authenticated stories of wolves attacking humans almost certainly involve wolves with rabies. Most of the animals they attack withstand or escape them.

The common attitude to the gorilla as the most extreme incarnation of aggression and violence is equally wide of the mark. Gorillas are shy, timid, easily put to flight. As for their alleged sexual excessiveness, male gorillas have very small genitals and are the least sexually active of primates. They spend most of their time pottering around in pursuit of vegetable matter to eat.

Elephants are, indeed, highly intelligent animals. They live in complex matriarchal societies. When there is trouble males are the first to run away. They live in families for the same reason that we do, because of a long period of infant dependency in which knowledge and skill are passed on. Elephants are profoundly affected by the death of their relations.

Hyenas are much less given to scavenging than lions and kill most of what they eat, a fact long obscured by the hyena's practice of hunting at night. They are, indeed, particularly gifted hunters and are helped in this by a social order that is at once sophisticated and companionable. Unlike lions they kill quickly and dine politely.

Bears, especially brown bears, are the carnivores most directly dangerous to man in the parts of the world they inhabit. Grizzlies are very dangerous but do much less damage than black bears, which are far more numerous. Dolphins, although they can learn tricks and, like parrots, are excellent mimics, are not really all that intelligent. The altruism they display in coming to the rescue of injured members of their species is by no means peculiar to them. The mechanism of kin selection has established it as well among elephants, baboons, and wild dogs.

Conservationist enthusiasm, encouraged by the teachings of Lorenz, has fostered the idea that man is uniquely aggressive, that, as is sometimes said, he is the only creature that kills for other reasons than self-defence and food. In fact, as E. O. Wilson observes, 'Murder is far more common and hence "normal" in many vertebrate species than in man.' The fact that the tide of informed opinion has completely reversed itself in the twenty years since Lorenz's ideas were first generally available shows how limited the development of the scientific study of animal behaviour is.

It was pointed out earlier that during the vastly greater part of the duration of the human species so far, the period of hunting and gathering, men's relations to animals were important but distant. Only in the agricultural epoch did the relations between them become close. But, even then, close relations were confined to domesticated animals. Wild animals were, if anything, remoter than ever. Men's ideas about horses and cows, dogs and cats, became reasonable enough once these animals had been domesticated. But the earlier fear of wild animals persisted in its error-fostering role, even if it was no longer intensified by anxiety about there being enough wild animals around for men to hunt and feed on.

Misconceptions of animal nature have been at least partly redeemed by aesthetic benefits in the visual arts. Kenneth Clark's casual but typically elegant essay that introduces the fine reproductions in *Animals and Men* (1977) runs through the main motives underlying the human interest in animals as it reveals itself in art. Clark lists fear, admiration (as in cave paintings), greed, cruelty (as in the bullfight and its celebrators in paint, Goya and Picasso), and love. Animals are prominent in ancient and classical art. But what I have called Christian anthropism excluded all but a few species picked out as religious emblems—lion, fox, eagle—from most medieval art. Leonardo's concern was formal rather than emotional. Only with Titian and Veronese are animals regular features of the human scene; they are not to be found in the work of Michelangelo and Raphael. It is the strength and energy of animals that usually attract the painter's eye. But some are concerned with animals as living things, not as visible structures: Dürer, Stubbs, and Bewick. With Landseer, and others in the nineteenth century, that measure of sympathy topples over into sentimental anthropomorphism.

3. Are Men Really Animals?

As things stand colloquially the correct answer to the question whether men are really animals is very simple. It is no. In ordinary conversation we use the word *animal* to distinguish from men those living things that can move themselves about and are not men. What is that moving around in the next room, crashing about in the undergrowth, disappearing over the skyline—a man or an animal? we ask. The two possibilities are taken to be mutually exclusive. Animal food is not appropriate for human consumption. Animal acts on the stage or at the circus must involve nonhuman beings. Remarks like *he prefers animals to men* or *they were behaving like animals*, phrases like *animal trainer* or *research animal*, would make no sense unless the fields of application of *man* and *animal* were distinct.

Those who say that men are really animals are not unaware of this fairly trivial, lexicographical fact. The first sentence of Mary Midgley's admirable *Beast and Man* is 'We are not just rather like animals; we *are* animals.' But, of course, not only does she understand the everyday and exclusive use of the two words perfectly well, she also adheres to it herself with the laudable purpose of being readily intelligible and of avoiding the cumbrous expression *other animals* to which her bold initial proclamation would appear to commit her.

A moderately unhelpful move at this point is to circumvent the collision between the two points of view by saying that it is simply the result of the word's having two different senses, an everyday one and a technical, zoological one. A familiar comparable case is that of the word *fish*. Most people are inclined to describe as fish any living creature whose usual habitat is the water. But many of them realize that those who have given most attention to the denizens of the water deny that whales are fish, although whales live in the sea. It is natural to acknowledge this fact by saying that although whales are often called fish, they are not *really* fish. A special authority is given to the technical sense of the word. It may be convenient for conversational purposes to call all water dwellers *fish*, but it is admitted that this is a formally defective way of speaking.

In the fish case, no one who is aware of the technical concept is much disposed to question its superiority to its everyday competitor. Apart from the single feature of their common habitat, whales have much less in common with sharks or cod than they do with elephants and cows. Whales, like the latter, give birth to live young, not eggs; they breathe air; they are warm-blooded. The superiority of the technical concept is admitted without protest because there is nothing much at stake. It incorporates a large number of important, if not immediately obvious, similarities between whales and other mammals, while the everyday concept takes note of a single, obvious likeness. The first is richer; it tells you more about something it is correctly applied to than the everyday concept does.

That peaceful state of affairs does not prevail in the case of *animal* and *man*. There is an impulse to say that men really are animals and a contrary one to say that they are not. It is not a case where the superior authority of a technical over an everyday sense is contentedly admitted. Nor, again, is it a case where two different senses can be allowed to coexist without a claim being made for the primacy of either, as is suggested by the move I described as unhelpful a little while ago. That kind of placid pluralism is to be found among those who do and do not take wildflowers to be flowers, admirals to be sailors, or library steps to be ladders. The animal and man case is more like disagreement as to whether or not Anglican clergymen are priests. Obviously they are not Catholic priests, but those combative Catholics who doubt the validity of Anglican orders would deny that they are really priests at all.

Modern studies of animal behaviour have indirectly illuminated one factor that may have contributed to the refusal to let the two senses peacefully coexist or to admit the superiority of the technical sense, in other words to an insistence that men are really not animals. Colloquially to describe someone as an animal or as behaving like one is to dispraise him for grossness. Much the same is true of the older synonyms for *animal*: *brute* and *beast*. To be brutal is to be cruel; to be beastly, to be disgusting. The adjective *wild*, with which we pick out animals who have not been rendered more or less acceptable by domestication, is also generally unfavourable, implying tumultuous violence.

Attentive and persistent observation of nonhuman animals in their natural state has shown that the conventional picture of them as violent, cruel, and disorderly is a gross misrepresentation. It was probably fostered by the fact that most casual observation of undomesticated animals was made by people who were attempting to kill them, a point of view to which no one is likely to give either an agreeable or a representative impression. Animals are not, in general, wild, beastly, or brutal, in the ordinary senses of these terms. Like men they can be violent in the pursuit of food, in self-defence, and in seeking and enjoying erotic satisfaction. But these, with them as with us, are exceptional episodes, standing out from a background of orderly routine, domestic affection, and simple torpor.

But, even if the emotional obstacle set up by this system of misconceptions is removed, reluctance to admit that men are animals will persist. The admission that there are numerous similarities between men and animals may be made less grudgingly if the libel that they are monstrous images of our worst passions is refuted. Still, it is maintained, these likenesses are outweighed by the much more important differences between animals and men.

There is an assumption, embodied in talking about similarities outweighing differences in importance as the justification for preferring one way of drawing conceptual boundaries to another, that should be brought into the open. This is that it is a matter of human convention, up to us, to draw conceptual boundaries as we choose. That is by no means the traditional view of the matter, which is that there are fixed natural kinds that it is the task of the intelligent observer to discern. The observer's only element of choice in the matter is the selection of sounds and marks to give spoken or written expression to the general, classificatory conceptions he registers.

The world, on this, more or less Platonic, view, is like a warehouse of motorcar parts in which there is a finite variety of kinds of item, each item falling squarely and unequivocally into one of the kinds in the inventory. The fixity of kinds in such a warehouse is the result of the fact that everything brought into it has been deliberately manufactured in accordance with previously formulated specifications. In the real world, of course, no warehouse is so perfect. Other oddments creep in with the people who work there; there are the ingredients of the warehouse itself. But if the world is conceived as the product of an intelligent creator, the notion of a fixity of kinds in it is a congruous one. Items that do not fit into the inventory are spoiled or anomalous and so detract, by implication, from the creator's perfection.

There are features of the world that lend some colour to the theory of fixed kinds. Many of the things we deal with are human artefacts, although they will pose classificatory problems from time to time, since their creators, or, more properly, fashioners, are imperfect. Another large group of things are members of living species of whom, in general, it is true that they can come into existence only through the sexual collaboration of two other, previously existing members of the same species. If that were absolutely true, together with the species-defining principle that every member of a given species has a set of properties that is uniquely definitive of that species, all living things without remainder would fall into fixed kinds. But since species evolve, it cannot be absolutely true. Finally, chemistry has established that all matter, living and nonliving, is made up from a limited repertoire of chemical elements, each of which itself consists, to oversimplify slightly, of a nucleus and an element-defining number of electrons.

There is, then, a lot of fixity about, simply as a matter of very general, natural fact. But it prevails at the level of element and species in a way that it does not at the level of the more general kinds under which the primary kinds are classified (metals or hawks, for example) or, again, at the level of classifications that are independent of the primary ones (into inflammable substances or carnivores, for example). Man is a species, but animal is not.

The doctrine of fixity of kinds has an extreme contrary opposite from whose evident unacceptability it may derive some undeserved support. This is the arbitrary variety of conventionalism which holds that the way we classify the things we come across is entirely of our own making, a purely subjective contrivance whose subjectivity is concealed by the fact that we all agree to adopt much the same conventions. It may well be doubted whether this is even a coherent thesis. Are our individual conventions really the same or do we merely surreptitiously agree to call them the same? And do we really call them the same . . . ? It is surely plain that many likenesses and differences are just matters of given, experienced fact: the likeness in colour of these two ripe tomatoes and the difference in colour between them and the lemon nearby.

But beyond this basic level we have room for manoeuvre. A traditional idea about classification associated with that of the fixity of kinds is that of their simplicity, the idea that each kind is defined by a unique set of characteristics. A strong form of this doctrine is that all but the most general kinds are defined by reference to the more general kind of which they are a species and the differentiating property that distinguishes them from the other species within that more general kind.

That idea cannot be sustained. Most actual kinds are defined by clusters of characteristics which do not all have to be possessed by an item if it is to count as a member of the kind, only a reasonable number or quorum, and then only to some extent or within a certain range. Lemons, for example, do not all have the same colour or the same shape or the same size. The concepts of kinds it is useful to have are those that are widely applicable. So they must embody clusters of characteristics that are frequently found in association. But in the actual world characteristics do not associate as neatly as the doctrine of simplicity assumes. As we get to know more about the way characteristics occur together, we can revise our notions of kinds in various different ways. Thus, old words get new senses, like *fish*, and new words come into use, like *neurosis* or *semantics*, which are not words for new or newly discovered things, such as *television* and *quasar*.

In experience, then, we find in the world a number of objective likenesses and differences which serve as the foundation of all our subsequent classificatory ordering of what there is. In moving on to more general and specific classifications we can choose what general sums and specific products of characteristics we shall pick out to give names to. They are not irresistibly thrust on us by the nature of the world, but there are objective reasons for preferring some choices to others.

When one considers how closely alike men and apes are, both in physical appearance and in behaviour—how much, indeed, men have in common with many of the mammals they have had good opportunities for observing—it is extraordinary how little headway the idea that men are animals has made. It is not just that the idea that man is a part of nature has been rejected as absurd when it *has* been advanced, as by Hobbes and, in a much more convincingly-based way, by Darwin, two hundred years later. It is that it has seldom been given serious consideration.

The main practical reason for this curious state of affairs has been, of course, the power of institutional Christianity. For Christianity, men are distinguished absolutely from animals and from everything else in the natural world by the fact that they have, or even essentially *are*, souls. The human body, animals, plants, and lifeless matter are all, according to Christian doctrine, provided by God for men to live with or among for a while, to make discriminating use of, to be tempted by, and, ultimately, to transcend, to leave altogether behind them at the end of the soul's earthly career.

The church could exercise control over the expression of thought and thus, to some extent, over thought itself, which is helped to flourish by explicit formulation and debate. But it was also able to call on intellectual support of a distinguished kind in its unrelenting resistance to naturalism of any kind. There have been two main streams of doctrine to uphold the division of the world into men and everything else. The first is the dualism philosophically articulated by Plato in his *Phaedo*, developed and incorporated into Christianity by St Augustine, and revived with brilliant dialectical force and economy by Descartes so as to become the almost universal persuasion of philosophers, even non-Christian and anti-Christian ones, until comparatively recent times. The second is the philosophy of Aristotle, which in its original form did not accord an overwhelming importance to the distinction it recognized between men and animals but came to do so in the Christianized form it was given by Aquinas, which has been for many centuries the official philosophy of the Catholic Church.

The philosophical dualism of soul and body does not inevitably imply that there is a fundamental difference between men and animals. In view of the excellent grounds we have for ascribing consciousness, sensibility, and intelligence to animals, it would be more natural to associate it with the view that both men and animals are on one side of the major division it affirms within the domain of what exists, while plants and lifeless matter are on the other. Descartes, clearheaded enough to see that this was a formally possible way of following out the consequences of the soul–body dualism to which he was committed, took the bold step of asserting that animals are automata and the mentality they seem to exhibit is only illusory appearance. More usually the problem of categorization posed by the fact of animal life has simply been ignored. Nothing is acknowledged to exist in the world surveyed by most philosophers but men and the material things they perceive and handle.

The continuity of men and animals is repudiated by the two most widely influential philosophers of the middle part of this century: Wittgenstein and Sartre, the most thoroughgoing of anti-Cartesians and the most uncompromising of atheists, respectively. Wittgenstein pertinaciously fought against Descartes's idea that mind and body are utterly different kinds of things because differently known. According to him, when we talk about the mind and its contents what we say must be connected to the observable behaviour of human bodies. Yet he ascribed only the most meagre mental life to animals, denying that they could form intentions or harbour any but the most rudimentary beliefs, on the ground that they are not users of language. Second, he maintained that human actions are radically distinct in character from what he called 'natural happenings', including all the activities of animals, on the ground that human actions, being done for reasons, are not susceptible of causal explanation. Sartre divides the field of existing things into those that exist for themselves and those that exist in themselves. The former, which are conscious of themselves and determine their own character, are exclusively human beings. The latter have fixed given natures. It has been suggested that the blindness of these philosophers to the close likenesses between men and animals is due to their respective sophisticated metropolitan backgrounds in Vienna and Paris. It seems unlikely that either of them ever owned a dog.

Aristotle influentially distinguished men, animals, and plants from lifeless matter in terms of the rational, animal, and vegetative souls they each possessed. These souls are what underlies reason; self-movement, perception, desire, and emotion; nutrition and reproduction. Aristotle took reason to be peculiar to mankind (and to any 'higher' intelligent creatures there may be), but no unfathomable abyss separated men from animals in his view. Men alone have rational souls, but they have animal souls as well. They are, in the words of the celebrated definition, rational animals. Reflection on his terminology prompts the thought that it is really very strange of Cartesian dualists to deny that animals have souls, given that the word *animal* is derived from *anima*, the Latin synonym of the Greek *psyche* or soul.

In order to incorporate Aristotle into Christianity, and, in particular, to find a place for human immortality within a system of thought that made no real provision for it, some casual remarks about the active intellect, suggesting that on the death of its possessor it would rejoin the universal reason, had to be elaborately developed and insisted on. A Christianizing revision, then, obliterated the naturalistic tendency of Aristotle's philosophy, with its emphasis on the graded continuity of all existing things.

The dualistic doctrine of the soul affirms not only that the soul is distinct from the body in a fundamentally important way and that human beings alone have souls. It also holds that human beings are essentially or intrinsically souls, capable of being attached to bodies but equally capable of existence independently of them. This prepares the way for the idea that the soul actually does continue to exist after the death and disintegration of a body to which it has been attached. The most general argument for that conclusion was put forward by Plato. The soul is simple and indivisible (perhaps because it is not in space); only what is composite and divisible can go out of existence (at any rate in the natural order of things and without divine intervention): therefore, the soul cannot go out of existence.

Descartes's argument for the thesis that I, or any human being, am essentially a soul, and only contingently a body, is that it is impossible for me to suppose that I do not exist, but I can suppose, without contradiction, that my body does not exist, so that it is possible for me to exist although my body does not. For the purposes of this discussion it is not necessary to ask if the argument is valid or not. If, as seems obvious, animals are conscious beings and have beliefs, it would simply follow that, if the argument were valid, then animals are essentially souls and only contingently embodied too.

The naturalist alternative to these dualistic ways of thinking may be of a strong, materialistic variety, holding that mental events and processes just are material events and processes of a particular, presumably cerebral, sort. It may, more moderately, admit a distinctness of character between the mental and the physical but contend that the mental never occurs without, and is causally dependent on, the existence of a physical organism in which it is embodied. But it will deny that any mental activity could go on without a physical basis, whether it were the mental activity of men or of animals.

4. The Soul: its Parts and Purposes

The traditional dualism of soul and body was not advanced by philosophers with any particular interest in distinguishing men from animals. Its main underlying purpose was to distinguish man, or an essential ingredient in man, from nature. Animals, unreflectively assumed to be parts of nature, were, by an easy transition of thought, supposed, for the most part with the same lack of reflection, to be without souls. Only when Descartes took the step of explicitly asserting that animals are automata did it become necessary to draw some distinctions, to work out in just what respect animals fall short of man.

What is it to have a soul? At its most inclusive a soul is simply a consciousness, a sensibility, in particular the capacity to enjoy pleasure and suffer pain. The disconcerting view of Descartes was that animals, despite appearances, lack even this. They cannot, of course, tell us in so many words that they are enjoying themselves or that they are suffering. Nor can a baby, or a retarded person, or someone suffering from aphasia, or even a foreigner whose language we do not understand. A monkey may well look much more like an adult human being then a baby does. Its behaviour when in pain may be much more like an adult human's than a baby's. It can identify the painful spot and rub it for alleviation. We have, then, much better reason for saying that the monkey is in pain than that the baby is. Indeed, it seems to me that we can reasonably suppose that we have a better idea of what it is like to be a monkey in pain than to be a baby in pain, despite the fact that in our unrecallable pasts we have all been babies in pain.

As philosophical investigators of the problem of our knowledge of other minds often remind us, we do not know the pains of others as we know our own. We feel our own pains, we directly experience them. But, for all the sympathetic wincing the pains of others may excite in us, we have to tell that they are in pain from our observations, which are painless in themselves, of their pain-giving circumstances and their pain-expressing behaviour, the cut finger and the sharp cry. The baby's cry may come from stomach ache or frustration. The monkey's expressions of physical pain and of anger are much more clearly differentiated. Our adult compatriots can, of course, tell us that they are in pain. But they do not always tell us the truth. Circumstances and behaviour are the ultimate, if seldom appealed to, tests of their veracity. Furthermore, they can and do deceive us by pretending to be in pain, or, more commonly, because of the exigencies of social life, to be enjoying themselves. Animal pretence is on a much more modest scale. Our evidence for animal pain is, then, much more unequivocal than that we have for the pains of our fellow human beings. To turn this point in the direction of Descartes: we have no less reason to think that other human beings are automata than we have to think that animals are, and no more either. And since the first belief is absurd, so is the second.

The Cartesian account of the nature of animals is clearly a philosophical grotesque, a paradox to be used simply as an incitement to further thought about the way in which we ascribe feelings to other sensitive beings. Any account of the difference between men and animals plausible enough to be taken as a serious contender for our acceptance must be Aristotelian. Aristotle ascribed to animals sensation and appetite (comprising desire, passion, and wish) but denied that they had reason or the power of thought. His position is not as clear as it looks. The familiar contrast of thought and feeling is not a sharp one; there is a debatable middle ground of mental activities that partake of both, essentially the region of perception and belief. Aristotle acknowledges that animals can perceive but denies that they have beliefs, denies also that they have the power of 'calculation and thought'.

Belief and thought are closely connected, as is suggested by the colloquial use of *think* for *believe*. 'I think he is married' means the same as 'I believe he is married.' Perception, again, is commonly distinguished from mere sensation, a wholly passive sensory receptiveness, as a matter of the formation of beliefs at the prompting of sensation. We do not need to explore these refinements, since it is quite evident that animals are capable of perception and belief. H. H. Price sensibly observes:

The point of being conscious, of having experiences, is that it enables one to *recognize* one's food or one's enemies when they are within the range of one's sense-organs, or to recognize other things which are biologically helpful or harmful (for example, a suitable place for concealment, a safe place for building a nest).... It is possible that in some creatures the capacity of recognizing their food or their enemies is unlearned, 'instinctive' as we say.... But in most animals, perhaps in all, sensation has another function as well. It enables one to learn from experience, and thereby to respond more effectively to one's environment. (*Thinking and Experience*, 41–2)

We all know perfectly well that a dog can believe, quite rightly, that its ball has rolled under the sofa; a cat, that one is about to feed it; a squirrel, that it can jump safely from one branch to another.

Belief and the kind of perceptual thought from which all our fundamental beliefs about matters of fact derive are plainly within the capacity of animals. So Locke is wrong when he says that 'brutes abstract not', that animals do not make sense of their experience with general ideas. Of course they do not use general *words*. But their behaviour gives overwhelming evidence of their ability to recognize things as being of particular kinds and of having predictive beliefs—expectations, set up by their recognitions, together with learnt beliefs about the further characteristics of what they recognize.

Where Aristotle and many others since have firmly dug their feet in is in their insistence that human beings alone have reason. But animals identify problems—the need to find a way out of a disagreeably confined environment, for example—which they go about solving much as human investigators do, namely, by the experimental procedure of trial and error. Nor are their enquiries always directed towards the solution of some immediately pressing problem. A predator may spend a long time carefully observing the regular movements of its prey in order to choose a good moment to strike. Animals reason, draw inferences, and display intelligence.

What they do not do is think for the sake of thinking. They are not speculative theorists but practical investigators. We may agree that science, or, more broadly and accurately, *theory*, is a special and distinguished achievement of our species without concluding that it amounts to some vast and estranging abyss between men and animals. After all, it is an activity of rather few human beings even now, and it is reasonable to think it has emerged only rather late in the evolutionary history of the human species.

The most favoured differentiator relied upon by those who still wish to maintain that the difference between men and animals is the most fundamental partitioning of the actual contents of the world is language. Its invokers have to admit that animals communicate. On the one hand there is the very precise signalling system of bees, with its admittedly limited repertoire; on the other, the chimpanzees who have been taught to say a large number of things in gesture. The bees can be discounted since their communications about the distance and direction from the hive of supplies of nectar has something of the mechanical rigidity of the thermometer or barometer. These minds are too one-track to count as minds at all. But the talkative chimpanzees are another matter. They can make up new sentences out of the elements of gesture-language they have been taught. In doing so, they have moved beyond mere signalling to an articulated, syntactical manner of using language which has hitherto been, so far as we know, a human monopoly.

It must be admitted that these linguistic achievements, although real, are very rudimentary although the chimpanzees' new sentences show that there is no incapacity in principle in nonhuman animals to use a means of communication that is a true language in being conventional and creative. I mentioned earlier that in the social life of animals there are to be found, in comparatively primitive form, the stable family, the organized economy, and the law-enforcing state. These are needed for the continuation of the species, its sustenance, and its protection from external enemies and internal conflict. But the other three great human institutions have no correlates in the animal world. We are unique in possessing theory, religion, and art. Theory comprises much more than science as Bacon conceived it, a body of methodically acquired and systematically organized natural knowledge for the more effective satisfaction of our desires. A main part of religion is theory, about the world as a whole and man's place in it, in large measure a response to the knowledge of the inevitability of death. Animals fear death when the danger of it is near at hand; they do not contemplate it from afar. They also have in some form the other main parts of religion: ritual and the instilling of codes of conduct. They have aesthetic preferences but do not seem deliberately to make things for the purpose of gratifying them.

Although it will be admitted that animal societies instil and enforce codes of conduct, many would rest their case for the uniqueness of man on the fact that he is a moral agent, that his conduct is, at least partially, governed by conscientious choice rather than instinct or the powerful sanctions of the tribe. But if we consider the content of morality, the forms of action and the types of virtue it generally enjoins, underneath all its anthropologically celebrated variations the contrast between us and animals is far from irresistibly evident. Animals are courageous, patient, affectionate, good parents, loyal companions, forgiving—very much in the way we are, that is to say, not all, not all the time, and in some cases never.

When the whole range of allegedly differentiating human powers and achievements is surveyed, the old ideas that animals are quite other than men because devoid of soul or reason shrink to manageable proportions. Of course there are differences. The modest peculiarities of human anatomy and physiology—the large brain, the comparative hairlessness, the habitually upright posture, and so forth—are associated with more substantial differences of mentality and culture. But these are not of a completely different order from the differences that separate species of nonhuman animals. What is strongly suggested by the straightforward physical likenesses of men and other animals is confirmed by the continuities of behaviour and of social life. It is plain that man is a special kind of animal. But it is blindness to believe that he is not an animal at all, or that some animals, at least, are not in most respects like him.

What are the underlying reasons for the deeply entrenched habit of considering men and animals to be in all that matters utterly distinct, a habit that, when challenged, turns into an anxious determination? The most fundamental has already been briefly mentioned in connection with philosophical dualism about soul and body: immortality. The survival of the death of his body by what is essential to his personal identity is the most metaphysically grandiose element in what is supposed to be the special dignity of man. Of almost equal antiquity and importance is the idea that men alone have free will. Animals, as much as running water and falling stones, are taken to be rigidly governed in their behaviour by causal laws. Given their natures and their circumstances they cannot but do what they do do. But men, it is believed, are different. They have free choice and are, generally, responsible for their actions. A libertarian or indeterministic conception of man seems inconsistent with the programmes of the human and social sciences, at least if these are conceived as undertakings of the same kind as the natural sciences.

Despite the relevance of human freedom of will to morality it is not, in itself, a moral issue. But there is a large array of connected moral problems about man's relation to and treatment of animals. He hunts, breeds, kills, and eats them. He compels them to work for him in various ways, as providers of food and muscular energy, for the most part. For the sake of entertainment, and a dash of instruction, he trains them to perform in circuses and locks them up in zoos. For purposes of scientific research he subjects them to all sorts of painful, mutilating, and lethal experimentation. These are all modes of treatment that are more or less unthinkable as applied to human beings. Some of them would be acceptable provided that the subject's consent had been obtained, perhaps in exchange for some consideration, monetary or other. Most of them would not be regarded as things for which consent could permissibly be sought or given. The issues must be looked at in a little more detail.

Immortality

The main philosophical point of mind–body dualism has always been the immortality of the soul, even if dualism has often been accepted by philosophers such as Hume and A. J. Ayer, who do not believe in the soul's survival of death. There has been a great deal of very involved discussion about the nature of the soul, which is held to survive the death and disintegration of the body, that is, its completely going out of existence as a body. Is the soul or mental aspect of a person the total set of his experiences, of the passing mental states of which he is conscious? Is it, as Aristotle hinted—in a way that made it possible to reconcile his philosophy with Christian doctrine—a part of his mental equipment, in Aristotle's case, the 'active reason', the bit of the mind that goes in for theoretical reasoning? Is it, as some have said, a mysterious something or other, a pure ego, as it is sometimes called, which has or underlies all the conscious states that make up a mind's history? A further difficulty is presented by the universally admitted, if not always explicitly acknowledged, existence of unconscious mentality—mental states and processes, that is to say, whose subjects are not consciously aware of them.

Even if sense can be made of the notion of a pure ego, which I do not think it can, its persistence after the death of the body would not be enough to count as a real continuation of an individual person's life. Locke and Leibniz, two major philosophers who disagreed about almost everything except that there was such a thing as spiritual substance or the pure ego, agreed also that survival required that souls should be connected to their previously embodied selves by memory of their former states. That is, the soul after the body's death would have to have conscious experiences, in particular memory experiences of former conscious experiences.

An obvious objection to the idea that a person's mental life can go on after the death of his body is that all the mental life we know of, or even have good evidence for, is associated with living bodies (and not, of course, only human bodies). Furthermore, some parts of it seem to be more closely and directly dependent on the body than others. Perception and sensation seem to require physical organs of sense. Emotion and desire, the domain of what used to be called the passions, have evident bodily manifestations and accompaniments. Aristotle's theoretical reason, on the other hand, is comparatively self-contained. It can be exercised without bodily expression and upon purely mental stores of information, without reliance on any immediate bodily stimulus. This lends some colour to the idea that the human reason, at any rate, can intelligibly be supposed to exist without a bodily support. But it does not do much more than that. It is plain that our reasoning powers are subject to bodily influence. For one thing they can be damaged or completely destroyed by injury to the brain, a fact that throws a sombre light on their prospects when the brain has completely disintegrated. They are also susceptible to the influence of drugs and other chemical substances that are introduced into the body.

What is more, the reason on its own suffers from the same defect as the pure ego or soul substance. Its survival would not preserve the individuality of its previous possessor. Separated by bodily death from the rest of his mental apparatus, it would be, as Aristotle himself saw, entirely impersonal, a consideration that led him to view it as being absorbed back, after embodiment in a particular human individual, into some kind of universal mind.

The fact that much of our mental life is unconscious is a further support for the thesis that an individual's mental life is causally dependent on his body. If I step carefully over an obstacle in my path when too interested in something else to be consciously aware of the fact, there is the same relation between the physical exposure of the sense organs to the obstacle and the ensuing avoidance of it that is present in the conscious case where I am actually aware of perceiving it. What can the unconscious perception of the obstacle be that we believe to have occurred but a registration of the obstacle in the brain which leads to a nerve impulse that alters my mode of walking?

Immortality, then, is an obscure notion and a somewhat protean one. All the same, it is something that many, perhaps most, people have passionately desired, and nearly as many have passionately believed in. It is also something that has been generally ascribed by those who believed in it to *all* human beings and *only* to human beings. Whatever view is taken of the nature of mind, the reasonableness of this restrictive belief will have to be examined.

Free will

Human beings, it is generally held, are the only moral agents, the only creatures that are morally responsible for their actions. That is really too sweeping. No human being is morally responsible for everything he does. All of us are sometimes subject to duress, irresistible physical force, breakdowns of consciousness of one sort or another. Some human beings are excused from responsibility, not just for particular acts by reason of special exculpating conditions, but for part or all of their lives: the badly retarded permanently, the insane from the time of going mad. Nevertheless, it does seem reasonable to say that most human beings are morally responsible for a good deal of what they do, and that nothing that is not a human being is morally responsible for anything it does.

It is a common conviction that a moral agent is absolved from responsibility for something he has done if he could not have done otherwise. But if there is a causal explanation, in terms of my nature and the circumstances, for my acting as I did, it follows that it is impossible that, given that nature and those circumstances, I should have done anything different from what I did do. If the scope of causal law, in other words, extends to cover the whole range of human conduct, nothing humans do is ever done freely, and for nothing that they do are they ever really morally responsible. *Ought* implies *can*, as the phrase is; it is incorrect to say that I ought to have done something other than what I actually did unless I could have done otherwise. But if I am a part of nature conceived as a deterministic system, then I can never do anything other than what I actually do do.

I believe, with many other philosophers, that this conclusion is incorrect, the result of a muddle. But many philosophers think otherwise, and they are by no means less well qualified to have an opinion on the subject. I do not intend to enter into debate with them directly since either view—that determinism is, or that it is not, compatible with moral responsibility—is itself compatible, I shall argue, with the view that men are enough like other animals to be counted as animals themselves.

Nevertheless, the attribution to men, by the libertarian opponents of determinism, of free will, of a faculty of making choices or decisions that are not causally determined by the nature and circumstances of the agent, has been thought to mark a crucial aspect of the distinction between men and animals. Animals behave, but men act. Animals are driven by instincts, brought into operation by immediately perceived stimuli. An animal that appears to be steadily working towards the realization of a plan, deliberately prepared in advance, like a spider spinning a web, a beaver building a dam, or a bird building a nest, is not a genuine agent but is simply going through a behavioural routine for which it has been programmed by evolution.

The possession by men of a genuine, that is to say, free, will is closely tied up by those who believe in it with man's allegedly unique possession of reason. Where the animal is instinctually driven to go through its built-in programme, we consciously formulate and adopt more or less long-term ends and select means to them in the light of our stores of general knowledge about how things are connected and from our calculations of the costs of these alternatives and their side effects. To do this we must be able to reason and to acquire and retain a good deal of more or less theoretical knowledge. Will and reason, in short, go together; will, properly so called, is simply reason in its practical employment, as Kant put it. Both are higher, distinctively (even if not quite universally) human faculties of the mind. The uniqueness of man as an agent preserves him in his deterministic natural environment as the sole bearer of moral responsibility.

The sciences of man

A disquieting implication of the thesis that men, as morally responsible agents, frequently act in independence of causally determining factors is that to the extent that man acts freely his conduct is not susceptible of scientific explanation. It follows that psychology and the social sciences, understood as they usually are, are doomed to failure as attempts to discover the causal laws of human conduct. Man can be a subject for science only in respect of those of his activities that occur independently of his will. These are for the most part bodily: breathing, the circulation of the blood, digestion, growth. There may be room for a science of abnormal behaviour, that of the naturally deficient in whom the will does not operate—the retarded and the mad—and also, perhaps, for child psychology, of the mental life and behaviour of those in whom the will has not yet emerged. Human freedom of will is part of what underlies the doctrine that history is not a science and is perverted by those who try to pursue it as if it were.

Two recent tendencies in philosophy, the Wittgensteinian and the existentialist, strongly opposed to one another in many respects, agree that human beings are not a proper or possible topic for causal enquiry in the way that, apart from man but including animals, nature is. The Wittgensteinian view is that human conduct has to be understood as issuing from motives or reasons and that these explanatory factors are not causes connected by law to the actions they explain. The existentialist asserts that man has no fixed nature for the supposed causes of his conduct to be found in. Men create themselves by free acts of will. Wittgensteinians share with structuralists the idea that the possession of language is the essential distinguishing mark of mankind, and they are led by this to the conclusion that to understand men and their institutions is more like interpreting a text than a matter of registering a natural regularity.

One recent attempt to bring men within the scope of a universally acknowledged natural science which has excited violent controversy is the sociobiology of E. O. Wilson. Wilson is an expert on the social insects and has brought the most sophisticated forms of evolutionary biology and population genetics to the business of explaining how a particular form of natural selection operates in favouring the development of various peculiarities of structure and behaviour. This is 'kin selection', the way in which evolutionary advantage goes to organisms that act so as to maximize the chances of survival of the genes that are distinctive of them and that they share in varying degrees with their blood relations.

Wilson's offence in the eyes of his most vehement critics has been to extend the application of his theories to the human species. In the interests of various ideological fads, such as anti-sexism and anti-racism, they have subjected him to a torrent of invective well outside the usually recognized limits of academic brawling.

It is not that they hold that human nature and conduct cannot be causally explained. Many of them are Marxists, constrained by their interpretation of that system of doctrine to hold that the historically varying properties of men are due to society and culture, more specifically to the interaction between the way in which economic production is carried on and the social organization that corresponds to it. Generally, they hold that man's genetic inheritance, a matter that falls within the scope of biological science, determines largely what is common to the species, while the variations that have taken place since the establishment of the species are largely due to culture. What culture has brought about, a changed culture can change in the direction of its heart's desires. To attribute aspects of the social life of mankind—an important instance is the comparatively specialized roles of males and females—to inherited factors excludes, or at any rate limits, the possibilities of what they see as desirable reform. No adherent of supernatural religion has assailed with greater ferocity than critics of sociobiology the idea that men and animals can be investigated in the same way.

The treatment of animals

The interests which have been considered so far as underlying the distinction between men and animals have all been concerned with safeguarding the dignity of man. He alone, among all that is to be found in the universe, can survive the death of his body, act freely as a morally responsible agent, and elude the net of scientific interpretation; thus, he alone can escape the dangers of having his actions predicted and, worse than that, brought under the control of technical manipulation. Another, more practical interest is human convenience. To see animals as wholly distinct from human beings is, among other things, to exclude them from the moral constituency, from the range of those whose well-being we ought morally to take into account.

Man's convenience dictates that animals should be used as part of the general bounty of nature in whatever way suits us, provided that we respect the property rights in them of other human beings. We use them, first of all, for food, as an unrivalled source of protein. With this in mind, we hunt and fish them in their natural habitats, breed, rear, and slaughter them in various environments—farms, batteries, and abattoirs. Second, we use them to provide us with dairy products and eggs, with wool and silk for clothing. Third, we use them for purposes of research, a work for which they are the more suited the more like us they are. We test drugs on them, use them to examine the course and effects of diseases that we induce in them, try out industrial products on them to see if they have unpleasant side effects. Fourth, we make use of them in a large number of ways for pleasure and recreation. We hunt, shoot, and fish them when we do not need or even intend to eat what we kill. We breed and train them to race against each other. In a more furtive way we still set them up to fight against each other, in spite of fairly widespread legal prohibition. We train them to appear as circus acts. We capture them in order to display them in zoos, frequently in conditions of unpleasant confinement. More genially we keep them as pets, but as well as the companionable side of this relationship there is also much cruelty, neglect, and abandonment. Finally, we use them to work for us, as draught animals, as aids in hunting, to guard factories and sniff out drugs, to herd sheep, to guide the blind, to control rodents, even, although to a decreasing extent, to take us about, but more for exercise than for purposive travel.

Traditionally, those who have reflected philosophically on the morality of man's treatment of animals have either, in the spirit of Descartes's theory of animals as mindless natural objects, taken the view that there is no moral issue here at all—that we are morally permitted to treat animals in any way that we like—or they have held that we ought not to ill-treat animals because to do so is to fall into habits of cruelty that could be harmful to other men. The first position is adopted unreservedly by Spinoza. 'The law against the slaughtering of animals is founded rather on vain superstition and womanish pity than on sound reason. . . . I do not deny that beasts feel; what I deny is, that we may not consult our own advantage and use them as we please, treating them in the way that best suits us.' The same belief is found in St Augustine, who defends it by reference to the incident of Christ's miraculous transfer of devils into the Gadarene swine.

The second position is that of Kant, who argued that we could have no duties to animals since they are not rational beings, but that we should not treat them cruelly because it fosters a habit of inhumanity to do so. That is not a very defensible point of view. Either animals are enough like us to deserve moral consideration because of what they actually are, or it is simply a sentimental illusion to worry about them, like pitying an old car as it grinds up a steep hill.

Many Eastern religions have condemned the killing and eating of animals, sometimes because they believed that the souls of human beings could be reincarnated in the bodies of animals. In the West, a concern for the well-being of animals for their own sake has been fitful. St Francis is a lonely medieval exception. In the Enlightenment, Voltaire and others revived the generous ideas of Montaigne, but, as Mary Midgley points out in *Animals and Why they Matter* (1983), this initiative was to some extent smothered by the preoccupation of the thinkers of the Enlightenment with reason. Most philosophers, she remarks, are town dwellers, have little to do with animals, and easily forget about them, despite their steaks and salmon and woollen sweaters.

5. Human Dignity and Convenience Examined

Now that the supposed marks of distinction between men and animals have been themselves distinguished and made more explicit, it is time to see whether they have the favourable implications that have given men an interest in drawing them. The idea that men have souls, a mental aspect that could be the form in which they survive the deaths of their bodies, has been interpreted as referring principally to three things: the whole of a subject's conscious experience, the pure ego or soul substance, and the reason, which is multiform, being identified as the ability to think, or the ability to theorize, or the possession of language. Then there is the idea that men are, or that most of them, at any rate, sometimes or even often are, truly free agents, moved by will and not merely by instinct, on the one hand morally responsible for what they choose to do and, on the other hand, because of their freedom, not to be made predictable and manipulable by having their conduct explained by their nature and circumstances together with laws of human and social science. Finally, there is the idea that men alone are the appropriate objects of direct moral consideration, the only bearers of rights, the only moral ends in themselves.

With regard to each of these ideas, I shall ask whether the actual differences between men and animals give an adequate foothold to the exclusive status accorded to human beings. I shall argue that in no case is the total exclusion of animals from the respect and consideration men are accustomed to giving themselves justified, although the differences that really exist between men and animals can be reasonably argued to have some qualifying consequences for the morality of our treatment of the latter. If that is right, there are, in the case of each of the interesting ideas involved, two possibilities. Either we can conclude that animals too have immortal souls, free wills, and moral rights. Or we can conclude that since they do not, we also do not.

The soul in men, which has been supposed to be the essential element capable of surviving the death of their bodies, can be understood in several different ways. The most comprehensive identifies the soul with the totality of an individual's conscious experience, the entire stream of beliefs, imaginings, desires, emotions, deliberations, and choices of which an individual can be introspectively aware as making up his inner, mental life. A soul in this sense can be denied to animals, and in particular to the primates and more evolved mammals who are physically and genetically closest to us, only by the heroically absurd expedient of maintaining that animals have no conscious experiences at all. The plain fact is that we have precisely the same sort of grounds for ascribing consciousness to many human beings—to babies, to the very old, to the mentally abnormal, to those, also, who are very alien to us in language and behaviour—as we have for ascribing it to many animals. And we have very much the same evidence, but some more besides, for ascribing it to people with whom we can communicate linguistically and whose customs and preferences we share. If consciousness is a reason for supposing immortality to be possible or actual for people other than ourselves, then we must admit that animals are immortal too.

The same conclusion follows from the assumption that the immortal element in a human being is a pure ego or spiritual substance. We can attribute such a thing to ourselves or anyone else only indirectly, inferring it from the fact that they are conscious together with some general principle to the effect that conscious states are inconceivable without a substantial something or other of which they are the states. If men have pure egos, then so do animals.

The idea that reason is the immortal ingredient in the constitution of men can itself be taken in at least three ways. The simplest is that a being has reason if it can draw inferences from the beliefs it acquires by perception. That is suggested by the adoption of appropriate means to bring about desired ends but is not clearly established by it. The well-adjusted routine of behaviour might be purely instinctive. But it is plain that much complex satisfaction-producing behaviour in animals is not simply instinctive but has been learnt, and not by a process of conditioning imposed by some external trainer, but rather as a result of the animal's own observations and trials.

There is, however, another, narrower conception of reason in which it does seem to be largely peculiar to human beings. This is theoretical reason, the power of developing logically articulated bodies of general beliefs about the world, carried on, for the most part, reflectively and by thinkers not in direct perceptual contact with a problematic situation. The purest product of theoretical reason is mathematics, of which animals plainly have no inkling. The special intellectual glory of our species is the theoretical natural science elaborated in the last three centuries in which mathematics is applied to the world by bringing calculation to bear on the results of measurement.

It was something like this that Aristotle had in mind with his conception of 'active reason', in his view the only possibly immortal element in the soul. Its impersonality was his ground for thinking it to be not really the property of the individuals who have the use of it, and so really universal and capable of surviving the death of the rest of the individual. At any rate, if it is distinctive of the human species, it is not distinctive of particular individuals. What those who find the thought of immortality attractive want for themselves and those they are attached to after death is not this thin and abstractly intellectual residue of personality. Immortality confined to this would not be worth having. Many human beings would not achieve it anyway; as a criterion it restricts immortality to a cognitive elite.

The most favoured conception of the distinctive reason of men at the present time is the type of rationality that is embodied in the possession of language. Animals, it is admitted, have signalling systems, but these are not languages proper. What is undeniable is that animal 'languages' are much poorer and more rudimentary than human language. It is much less clear that, as is often claimed, animal languages have no real grammar but are just a desultory repertoire of unrelated message-units and, again, that animal communication is not the expression of an intention to communicate. And we must remember that many human beings, from great youth or age or some other reason, have no capacity to use language, so they could be denied humanity on this ground. Thus, the possession of language has all the weaknesses as a criterion that theoretical reason has, and more, since it is far from clear that animals are wholly without it.

Defenders of immortality are not usually very precise about what it is that they expect to survive death. One who did try to think the matter through was C. S. Lewis. In his book *The Problem of Pain* he felt constrained to admit that animals had something of what he hoped would survive death in human beings. He consistently drew the conclusion that animals, or at least animals that had been to some extent humanized by human companionship, would survive death too.

Although animals are conscious, often intelligent, and modestly rational as well as, it seems, the intentional users of systems of communication, there is one important limitation to their mental lives which must be considered. This is that their awareness is generally restricted to what is going on in their immediate spatial and temporal environment. They are not given to what is variously called 'free thinking' or 'thinking in absence'. To the extent that they do think about what is absent, it has to be tied by a strong associative link to what is present to their senses. It is the currently visible lead that makes the dog think of a walk and a swim, the heard sound of the refrigerator door that puts the cat in mind of a drink of milk. It might be said that a dog who snuffles and whimpers and shakes his legs in a dream is thinking about rabbits pursued long ago and, at any rate, not sensibly present to him. But this familiar speculative possibility does not undermine the point. The dreaming dog thinks of the rabbits, if he dreams about them, as actually present to him, just as we should.

A consequence of this parochialism of conscious scope in animals is that their memories are limited in a way that ours are not. They remember how to do things that they have learnt, in particular to recognize individual people and places. Past experiences can affect their current reactions. But, like the burnt child, they do not have to recall the particular fire that burnt them and caused them to dread this fire now. In other words, they do not appear to have much in the way of a personal memory, the power to recollect particular events in their own pasts. Philosophers have often seen the power to recall past experience as an essential element in the identity of a person, sometimes as *the* essential element. It was animal deficiency in this respect that led Leibniz's follower Wolff to deny that animals are persons. They do not have, he said, 'a consciousness of having been the same thing previously in this or that state'.

Locke defined a person as 'a thinking intelligent being, that has reason and reflection, and can consider itself as itself, the same thinking thing, in different times and places'. I should hold that some continuity of character is also part of the idea of a person, but some continuity of personal memory is at least a necessary condition. It is this and the memories they do have, particularly of us and of what we are like, that makes companionable relationships possible with animals that at least marginally approximate to those we have with human beings we are attached to. The limitations of animal memory cast doubt on the conceivability of animals' survival of bodily death. A convenient way to think about the problem is to compare the ways in which we might be led to suppose that a man or an animal, known to have died, has been reincarnated. If the new animal enthusiastically recognized us and displayed the same character as the dead one, we might well identify the two. But we should lack the corroborating evidence of specific recollections of our shared past which would be available in the parallel human case. This little thought-experiment is not as far-fetched as it might seem. It has a realistic analogue in the problem of identifying a physically unrecognizable man or animal, who, in the way appropriate to him, claims to be a man or animal we have known in the past but have long lost touch with.

I conclude that the limits of animal memory do not absolutely exclude, as Wolff believed, the conception of animals as continuing personalities of a rudimentary kind, nor do they make the survival of death inconceivable for them in a way that it is not inconceivable for men. But, like the animal's lack of theorizing power, a form of intellectual detachment from the immediate environment comparable to personal memory, it is a real difference between the two.

Before we can ask whether animals are free agents we must ask whether they are agents at all. The contrary view is that their behaviour is entirely driven by instinct, by fixed and innate dispositions manifested under the influence of perceived external stimuli—the mouse in the cat's field of vision—and internal ones, such as a felt emptiness of the stomach. There are two points to be made here. The first is that it is certainly not true that all animals are wholly run by instinct. Many of them plainly learn from experience—from early life, in which they imitate or are trained by their elders, onward. Second, it is certainly not true that instinct plays no part in human life. There is no hard and fast dividing line between instinctive animals and deliberative men. We start with an instinctive set of dispositions, these are conditioned in various ways by our culture, that is to say by parents, by companions, by schools, by the state. Over and above this passively undergone modification of our springs of action, we also actively modify our own modes of conduct through experimentally pursued experience of life. Animals, too, try out new things and new ways of doing things.

But, just as they lack explicit theory, so they lack explicit codes of conduct—technical, prudential, and moral. Since their codes are not explicit and, so to speak, externalized, they are not available readily for critical examination, and animal means of communication are not rich enough for them to be discussed. That, however, is not to say that they do not have such codes, in the form of rules, or, if the word is preferred, habits of action, which are susceptible of change through intelligent adaptation to the experienced results of acting in accordance with them. It is not anthropomorphic fantasy on our part to speak of the cunning of the dog who comes to know how to shame us into taking him for a walk, or the cleverness of the cat who slips out of the house when we want him to stay in.

Animals, like us, envisage alternative possibilities of choice and, after reflection and perhaps some tentative tests, make their selection. Sometimes they just do things, but at others it seems more reasonable to say that they decide to do them. We can tell what they are thinking about and that they spend some time at it before they do it. Often, like us again, they are impulsive or act in an automatic, unreflective fashion. They passively acquire and also actively develop more efficient ways of doing things. They also come to be more prudent with the passage of time, take care to avoid pain and achieve pleasure, to maximize their long-run advantage, even if they have no conception of such a thing.

Do they have wills? The will, as such, is something of a philosopher's speciality. In ordinary life we talk about good and bad will, strong and weak will, but not of the will on its own. Animals can unquestionably be compared in respect of the relative goodness or strength of their wills. They are more or less amiable, more or less resolute and determined. They have characters. Kant confined will to human beings on the ground that to act on will is to act in accordance with the *idea* of a rule, and not merely in accordance with a regularity. But that is a perverse limitation; the relevant point is whether the rule is part of the agent's given constitution or is an intelligent acquisition, susceptible of intelligent amendment.

Are animals moral? They exhibit forms of behaviour that would undoubtedly be accounted moral in human beings and have what are very like virtues and vices. They show self-sacrificing concern for their offspring, suppress aggressive impulses, tolerate the tiresomenesses and minister to the needs of one another. In all this naive, primitively moral activity they are, after all, like a great many unsophisticated human beings who do not reflect about moral issues in the abstract but know what they ought to do and try to do it with more or less success. It is no more true of animals than it is of human beings that, in general, they behave in formal accordance with the generally recognized principles of morality only in order to avoid trouble and secure material rewards. They, like us, are capable from time to time of a disinterested concern for the well-being of others.

I do not want to suggest, however, that animals are fully fledged moral agents. For that, I think, a capacity to stand outside oneself and consider one's conduct and character in a critical manner is required. For that, in turn, a kind of self-consciousness is needed which animals do not possess because of their lack of personal memory and also, perhaps, because, if they have language at all, it is confined to the particular features of the here and now. What I do maintain is that there are the preliminaries of moral agency in animals, just as there are in young children, a fact that makes both of them susceptible to moral training in good habits and proper objects of praise and blame, to which both animals and young children are responsive.

None of this implies that the wills of animals are free, in the sense that any of their actions are intrinsically unpredictable, unconnected by law with their character and circumstances. Much of what they do is, of course, unpredictable in practice, but that can be attributed to the limitations of our knowledge, not to an objective deficiency in what there is to know. It is true that their repertoire of conduct is narrower than that of human beings, particularly of civilized human beings in the modern world. The gap is narrower between them and primitive human beings. It can be reasonably held that human beings are uniquely creative, as long as it is acknowledged that only a few human beings actually are.

But, if animals are not free agents in the sense of being able to act in an uncaused way, neither, I should argue, along with many other philosophers, are human beings. It is not necessary, fortunately, to discuss the problem here. In general, the reasons adduced for attributing this kind of freedom to human beings, like true creativeness or the habit of explicit moral self-criticism, apply to few, or at best a minority. Or, as with the power of deliberation and choice, the possession of wills of varying degrees of strength and goodness, the habit of acting efficiently, prudently, and virtuously as much may be said of many animals as of human beings.

A science does not require that the field to which it is applied be perfectly deterministic. All that is presupposed as a condition of possibly fruitful scientific investigation is some measure of order. As with the other kind of law, the one which human societies impose on their members, the whole undertaking is not undermined by the fact of a number of exceptions, so long as they are exceptions and not the usual case. Social and human science in general, and sociobiology in particular, are compatible with a measure of contra-causal freedom. Although such freedom has, in my view, nothing to do with moral responsibility (I agree with Hume that responsibility presupposes determinism—or a good deal of it—and is inconceivable without it), human creativeness and some novelties in nature do count in favour of there being such a thing in fact.

But the usual objection to sociobiology is not that it is deterministic. It is, rather, that it rules out all sorts of beneficial changes in the human world as impossible, or immensely costly, by connecting things it would be good to change—the relations of the sexes, classes, and races—with aspects of genetic inheritance which cannot in practice be altered. The most vociferous critics of sociobiology hold that human nature is not a constant, unalterably fixed in our genetic constitution, but, at the present stage of human evolution at any rate, is a product of culture, which is various and within our power to change. E. O. Wilson's extrapolations from the genetically programmed features of the social life of the hymenoptera are undoubtedly rather extravagantly speculative. More reasonably applicable lessons would be available from study of our closer relatives, the mammals and, particularly, our fellow primates. These higher animals, as we have seen, have a culture too, of an elementary and, as it might be put, nonspiritual kind. There is no absolute gulf between men and animals that rules the project of sociobiology out in principle. Its speculative excesses should be curbed by rational criticism, not quasi-religious hysteria.

Very much the greater part of our conduct that affects animals contravenes principles that would universally be agreed to apply to our treatment of human beings. We kill them, eat them, cause them great pain for no compensating advantage of their own, and enslave them. There is in many advanced countries, where the keeping of pets is much more widespread than participation in the hunting and rearing of animals for food and sport, a general persuasion that animals should not be treated cruelly. Laws against cruelty to animals are enforced and offences against them are energetically sought out and prosecuted by voluntary societies. Many people are induced by moral considerations, and not for the sake of their own health, to abstain from the eating of animal flesh. In our moral environment, alive and well, there is to be found a whole range of attitudes from that of the dedicated vivisectionists and happy steak enthusiasts at one extreme to that of the committed vegetarians at the other.

The animal-users have the weight of our moral tradition behind them. If called on to justify their exclusion of animals from the domain of moral consideration, they would appeal to the familiar distinguishing features. If the Cartesian view were correct, their position would be impregnable. Since it is not, they must rely on the allegedly nonrational nature of animals in one of its forms.

But the relevant fact is that animals suffer and feel, can experience pain. If that is denied, it follows that it is morally permissible to eat, hunt, torment, and work to death nonrational human beings. The fact that animals are not moral agents is sometimes invoked to support our manner of treating them. I have admitted that the moral agency of animals is at most rudimentary and, for the purposes of this argument, I am quite content to allow that it does not exist at all. Animals have no rights, it is said, because rights imply duties and animals, not being moral agents, can have no duties. Therefore animals have no rights; there can be no moral aspect to any action of ours that affects an animal except to the extent that the rights of another human being are involved—its owner, perhaps.

This is just a sophism. Rights imply duties, not in the sense that I can have rights only if I can also have duties, but in the sense that if A has a right against B, then B has a duty toward A. Children too young to have duties obviously have rights; there are things we have a duty to do for them and things we have a duty not to do to them.

A more defensible point of view relies on the fact that animals in general, having no personal memory, have no real self-conscious awareness of their own identity as continuing things. (They lack the existentialist's most dramatic human feature; they have no conception of the ultimate inevitability of their own death.) This may also have implications about the nature of an animal's experience of pain. Preoccupied with our own continuing futures, we fear and dislike pain, at least in part because of our fear of its consequences in terms of disablement, mutilation, and death. An outward-reaching anxiety is added in our case to the painful sensation. The lives of human beings are seen by them as continuing projects, where those of animals are a sequence of immediacies.

The moral prohibition of killing people is so fundamental that it seems almost absurd to try to make the reasons for it explicit. Its primordial nature is shown by the fact that in order to show that some forms of killing are morally permissible, we normally appeal, with more or less plausibility, to their being the means to the prevention of other deaths. That justification is most powerful as applied to killing in self-defence. It is weaker as a basis for capital punishment. Even if confined to those who have killed others or tried to do so, it has to assume that that makes it likely that they will kill, or try to kill, again. Once a war has started, the self-defence argument applies, in a collective fashion, although, for one side at least, it is not available as war breaks out.

The fact of being killed abolishes the system of expectations within which the individual's conduct of his life was carried on. That will be of no (earthly) disadvantage to him, but it will to all those who were rewardingly involved in that system, most acutely those who loved or liked him. The fear of an unnaturally precipitate death, not quietened by the effects of mortal illness or old age, must shadow and undermine his life. The right to life is traditionally given first place in lists of the supposed natural rights of man. Its being respected is, after all, an indispensable condition of the exercise or enjoyment of any other rights. Perhaps an underlying assumption is that the future will contain a positive balance of satisfaction over suffering. Even in cases where we are convinced that this is incorrect in some particular case, we do not give serious consideration to the thought that, since the person would be better off dead, we should take steps to kill him, unless mental collapse has unfitted him for making such a decision. *Arsenic and Old Lace* was a farcical comedy, not a dramatized policy recommendation.

Insofar as we kill animals for food or sport we can reconcile this with our convictions about the taking of human life only by relying on the difference between a man's conception of his future and an animal's, and as far as the indirect effects of killing are concerned, on the belief that the individual attachments of animals to one another are of an altogether different order of magnitude in intensity from those that connect human beings. It is not a very substantial moral basis for the meat industry, but it is at least an open and rational one. Vegetarians are right to reject the suggestion that kindly treated meat animals would not have the pleasant, even if foreshortened, lives they do—fed, warmed, protected from harm—unless men wished to eat them. We should hardly endorse the practice of replacing abortion by the rearing of unwanted children for the table.

The not unreasonable idea that animal pain is very different from ours, for the same reason that animal fear of death is, must also be invoked in any rational attempt to defend vivisection. The genuine, if often circuitous, contribution it makes to the saving of human lives is not enough, any more than it would be for a practice of using involuntary human subjects—prisoners, for example.

Moral progress, in its most important dimension, has always been a matter of enlarging the moral constituency: from family to tribe, from men to women, from adults to children, from compatriots to mankind at large. It is probable that, as we shake ourselves free from our habitual illusions about the differences between men and animals, we shall increasingly regard both as members of a single moral community.

18

The Past and Future of Freedom

The preservation of the freedom of the individual in a social order characterized by massively concentrated industrial undertakings, in which a hundred firms account for more than half of the national product, and by a state which has taken on an unprecedentedly large array of public responsibilities, including extensive control of and participation in industry, is clearly a crucial issue in any discussion of the relations between the three. But there is a sense in which the topic of the freedom of the individual is too confining in this connection.

Let me approach this point indirectly with a comment on what philosophers have to say about God. To put it shortly, the God whom philosophers prove to exist usually turns out to be very much a philosopher's God. The extreme case is that of Aristotle, whose God is really very much like Aristotle himself, if on a rather larger scale. He is a disembodied intelligence, engaged in uninterrupted contemplation of himself and of the most abstract truths about the world. It took all the persevering intelligence and inexhaustible theoretical resource of the medieval schoolmen to accommodate this notion, as they felt bound to do, with the fundamental teachings of Christianity. The Christian God, after all, is very much a person, one we are invited to conceive as a father, actuated by love and concern for his children.

Now something very similar is true about the views of philosophers about social values, about the ends which a properly constituted society ought to aim to realize. Many of them, to put it a little brutally, seem mainly concerned to make a world safe for intellectuals. The two greatest names in the tradition of British liberal thought, John Locke and John Stuart Mill, are both primarily interested in intellectual freedom, freedom of thought and expression, and, in Locke's case in particular, in religious freedom, freedom of worship and belief. Take Mill's great essay *On Liberty*. In the course of it he enumerates three main kinds of freedom: personal freedom, or, as he puts it, 'freedom of tastes and pursuits'; political freedom, above all of association for political purposes; and intellectual freedom of thought and expression. The last of these is clearly by far the most important in his view and the great bulk of the argument of his essay is consecrated to it.

There is, of course, an opposed tradition in the history of political thought: one which rates order above liberty, takes security to be the essential precondition of man's life as a social being and regards its preservation as the prime and overriding end of the state. In the work of Hobbes this attitude finds its most stark and memorable expression. For Hobbes liberty is simply 'the silence of the law', it is that residual area which the state believes it to be safe to leave to individual choice. The right of private judgement, especially in matter of religion, which for Locke is one of the three natural rights of man that no legitimate state may interfere with, was in Hobbes's view the prime cause of the Civil War, that most immediate and terrible breakdown of public order which provoked him into thinking about politics.

What I am inclined to suggest is that this dimension of thinking about politics, where the claims of individual freedom are balanced against the claims of peace and order as secured by the constraints of the state and its laws, important as it is, leaves a great deal out. It more or less ignores man as a worker and producer, as an economic being. Preoccupied with liberty, security, and equality, it pays only the most fleeting and marginal attention to prosperity, which is, after all, the object of the great part of men's actions and so primordial a constituent of human well-being.

I should not seriously ascribe this curious limitation of interest simply to a kind of intellectual myopia or *déformation professionnelle*. Until comparatively recent times the economic order was very much thought of as part of the natural order of things, as something not particularly amenable to human interference and modification, something, indeed, more or less given, like the weather, available for discussion, perhaps, but not for deliberate improvement. Governments have, indeed, for a long time exercised a powerful influence on the conditions of economic life, by such things as the debasement of currencies, the fixing of 'just prices', the granting of monopolies, and, above all, by the maintenance of a level of public security which made the activities of merchants safe enough to be worth engaging in. But there was until the eighteenth century little theoretical understanding of the way in which the economy worked and when a theory was developed it was one which argued that the best results for all would ensue if individual agents were left alone to pursue their own individual interests, the role of the state being that of preserving a secure and honest framework for the interaction of individual decisions about production and exchange.

Before continuing with the issue of theory, in particular of the principles to which we can or should appeal in seeking to work out a more satisfactory view of the proper relations of industry, state, and individual, a glance at some matters of historical fact may be useful. It will have to be a very schematic glance but its crudity and oversimplification need not deprive it of point.

The first type of economic system which we encounter in recorded human history is the slave economy in which the bulk of the population are scarcely regarded as human beings at all, but essentially as instruments of production, as, in effect, a kind of useful domesticated animal, puzzlingly similar in physical appearance to human beings proper. The great political thinkers of the ancient world, members and beneficiaries of slave economies, concerned themselves wholly with the well-being and self-realization of *citizens*, free citizens, that is to say. The enslaved masses were not, so to speak, part of their constituency. It is an essential feature of the life proper to a free citizen, according to the ideas of Plato and Aristotle, that he should be leisured, or, at any rate, that he should not be involved in any sort of economic production. Plato's ideal human being is a ruler, Aristotle's a sequestered theorist. The material conditions of life, and the well-being of those who actually secure those conditions, do not enter into consideration.

In due course slavery gives way to serfdom, the worker as chattel is replaced by the worker as more or less infantile dependant. The landlord determines where the serf lives and what he can and must do. His thinking, as far as it ranges beyond immediate, everyday, practical concerns, is done for him by his priest. The influence of Christianity is shown in the fact that lord and serf are at least seen as both being immortal souls. But the equality of status and consideration that is accorded to both at the ultimate seat of divine judgement does not manifest itself very conspicuously in terrestrial affairs.

The great change occurs, of course, at the beginning of what is still conventionally regarded as modern history. The conception of the individual as the responsible determiner of his own economic fate begins with the merchant, is extended to the craftsman or artisan, and appears in the agricultural sector, which is still the very much largest part of the economy, in the peasant proprietor or free tenant or yeoman, who is not formally bound to the soil he cultivates like his predecessor, the serf, but holds it by reason of a fairly straightforward commercial, contractual relationship.

It is at this stage in history that our concept of the individual, however much it had been abstractly anticipated by Stoic or Christian notions of equal humanity, really becomes effectively applicable to the life of mankind. The individual, as we still conceive him, is an invention of the Renaissance. It is closely tied up with those cognate Renaissance concepts of the genius and of personality. Hitherto individual human beings may have been the atoms of the social whole but they have always been bound up together into some kind of social molecule: the tribe, the slave-run estate, the manor.

The enormous liberation of human energies brought about at this early, mercantile and craft, stage of capitalism is a commonplace of liberal historiography. It is also, I believe, a great historical truth. It involved, not just a change in social organization, but a change in human nature. Anonymous balladeers and cathedral-builders give way to named poets and architects. Inventions flow from the minds of some imaginative and enterprising individuals and are put to the task of relieving man's estate by others. A vast accession of power to improve what had been thought of as the effectively immutable conditions of human life takes place and with it a general diffusion of the idea of ambition, of self-improvement, almost a kind of general human coming of age in which men at large come to think of themselves as responsible for their own fates on earth.

Now it is perfectly reasonable to describe this movement from slave to serf to free merchant, craftsman, or farmer as a progressive augmentation of human liberty. But the curious fact is that it is not this kind of freedom, this self-direction or self-management as a productive or economic being, with which political theorists preoccupied themselves. In the aftermath of the Reformation it was with religious freedom, specifically with freedom of styles of worship and of modes of ecclesiastical organization, that the theorists of liberty were for the most part concerned.

Marxists would say that the explicitly religious issues I have mentioned are only the apparent or manifest content of the thinking of that age. This thinking is really, in their view, an encoded public expression for more basic, practical, material interests. Progressive thinkers might talk about a vernacular Bible, the replacement of an altar at the east end of the church by a table at the side and the removal of sacred imagery. What they were actually concerned with was replacing the notion that usury was sinful by the idea that the rate of interest should be determined by supply and demand. In the sense in which this view is intended, in which there is no imputation of conscious deception by the thinkers involved, I should not quarrel with this. Its effects on ideas about how productive, economic activity should be carried on were at least as important for the character and quality of human life as its effects on its ostensibly devotional field of reference.

At the level of public expression and debate, concern with freedom moved from religion to politics without seriously touching the economic aspects of man's life in society. Both Catholics and Protestants were converted from more or less theocratic notions about the state, which saw it as either dependent for its legitimacy on the church's endorsement or, more extremely, as with Calvin, identified it with the church, to the secular idea of the state as a human contrivance set up for earthly, human ends and to be justified by its service of those ends. The process was encouraged by the phenomenon of dynastic rulers being of one religious persuasion while most or many of their subjects were of another. This was to be the main topic of political theorizing in the eighteenth and nineteenth centuries.

In the eighteenth century, inspired by Locke, the secular political thinkers of the Enlightenment developed the idea of the separation of church and state, and with it that of the essentially private, voluntary character of religious subscription, and the idea of the limitation of the state's powers by the imprescriptible natural rights of individual human beings. The two great themes of the nineteenth century were democracy, justified as the only form of government with an automatic concern for the rights and well-being of the population at large, and nationalism, the idea that the boundaries of states ought to coincide with natural social groupings and not be determined by the accidents of dynastic inheritance. The Enlightenment prepared the agenda for the American and French Revolutions. The democratic and nationalist thinking of the nineteenth century prepared the way for the mass societies, both democratic and totalitarian, of our own century of terrible wars and frustrated hopes of progress.

Now while all this was going on the economic order was undergoing a massive transformation, mercantile capitalism was giving way to industrial capitalism. The liberation of human creative energies I spoke of earlier, although most evident and emphasized in the domain of culture, in the plays of Shakespeare and the French tragedians, the invention of orchestra music and the secularized or at least humanistic painting of the Italian Renaissance, also produced a flow of mechanical and technical invention which was to transform the social conditions in which the liberation had occurred. The small craftshop, where the apprentices could look forward to becoming master craftsmen on their own account, the small merchant house whose agents might hope in time to become independent merchants themselves, increasingly found themselves replaced by ever-larger factories and by institutionally massive trading and banking corporations. The process of industrial concentration extended to the agricultural sector where it was facilitated by enclosures and clearances. Marx noticed the tendency and over-apocalyptically projected it, with his prophecy of a minute class of hyperbolically wealthy monopolists confronting a huge, industrially organized mass of increasingly miserable and impoverished proletarians.

Three things were left out of his calculations. The joint-stock company made it possible for great industrial economies of scale to be combined with a comparatively large diffusion of ownership. Increased productivity and non-revolutionary trade unions making demands that could be conceded without a fight meant that his 'law of increasing misery' did not come into force. The increasing technical complexity of manufacturing processes and the enormous enlargement of the services sector of advanced economies created a new intermediate class of managers and technicians. But, for all that, economic concentration proceeded inexorably and, if it did not bring about the kind of obviously explosive situation which he predicted for advanced industrial societies, it left us with the problems of frustrated desire for autonomy, of alienation from work, of what one might call massive occupational disappointment with which we are confronted today.

I said earlier that it was perfectly reasonable to describe the movement from slave to serf to independent merchant or artisan or yeoman as a progressive augmentation of freedom. Even if it was not a kind of freedom that traditional theorists of state and society have given much attention it is one to which their specific conception of freedom, which is the one which governs our thought and speech on the subject, unquestionably applies.

I am afraid a short terminological digression cannot be avoided at this point. It is clear, once one reflects on it for a moment, that we often talk in everyday life about freedom when we are not in the least concerned with freedom as a social value, as a proper end, or standard of political action. We speak of a road being free from holes, a central heating system free from leaks or stoppages, of a person as being free from financial worry. All we mean here is that whatever it is that is said to be free does not have, perhaps no longer has, something that is, or is thought of, as bad. Thus we should only say ironically that a child was wholly free from any consideration of its parents or that the hotels somewhere were entirely free from modern plumbing.

Freedom as a social value is a more confined and limited notion. It is ascribed only to people, to rational agents. It asserts the absence of obstructions to their doing something they want to, or might reasonably be expected to want to do. It is not that I am not free, because of my bodily constitution, to live without air; it is just that I cannot, I am unable to.

Similarly, although I may wish, on leaving Oxford, that I could be in London a minute later, the fact I cannot get what I want is no limitation on my freedom, it is simply a deficiency of power. Freedom as a social value is the ability to do what one wants, unobstructed by human interference. And even that is not quite enough. If someone prevents me from having a picnic in a certain spot by getting there first, in ignorance of my competing desire and even of my very existence, he is, no doubt, a nuisance, but he has not diminished my freedom. Freedom strictly so called, and as we commonly understand it, is the absence of intentional prevention of people's doing what they want to do.

Now the slave of the ancient world was utterly unfree in this sense of the term. The move from slavery to serfdom was accomplished by the removal of legal and customary constraints, intentionally imposed and deliberately sanctioned, on the ownership of property, the employment of much, at any rate, of one's own labour, of choice of a marriage-partner. Further intentional constraints were removed at the next stage. The free man of the post-medieval epoch was not compelled by deliberate human agency to live in a certain place, to perform certain fixed services for a lord whom he no more chose than he chose his place of birth. He could change his place of residence, his occupation, his style of life.

Under advanced industrialism of the highly concentrated sort we have today it is not that these freedoms have been abrogated. It is rather that they have become difficult to exercise because circumstances have arisen with no forethought of such consequences, which are very different from those that prevailed when the freedoms in question were first won. It is harder for dissatisfied but enterprising people to make their way to an unoccupied or unexploited part of their country or the world to make a new start on their own. Skills are more specialized, so that the heavy investment in their acquisition cannot lightly be cast aside in pursuit of a new and more satisfying occupation. In general opportunities for satisfying or at least remunerative employment are more and more concentrated in vast organizations where the precise manner and style of working has been laid rigorously down by some remote and impersonal directing authority.

This is not, in terms of our ordinary understanding of the word, a loss of freedom. But it is a loss of something important, of something, which if not freedom itself, is what made freedom in its economic aspect really worth having.

What possible ways are there of alleviating this state of affairs? One is to put the clock back and to revert to an altogether smaller scale of operation in our institutional arrangements. This small-is-beautiful theory was affirmed with prophetic vehemence by Rousseau, even if as a cure for a rather different disease than that with which we are concerned. Rousseau thought urban civilization with its sophisticated luxuries morally corrupt. His ideal was for men to live simply by subsistence agriculture on their own land in the manner of early American and Australian frontiersman. That ideal could hardly be realized with anything like the thoroughness with which he envisaged it without genocide. Even in more modest and manageable terms it would surely involve a reduction in living standards, an ascetic discarding of the productive fruits of human inventiveness and effort, which the broad, unidealistic mass of mankind (amongst whom I may say I include myself) would refuse to countenance.

Another possibility is suggested by some descriptions of the life of employees of large, paternalistic concerns in Japan. This is a kind of neo-feudalism in which the old responsibilities of the manorial lord to his villeins, the often-mourned counterpart of the bondage of the medieval villager, are discharged, in modern dress as it were, by the giant firm to its employees. Housing, leisure, and recreation, the provision of a host of socially valuable and humanly supportive services, are left not to the agencies of the state but to the employing organization. I think this would not really solve the problems of alienation in a world of organizational giants, at any rate in the West with its long tradition of partly actual, partly devotional individualism.

There is, surely, no serious prospect of dismantling the great institutions that dominate our lives in advanced industrial societies. What is needed is to impart a degree of autonomy to their constituent parts so that they function in it more like the elements of a living organism than the pieces of a machine.

A consolidated balance sheet is too insensitive a measure of the health of a large industrial organization. Yet it tends to be the basis of central decisions which wipe out the whole of the employment of a given kind that there is in a particular neighbourhood. We need, in other words, to be anxious to find out ways of including the social and human costs of industrial decisions in the balance sheets of particular enterprises.

The giant corporation has brought into existence, as an inevitable dancing-partner, the giant union, insisting on national wage bargains against the real interests of those who live, and wish to continue to live, in more or less remote or industrially backward regions. To match an increased concern with the social costs of industrial concentration on the part of employers they might be expected to take up a less predominantly adversary stance towards those employers, for both parties have an interest in higher productivity and, in the largest sense of the phrase, better working conditions. Resentful and suspicious insistence on solidarity at all costs is an anachronism with the present distribution of industrial power.

Economic freedom has always been the Cinderella of political theory, overshadowed by the two ugly sisters of religion and politics. In a way the fight for economic freedom was won a long time ago. The trouble is that one of the fruits of victory was a kind of industrial development which has made the freedom attained of increasingly reduced value, for all its astonishing transformation of the material conditions of life. The fact that Marx gave a perceptive diagnosis of the disease when it was still not very far advanced should not obscure the fact that his prognosis of its future course was largely mistaken and his therapeutic recommendations, to the extent that they have been followed, have turned out to be repulsively barbarous. Let us see if we can do better.

19

Culture, Education, and Values

Introduction

The subject of this and the next chapter, originally the first two lectures in the Cook Memorial Series, is not the three abstractions that feature in their general title on their own, apart from a brief preliminary canter around them. What they are really concerned with is a crisis in contemporary culture in our part of the world, which has first made itself felt in the domain of education and which consists essentially in the repudiation of values that have been usually accepted. I believe that if this revolution against familiar values prevails there will be a break in the continuity of our culture, larger even than that which constituted the Renaissance, and really more comparable to that which accompanied the fall of the Roman Empire and its replacement by the barbarian kingdoms.

A Cultural Crisis: The Devaluation of Values

With the Renaissance the focus of cultural interest moved from heaven and the soul's eternal destiny to the earth and to the embodied life of human beings upon it. Educationally it led attention away from the abstract studies of logic, metaphysics, and theology to rhetoric, from dog Latin to the style of Cicero, from the fathers of the church and the commentators on the Sentences to the poets and orators of Greece and Rome. The idea that the classical imaginative literature of Greece and Rome was the ideal and total completion of the educational process turned out to be remarkably durable. It prevailed in all but the most humble and rudimentary schools until well into my early life.

The current revolution directs itself against the values incorporated in the literary canon, in the first instance, that is, against the generally accepted, if constantly revised, list of masterpieces of literature. That canon defines what one ought to have read and understood, at least in reasonably large part, if one is to count as an educated person. Loosely associated with this attack, and conceived in much the same spirit, is a less coherent assault on the values of the intellect. I mean in talking of these to refer to the values implicit in the ideas of speaking rightly and thinking rightly, of conformity to the rules of language and the rules of logic and method.

The prophetic figures of the Renaissance saw themselves as leading a march back to a glorious past, to the more golden passages of the histories of Greece and Rome. The current revolution seems to go back much further, to the primitive, to what may be described as natural or barbarous, according to taste. Barbarous rather than savage, in terms of Collingwood's distinction between them, since where the savage is untouched by civilization, the barbarian is determined to destroy it.

A brief parade of symptoms of the crisis may help to make it more vivid and concrete. There is the scene of the Revd Jesse Jackson leading a crowd of 500 students at Stanford University, the major private university of California, as they chanted 'Hey, hey, ho, ho, Western culture's got to go'. There is the widely used formula, purporting to describe the authors of the books making up the canon: Dead White Males. There is the project of replacing the familiar style of study of English or other literature with something called 'cultural studies', a pseudo-sociological pursuit of alleged political content in imaginative literature, the arts (fine but preferably popular), and mass entertainment. There is the censoring by local government library committees of ideologically unacceptable works from the shelves. At a more basic level there is the failure in primary education to develop literacy, or, where that is achieved, to encourage reading. In its place there are intruded collective activities or 'projects', which seek to make the classroom and the playground as much like each other as possible. Emphasis is laid on self-expression, which, in the case of those too young to have much in the way of selves to express, has to be valued more for its simple noisiness or amplitude than for anything it may objectively achieve.

The same kind of indulgent antinomianism prevails in the teaching of the English language. The perfectly reasonable view that dictionaries should not be anachronistically prescriptive, should not lay down as correct senses of words which have largely fallen out of colloquial use, is blown up into the doctrine that there is no distinction between correct and incorrect at all. Grammar is similarly seen as oppressive, an attempt to destroy the self-esteem, and even identity, of the working class by imposing middle-class habits of speech on them.

The assault on rationality is a many-faceted one and less explicit than the corresponding attacks on literature and language. To a considerable extent it is a matter of exemplary practice rather than of conscious theory. When Heidegger and Sartre entered the British field of consciousness after 1945 they astonished those who read or read about them by their lack of intellectual decorum. Their successors in the leadership of intellectual fashion on the continent of Europe have kept up the bad work: Habermas, Foucault, Derrida. The gratuitous obscurity which is offered as a challenge and a reproach to the naive lucidity and pedestrian argumentativeness of Anglo-Saxon empiricism more or less guarantees that what is said will be misunderstood, or, in the face of criticism, be held to have been misunderstood.

There are, however, some bodies of explicit anti-rational theory about. At a fairly manageable distance from the conventional intellectual tradition there are objectors to the supposedly supreme objectivity of natural science, moderate in the case of Kuhn's theory of successive paradigms, wildly extreme in Feyerabend's doctrine that anything goes. The assumption that there is such a thing as objective truth and an objective reality for it to be true of has been undermined from various directions, by anti-realism and by Rorty's dismissal of the pretensions of philosophy to be some kind of intellectual judge or referee. If this is the persuasion of the intellectual elite, it will soon filter down to the classroom and encourage the belief that thought is simply the expression of what one feels, that it does not have to submit to any controls of logic and method.

Before setting out to expound these cultural forays in greater detail there are two other preliminary matters to be dealt with. First, I shall consider the relations between culture, education, and values in general, not so much to vindicate my choice of a title for these lectures as to focus definitely on what is at issue, which is, briefly, not culture in its most inclusive sense, but high culture. Secondly, I shall seek to put our present situation in some sort of comparative context by outlining an extremely short and selective history of education. This will, I believe, show that our crisis is unique in its destructive potential.

Culture, education, and values are intimately connected. Culture is what is transmitted from one generation to another by education. The rest is biological inheritance. Values are central to, although not wholly constitutive of, education. Therefore values occupy a central position in culture. That culture is what is handed on by education would not be disputed, I imagine, so long as some appropriate qualifications are made. I shall force myself not to linger over these since they are needed only to prevent misunderstanding. First of all, the education that conveys culture is very far from being all formal, that is to say carried on in some kind of school. Much of it will come from parents and other adults or contemporaries whose activities may be observed and imitated. Furthermore education need not be intentional or, if you feel that it must be, learning does not presuppose an intentional educator. One can learn from someone who has no idea that one is watching him.

What are the main kinds of cultural items that are learnt? Above all they are items of practical knowledge or skills: how to speak meaningfully and grammatically, and the associated arts of reading and writing, how to reason, investigate, and criticize one's own beliefs and those of others, how to get the most out of things, for example by attention. Values have a double application to skill or practical knowledge. In the first place, the fact that they are intentionally taught, if they are, shows that somebody thinks they are worth learning or, at any rate, teaching. That is an external value, one might say, of a taught and learnt capacity. But a skill also has an internal value, since to have acquired the skill is, to some extent at least, to have mastered the *right* way to do the thing in question and to have come to know what that right way is, even if one has not yet fully mastered it. These internal and external values are not wholly distinct. In the standard case, that of sincere or committed teaching, it is just because the teacher thinks that what the skill defines as right is right that he thinks it worth imparting.

Everyone who thinks at all about education nowadays is so conditioned to denying that to be merely informed, to know a lot of facts, is to be educated that it is worth saying that, if not the central element in education, information or knowledge is still essential to it. In part that is because the more theoretical or cognitive skills need information to work on. To speak and write, to reason and investigate, you need some raw material of fact. A kitchen is not a larder, but it is no use without one. But to admit that is not to deny the primacy of skill or know-how.

All cultures teach the prevailing language, approved and customary modes of behaviour, and how to do things that need to be done and that people know how to do. None of that requires formal education, which comes in with literacy, the first schools in the original river-valley civilizations having been schools for scribes. Once there is writing the range of cultural achievement is much increased. There is great oral poetry, some oral law and aphoristic wisdom, simple crafts do not need writing. But science, mathematics, articulated philosophy, history that is not legend or memorized chronicle, the novel—all have to be written down. It is largely from these that a conception of culture altogether narrower than the comprehensive anthropological one under consideration so far develops, that is to say Arnold's conception of culture as high culture.

He defined it, in effect, as 'the best that has been thought and said in the world' and thought that to pursue it is to pursue human perfection. I propose to modify Arnold's formula and define high culture as *what has been best thought and best said*, in other words as the greatest intellectual and literary achievements or, if culture be thought of as a characteristic of an individual and not as an objective body of work, as familiarity with those achievements. That is close to T. S. Eliot's list of the ingredients of high culture: first learning, then 'philosophy in the widest sense', as he puts it, 'an interest in, and some ability to manipulate, abstract ideas', and next the arts, literature in the first place, no doubt, but also painting and music. A fourth ingredient for Eliot, urbanity or civility, I shall ignore as really being nothing like and having nothing at all to do with the others. It is high culture, understood as the summit of intellectual achievement, measured by established intellectual and literary values, that is currently in danger.

I turn to my threatened very short outline history of education to show that in literate communities high culture is identifiable at an early stage of their development. It is most readily seen in education where it forms the curriculum of the most highly esteemed and most ardently sought teaching.

In archaic Greece serious formal education was much the same thing as the study of Homer, with his lessons in knightly honour, appropriate to a warrior society. In due course Euripides and Menander as well as orators, philosophers, and historians were added to the canon. There emerged an oscillation between stress on cognitive rationality, as in Plato and Aristotle, and stress on style and eloquence, nourished by rhetoric rather than logic, as in the sophists and Isocrates, that was to persist until modern times. The Roman emphasis was on rhetoric, as befits the greatest nation of legal thinkers and practitioners. In taking over the Greek canon they made it a condition of being truly educated that one should know Greek. The Greeks had seen no point in knowing any language but Greek.

Monastic and cathedral schools kept education going after a fashion. The difficulty of incorporating pagan literature into the education of Christians was gradually overcome. Greek had died away. The literacy required for reading the Bible became the defining characteristic of the clergy. Around the twelfth century the large part of Aristotle's works which had until then not been available in the West came in from the Arabs and was translated. Universities emerged for Aristotle's logic, metaphysics, and physics to be taught in and applied to the exposition of church doctrine. Medieval higher education was strongly cognitive or logical in emphasis. Vocationally considered, its aim was to turn out administrators for partially literate feudal kings and nobles. There was nothing much of a literary side to it.

With the Renaissance rhetoric replaced logic, purity of style replaced validity of reasoning. Yet the revised and enlarged classical canon had a marked cognitive element. It called for translation from, and into, classical languages and so inspired a sense for exact meaning and conscious adherence to the rules of grammar. The Renaissance curriculum prevailed in the teaching of the upper classes until very recent times. Other fields of study were introduced and took some time away from Greek and Latin—science and history and modern languages—but the classics retained their leading place. And the medieval, Aristotelian tradition was not obliterated. It continued to dominate the universities, despite the exasperated criticism of major thinkers like Bacon, Hobbes, and Locke. It was, indeed, an aspect of the general decline of the universities after the Renaissance, reaching its nadir in the eighteenth century.

At a lower social level much increased literacy understandably coincided with the mass production of books by the printing press and the appearance of vernacular Bibles to allow for the cultivation of Protestant religious self-reliance. Vocational teaching became available for more of the general mass of the population.

In the nineteenth century economic requirements encouraged vocational pressure on the curriculum of the more exclusive schools, but the classical canon preserved its status. In this century more and more people have received higher education, so more and more schools have had to prepare pupils for it. That has led to the introduction of useful subjects, such as engineering, and widely accessible ones, such as English. The canon these lectures are concerned with is largely a combination of the Greek and Roman classics with the acknowledged classics of English literature, with some European supplements. The modern part of this compound was not invented to serve the needs of newly created English departments. It was an established tradition, something that every educated person had previously been expected to get up on his own. Such works as Johnson's *Lives of the Poets* helped to form it. So our canon is not new. It is continuous with what was picked out as the best by Greeks and Romans, as revived at the Renaissance, and has been added to and otherwise varied in composition ever since.

Such a canon is not peculiar to the West. The most notable canon is that of the Chinese classics. Assembled partly by and in the lifetime of Confucius, they later became the crucial examination subject used to select mandarins, surviving the energetic attempts of an emperor to suppress them. The Chinese canon, like that of the

West, goes back more than two and a half thousand years. They arrived at the novel, however, three hundred years before we did.

The history of formal education can be looked at from two points of view, one concerned with what is taught, the other with whom it is taught to. The second factor does not have to affect the first. If what has hitherto been taught only to a few is the best there is, why should it not be made available as numbers expand, to a larger number? In the nineteenth century, when literacy became pretty well universal in Britain, there was a vigorous movement for self-education in the lower ranks of society. They were not to be satisfied with any watered down version of the literary canon. They wanted the real thing and Ernest Rhys was there to supply it, with his Everyman's Library. In what follows that should be kept in mind.

I have slightly adjusted Arnold's definition of culture, in the narrow sense of high culture, to read: what has been best thought and best said. That covers both sides of the long oscillation I have recounted between the primarily intellectual and the primarily literary content of the highest kind of education. Intellectual higher education is now more a matter of studying a subject in its current process of development than of mastering a set of classic texts. The older way of doing things still prevails in ancient history and in philosophy, but not very much in modern history, hardly at all in economics and the social sciences and only vestigially in the natural sciences.

The three challenges I am going to consider to high culture are directed against what, following Arnold, I see as its two main ingredients and, in the third place, against the seriousness about language, about speaking and writing, which is required for effective study of either of the other two. The challenges in question are distinct. The rejection of the canon is vocal, explicit, and clearly identifiable. The war against language and the intellect is more diffuse, more embedded in practice than polemically articulated. But they have some common elements which can be mentioned at the outset.

Both are, to start with, essentially political. The forms of culture attacked are seen as the possessions of a minority—it would be more accurate to say: several minorities. Since that is so it is assumed that they must be instruments serving the interests of the minority or minorities involved. To impose them on people outside the minority is, therefore, oppressive: it ignores the needs and experience of the outsiders or it causes them to think of the world and human society in a way that confirms their domination by the minority.

The excluded majority is divided into a now familiar number of categories: women, sexual deviants, blacks, non-Westerners generally, sometimes the young. There are various apparent ideas about to what extent and in what way ordinary high culture should be handled. Should it be allowed to continue in a suitably humbled form, like a former aristocrat in a communist country, acting as caretaker of the museum that was once his palace? That is what the establishment of university departments of women's, black, or gay studies would seem to point to. Should the canon simply be augmented with works by authors from the groups said to be inadequately represented? Or should some disciplines be altogether given up in favour of others: literary criticism by 'cultural studies', philosophy by conversation in the manner of Richard Rorty? The votaries of high culture, it is believed, are on to a good thing, to the extent that it helps to protect their dominant social status, and, in the interests of justice, they must be expropriated.

Let me turn to the sharp leading edge of the attack on high culture: the rejection of the canon. It has been much more evident and has gone much further in the United States than here. One reason for that is that the idea of the canon is very obtrusive in American education, where it is usual in universities to offer a 'required' or compulsory course on Western civilization. The heart of these courses is a list of selected readings from 'great books': Plato, Augustine, Erasmus, Pascal, etc. Their purpose is to make up for the deficiencies of American high schools in acquainting their students with anything that could count as knowledge of their cultural inheritance.

The critics point out that these lists of great books are of writings by dead white males and are put together by white males, who are ordinarily alive, but much under the influence of their dead predecessors. It may be added that both the selected and their selectors are for the most part bourgeois and straight. It should be admitted that this observation is broadly correct. There are a few women in the canon (many more than in the parallel canons of painting and music, but, of course, in nothing like their proportion in the population at large). There are no blacks at all. That there are no Chinese, Indian, Arab, or Persian representatives, a defender of the canon would say, is not from lack of merit but because of linguistic remoteness. It is not a perfect answer. But works of these four great literatures are available, indeed in cheap, canon-sustaining series like Everyman's Library or Penguin Classics. The gay have no real statistical cause for complaint. Five canonical poets in English were homosexual: Marlowe, Gray, Hopkins, Whitman, and Auden (six, if Housman is reckoned great). Nearly all canonical writers were middle-class, although an occasional Villon or Burns breaks through.

There are obvious explanations of the fact that the contents of the canon should be largely by, and even more largely selected by, white, middle-class males. It is selected by literary intellectuals, like Johnson, Coleridge, and Arnold, or, more recently, by university teachers. These are occupations into which women have only recently made their way. The poor have had neither the conditions of life, nor in many cases the literacy, for serious reading and writing. But do these limitations on those selected and their selectors undermine the claim that the works in the canon are of conspicuous excellence?

The critics of the canon do not really engage with it on that level. What they do first, is to attack the credentials of those who select the canon and then proceed to their main business which is the alleged bad consequences of canonization. One way of seeking to undermine credentials is the familiar manoeuvre of scepticism about value judgements. In this case it relies on the distinguishing marks of the selectors to prove that their shared interests must underlie their valuations. For that to be effective the critic would have to show that there is a connection between the two. And that is usually just assumed. The thought that the selectors prefer works written by people like themselves over works written by other kinds of people *which are of equal or greater merit* is not available to the sceptic about value. In fact something like it is to be found in polemically feminist writing about literature, because in their case there really is a body of arguably undervalued work to appeal to. But that recourse is not available to blacks or the poor.

What are supposed to be the bad consequences of canonization? Accounts of these are sometimes positive or direct, sometimes negative or indirect. The positive view is that teaching the canon forces on the oppressed outsider a white male middle-class way of viewing the world which falsifies his experience and obliterates his own view of the world. That, it is argued, manipulates him into putting up with the subordinate role which outsiders are held properly to occupy in the dominant viewpoint, as a Victorian family servant might say 'we go to Menton every winter'. A milder variant of this position says that a canon made up of books by white, middle-class males obstructs the development of imaginative sympathy with those outside the privileged circle. Thus in Shakespeare the poor serve the purpose of light relief; the rustic actors of *Pyramus and Thisbe* in *Midsummer Night's Dream* for example or Dogberry and his colleagues in *Much Ado About Nothing*. The same could be said of Hardy's peasants—and he was one himself, as Shakespeare was not.

The indirect bad consequences alleged are somewhat easier to grasp. Essentially they are that the literature of the canon diverts attention from the clamorous and crisis-ridden present either to timeless beauties and eternal verities or an idealized, imaginary past. To put the point more forcefully; it does not merely divert attention that could be better placed: it acts as a palliative to social evils, provides a bogus substitute satisfaction for real needs. Even more indirectly, high culture is criticized for its failure to be primarily directed towards the emancipation of the oppressed. That is reminiscent of Tolstoy's doctrine that the excellence of a work of literature is determined by the contribution it makes to the brotherhood of mankind. Acting on that principle he judged *Uncle Tom's Cabin* to be supremely good.

These conclusions about the bad consequences of canon lead to proposals of reform which are of various degrees of vehemence. The most moderate is that of enlarging the canon, or revising it, so as to include works by authors from the oppressed groups. Thus Frantz Fanon joins John Stuart Mill, or replaces him. But that is really at best a practical makeshift, like the participation of totalitarian parties in parliamentary government. In so far as it is believed that all valuation is irremediably biased and subjective, anything that claims to be a canon will be no more than an expression of the preferences of an individual or group.

Consistent with that is the extreme conclusion that evaluative literary criticism should be abandoned. It should be replaced by the new discipline of 'cultural studies' in which literature and other broadly comparable things like films, television shows, videos, and comic strips should be examined to determine their political significance, their contribution to or their impairment of the interests of the oppressed. By that stage, quite evidently, no other characteristics of a literary work make it worth study

CULTURE, EDUCATION, AND VALUES 227

apart from its political bearing. Mere revision of the canon still allows for a significant difference between literature and other objects of cultural study.

The attack on intellectual values is many-pronged. To be complete it needs to be since they are numerous and varied. Some, like those of clarity, simplicity, and unambiguity, are comparatively informal, although they can, of course, be formally taught. But this aspect of rhetoric is not a systematic discipline. It is like good manners, in that while some broad rules of thumb can be laid down, the skill involved is not a technique, but a capacity to adjust behaviour in the light of its effect on the sensitivities of others. In the case of these informal values of discourse consideration for the reader is the governing factor.

These values have not, I think, been directly challenged. But the pursuit of them has been abandoned by a large number of vocal and admired thinkers. Much German philosophy has been evilly written since Kant's unfortunate example. But Cartesian clarity persisted in France up to Bergson's stylish communication of his elusive message. Sartre, importing Heidegger, initiated a catastrophic rout of the French intellect which reached a high point with Foucault and Derrida. The German critical theorists, from Horkheimer and Adorno to Marcuse and Habermas, wrote in a mixture of the styles of Hegel and Marx.

Degeneration of style has been accompanied by degeneration of structure. Terms indicative of logical organization abound in the writings of the unmasking thinkers of contemporary Europe: *thus* and *so*, *therefore* and *it follows*, *contradictory* and *incompatible*. But, when examined, these prove to be a kind of ornamentation. Where an effort is made to extract an intelligible line of argument it turns out to be absurdly fallacious. John Ellis has painstakingly reconstructed the way in which Derrida recommends to the reader his paradoxical conclusion that writing is prior to speech. What Derrida does is progressively redefine 'speech' so that it means 'writing' and 'writing' so that it means 'speech'. His technique is to pronounce some amazing but fairly intelligible thesis—for example, that there is nothing outside the text—and then surround it with a tissue of highly obscure and not discernibly relevant matter so as to intimidate the reader into swallowing the amazing thesis.

To show that this is not just casual abuse, I shall consider an example.

A written sign is proffered in the absence of the receiver. How to style this absence? One could say that at the moment when I am writing, the receiver may be absent from my field of present perception. But is not this absence merely a distant presence, one which is delayed or which, in one form or another, is idealized in its representation. This does not seem to be the case, or at least this distance, divergence, delay, this deferral must be capable of being carried to a certain absoluteness of absence if the structure of writing, assuming that writing exists, is to constitute itself. It is at that point that the *difference* as writing could no longer be an ontological modification of presence. (Derrida, *Limited Inc.* (1988), 7)

That starts intelligibly enough. Something written need not have an audience which is present at the time and place of writing. The audience may be somewhere else. The suspicion is voiced that he is not just a distant presence, i.e. presumably present somewhere else, but is capable of absolute absence, i.e., presumably, of not existing at all. All this to express the truism that something can be a piece of writing even if nobody ever reads it. But why dramatize that by saying that the possibility of a piece of writing's being unread is *necessary* if it is to constitute itself as writing. It gives a wholly superfluous air of menace to the concealed truism. To say that something does not have to be read to be a piece of writing is not to say that it *must* be capable of being not read, only that it is capable of being not read. Another truism lurks in the final sentence, namely that what makes a cluster of marks into piece of writing is not present where and when the marks are. For one thing there is the intention of the writer: another, more important item is the set of social conventions about the making of such marks which endows them with meaning and so enables the writer to carry out his intention to communicate. But nothing in the passage about unread writing has any bearing on this second truism at all.

Derrida is the most extreme and, in his curious way, distinguished of stylistic debauchees. He is further down the road of self-indulgence than Sartre or even Foucault. But he is not alone. He has many imitators in American academic life and some in this country. Here is a ripe specimen of this new form of discourse. It comes from an essay about the Turin Shroud.

What we need is a concept of figurative *Aufhebung*. We would have to consider the dichotomy of its field and its means, and how they employ a dialectical mimesis as initiation of absolute knowledge: how it attempts to transform sensible space and so begin a movement (Hegel would have said automovement) in the direction of a certitude, figural certitude. An absolute seeing that would transcend the scansion of seeing and knowing... (G. Didi-Huberman, *October: The First Decade*, ed. Michelson et al. (1987))

If Derrida hides truism, and falsisms, in his prose and serves them up with an illusion of logical connectedness, that last quotation is simply babble, a sort of verbal delirium. Those who write like that, and also the somewhat overlapping group of those who repudiate the canon, share a common assumption that there is no such thing as objective truth, that all systems of belief reflect interest and bias and that there is no fixed and solid reality for our beliefs to be true about. It follows that the beliefs which we dignify with the title of knowledge in the light of the methods by which they were arrived at, methods dignified in their turn by being labelled rational or scientific, have no objective validity, but are relative, or even subjective, and the associated methods are too.

Scepticism is almost as old as philosophy, but traditional scepticism was based on supposed limitations of human intellectual power rather than on the emptiness of the goals pursued by the credulous believers whom sceptics were criticizing. In the current view there were three great masters of deception or unmaskers of illusion in the nineteenth century: Marx, Freud, and Nietzsche. For contemporary relativists the greatest of these was Nietzsche. It took time for the European mind to be prepared for the heart of his message. Marx's theory of the superstructure and Freud's of the unconscious emotional determinants of conscious mental life were needed to prepare the way for acknowledgement of Nietzsche's conception of beliefs as instruments in the service of the will to power. All our experience of the world is from some perspective or other and a perspective is a way of imposing order or form on a reality which in itself has none.

In Foucault's work there is an attempt to identify a sequence of such perspectives, which he calls *epistemes*, in the history of European thought. He closely followed Nietzsche's notion of what we call knowledge being really in the service of our will to power, by examining the ideologically-driven variations in prevailing conceptions of what it is to be mad, ill, criminal, or sexually deviant. In the case of each of these social rejections allegedly objective science is used to force a set of people to the margins of society. There is a parallel between this and Thomas Kuhn's account of the history of science as a succession of periods in each of which a certain paradigm or standard, acceptable form of theorizing prevailed to the exclusion of all others until a scientific revolution replaced it with a new paradigm.

Less farouche than Foucault and less confined in scope than Kuhn is Richard Rorty. His principal target is epistemology, the theory of knowledge, to the extent that it supposes itself qualified to bestow certificates of cognitive respectability on other disciplines, or, as he might put it, other bodies of participants in the cultural conversation. The mistake of epistemology is to suppose that it is possible to compare the world in itself (nature) with the ways in which we represent it to ourselves (the mirror) to see if those representations correspond to what they refer to and are, therefore, true. The unsatisfactoriness of that account of the way in which we ascertain the cognitive value of our beliefs is familiar as a legacy of nineteenth-century absolute idealism as well as of Viennese logical positivism, at least until Tarski came and, supposedly, removed the scales from the eyes of the critics of correspondence. What is new is Rorty's adoption of a rather sedentary version of pragmatism in which the representatives of different disciplines converse with each other on equal terms.

Another American opponent of the alleged illusions of objectivism is Stanley Fish, Professor of Literature and of Law at Duke University and generally assumed to be the original of Morris Zapp in David Lodge's novel *Small World*. Inspired by Marx rather than Nietzsche, his argument against objectivism is short and simple. The factors which relativize our beliefs to our biases and interests are just as calculated to affect any principles or criteria of truth or justification or rationality to which we might appeal to modify our beliefs. So, for Fish, any such principles have no more authority than 'mere belief and unexamined practice'.

Foucault, Rorty, and Fish may be described as undiscriminating relativists. They do not apply their relativism to any particular body of beliefs, but spread it around in a wholesale fashion. Nietzsche came to that position eventually. But earlier in his career he excepted science from invalidation and confined his perspectivist doctrine to religion, metaphysics, art, and morality. In that he was at one with the more militant and orthodox positivists, who took religion and metaphysics to be empty and took moral and other value judgements to be no more than expressions of emotion.

Nietzsche based his perspectivism on the idea that interpretation is always from a point of view. He extended the doctrine to science on the ground that science is as much an interpretation of experience as metaphysics or poetry. Two other factors have, I believed, encouraged thinkers of the present day to follow him in this respect. One is ideological hostility to science. It is seen not merely as an intellectual precondition of such deplored developments as nuclear warfare, industrial pollution, and genetic engineering, but as somehow in favour of them. A little more cautiously, it has been held that scientism, the view that scientific knowledge is the best or the only real kind of knowledge, is implicitly propaganda for the application of science-based technology. The other is the curious hold, on philosophers of science who take science to be the best kind of knowledge, of non-realistic accounts of scientific theory, which regard such theories as useful fictions, readily replaceable instruments of prediction.

If science, the last stronghold, is given up, then rationality, objectivity, disinterestedness in general are exploded, revealed to be devices, at best unconscious, for the pursuit of group or personal interests and the achievement of power over others. What practical implications it is sensible to see that revelation as having is a complicated matter. Perhaps it need have no practical effect. A reflective scientist might simply carry on as before. For, even if his chosen pursuit is, he is now persuaded, inevitably biased and perspectival, it is no more or less so than anything else. But many, perhaps, will be persuaded by this line of thought that, since it is only a kind of sophisticated fairy-tale, it is not worth while going through the efforts involved in qualifying oneself to do it and in carrying it on in a professionally recognized way.

The attack on the intellect, or on its pretensions to rationality and disinterestedness in the most elevated fields of its application, bears on it as it is to be found in the domain of higher education. But any encouragement it gives to the indulgence of subjective whim and impulse there will make itself felt at the more primary levels of the educational system. And there have been reverberations. Relativism is in a naturally sympathetic relation to the development of multicultural studies. Equally the denial of objectivity, Derrida's view that interpretation, the essential work of the intellect, is play, or Rorty's that it should take the form of social conversation—all these ideas are in tune with educational practices which reject disciplined processes of learning in favour of exploratory self-expression.

I am not going to pursue the topic of elementary educational changes in general. But I want to consider the changes that have taken place in the teaching of language, since linguistic capacity—the ability to read with understanding, to speak and write with lucidity and order—is an indispensable requirement for effective literary study of the canon and for work in the fields in which the highest achievements of the intellect have been made.

The aspect of change with which I am particularly concerned is that which opposes the notion of language as being governed by rules. It sees the idea that an adequate capacity for speech requires the internalization of these rules as constraining and elitist. They are taken to stunt or obstruct the free self-expression of speakers, on the one hand, and either to confirm the position of the elite by excluding the masses who do not speak as they do or, alternatively, and conflictingly, by imposing an artificial manner of speech on them which cuts them off from their roots. The apparent conflict between exclusion and admission can be eliminated by distinguishing those who qualify for admission to the elite by learning effectively to speak as the elite do and the large remainder, the excluded, whose non-elite status is audibly marked by their failure to learn.

The matter is complicated, in England at any rate, by the way in which accents are distinctive of social classes. But that is not the kind of 'speaking properly' that is at issue here. What is in dispute are the requirements that a competent speaker should have a large vocabulary of words which he can use in their established meanings and that he should be able to assemble them in discourse in accordance with the rules of grammar. A teacher primarily concerned with expressiveness will give little or no attention to these things. That indifference may be solidified into hostility by the ideas that dictionaries should not be prescriptive and that grammar, like the operative meaning of words, is constantly changing.

It is persuasively argued that language is a natural, evolving phenomenon and that the function of dictionaries and grammars is simply to record how it is actually used. The way it is now is the outcome (to a large extent, for there are also neologisms to take account of) of individual deviations from what was, at the time, the prevailing practice. If most people use 'disinterested' as a synonym for 'uninterested' or say 'they invited Mother and I' rather than 'they invited Mother and me', that is all that the newer way of speaking requires for correctness.

Education is the transmitter of culture and the inculcation of values is at the centre of education. Traditionally, high culture, as embodied in the canon and the more theoretical academic disciplines and made possible by developed linguistic capacity, has been assumed to be the supremely valuable part of education. Hitherto those who wished to extend education from the few to the many aimed to enlarge the constituency for high culture. But now, by those who would unmask it as an elitist device, it is under the threefold attack I have described. In my second lecture (see Chapter 20) I shall address myself to the cogency of this attack.

20

A Revaluation of Values
Keeping Politics In Its Place

In the previous lecture (see Chapter 19) I described various directions from which the high culture component of the traditional content of education is under attack. The canon of supposedly supreme works of literature, the intellectual values that are most concentratedly pursued in the higher theoretical disciplines, the linguistic skills needed for effective study of the canon and the higher disciplines are all repudiated from the point of view of a militant egalitarianism which seeks to undermine their respective claims to superiority as compared with rock videos, women's or gay studies, and the discourse of Derrida, Dave Spart, or Raymond Williams.

Before taking a critical look at the objections raised against high culture I shall briefly do two other things. First of all, it might be interesting to reflect on possible explanations for this violent cultural insurrection. Secondly, I want to consider, in bare outline form, what might be the consequences, for education and for culture, and, therefore, for the community at large, of the revolution's success. Early in the first lecture I hinted darkly that it is a kind of incursion of the barbarians and that thought needs to be substantiated.

The denial of objective truth, of real knowledge, and of a real world to be known is, perhaps, an understandable, if delayed reaction to the uninterrupted diminution of anything like literal religious belief among the more reflective and thoughtful. It is not surprising that Nietzsche, who took the death of God seriously, should be the inspiration of those who seek to unmask the pretensions to objectivity of the Western mind. More fundamentally than in the role of an authorizer of morality, God served to guarantee the orderliness and intelligibility of the world. A world created by an intelligence in essence like that of human beings, even if infinitely more powerful, ought to be intelligible to them. But, of course, the absence of a cosmic guarantee of order and intelligibility is not a proof, or even much of a reason to believe, that those things are not to be found in the world, but are arbitrarily imposed on it.

An entirely humdrum and respectable conviction that the canon is a fairly parochial affair could be excited by enhanced communication and travel. As things are, *The Thousand and One Nights*, *The Dream of the Red Chamber*, *The Tale of Genji* are, so to speak, already associate members, although they are not exactly required reading. There

---

I want to acknowledge my heavy dependence on *Tenured Radicals* by Roger Kimball for illustrative material from the United States.

have always been a few Europeans interested in non-European literature: Sir William Jones, Goethe, Edward Fitzgerald, Arthur Waley. Through their translations they have supplied narrow glimpses of other canons than our own. It must be an anachronism to imagine that a canon composed exclusively of European works is comprehensive. But to arrange greatly enlarged membership of the canon is quite another thing from dismantling it altogether. Nor would the need for such an enlargement call for the degree of passion that the very idea of a canon excites in its current critics.

It is plain that the chief force behind the attack on high culture is a vehement and comprehensive egalitarianism. The question is: why should Western intellectuals and academics—particularly French and American ones—have embraced it with so much enthusiasm? They would reply, no doubt, that it is an entirely intelligible response to the evils of contemporary capitalism: nuclear weaponry, industrial pollution, neo-colonial exploitation. But these offences are hardly specific to capitalism, unless somehow China and the former Soviet Union can be made out to be really capitalist societies. The Vietnam War had a very disturbing effect on the American university scene. Students were first made guilty, and then angry, by exemption. Opposition to the war, for which there were anyway good reasons, was exacerbated by the fact that others were fighting it for one. That accounts for the unattractive flavour of the following description of the war, many years after, by a left-wing feminist. 'It was', she says, 'fought for the most part by ghetto residents commanded by elements of the southern lower-middle-class.' The word 'elements' for some disliked class of human beings, as Orwell pointed out, is often to be found in the vocabulary of totalitarians. Observers of the present cultural crisis as it has taken form in America at the moment have noted that its instigators are those, now in their late forties, who were rebellious students of 1968. They are at the height of their professional careers. Their conception of theory and literature as of pre-eminently political significance is combined with a corresponding determination to control the centres of power in the university and in what were once scholarly organizations. In line with their unembarrassed assumption that the life of learning is a political struggle, they ensure that appointments and promotions go to people of their way of thinking.

The launching of *Sputnik* in 1957 awoke a feeling in the United States that the country was falling behind its main adversary in intellectual competitiveness. The outcome was a great increase in government support for universities and an associated shift from the conception of them as ivory towers set in elite playgrounds to one which took them to be a vital component of the nation's strength. The humanities benefited from the new prosperity, but not gratefully, perhaps because it was not really intended for them. The events of 1968 saw a large reversal in the public perception of universities, which recent disclosures of misapplications of public funds within them can only have intensified. In an unsympathetic public environment dissidents within them have made effective use of the autonomy of universities, which was designed to protect them from political pressures, to turn them into citadels of political revolt in cultural clothing. That is not going to enhance public esteem for them.

What will happen if the kind of domination of intellectual life the dissidents have secured in some of the most prominent and sophisticated universities in the US becomes general? What will be the effect of the abandonment of disciplined, rule-observing speech and writing in schools? No great penetration is needed to answer these questions, but, in order to develop an organized and reflective response to what is going on, it is necessary to set the probable results out in an explicit way.

The canon will be expelled as an elitist imposition. In its place 'cultural studies' of a special kind will reign. The simple mental fare served up by the entertainment industry in a large sense of the word will be scrutinized for its political content. The productions of members of oppressed or unprivileged groups will be required for study, to the extent, at any rate, that they bear a politically correct intention on their faces. Oral poetry and folk art that is calculated to function in the style of a rock concert in obliterating individuality in a kind of communal ecstasy will be encouraged. The ideal graduate of the new-style university is already approximated to by the kind of semi-literate partisan that infests television, the world of documentary photography, and a good deal of journalism.

The assault on intellectual values will assimilate the study of the older humanities—philosophy, history, literature—on the one hand to the delirious obscurity and incoherence which pervades their practice in France and also to the unapologetic tendentiousness of certain kinds of 'committed' social science. What might happen in the natural sciences is more shadowy in outline. On the one hand equal status will be accorded to beliefs and techniques that are currently regarded as unscientific, an evaluation which dissidents regard as mere elitist prejudice. All sorts of alternative medicine will be accommodated alongside what we now think of as scientific medicine; not just acupuncture and homoeopathy, but diagnosis from spots of blood or pieces of hair, the use of spells, anything that any culture has used to identify and treat illness. On the other hand, certain established fields of scientific enquiry will be run down as contributory to such evils as nuclear warfare and environmental pollution: space exploration and industrial chemistry, for example. In an egalitarian spirit, alchemy and astrology might well be brought in from the cold and rehabilitated.

That scenario for the natural sciences is perhaps a bit hyperbolic. It is hard to imagine that any substantial progress along the road indicated would not evoke a powerful counter-reaction, not just from directly threatened groups like the medical profession and the existing scientific community, but also from their clients, from government, in the first place, and beyond that from the rational part of the general population.

But a dissolution of the humanities into a compound of political indoctrination and self-expressive, antinomian play is far from inconceivable. Even that, it could reasonably be supposed, would not be likely to last for very long, provided that the dissidents did not secure control of the state as well as the university. Public and private finance would dry up. Doctors, engineers, and other needed professionals could be taught in straightforward professional schools. In fields where hard research is possible it could go on in specialized research institutes. The university could simply fade away, as it nearly did in England in the eighteenth century. The humanities and literature could be kept going in an informal way as they were then.

But, even if complete success for the revolution seems unlikely because of reaction against it or simple self-destruction, there are intermediate positions which are not attractive. An example is the weird division of the Philosophy Department at Sydney, Australia, post-1968, one bit being standard, the other ideological. A larger one was the coexistence in the universities of the Soviet Union and its satellites of sumptuously provided instruction in the gibberish of Marxism-Leninism, as defined for the time being by Stalin and Suslov or whoever, and perfectly rational work in mathematics, physics, and logic.

The effect, finally, of the abandonment of disciplined language teaching would be that those touched by it would be unequipped to study the canon or the higher theoretical subjects anyway. This it is easier to foresee since the process is already so far advanced. In their anxiety not to subject their pupils to any kind of constraint some primary schools do not try to improve their speech but let it pour forth in all its semi-articulate disorder. To do that and to fail to teach effective reading or promote the reading of any but the most pictorial and colloquial of printed matter is to make grammatical and verbally rich discourse, spoken or written, unintelligible to the victims of the process.

I turn now to a critical examination of the way in which the displacement of the canon is recommended. Despite the professed disdain of the displacers for ordinary rational argument, it is impossible, or at any rate unsatisfactory, for them to demand its removal as a blank imperative. Facts, or alleged facts, about the content and the motives for the composition of the canon are stated and are implied to be reasons of some kind for getting rid of it. The first of these facts really is a fact, as has already been conceded. This is that the canon is parochial, or, more precisely, Eurocentric. It could be said as well that the canon in any particular European country is top heavy in its representation of that country's language.

The circumscription involved is not altogether unreasonable. Not many students or readers, even students studying the canon in higher education, can be expected to know more than one or two languages other than their own well enough to read effectively in them. So, if they are to read outside that narrow linguistic area, they must rely on translations. There is a tiresome puristic doctrine which regards translation of imaginative literature as acceptable only as an aid to limited capacity to read the original, as in bilingual editions, or as a kind of literary exercise on ready-prepared literary raw material for autonomous imaginative writers like Dryden and Ezra Pound. A kind of answer to this purism is provided by the Authorized Version of the Bible, which is at once a supreme ingredient of the canon in English and, as a translation, the work of a fairly anonymous group of no independent literary standing. One could ask the question: is it not better to read Homer and Virgil in translation rather than a minor work of Dickens or Thackeray—*Barnaby Rudge* or *The Newcomes*, for example—or than not to read them at all?

But the extent to which the canon, as acknowledged in any particular country, is confined to writing in the language of that country should not be exaggerated. In Everyman's Library or the Éditions de la Pléiade, which may serve as rough institutional realizations of the English and French canons, a large proportion of the books included was originally written in neither English nor French. Each contains substantial representation of the literature of the other and also works from other major European literatures: Russian, German, Italian, and Spanish. Everyman has also contained, and may contain again, the Bible (described as Ancient Hebrew Literature), Persian poems, the Koran, Hindu scriptures, and Chinese philosophy in classical times. Non-European literature, from the *Epic of Gilgamesh* onwards, is even more fully represented in the Penguin Classics series.

The canon is not the fixed repertoire of works in Greek and Latin it was four or five hundred years ago. It is constantly under revision and, in particular, is constantly being extended. Even those like Leavis, who interpret it in the most exclusive, little-Englandish form, do not deny the existence of literature of the highest value outside the restricted range of what they suppose it to be practicable to teach.

Other allegedly excluded groups are also present to an even more defensible extent. Certainly women are not to be found in it in direct proportion to their numbers in the population, except perhaps in fiction. If there are unfairly kept out women, who, as it is said, express a genuinely feminine point of view in a way that Sappho, Jane Austen, Emily Brontë, and Virginia Woolf do not, let them be brought forth for consideration. Homosexuals probably do have a proportionate presence, although not as campaigners for gay rights. Gide's *Corydon* and Forster's *Maurice* are passed over in favour of *Les Faux Monnayeurs* and *A Passage to India*, for literary reasons, not as a piece of homophobic repression. Societies of the Third World that are minimally, and only very recently, literate are absent on the same grounds. Stories about animal tricksters, orally conveyed, are part of the childhood of mankind and, apart from anthropologists, are principally of interest to children.

Opponents of the canon draw critical attention to the social type of its selectors as much as to the writers whose work is included in it. These canonizers too are 'dead white males'. The first thing to notice about them is that although, inevitably, educated, they are not from the social and political elite. Johnson was the son of a man who ran a market bookstall and was desperately poor for much of his life. Coleridge went to a charity school, Christ's Hospital, and spent most of his life dependent on charity. Arnold, better born than they, no doubt, worked at the full-time drudgery of school inspection; Eliot for many years held a minor position in a bank. Leavis, son of a man who had a piano shop, did not get a decent university appointment until late in life, and lived on his meagre college income. Certainly they were not subsistence farmers in the tropics, but subsistence farmers have no literary opinions, although it would be a fine thing if they did.

Women have contributed to the canon much more than they have managed to define it. No doubt they were discouraged from thinking they could do so by way of a conception, imposed on them by men, of what their proper role was. The assumptions and institutional barriers which brought this about have now been largely dismantled. If Mrs Leavis is to be believed, she, rather than her husband, was the driving force behind the most resolute canon-defining and canon-preserving movement of this century.

It is not, of course, the bare fact that the authors of the canon and the critics who select them for it come from a particular and limited social domain that is the fundamentally objectionable thing about it. It is rather the kind of writing written and preferred by such people which is seen as defective. White, male, middle-class, and mostly straight, they impose a view of the world determined by those characteristics on those who are educationally subjected to the canon.

At the superficial level of subject matter there is something in this, so far as the non-white are concerned. *Huckleberry Finn*, *A Passage to India*, and *Burmese Days* are exceptional books. But, since so much imaginative literature is about romantic love between the sexes, women are abundantly present, at any rate, and by no means universally represented in a meek and subservient light. Some major male novelists are more memorable for their accounts of women than for their accounts of men: Tolstoy and Hardy are examples.

Nor do fictional characters at the lower end of the social scale always figure in a more or less ornamental way as light relief. In Scott's novels, what may be called the vernacular characters are always more solid and vital than the rather pallid representatives of the ruling class, unless the latter are villainous like Balfour of Burley in *Old Mortality* or the character who gives his name to *Redgauntlet*.

The thought implied by the opponents' claims of bias in the canon is that it serves the interests of the ruling class. Not much of it indeed is outright revolutionary propaganda, although some is, much of the poetry of Shelley, for example. But then nor is much of it reactionary propaganda, either. Even as conformist a writer as Galsworthy is critical, in a limp, high-minded way, of the established order. Evelyn Waugh, explicitly reactionary in his political views, hardly glorifies the most socially elevated and powerful of his characters. For the most part, where it is not politically indifferent, the canon is hostile to the status quo. That is why there was resolute opposition to state support for public libraries in the mid-nineteenth century.

But references to such things as the somewhat unorganized reforming impulse in much of Dickens will not placate the opponents of the canon. At one level, the fault of the works that make it up is that the criticism they make or imply of the status quo is largely confined to the realm of individual morality. In its concentration on particular people it fails to address the grand collective issue of emancipation. The great bourgeois novelists of the beginning of the century all take the general structure of the social system for granted. When they do cast an eye on those with truly revolutionary sentiments it is a violently hostile one, as in *The Possessed*, *Princess Casamassima*, and *Under Western Eyes*. Even where not directly engaged in the defence of things as they are, they suggest, it is alleged, that the ideal form of life is that of the rich, cultivated bourgeoisie, sustained by the exploitation of others.

That is really a somewhat ridiculous anachronism. The novels of James and Proust are now historical fiction, no more recommending an immediate return to the social conditions they describe than *Ivanhoe* proposes a revival of the feudal system. Those few who are rich enough now to live as well as Swann or Milly Theale pursue the pleasures of the Marquesses of Bristol and of Blandford or of Lord White and Sir Ralph Halpern. But even a vanished world can have a bad effect in the critics' view. Its essential fault is that it does something other than excite impulses directed towards the emancipation of the oppressed, diverts attention from the overwhelming primacy of that political purpose. That is the one standard by which everything is to be judged.

Is the dismantling of the canon really going to do anything for the great cause? Is it not part of the point of emancipation that it should enable many more people to have effective access to the canon and other ingredients of high culture than they have now? If furthering emancipation of the oppressed is the overriding purpose why concentrate on high culture as something not totally committed to it any more than on ice-skating or mountain-climbing? The critics of the canon are simply repeating in a modernized form the message of Tolstoy's *What is Art*, that the entire and exclusive value of art resides in its enhancement of emotions of human fraternity. One could perfectly well sympathize with emancipation or fraternity without taking them to be so uniquely and overridingly important that nothing is of any value except in relation to them. If one believed that then all but the most primordially self-preservative things people do would have to be abandoned or transformed out of recognition. That would make the question—emancipation for what?—unanswerable. It would lead to the misuse of things that are of independent value in themselves to make some minute contribution to the primary aim, as revolutionary soldiers might burn some Raphaels to keep warm.

Critics of the canon, however, would dispute the independent extra-political value of the works that compose it. There can be no formal disproof of that claim. What can be said is that the high estimation of the canon is the result of a convergence over a long period of the judgement of those who have attended most closely to the items in question. That is really all the answer that is needed for value scepticism that rests on the fact that opinions differ. What more could be asked for? Does anyone seriously question the principle of convergence of experienced judgement in the evaluation of cricket players or opera singers or holiday beaches? There are many different kinds of thing in which people have an interest or which they want, many different kinds of thing are sources of satisfaction, enjoyment, or fulfilment. Some of them can be enjoyed directly, without preparation. To enjoy others we need some kind of training. To the extent that we are untrained or unprepared it is only sensible to follow the guidance of the initiated.

Furthermore, the supreme value exalted by the opponents of the canon is inevitably a secondary, derivative one. Redistribution has a point only if there are things other than the form of the redistribution aimed at which are of value in themselves. The politically obsessed confine these goods in themselves to power, first of all, and to wealth and status after that. But these too are all primarily means to ends. The possession of power, wealth, and status is, of course, pleasant to contemplate if one has it. But the main point of power is its exercise and of wealth its expenditure. Their charm as objects of contemplation is entirely derived from the possible uses to which they can be put. Cultural revolutionaries, by sanctifying emancipation, deprive it of purpose. If their seizure of cultural and educational power were to succeed it would ensure that people generally were unequipped to enjoy a large range of available satisfactions.

It must, then, be admitted that the canon is limited. But it is not closed: its membership is perpetually changing. Its limits, furthermore, although they skew it in a Western direction, are not such as to exclude non-Western writing and, in view of the difficulties of translation, which increase with cultural remoteness, they are not unreasonable. The selectors are not members of the ruling elite. The canon selected does not deal much with the people of the non-Western world and their experiences, but women and sexual deviants are well represented both as subject matter and authors. Far from being apologetic or propaganda for the status quo, much of the canon is, in Lionel Trilling's phrase, adversarial, particularly since a large reading public replaced princes as the ultimate dispensers of literary patronage. Its value does not lie in any directly emancipatory purpose it may serve. But unless it had its proper, literary value an important part of the point of emancipation would disappear.

So much for the canon. I turn now to the attack on intellectual values, on the belief that there is such a thing as objective truth or as objective rationality or justification. The obvious and repeated objection to that is that it is self-refuting. There are several ways in which the point can be made. One is that it is absolutely self-refuting, in other words, a straightforward self-contradiction, since 'there are no objective truths' is logically equivalent to 'it is an objective truth that there are no objective truths'. The relativist could reply that he does not deny that 'p' and 'it is true that p' are equivalent, only that 'p' and 'it is objectively true that p' are.

The objectivist can respond in a number of ways. First, he can ask if it is objectively, or only relatively, true that all truth is relative. The first option is self-refuting. The second prompts further interrogation. What does it mean to say that something is relatively true? Is it to say anything more than that something is believed by some person or group? It is hardly news that the beliefs of different people and groups are often in conflict. But when this is forced on their attention they ordinarily try to do something about it, to find out which belief is correct and then persuade the incorrect of their incorrectness.

A further question arises at this point. Is believing something intelligible without the notion of objective truth? Is to believe something not to take it to be objectively true? One could even go further along that line of criticism by asking whether the idea of meaning is not necessarily tied up with that of objective truth. To understand the meaning of a sentence is to know what circumstances license its affirmation, as constituting to everyone the conditions of its truth, at least in fairly elementary cases, but, perhaps, in more complex ones, the conditions of its justification. The meaning we attach to the utterances of someone else is a matter of what in the circumstances of utterance makes them true. That is most obvious in the anthropological case of working out what is meant by utterances in a wholly unfamiliar language. We effect an entrance into it by picking out some commonly uttered sentences—'it is raining', 'that is a dog', and things of that sort—whose circumstances of utterance have something evidently in common and work up to less context-bound remarks from there. There is no difference in principle between the anthropologist's situation and that of an English speaker who hears someone emitting sounds that form part of his own familiar vocabulary. But, in practice, just because he already has an elaborate, if inarticulate, theory about a language that has that vocabulary, he assumes that the meaning attached to the sentences emitted by others made up of that vocabulary is the same as he attaches to them. And, of course, he is usually, although not quite always, entirely right to do so.

The point of the inescapability of truth can be made in a more concrete and straightforward way by considering what someone might be doing by uttering an indicative sentence like 'it is raining' or 'people in the Third World are exploited' or 'there is no such thing as objective truth'. One can use it to assert something, to make a statement. One can alternatively use it to pretend to assert something, as in telling a story. One can use it, again, to test a microphone or to supply evidence to the appropriate sort of specialist about the state of one's throat or the quality of one's pronunciation. What distinguishes its use as an assertion is that it is uttered as true, or, at any rate, as something there is reason to think is true. A claim to truth, even if tentative, is essentially involved in an act of assertion. To assert something is to invite or encourage one's hearer to believe what one is saying, to take it to be true, whether or not it is true and whether or not one believes it oneself.

For the most part relativists simply ignore these objections. But, since relativists do not, for the most part, just blankly assert their relativist doctrine, but offer reasons in support of it, they really ought not to ignore them. They contend that their opponents do objectively believe certain things which are inconsistent—really inconsistent—with things they themselves believe and that these errors can be explained, really, objectively explained, by the biasing circumstances of the misled believers.

The sociologist Mannheim tried to preserve the consistency of his position by claiming that some people, of whom he was one, were a 'free-floating intelligentsia', epistemically privileged and above the strife of contending relative truths. Current relativists repudiate this implausible claim to a unique privilege and, like Rorty, admit that their own beliefs are on the same relative level as the beliefs of their opponents. To do that is to assimilate what they are saying to story-telling. Derrida talks of the *play* of interpretation. Rorty says discussion should be understood as conversation, free contributions to a pool of discourse, offered in a spirit of take it or leave it.

There are two objections to that. In the first place it is, self-refutingly, to claim that it is objectively true, on objectively true grounds, that there is nothing better than this, no such thing as real, serious disagreement. Secondly, and more important, the idea that communication is the exchange of utterances which the participants in a conversation find it agreeable to believe raises the question of what it is that they are playing at. Non-assertive uses of indicative sentences are parasitic on their assertive use. To understand a story one has to have an understanding of what the sentences that compose it mean, of what they could be used to assert, even though they are not being so used in the story-telling. In a more down to earth idiom, one has to know what it would really be like if the story were true. Without real assertion there can be no pretence of assertion.

All this anti-relativist argumentation, it might be held, is to make unnecessarily heavy weather of what is going on. When someone utters something which would, taken at its face value, be self-refuting it is surely natural, tolerant, and constructive to reinterpret what they are saying. The difficulty in this case is that the self-refutation is so fundamental, not just a local blur or piece of noise in a generally intelligible context, that the whole communicative project is undermined. What can be admitted is that there are certain considerations which lend a little colour to the relativist doctrine, even if they do not in fact justify it.

Much of what we now believe was not believed before. Much was believed which is now disbelieved. We may conclude that our own beliefs will be lavishly revised in the course of time (sometimes wrongly, perhaps). But that does not show that those of our beliefs that will be correctly abandoned in the future will be shown by that fact to have been only relatively true. What will be shown is that they were not true, but only believed. And a great deal of what we believe has always been believed and always will be: that human beings feel pain, while stones do not; that water quenches fire; that apples are edible; that sea-water tastes salty.

All beliefs are, indeed, first arrived at from a particular point of view. Often the falsity of a belief can be accounted for by some peculiarities of the point of view of the believer. But must the fact that all beliefs are in this way perspectival universally invalidate or relativize them? Are not some perspectives epistemically superior to others: daylight to darkness, calm to excitement, curiosity to anger? What is more, if beliefs originate from a particular point of view they are not locked into it. The believer can consider the matter from other perspectives and can incorporate the perspectives of others by critical interchange with them.

An important and generally ignored case of apparent disagreement which is not genuine inconsistency is the selective operation of our interests. For example, two people may disagree about the cause of increasing crime, one attributing it to social deprivation, the other to an insufficiently strong police force. But both may be right, not, of course, in believing that their respective diagnoses give *the unique* cause of rising crime for there is none, but that both are parts of the complex cause of the phenomenon. Either of the suggested policies for reducing or containing crime could have the desired effect, but the costs of the two policies may well be differently viewed.

The same selective factor is at work in what might be called competing descriptions of a given thing. I am an Englishman, a male, a human being, a mammal, a living organism. It is objectively correct to describe me in any of these ways, but in different contexts different descriptions may be appropriate. This fact is the basis of a familiar kind of joke, like that of the tailor who measured Stalin for a suit and, when asked what the tyrant was like, replied 'he was a short 42'. Not all truth is interesting or important, in fact very little of it is. To assert something is to suggest, outside the smallest small talk, that what is said is of some interest and that is often disputable. But to be uninteresting is not to lack objective truth.

Confronted by the self-destructiveness of intellectual nihilism it is possible to question the sincerity of those who propound it. If Derrida, who takes a notably possessive attitude to his writings, were to bring a case against someone for plagiarizing him, would he look tolerantly on a judge who deconstructed the statement that the plagiarist had copied his work, interpreting it the other way round as meaning that Derrida had somehow prospectively copied the work of the alleged plagiarist, along the lines of his own thought that writing is prior to speech? Would he not feel indignant about a chemist who had deconstructed a doctor's prescription for a bilious ailment from which he was suffering?

The lavishness of his claims about the unconstrained freedom of interpretation invites pedestrian, one might even say insensitively philistine, comments of this kind. Are we then to suppose that the claims carry a hidden rider to the effect that they cover only theoretical discourse? It should be noted in passing that, being part of theoretical discourse themselves, they would still be self-undermining. The main point is that this would be to trivialize theoretical discourse by segregating it from rational control.

An entertaining example of this kind of implicit limitation of scope is provided by the unfavourable remarks of Stanley Fish about the practice of peer review of work submitted for publication in scholarly periodicals, which are presented to reviewers without their authors' names on them. He says he should be exempted from this kind of equal treatment because, as he puts it, he 'has paid his dues': what he puts in should be accepted simply because he is an academic star. That is possessive individualism in its purest form. It resonantly affirms the bourgeois principle that justice rests on desert, not on need.

The third and final element of the assault is its egalitarian-cum-libertarian view about language. The oppressed masses, it is held, are kept in subjection by having prescriptive dictionaries, the rules of grammar, and Fowler-like principles of style imposed on them. Children should be encouraged to express themselves freely and impulsively, in whatever way comes naturally to them, and not be fettered in the bonds of bourgeois utterance.

There is, indeed, a case to be made against rigidly prescriptive dictionaries, grammar books, and manuals of style. Language is constantly evolving. To be rigidly prescriptive about it is not to give useful instruction but to imprison learners in a kind of semantic museum. A dictionary that beside the entry for 'discover' put only 'reveal', or beside 'nice', 'exact' would be like a twenty-year-old copy of the *Good Food Guide*: a recipe for disappointment.

But if meanings and rules of grammar change over the long run they must have a fair degree of fixity at any given moment for effective communication to be possible. The gravitational pull of idle, careless speech and writing is constant. Educational insistence on the rules is needed to counteract it, quite as much as the discipline of hygiene is needed to stem the easy solicitations of dirtiness. The fact that it is needed means that there are conflicting practices. It may be that a new practice, originated by ignorant neglect of a distinction, like the assimilation of 'disinterested' to 'uninterested', will eventually become too widespread to rule out. There are, after all, other words near enough in meaning to 'disinterested' in its traditional sense to serve as approximate substitutes for it, 'impartial', 'objective', 'fair-minded'. What is unfortunate about the assimilation is that it suggests that the only way of being impartial is to be indifferent to the matter in hand or emotionally uninvolved with it. A change of usage is powered here by a false belief with bad practical consequences.

The alternative to the kind of temporary fixity and definiteness of meaning I have called for is a kind of generalized floating ambiguity. Ambiguity is not always to be deplored. It is economical, using one thing to do two jobs, like stirring soup with a tyre lever. But that is only really safe where one word is used for two very different purposes, such as Mill's favourite 'bank', or when used for two related but syntactically distinct purposes as in 'drop' used of what is dropping and of the space through which something is dropped. In these cases there are clearly demarcated boundaries of application.

But in what I have called 'floating' ambiguity, users of the words infected by it will confuse themselves and confuse others. A few years ago politically enthusiastic people often said that bad housing is violence. It is, of course, nothing of the sort. Like violence, it is deplorable. Unlike violence, however, it is not intentional, although it can be remedied by human action. Furthermore it is avoidable by its victims in a way that violence, which is ordinarily peremptory, is not. And the kind of harm it does is slow and cumulative; no sudden, painful, and disabling shock is administered to the victim. What this loose way of speaking objectionably suggests is that since bad housing is violence it is appropriate to respond to it with violence in its standard meaning in virtue of an underlying principle of an eye for an eye.

A less clear-cut, but more obviously floating, example of ambiguity, one which has floated to the outermost limits of vagueness, is 'society', as in such formulae as 'it's not the criminal's fault, society is to blame'. It is not at all clear, either to speaker or hearer, what is being referred to. Is it everyone else or some particular group of people? At the back of the speaker's mind, perhaps, is the idea of the ruling class, the people who are supposed to dominate society. The implausibility of this is concealed by the loose reference which takes in the more obvious fault-sharers, the criminal's parents and associates, but loses them in the crowd.

In the affairs of practical life there is too much immediately at stake for linguistic corruption to get much of a hold. People are still going to be saying the same things when they say a sparking plug is wet or that a piece of fish has gone off. But at a more general level there is no such practical limit set to the looseness of speech. Disputants will be at cross-purposes with those they dispute with and even with themselves; sometimes in supposing something to be relevant to the matter in hand when it is not (as with the two aspects of the passage from Derrida I looked at in the first lecture), sometimes in supposing that they have actually asserted anything at all.

Language is an instrument for articulating our awareness of the world and ourselves and for communicating that awareness to others. The reality it works in is hard stuff, not indefinitely malleable. To cope with it the instruments of articulation need to be kept in good order, which in their case is a matter of preserving their common currency and of preserving the distinctiveness of their individual uses. At the far end of linguistic anarchism lies the reduction of communication to the expression of feeling, like the gruntings and chirpings of beasts and birds. That would be the final erosion of the most distinctively human thing about human beings.

The celebrated Third World thinker Confucius, when asked what counsel he would give if he were appointed adviser to Prince Mei, said he would ask, first of all, for the rectification of language. In what we may see as a too prescriptive spirit he said that things should be called by their right names, as if the name of a thing were something fixed eternally, once for all. Convinced, with the author of Genesis, that names are man-made, we admit that meanings depend on convention. But a convention is nullified if it is not generally observed.

I have been arguing against the relaxation of several large bodies of cultural constraints. The canon constrains by laying down that some books are supremely worthy of being read. The principles of rationality constrain us to sift our beliefs critically and in an orderly way and to make them as accessible as possible to this treatment by stating and arguing for them clearly and simply. Linguistic discipline constrains us not to take the easiest way out in discourse. It is always pleasant to relax constraints and, therefore, kindly to relax their application to others. But the pleasure and kindness involved here are short-lived and lead to pain in the long run. The achievements of the human species have been brought about by active effort to master ourselves and our environment. Culture, in its most inclusive sense, is the accumulated capital that has emerged through that effort. High culture is the most demanding and self-critical part of the general cultural accumulation in which the best, the most systematic and penetrating, knowledge of ourselves and the world is developed. It is a certain good. The emancipatory triumph to which its destruction is supposed, by it attackers, to contribute, is only a remotely possible outcome of its destruction.

In fact, its destruction is no more likely a result of the cultural revolution I have been considering than general emancipation is of the trashing of high culture. If the revolutionaries succeed in capturing power in the universities, it will be the universities that will be transformed, not the community at large. Universities do not sustain themselves, they have to be paid for by governments—and, therefore, in the end taxpayers—and by private benefactors. They will not go on indefinitely supporting centres of intellectual and aesthetic carnival. Who ever heard of a successful revolution that began by seizing the university, rather than the central telephone exchange or the main repository of arms? But the oldest medieval institution still in recognizably the same sort of working order as it originally was, which, in its eight hundred-year history, has often served high culture well, even if at times it has slept, is, in our present world, its principal citadel. If the university is undermined high culture will have to regroup itself elsewhere and it may be badly damaged in the process.

In these lectures I have said nothing directly about moral values, but some moral values are involved in the activities I have been talking about. The most important is honesty. It is important to realize that it is not the same thing as sincerity, although they are related. The most full-heartedly sincere expression of belief falls short of honesty if the belief in question is inadequately formulated and inadequately examined. Part of honest communication is putting what you are trying to get across so that what you actually mean is apprehended by your hearer.

I do not want to end either on a despondent or on a merely edifying note. As to despondency, I believe that the revolution can be contained, if it is recognized and resisted, not meekly submitted to from fear of unpopularity or of simply being out of the fashion. The roots of the revolution are fairly shallow. It is loosely anchored in the various groups of the really or apparently oppressed it purports to speak for. The passive multitude its exponents rather condescendingly wish to emancipate should not be satisfied with the disembowelled substitute for high culture their emancipators are preparing for them, and there are signs that they will not accept it, such as parents' revolts against playful schooling and the falling numbers of applicants for humanities courses in the United States.

As for edification, looking back on what I have said it reminds me uncomfortably of elderly persons in my own youth going on about the decay of standards and, in particular, of the slightly risible figure of C. E. M. Joad. He settled down in later life to the production at regular intervals of books with such titles as *Return to Philosophy* or *Philosophy for our Time* in which the absolute values of truth, goodness, and beauty were defended in a dilutedly Platonic manner. In holding that truth is not relative, but that only belief is, I have not assumed that truth or knowledge is an absolute value or, again, that the literary merit of the canon is. I think these values are rooted in human nature, not part of the eternal architecture of the world. But I still think them really valuable, not least as stepping-stones on the way to more comprehensive knowledge and a more inclusive canon, understood as a possession of the human species in general and not just of some biased and self-interested group of exploitative power seekers.

21

Morals and Politics

I

My title, as it stands, is not very informative. The two terms that occur in it are so commonly conjoined in the philosophical world, at any rate, that it can be no surprise to find them together. My aim, however, is to go some way, at least, towards disconnecting them. My thesis is, to put it briefly, that it is a mistake to see political philosophy as a subordinate part of moral philosophy and thus to suppose that the characteristic problems of the former are of the same kind as those of the latter. More concretely, the problems of politics itself are not generally or primarily, let alone exclusively, moral in nature. We all know that political problems are not, to any great extent, approached by those involved with them, from a moral point of view. I shall argue that it is not reasonable that they should be. But the philosophical habit of running the two things together encourages a kind of moral absolutism in political thinking, and from time to time in political practice, which has bad results, not necessarily morally bad, just bad.

The most obvious symptom of the unreflective institutional jumbling of morals and politics is the common exposure of students to courses, and subsequent examination papers, on 'moral and political philosophy'. This compound is correspondingly present in textbooks. It may be explicit as in Windelband's *Introduction to Philosophy* (1921) (where they stand cheek by jowl under the general heading 'practical philosophy'); in E. F. Carritt's *Morals and Politics* of 1935 and his *Ethical and Political Thinking* of 1947; and in C. E. M. Joad's *Guide to the Philosophy of Morals and Politics* of 1938 (a work to which many philosophers of my generation perhaps owe rather more than they would readily admit). More usually, comprehensive books on moral philosophy will contain a political section. Two of the twenty chapters of Brandt's *Ethical Theory* (1959) are about distributive justice and human rights, two of the eleven parts of Hospers's *Human Conduct* (1982) are about political ethics and justice, one of the five sections of Raphael's *Moral Philosophy* (1981) is called 'ethics and politics' and covers justice and liberty.

One indication of what I take to be the fairly far-reaching distinctness of moral and political philosophy is the large disparity between the lists of the classical contribution to the two disciplines in the post-medieval period. The major moral philosophers are Butler, Hume, Kant, Mill, Sidgwick, and Moore. The major political philosophers are Machiavelli, Hobbes, Locke, Burke, Rousseau, Hegel, Mill, and Marx. Mill is the only member of both lists. Hume and, in a smaller way, Kant contributed something to political philosophy. Hobbes and Hegel have some standing as moral philosophers. But the majority of these philosophers are either one thing or the other. In my experience, the same segregation is to be found among common or garden philosophers in the present age: those who teach one subject are seldom willing or able to teach the other. In the last few decades, however, the work of Rawls, in particular, and to some extent also that of Dworkin, has tended to bring the two subjects together.

II

These are fairly external considerations. To disentangle moral and political philosophy it will be best to go directly to a comparison of the nature and main problems of the two disciplines as they are ordinarily conceived. The disentangling of their objects, of morals and politics themselves, will be taken up later. The central issue of moral philosophy is that of how, if at all, moral beliefs, whether general rules or judgments of particular cases, are to be justified. That enquiry presupposes a clear conception of what makes a belief moral. But it is seldom adequately supplied with one. It is very commonly assumed without qualification that a belief is moral if its natural expression contains the words *good*, *right*, or *ought*. That is an error and one that has undesirable consequences. The fact is that these words occur in all the varieties of practical discourse; in what Kant called 'counsels of prudence' and 'rules of skill', in bodies of guidance that do not all comfortably into either of these categories such as the rules of healthy living, and, of course, in political reasoning and judgement. (There are some exclusively moral words—*obligation*, *virtuous*, and *praiseworthy*, for example—but they are to be found in only a small fraction of recognizedly moral discourse.)

Whether preceded by an account of the domain of the moral or not, the central issue of moral philosophy is that of the justification of moral beliefs. To some extent that is a matter internal to morality, that of basing one kind of moral belief on another, as when the rightness of an action is derived from the rightness of the action to which it leads. The harder question, as we all know, is how ultimate moral beliefs, whatever form they have, are to be established. To make any headway in either of these types of enquiry it is essential to be clear about the meaning of the terms involved.

Political philosophy, as ordinarily practised, does, or should, begin with a delimitation of its scope, and is to that extent parallel to moral philosophy. Usually that concentrates on the problem of defining the state, often by way of an investigation of the notion of sovereignty. That way of proceeding assumes that politics is activity related to the state: obeying its laws, securing control of it for oneself or others, actually running it. Other institutions have their politics too; businesses, clubs, churches, trade unions, professional associations, and so on, even perhaps families. But the convention of taking activity related to the state as literal or primary politics is a reasonable one.

But at that point the two philosophical disciplines diverge. There is no identifiable field of study which enquires into the justification of political beliefs. They are far too various for it to be a coherent undertaking. That is because the varieties of political activity are so varied. They can be classified without too much squeezing under four heads. First there is the activity of obeying the law, expected of one who may be called, with only the appearance of paradox, the passive citizen. Secondly, there are the characteristic activities of the active citizen: voting, first of all, in constitutional systems where it is provided for and equipping oneself to vote effectiviely by acquiring the relevant political information. (Even where there is no voting or it is merely an empty ritual it is worth becoming politically informed. Voting is not the only way of bringing presure to bear on governments and it is a good thing anyway for the passive subject to have some idea of what they are likely to do.) Thirdly, there is the activity of the politically involved: persuading, organizing, running for or otherwise seeking office. Finally, there is the work of running or governing proper, most conspicuously as legislator or policy-maker, but also as administrative subordinate.

The traditionally central problem of political philosophy concentrates on the passive citizen. It asks why the citizen should obey the state and conform his behaviour to its laws, poses, in other words, the problem of the grounds of political obligation. To describe the problem in that second, polysyllabic way begs the question in favour of an answer in moral terms. There can be, and obviously are, several good reasons of a non-moral character for thinking that one ought to obey the state, a matter that I shall look into more fully later.

Since Locke, at any rate, the theoretical function of the problem of philosophical obligation has been to set limits to the legitimate activity of the state by laying down conditions for the citizen's obligation. These take the form of retained natural rights which the state may not infringe on pain of forfeiting its legitimate authority. These natural or 'human' rights are in current political philosophizing argued for directly. They are still seen as limits to the authority of the state but not arrived at by an argumentative circuit through a mythical agreement. The instances usually concentrated on are liberty, justice and its close associate equality, property, the political right of demonstrative participation. The most important of all, namely security, seems to be taken for granted. That can be explained, but not entirely excused, by the fact that a state that does not provide a fair measure of it does not simply lose its legitimacy, it ceases to be a state altogether. That is the point made by the reference to 'habitual obedience' that occurs in the definition of sovereignty given by the nineteenth-century John Austin. More attention could be paid to the right, or any rate value, by which ordinary citizens seem to set most store: prosperity.

Moral and political philosophy, then, both should start with an explicit demarcation of their respective fields. When they do, the demarcations, however, are of very different kinds of thing. Moral philosophy needs to pick out moral beliefs from other practical beliefs (prudential, technical, and so on) and from beliefs generally. Political philosophy needs to pick out political from other forms of activity or, more usually, state-related activity.

The traditionally central question of political philosophy, that of the grounds of political obligation, or, less question-beggingly, of why citizens should obey the state, has a parallel in moral philosophy: the question—why should I be moral? But while the political question seems to be a substantial one, although, I shall argue, not a mainly, let alone exclusively, moral one, the moral opposite number is either a prudential question or it is empty. Of course I morally ought to do what I morally ought to do.

Up to this point, then, there are parallels between moral and political philosophy, but they go no way towards showing that the second is part of the first. That is clearly shown by the fact that there are the same parallel elements in the largely hypothetical discipline of prudential philosophy. There is, of course, a great deal of prudential thinking, much of it stored in works of practical wisdom. Prudential philosophy, were it to come into existence, would need to delimit its field, to judgements or actions directed towards the long-term interest of the agent, and to confront the question: why should I be prudent?

After these first two, more or less parallel elements moral and political philosophy begin to diverge. Philosophers who explicitly assimilate them tend to conceal the fact by various emolliently general formulae. Both, says D. D. Raphael, are concerned with 'beliefs about what is right and good for man and society'. Something a bit less efficient in covering up the differences is Joad's claim that moral philosophy deals with the nature of the good life for the individual, political philosophy with the principles that should govern the association of individuals in societies. The assumption behind these quotations seems to be that because both deal with what is right and good or with what is good and what should be done they are, therefore, fundamentally the same. But counsels of prudence and rules of skill also deal with what is right and good and what should be done.

The moral appropriateness or requisitioning of the words *good*, *right*, and *ought* is particularly blatant in J. L. Mackie's *Ethics: Inventing Right and Wrong* (1977). He says 'if ethics is the general theory of right and wrong in choices and actions ... then political actions and aims and decisions come within its scope'. The antecedent of this conditional is false, it is not ethics, understood as moral philosophy, that is the general theory of right and wrong in actions but a more general discipline, the theory of value. Political activity does, indeed, come within the scope of morality, it can be properly condemned in appropriate cases as wicked, dishonest, cruel, and so forth. But so, equally, can actions motivated by prudential consideration or chosen as instances of technical skill. It does not follow from the fact that political activity can be morally judged that the politically right and good are the morally right and good.

III

I shall now turn to a comparison of morality and politics, understood as state-related political activity. Both are, certainly, forms of decision and action. In both there is the preferred decision, which is the right one or the one one ought to make, and it is, typically, intended to bring about a good result. But that, for reasons I have given, does not subordinate the second to the first.

An initial difference is that morality is universal, in the sense that its rules are taken to apply to everyone. Or nearly everyone: its rules are not incumbent on infants, the insane, or the mentally defective. We do not always do what we think right, let alone what really is right (if there is such a thing). But we all have some idea of what is right, which has more or less influence on our decisions. In politics there are very various levels of activity, involving various proportions of the population as a whole (with much the same exceptions as in the case of morals). The only comparably universal one to morality is passive citizenship, obedience to the law.

Against that it might be objected that in a democratic state in which citizens are not legally obliged to vote, they have a moral duty to do so. But that is far from obvious. If they have no definite political opinions and are politically uninformed it could just as well be said that they have a moral duty to abstain from voting. Well, then, the objection might go, they then have a moral duty to acquire some political knowledge and to base some political opinions upon it. I can see that it might, in some large sense, be a good thing if all adult citizens of a state had enough political knowledge to vote reasonably (by which all I mean is that they have some ideas of what they are voting for and against) and voted. But the fact that in most states many have not does not strike me as an obvious moral deficiency on their part. The fully politically involved, at any rate, are, and in a large state must be, a fairly small minority and rulers, who are not mere functionaries, a smaller one still.

Another marked difference is that where moral convictions are comparatively uniform, at least as regards a broad array of fundamental principles of conduct, political convictions typically clash. There are two ways in which this apparent difference could be played down. The first is that in democratic systems of government that are organized on party lines political disagreement is institutionalized and exacerbated. Moral disagreement does not have to be settled in the way political disagreement does. I can drink and you can abstain. We may deplore each other, but go our own ways. In the business of government a single decision, binding on everyone, has to be arrived at. As it happens, sensible governments do not push the opposition too far, but go some way to meet them with a compromise. The stark collision of party is, it could be said, part of the game of democratic politics, like a vendor's exaggerated initial price which gets the bargaining going.

That leads to a second consideration that tends to weaken the contrast. Just as there is a central core of morality which no one seriously challenges in principle, whatever they may do in practice—you should not kill or injure people, steal from them, lie to them, cheat them, break promises you have made to them—so there is a central core of agreed political beliefs: that there should be a government, that it should enforce the central core of morality by legal sanctions for the security of citizens from their neighbours, that it should protect the nation as a whole from attack by foreigners, that it should come to the assistance of the seriously disadvantaged by transferring to them some of the wealth of the better off.

But despite these two diluting considerations the difference of nature and scale between moral and political disagreement is still substantial. It can best be brought out by the fact that people are not as indignant with those with whom they disagree politically as with those with whom they disagree morally. And the more professional political disagreers are, the less indignant they are. That is more true of politicians proper than of those I have called the politically involved, who tend to have the ferocity of football supporters. To the extent that it is so it is because these last, of all kinds of people in some way touched by politics, most ardently identify politics with morality.

It is an aspect of the universal application of morality that it does not require more than common knowledge. A moral agent could benefit from special knowledge, of psychology, for instance, but is more likely to benefit from a natural sensitivity to the feelings of others. But above the level of passive obedience to the law political activity requires uncommon knowledge. Another way of making the same point is that there are really no experts in morals as there are in politics. Priests were long supposed to be moral experts. That may have been in part because they were thought to have the power of absolving and remitting sins. The discharge of that function, particularly where it was tied up with individual confession, caused them to spend a lot of time thinking about moral problems and to equip them with a large and varied, if mainly vicarious, moral experience. Their training, however, exerted an influence in the direction of legalism, both in identifying the wrongs done and in the imposition of penitences. Many humane priests have always risen above this. But priests are primarily experts in theology and ritual. Political expertise, on the other hand, is an evidently limited acquisition.

A final difference will prepare the ground for a later discussion of morality in the relations between states. I imagine that most people are utilitarian enough to agree that morality is, in an ultimate if not exclusive way, concerned with the interest or well-being of all humans, even all sentient creatures. Politics, except in very unusual circumstances, is concerned with the interests or well-being of a particular group. That group, ordinarily in the modern world a culturally coherent nation, is, and is seen to be, in competition with other groups like itself. That competition can be of varying degrees of ferocity. But it is always present in a ruler's mind. His task in managing the relations between his own country and others is that of pursuing and protecting the national interest.

Politics, as the pursuit of the national interest, is, then, impersonal like morality, but it is inevitably not universal in a world where there is a plurality of states. Let me repeat that, generally, it is not my purpose to deny that morality has a place in politics, only that politics is a part of morality, to be wholly guided and appraised by moral principles and to be directed exclusively towards moral ends.

IV

The idea that politics is a department of morals rests to a great extent on the identification of what is taken to be its central issue—why should one obey the state?—with the pursut of the ground of political obligation, that is of the moral duty to obey it. These are, as I have argued, by no means one and the same.

It is not directly to the purpose that in determining why people in fact obey the state any moral obligation that they recognize to do so does not bulk very large. At the crudest level they obey it because they fear it, because it has the power to apply painful sanctions where obedience is not forthcoming. That is prudence at its most primitive. But there is another good general reason for obedience of a prudential kind. This is that the state provides security and protection of one's life and property which would be in constant danger without it. As things have turned out it does a number of other valuable things as well, but security is the fundamental consideration without which the other things it provides are barely worth having. Now this reason for obedience is essentially self-regarding. It is not exclusively self-regarding, except in the case of an emotionally isolated person. It derives much of its strength from one's concern for those, inevitably a minority, to whom one is linked to ties of personal affection. Even if it extends in some degree to one's compatriots at large it still falls short of the human or sentient community as a whole, which is the essential moral constituency.

The fact that this prudential consideration in fact weighs much more strongly than any strictly moral motive for obedience cannot be ignored in any enquiry into the reasonableness of obedience. The alternative, anarchist, option is to suppose that most people's obedience is unreasonable. There is an argument, the free-rider argument, which holds that it is. So long as most people obey the state, it is said, although, on some particular occasion of occasions, I do not, the protective power of the state will not be seriously or even perceptibly undermined.

Hume argued that what he called allegiance, obedience to the state, is, like promise-keeping and respect for property, something that is advantageous only if the principle involved is generally adhered to. I cannot reasonably allow my private desires to override it unless I am prepared to admit that others may reasonably do the same in similar circumstances. In that case, of course, the protective capacity of the state dissolves. That is not a moral argument, however; it still turns on the advantage to me and to those I care about. As it happens, people are not always reasonable in this way. That is where the other self-regarding consideration comes in, the directly prudential consideration of fear of the state's sanctions.

To say that is not to say that there is not also a genuinely moral reason for obedience. That is dependent on the fact that the law, or more accurately the criminal law, forbids or requires conduct that is ruled out or dictated by morality. The state is fundamentally in the business of the enforcement of morals. The main content of the criminal law coincides with the principal requirements of what is generally recognized as morality: the prevention of harm to others by killing or injuring them, stealing from them, breaking promises to them (the law of contract), defrauding them, defaming them, and so on.

It does not enforce the whole of morality, although it comes near to doing so in theocratic states. It limits itself, ordinarily, to those offences which are large enough to excite this sort of revengeful impulse and, it might be added, those which it is practicable to identify and penalize. It is morally objectionable to be impolite. The law confines itself to the much more narrowly defined offence of insulting behaviour.

Those who have discussed the enforcement of morals recently have curiously neglected its central place in the content of law. Hart, in his *Law, Liberty and Morality* (1963), enumerates four questions about the relation between law and morals. There is, first, the question of the causal influence of morality on law. Secondly, there is the question of whether some reference to morality must enter into any adequate definition of a law or a legal system. Thirdly, there is the question of whether law is open to moral criticism. Finally, there is the question of whether conduct which is by common standards immoral ought to be punishable by law.

In connection with the second of these he makes the peculiar remark, 'is it just a contingent fact that law and morality often overlap (as in their common prohibition of certain forms of violence and dishonesty)?' The suggestion here is that the prohibition of 'certain forms' of violence and dishonesty is somehow a comparatively minor aspect of morality and of law. In fact it is the central and crucial part.

What helps to conceal that fact is the cavalier way in which moral philosophers approach the phenomenon they are investigating. For the most part they take it for granted that we all know what the main types of conduct which are morally enjoined or prohibited are. When they do address themselves directly to any kind of descriptive survey of common morality the results are unpersuasive. W. D. Ross, for example, lists five kinds of prima facie obligation: keeping promises, telling the truth, being grateful for benefits received, making restitution for injuries done, and, as a kind of utilitarian bedspread, designed to cover the very large area of the field left uncovered, doing as much good as possible. It turns out that this list, apart from its last item, is derived from Grotius and is not the outcome of any independent enquiry.

If one actually looks at the range of widely accepted moral beliefs the inadequacy of the Grotius–Ross list is obvious. Making restitution is parasitic on the far more important matter of not inflicting the injuries in the first place. Do not harm or injure others is, in actual moral life, the bedrock and first principle of morality. It embraces truth-telling and promise-keeping. Next in order of importance is what may be broadly described as charity (but in a narrower sense than that of the Charity Commissioners). The imperative here is to minimize suffering caused, not by oneself, but by other people or nature. The conferring of positive advantage on others (the leading implication of the phrase 'doing as much good as possible') is not, I would maintain, a requirement of morality at all. Mr Wardle of Dingley Dell was a very nice man, but one might feel that his beneficence could have been more thoughtfully and productively distributed.

Everyone knows that the ten commandments, a kind of moral archetype for Western civilization, are almost exclusively negative, a matter of prohibitions, of thou shalt nots. The first four are of a purely religious nature: the ones about no other gods, graven images, taking the name of the Lord in vain, and not working on the Sabbath. The remaining six—forbidding murder, adultery, theft, false witness, coveting, and requiring one to honour one's parents—are all, with the exception of the last, negative. They are also much the same as the varieties of harm to others which I have said it is the common purpose of law and morality to prevent. It is interesting that there is no reference to charity or alms-giving in this list, but it makes an appearance later on in Deuteronomy.

Now the fact that Law has as its first aim the enforcement of the fairly accepted core of morality is the best reason I know of for believing that one morally ought to obey it. For I have not denied that there is good moral reason for obeying the law and more generally the government that upholds it. I have been concerned only to deny that it is the only good reason for obedience, as if the reasonableness of obedience stands or falls with the moral appeal it has for its citizens.

But the politician, or, to use a politer and in this connection more relevant term, the statesman or ruler, is not a moralist. He does not discover or invent the moral principles it is the primary purpose of the law to enforce. For the most part they are a traditional, customary inheritance. He will seek to change them from time to time in accordance with shifts in the prevailing moral consensus. He needs, to be successful, to be sensitively perceptive about doing so. If not he will cause social disasters like Prohibition in the United States.

As a ruler, furthermore, his motive will not be principally the moral improvement of the citizenry but the preservation of public order. As I said, one of the prevailing limitations on the amount of commonly accepted morality he will call upon the law to enforce is that only offences liable to excite violent reaction should be legally prohibited. Just like anyone else he ought to guide his personal conduct by basic moral principles, but he does not have to be a crusading moral enthusiast to perform his task well. In areas of lively moral controversy it is perfectly proper for him to sustain a law with whose moral correlate he does not agree, on the ground that it is necessary for the preservation of peace.

In fact, not much of the legislation of a modern state is concerned with moral, rather than administrative or procedural matters. That is even more the case with the business of government in general. That is partly administrative, where the criteria are convenience and efficiency, and partly assistance to the nation's prosperity, which is not a matter of morality, being neither harm-prevention nor the relief of suffering (although it may indirectly contribute to the second of these). As the supplying of positive benefits, it is, rather, a matter of collective prudence. A further aspect of the government's business, which will need some special consideration, is the provision of national defence and the conduct of foreign relations. Some of those who are acknowledged to have been great statesmen have been moral enthusiasts. Cromwell and Gladstone stand out in British history. Walpole and Disraeli are at the opposite extreme, along with Palmerston and Churchill to a less insistently non-moral extent. On the whole it would probably be agreed that the more non-moral (but not conspicuously immoral) rulers do less harm than enthusiastically moral ones. The main tasks of the ruler are three: internal and external security and prosperity. Only the first of these is a moral purpose, although strictly defensive military policy is harm-preventing. And it is not the moral aspect of these tasks that should preoccupy a ruler. A good ruler is not a moral teacher or a pioneer, he is the skilled practitioner of a technique, that of preserving public order, protecting the community against its rivals or enemies, and enhancing its prosperity.

In the matter of conducting a country's relations with others, peaceful or belligerent, the ruler claims to be pursuing the national interest. That does not mean that he should repudiate treaties whenever he thinks he can get away with it. But he will abstain from doing it only in the spirit of A. H. Clough's lines about adultery: do not adultery commit, advantage rarely comes of it.

A different idea of the moral responsibilities of a ruler in international relations has, of course, often prevailed in practice. In our day the leading moral imperialist is, or has recently been, the United States. The policy has had two large apparent successes, the imposition of liberal-democratic institutions by force of arms on Germany and Japan. Our own predilection for the same sort of thing in the past has one large disaster to its discredit: the post-colonial regimes of sub-Saharan Africa, and one slightly unstable success: the still surviving democracy of India.

To question the wisdom of this kind of thing is not to rule out there being good moral reasons for assistance to countries in desperate need in other parts of the world. But the provision of relief for the destitute must be realistically tailored to the balance of altruism and self-interest in the population who have to foot the bill. And there are also good prudential reasons for such policies, to prevent distress taking the form of a violent reaction. In any case, the moral grounds for aid do not suffice for a complete resolution of the problem.

In seeking partially to disentangle morality and politics I have not been aiming, in a Machiavellian spirit, to separate them altogether. I have agreed that the state has a moral function, even if it primarily pursues it in the interests of public order. But it has other functions as well. Again, although there are good moral reasons for obedience to the state, they are supported by prudential ones, which are probably in practice the stronger. I have left much undiscussed: for example, the validity and strength of the moral claim for what is called social justice, conceived as the establishment of some kind of economic equality. But I hope I have gone some way towards showing that the usual assimilation of moral and political philosophy is a mistake.

22

Words on Words

I

The name of God was revealed to Moses as Yahweh, or, as we used to say, Jehovah. Some doubt is cast on the idea that Moses was the first to learn of it by the fact that the name of Moses's mother, Jochebed or Yokheved, already contains the name of God within it. At any rate in the post-Exilic period the Jews ceased to refer to God as Yahweh because the word came to seem too sacred to be spoken. What took its place was roughly God's title: Adonai, or Kyrios in Greek, that is, the Lord.

The instinct of the post-Exilic Jews was correct. The nature of one's ideas about religion is strongly conditioned by the words in which they are expressed. To be, mentally, on first-name terms with someone brings them down to a humdrum everyday level.

In English 'God' is surely the best, the most appropriate, of God's names. The stark and uncompromising monosyllable has a direct, categorical quality that is missing from such comparatively euphemistic, circumlocutory designations as 'Our Lord', which has a slight element of feudal quaintness. With such Augustan terms as 'Deity' or 'the Supreme Being' God is, as it were, put into commission, like 'H. M. Government' or 'the Sublime Porte'.

In French God takes on a stylized, courtly aspect. 'Dieu' is a more melodious, civil, and insinuating word than 'God' and to think of God as 'le Seigneur' immediately puts him into a long silk coat and knee-breeches and makes him capable of observing, with elevated eyebrows, 'L'univers, c'est moi'. The Italian 'Dio' seems most apt as the beginning of passionate entreaties. The Russian 'Bog' suggests something obscure, shapeless, and terrible.

More generally our religious vocabulary has its source in the Authorized Version of the Bible. From it we derive a great mass of words and phrases which are more or less peculiar to religious discourse. 'Amen', 'damsel', 'wrath', the pronoun 'ye', the verb-ending '-eth', 'serpent', 'woe', 'which being interpreted', 'I say unto you'. If these are messed about with in alternative translations of what it is here natural to call Holy Writ we feel that something essential has been lost.

In his recent book of selections from translations of the Bible between Tyndale's of 1534 and William Barnes's of 1859, Father Peter Levi provides interesting material for reflection. The Authorized Version is a splendid counter-instance to the law that committees always produce weak compromises. But its compilers did somewhat water down certain aspects of the language used by Tyndale and Coverdale, two earlier Protestant translators on whom they greatly relied. They turned 'thy staff and thy sheephook comfort me' into 'thy rod and thy staff they comfort me'. Neither rods nor sheephooks seem ideally calculated to yield comfort but the older word is more concrete and forceful. Those unapproachable damsels of the familiar Old Testament were prettied-up versions of the wenches of earlier translations, just the sort of person one would chat up at the well. 'Whosoever lieth carnally with a woman' is bleaker and more legalistic than 'whosoever lieth and meddleth with a woman'.

Two oddities quoted by Father Levi are the translation of the Song of Songs by William Barnes into Dorset dialect and the 'Liberal Translation' by Edward Harwood of 1768 in which the New Testament is put into the most stilted sort of eighteenth-century diction. For 'thy cheeks are comely with rows of jewels, thy neck with chains of gold' Barnes has 'your cheäks be comely wi' beäds, an' your neck wi' your chaïns'. Harwood sets about the following passage from St Matthew: 'then shall the righteous answer him, saying, Lord, when saw we thee an hungred and fed thee, or thirsty and gave thee drink?' In Harwood's version this becomes: 'The righteous, alarmed at such an unexpected discourse, will then answer—Blessed Messiah! when did we see thee languishing with hunger, or fainting with thirst, and in these extremities relieved thee?'

To me it seems that the New English Bible was composed in a contemporary version of Harwood's spirit. When I found that 'And when he was come into Jerusalem all the city was moved, saying, Who is this?' had been changed into 'When he entered Jerusalem the whole city went wild with excitement' I meditated further translations in the same vein. 'In the beginning was the Word' might become 'To start with there was the remark'. 'I am black but comely O ye daughters of Jerusalem' in the language of a Gas Board leaflet might turn into 'I am coloured but physically attractive, you Jerusalem teenagers!

II

A particular aspect of the general bigness of America is attractively presented at the dinner of the Junta in chapter 8 of Max Beerbohm's *Zuleika Dobson*. The guest of its superb presider, the Duke of Dorset, is Mr Abimelech V. Oover, a Rhodes scholar from Trinity. 'Gentlemen', he says, when greeted upon entry, 'your good courtesy is just such as I would have anticipated from members of the ancient Junta. Like most of my countrymen, I am a man of few words. We are habituated out there to act rather than talk. Judged from the viewpoint of your beautiful old civilisation, I am aware my curtness must seem crude. But gentlemen, believe me, right here—'

'Dinner is served, your Grace.'

'Thus interrupted, Mr Oover, with the resourcefulness of a practised orator, brought his thanks to a quick but not abrupt conclusion.' A little further on Max Beerbohm allows himself a few general reflections on the national tendency Mr Oover representatively displays. 'Americans', he says, 'individually, are of all people the most anxious to please. That they talk over-much is often taken as a sign of self-satisfaction. It is merely a mannerism. Rhetoric is a thing inbred in them. They are quite unconscious of it. It is as natural to them as breathing. And, while they talk on, they really do believe that they are a quick, business-like people, by whom things are "put through" with an almost brutal abruptness.'

And before Beerbohm the rhetorical abundance of Americans had caught the attention of Dickens. When Martin Chuzzlewit tells General Choke that Queen Victoria does not, as the General supposes, live in the Tower of London he is deluged with the following reply.

Hush, pray silence. I have always remarked it as a very extraordinary circumstance, which I impute to the natur' of British institutions and their tendency to suppress that popular inquiry and information which air so widely diffused even in the trackless forests of this vast Continent of the Western Ocean, that the knowledge of Britishers themselves on such points is not to be compared with that possessed by our intelligent and locomotive citizens. This is interesting and confirms my observation. When you say, sir, that your Queen does not reside in the Tower of London, you fall, into such an error, not uncommon to your countrymen, even when their abilities and moral elements air such as to command respect. But, sir, you air wrong. She *does* live there.

What is the explanation of this insupportable loquacity? One possibility is that it was established as a national practice by the first settlers, extreme Protestants of an opinionated kind, given to the production of and attention to gigantic sermons, and inspired to endure the hazards of early colonization by a desire to discharge their ignorance and presumption without interference in the wide open spaces. In a community of half-educated people where there is no one to correct gaseous folly it will inevitably thrive and proliferate.

America is as diverse as it is large and the other side of the picture should not be forgotten. Men from Vermont are notoriously short-spoken and non-garrulous. President Coolidge was such a man and can stand comparison with the legendary Yorkshireman who when asked 'where's the wife, then?', replied 'upstairs'. To the further question 'restin'?' he answered 'No, she's dead.' A young woman turned to Coolidge at a dinner party and said she had made a bet that she would get three words out of him. His reply was 'You lose.'

But this is really just deliberate resistance to the prevailing current. I read in an American newspaper recently of a prisoner being taken by the arresting officer to 'the downtown detention facility'. More generally, it seems that almost any American can make a speech that sounds like a speech. Their readiness to take the stand compares very starkly with the fumbling and broken sentences brought forth by Englishmen on festal occasions. This thought suggests a more genial interpretation of American talkativeness than the persistence of a practice established by opinionated dissenters.

Consider the American social introduction. Names are ringingly and memorably pronounced. And as soon as they are put in circulation they are boldly and audibly used. 'Hi, there, Anthony,' they will say, 'and is this the first time you have visited with us in the state of South Dakota'. In England the principle appears to be that either you know the person already or do not really want to know them. Talk is a function of sociability and the more widely people are spaced the keener they are to be sociable. The volubility of Americans is a form of welcome; the mumness of Englishmen a device for the protection of menaced privacy.

III

Once upon a time the word 'society' was mainly used to refer to the most prominent, or at any rate the richest, section of the community. 'They are not in society' did not mean that they were hermits but that they did not go to the most sought-after parties. 'Society Notes' in a paper would recount the doings of titled persons: their divorces, their Swiss holidays, the prospects of their racehorses for the coming season, the places they went to for mudpacks and tango lessons. Today a column with that title might just as well be about the problems of meths drinkers in Nuneaton or the incidence of vandalism in the public conveniences of the Scottish Lowlands.

Behind this wider use of the word lurks a mythology: the idea that a mysterious abstract object called Society is the ultimate cause of everything humanly interesting that happens in the world. The nineteenth-century philosopher Feuerbach maintained that the idea of God was an unconscious projection by men of the attributes of ideal humanity. In worshipping God, men were really worshipping mankind in an idealized form.

As it is now conceived, Society, in the abstract, is an object of more or less religious emotions, but of a more ambiguous kind than was Feuerbach's idealized humanity. Sometimes, when it is taken to mean just other people in general, it is favourably viewed. The judge says to some unpleasant criminal 'society needs protection from people like you'. He could just as well have said 'people in general need protection from people like you'. Here society is that whose interests and welfare are the ultimate criterion of what is right or wrong.

But there is a more questionable way of using the word. Confronted by some person who has acted in a vicious or disastrous way, people sometimes observe in a philosophical tone 'it's all society's fault really, isn't it?' What do they mean by this?

Consider some youth who has battered two old people to death in the course of stealing the savings they had hidden under the mattress. Are those who say it's all society's fault wanting to put the blame on everybody apart from the primary offender or what? That he is what he is and not another kind of person, in particular some kind of person who would not have killed the old couple or even set out to rob them, is indeed causally due to a great many other people in varying degrees. In the first place his parents, pretty much inadvertently, supplied him with his genetic constitution. They will ordinarily have had a more controllable effect on him through the way in which they brought him up. The next set of people likely to influence his ideas about what it is natural or acceptable to do, whether positively or negatively, are his teachers and friends. More remotely the advertisers and television producers who helped form his ideas about possible objects of desire and attractive styles of living could be brought in. And beyond them lie the shareholders and so forth on whose behalf the advertisers and television men were filling his mind with dangerous images. But even if we go this far we are still well short of society as such, the whole totality of human beings with whom our thief is in some sort of social relations.

More important is the fact that in shifting responsibility from the primary offender to other people in general, this way of thinking really eliminates the concept of responsibility altogether. For if society is responsible for his bad conduct surely it must also be responsible for the particular bits of misbehaviour by which its members led him into bad ways? This line of argument has everyone taking in everyone else's moral washing, or, to vary the image, the buck passes from hand to hand without ever coming to rest.

Schopenhauer neatly observed about those who say that since every event has a cause there must be a first cause which is itself uncaused, 'we cannot use the causal law as if it were a sort of cab, to be dismissed when we have reached our destination'. The same is true of the principle of transferred responsibility.

It is perfectly all right to talk about particular societies or social groups: families, classes, firms, associations. But talk of society in general is almost bound to be rubbish. Man is an essentially social being, in the sense that men would not have their characteristically human qualities, intellectual and moral, unless they had had social relations to other men. Like air, society is always somehow present, however unnoticeably. To try to explain things by it is no more substantial and informative than saying 'well, that's the way things are'.

IV

One of the most noticeable defects of other people's conversation is that usually about a third of it is made up of words that appear to do no work at all. The phrase 'sort of' is the most prominent of these expressions, although it is not the most representative. For it does have a function, even if only a negative one, that of disclaiming responsibility for a feeble or imprecise choice of words. 'She was wearing a sort of cloak' is an economical and ordinarily quite adequate substitute for 'she was wearing an Inverness cape'. Indeed it can be perfectly respectable, as when it is used to show that something is not a standard sample of the kind of which it is said to be. 'He is a sort of policeman' is an entirely acceptable description of a full-time laboratory technician at Scotland Yard. A First Sea Lord's wife who said 'my husband is a sailor' would be speaking more loosely than if she had said 'my husband is a sort of sailor'. 'A sort of so-and-so' can usefully mean 'a so-and-so of an unusual kind'. All the same the phrase is more common as a mild gesture of defeat, as is its more demotic equivalent 'like'. 'It's at the back of the cupboard, like', or even 'he doesn't know where he's put it, like'.

There are, however, some expressions that are almost completely versatile. The phrases 'I mean' and 'you know' can occur without comic effect and quite naturally in the midst or at either end of any but the shortest remarks. 'I mean I didn't plan to do it', 'he's older than that, you know'. And they can pass unnoticed even with very brief remarks. 'When are you leaving?' 'Friday, you know'. 'What was the meal like?' 'I mean horrible'.

I suppose that the common use of these phrases is a degenerate version of a way of employing them in which they have a real communicative point, 'He treated her very badly, I mean he gambled away all her money as well as his own.' Here 'I mean' serves to spell out more fully and more specifically what has hitherto been no more than sketched, it is equivalent to 'to state my meaning more fully'. Or again it can be used to correct a careless or exaggerated utterance. 'He's quite mad, I mean you never know what he's going to do next'. Here it amounts to 'or rather, what I should have said'. In these, more functional uses, then, 'I mean' is an instrument for developing or correcting what was said too generally or too hastily in the immediate pressure of conversation.

'You know' likewise can be used to carry out the more positive task of reminding. Emphatically said—'*you know*, they used to live at number 16'—it expresses mild exasperation at a question the speaker feels need not have been put if the questioner had made a little mental effort. On other occasions 'you know' is an indicator of imprecision—'she's, you know, old-fashioned', where the point being made is that she is what I or we mean by 'old-fashioned', non-promiscuous perhaps, rather than what the dictionary would give for it.

For the most part, however, these expressions serve as the linguistic equivalents of what the pharmacist knows as excipients, namely 'that ingredient in a compound medicine which takes up or receives the rest', the neutral matter, in which the acetlsalicylic acid is contained, which makes up the manageable bulk of the aspirin. There are obvious reasons why therapeutic acids should be dressed up for the consumer. Does the same hold of conversation? Should we not strive to speak straight? Are these lumps of verbal chalk no more than devices to prevent someone else breaking in and to provide time for thinking up what to say next?

There is a possible justification, or at least explanation, for the universal reliance on these bits of linguistic junk, apart from mere loquacity and laziness. Stated baldly, a lot of what we have to say is more or less offensive. 'I am, I mean, a very experienced player' is less wounding to a defeated opponent than its untreated version. 'She was, you know, drunk' acknowledges a proper degree of embarrassment at having to convey the information in question.

The most charming of these verbal blushes to my mind is the adverb 'actually' 'Where did you go to school?', 'Eton, actually'. 'Is your father a duke?', 'Actually, yes'. Here it means 'I am slightly embarrassed at having to admit it but . . .' It is real English English and a source of constant delight to linguistically sensitive Americans. But embarrassment, of course, is a sort of very English thing. I mean Americans, you know, aren't actually embarrassed about anything, on the whole really.

The Balliol rhyme about Nettleship, a fellow there in the late nineteenth century makes him sound very nice and English.

> So to say—at least—you know
> I am Nettleship or so,
> Or, in other words, I mean
> What they call the Junior Dean
> You are gated after Hall:
> That's all: at least that's nearly all.

V

Theorists of the development of language seem to agree that its employment for purposes of factual description and rational argument is the last and highest stage of its evolution. Before that stage was reached it was used to incite action by other people and revoke feelings in them, as in 'clear off' and 'rotten swine'. The earliest form of articulate speech was purely expressive, an uncalculating business of venting the emotions of the speaker, not directed at anyone in particular, or, perhaps, at all, a system of ritualized cries.

Cursing and swearing are the most conspicuous conversational residues of this earliest period in man's history as a discursive being. Now the ordinary repertoire of swear-words is almost exclusively composed of terms connected with religion and sex. 'Damn' and 'hell' are eschatological imperatives, one mentioning the ticket, the other the destination, of a trip to the place of eternal punishment. 'Bloody', we have all been brought up to believe, is a contraction of 'by Our Lady'. I am sorry to say that that piece of homespun etymology is not endorsed by the *Shorter Oxford English Dictionary*. That authoritative work divides the imprecatory use of the word into, first, 'in low English, an epithet expressing detestation' and, secondly, 'an intensive (adverb): very... and no mistake, abominably, desperately, colloquial to c 1750, now low English'. Both adjective and adverb are said probably to derive from 'sblood', that is to say, 'Christ's blood', so at least the religious connection is maintained.

Stronger maledictions are of sexual origin and character. Normal and abnormal varieties of sexual intercourse provide the two good old stand-bys. With the preposition 'off' attached they serve as forceful commands to go away. A thing mentioned as the grammatical object of one of these verbs is thereby said to be ruined, spoiled, or even destroyed. The sexual parts of the body are the other main source of swearwords. A person who is described as being either a male or a female genital organ is thereby said to be a fool, idiot, or generally incompetent person. Where the aim is to convey moral, rather than intellectual, disapproval the person is described as a quantity of excrement. Breasts do not figure much in swearing under that name, but as tits or boobs are used for the makers of silly mistakes and for the silly mistakes that they make. The word boob acquires such a use very naturally from its likeness to booby; a boob is the sort of folly a booby is qualified to perpetrate. I do not really suppose that boob so applied has anything more in common than identity of sound and spelling with its use (usually plural, as a dictionary would say) to refer to the breasts. In the latter sense it must be an up-to-date version of bub or bubby, which comes from the German colloquial *Bübbi* for teat.

Blasphemous swearing is clearly of great antiquity. The first medieval knight to have been dismounted in a joust must have cried 'Zounds' as he hit the greensward. It is not clear to me when low, colloquial, non-medical words of a sexual nature began to be used for purposes of imprecation. There are fine old, improper Anglo-Saxon terms in Chaucer but they seem to have been employed only in a straight-forward descriptive way. The miller did not say 'well I'll be swived (or swiven)' when he found out how he had been bamboozled.

The prime purpose of swearing is to express strong unfavourable emotion. It is natural, therefore, that swearwords should be drawn from dangerous, forbidden, consecrated domains. It may be that the supplanting of religion by sex as the supplier of strong language reflects the decline of literal religious belief. Does current sexual permissiveness spell the end of standard obscenity? If so, what will take its place?

It is sometimes said that the two great unmentionables in the present age are death and class. In time to come will the infuriated drivers of non-polluting electrical cars shout 'corpse' and 'putrefy off' at each other at the traffic lights, or foremen (elected, of course, by the factory council) address fumbling neophytes with 'look what you've done, you silly gentlemen'?

VI

There is, or used to be, a regular feature in the *Reader's Digest* called 'How To Increase Your Word Power'. It took the form of a handy, portable version of the television game 'Call My Bluff'. A list of unfamiliar words would be given and one was invited to choose between a group of suggested definitions of each of them. No doubt this served its purpose in a quiet way but there is a more direct method. I refer to discriminating use of *Roget's Thesaurus*.

Plato said that thinking is the soul's dialogue with itself and to many philosophers nowadays a natural interpretation of that remark is an article of faith. Thinking, they believe, is something that is essentially done with words. We do not have to suppose that the proper and immediate objects of thought are ideas or concepts to which words are attached. Thinking is just using the words themselves, but silently.

The chief objection to that view is that very often one knows somehow what one wants to say but can't find the right word for it. It is here that *Roget's Thesaurus* comes into its own. When I was preparing an earlier talk in this series, I wanted a word that meant 'having the capacity for doing many different things'. I tried 'all-round' in the index but it wasn't listed. So I tried 'many-sided', realizing that it wouldn't do but thinking it was in the right semantic neighbourhood. It led me to section 698, Skill, and there I found a wealth of suggestions. Able, accomplished, talented, versatile, many-sided, resourceful, ingenious, inventive, and so on for a column and a half.

The usefulness of Roget does not, of course, really disprove the Platonic theory about the nature of thinking. After all I had no difficulty in putting what I was in search of into words, viz. 'having the capacity for doing many different things'. It wasn't that I had *no* words; I had too many. I was looking for a single word and Roget supplied one, versatile.

Not that Roget confines his attention to single words. A delightful feature of each section is a list of what are called phrases. The edition that I have says that 'all obsolete words (some amusing curiosities excepted) have been removed' but either language has moved on a good deal since that revision or the reviser was pretty indulgent to amusing curiosities. Take this list of phrases in the section Disuse: to lay on the shelf, to lay up in ordinary, to lay up in a napkin, to consign to the scrap-heap, to cast, heave, or throw overboard, to cast to the winds, to turn out neck and heels, to send to the right-about, to send packing. I have never heard anyone say that he was laying something up in ordinary or sending something to the right-about.

Italicized foreign expressions stand out among the phrases, mostly in French or Latin. Thus under Obstinacy we are offered: *coûte que coûte, quand même, per fas et nefas, à tort et à travers, vestigia nulla retrorsum*. Occasionally there's a bit of Italian ('Natura il fece e poi roppe la stampa', which is 'after they made him they broke the mould') or even a bit of Greek.

For the most part Roget does not teach one new words: he reminds one of words one knows already, but has lost or never acquired the habit of using. It is not so much that one falls in love with words as that one subsides into a kind of steady matrimonial habit with them and makes do with them when there are, to use a Roget-like phrase, better fish in the sea. There are words one falls in love with. I have had affairs with 'rebarbative' and 'insidious' and 'eleemosynary' at various times. But tiresome as these passing infatuations may have been they are less to be deplored than failure to use and thus help keep alive the marvellously full, ample, copious, plentiful, abundant, flush, lavish, liberal, unstinted, rich, luxuriant, resources of our language. What Roget's groupings show is not that we have in English a large number of pure synonyms. If that were all his *Thesaurus* would serve only to assist us in elegant variation, although that is not something that is wholly to be despised. What it does make clear is that there is an immense number of near-synonyms, a vast variety of different verbal fittings in which our thoughts can be more or less exactly clothed.

The linguistic pliancy of English is, no doubt, connected to a certain nebulosity of thought. Roget's word-assemblages, studied persistently, have a slightly sinister effect in which distinctions run together. It was a good idea of Patrick Hamilton's to preface the chapters of his *Hangover Square*, a novel in which a man goes mad, with large chunks from Roget. With it as with other valuable medicines it may be dangerous to exceed the stated dose.

Select Bibliography of the Works of Anthony Quinton

1952: 'Seeming', *Proceedings of the Aristotelian Society*, 26: 235–52.
1954: 'On Punishment', *Analysis*, 14: 133–42.
1955: 'The Problem of Perception', *Mind*, 64: 28–51.
1957: 'Properties and Classes', *Proceedings of the Aristotelian Society*, 53: 35–58.
1958: 'Linguistic Analysis', in R. Klibansky (ed.), *Philosophy in the Mid-Century* ii. 146–202.
1958: 'The Neglect of Victorian Philosophy', *Victorian Studies*, 1: 245–54.
1960: 'Russell's Philosophical Development', *Philosophy*, 35: 1–13.
1960: 'Tragedy', *Proceedings of the Aristotelian Society*, suppl. vol. 34: 145–64.
1962: 'Spaces and Times', *Philosophy*, 37: 130–47.
1962: 'The Soul', *Journal of Philosophy*, 59: 393–409.
1963: 'The A Priori and the Analytic', *Proceedings of the Aristotelian Society*, 59: 31.
1964: 'Matter and Space', *Mind*, 73: 332–52.
1964: 'Contemporary British Philosophy', in D. O'Connor (ed.), *Critical History of Western Philosophy*, 531–56.
1964: 'Thought', in S. Nowell-Smith (ed.), *Edwardian England*, 253–3.
1965: 'Mind and Matter', in J. R. Smythies (ed.), *Brain and Mind* (London: Routledge) 201–33.
1965: 'Ethics and the Theory of Evolution', in I. T. Ramsey (ed.), *Biology and Personality*, (Oxford: Blackwell) 107.
1966: 'The Foundations of Knowledge', in B. Williams and A. Montefiore (eds.), *British Analytical Philosophy* (London: Routledge), 55–86.
1967: *Political Philosophy* (Oxford: Oxford University Press), ed. with introduction, 1–18.
1967: Articles in Edwards (ed.), *Encyclopedia of Philosophy* (New York: Macmillan): British philosophy (i. 369–96); Knowledge and belief (iv. 349–52); Popper, Karl (vi. 398–401).
1968: 'Two Conceptions of Personality', *Revue Internationale de Philosophie*, 22: 387–402.
1968: 'Perceiving and Thinking', *Proceedings of the Aristotelian Society*, suppl. vol. 42: 191–208.
1970: 'The Bounds of Morality', in *Metaphilosophy*, 122–41.
1970: 'Ryle on Perception', in G. Wood and P. Pitcher (eds.), *Ryle*, 105–35.
1971: 'Absolute Idealism', *Proceedings of the British Academy*, 57: 303–29.
1972: 'Russell's Philosophy of Mind', in D. Pears (ed.), *Russell*, (Garden City: Doubleday) 80–109.
1972: 'Social Thought in Britain', in Cox and Dyson (eds.), *The Twentieth Century Mind, 1900–1918*, 113–35.
1972: 'Freud and Philosophy', in F. Miller (ed.), *Freud*, 71–83.
1973: *The Nature of Things* (London: Routledge), 394pp.
1973: *Utilitarian Ethics* (Basingstoke: Macmillan), 117pp.
1974: 'Critical Theory: On the Frankfurt School', *Encounter*, 8: 14–36.
1974: 'Has Man an Essence?' R. I. P. Supplementry Volume, 8–14.
1974: 'Maurice in America', in Lloyd Jones (ed.) (London: Duckworth), *Bowra*.

1975: 'Social Objects', *Proceedings of the Aristotelian Society*, 72: 1–27.
1975: 'Popper: Politics without Essences', in de Crespigny (ed.), *Contemporary Political Theory*, London: Nelda 1971, 147–67.
1975: 'The Concept of a Phenomenon', in Pivčević (ed.), *Phenomenology and Philosophical Understanding*, 1–16.
1976: 'G. Croom Robertson: Editor 1876–91', *Mind*, 85 (337): 6–16.
1977: 'In Defence of Introspection', *Philosophic Exchange*.
1977: 'Inquiry, thought and Action: John Dewey's Theory of Knowledge', in R. S. Peters (ed.), *John Dewey Reconsidered*, (London: Routledge) 1–17.
1977: 'The Image of Man in 20th Century Literature', in *Purnells History of the World*.
1978: *The Politics of Imperfection* (London: Faber), 105pp.
1978: 'Objects and Events', *Mind*, 88 (350): 197.
1979: 'The Philosophy of Kant', in *Great Ideas Today*.
1980: *Francis Bacon* (Oxford: Oxford University Press), 90pp.
1980: 'Philosophers and Intellectuals', in Alan Bullock (ed.), *The Face of Europe* Oxford: Phaidon.
1980: 'Reflections on the Graduate School', in W. Frankena (ed.), *The Philosophy and Future of Graduate Education*.
1980: 'A Schoolmaster: John Davenport', in S. Hill (ed.), *People*.
1982: *Thoughts and Thinkers* (London: Duckworth).
1982: 'Wittgenstein', *Social Research*, 49: 4–31.
1983: 'Dewey's Theory of Knowledge', in R. S. Peters (ed.), John Dewey Reconsidered. London: Routledge.
1984: Introduction to Michael Roberts, *T. E. Hulme* (Manchester, Carcanet).
1984: 'Madness', R. I. P. Suppliment. 18: 17–41.
1984: 'Orwell's 1984 and Ours' (keynote speech to conference).
1985: 'The Inner Life', in P. Horden (ed.), *Philosophy and the Novel*.
1985: 'Science and Religion in Three Great Civilisations' (NYU).
1985: 'Philosophy', in *Encyclopedia Americana*.
1985: 'Schlick Before Wittgenstein', *Synthese*, 64: 389–410.
1986: 'Dr John Radcliffe', *Journal of the Royal Society of Medicine*, 79.
1986: 'Animals and Men', in *Great Ideas Today*.
1986: 'On the Ethics of Belief', in Heydon (ed.), *Education and Values*.
1986: 'Character and Will in Medical Ethics'.
1991: 'Ayer's Place in the History of Philosophy', RIP Supplement 30: 31–48.
1991: 'Coleridge and Nether Stowey', in *Writers' Houses* (London: Arts Council).
1993: 'Morals and Politics', R. I. P. Supplement 35: 95–106.
1994: 'Homosexuality', in Griffiths (ed.), *Philosophy, Psychology and Psychiatry*, 197–212.
1994: 'Political Philosophy', in A. Kenny (ed.) The Oxford Illustrated History of Western Philosophy.
1997: 'The Trouble with Kant', *Philosophy*, 72: 5–18.
1998: *From Wodehouse to Wittgenstein* (Manchester: Carcanet), 360 pp.
2001: 'The Rise, Fall and Rise of Epistemology', *Royal Institute of Philosophy Supplement*, 48: 61–72.
2004: 'A Cultural Crisis: the Devaluation of Values' and 'A Reavaluation of Values: Keeping Polities in its Place', in Haldane (ed.), *Values, Education and the Human World*, 33–67.

Index

Acland, Henry 32
Adams, Charles F. 77
Adams, Henry 68, 74, 77
Adams, Richard 186
Adler, Alfred 28
Adorno, T. W. 227
Aesop 186
Agricola, George 7–8, 11, 13
Albert, prince (husband of Queen Victoria) 74
Aldrich, Henry 29
Alexander, Samuel 138
analytic v. synthetic, analyticity 123–4, 130, 134–5, 141–2, 150–1
Anderson, John 138
animals 38–9, 180–211
Anne, queen of England 26–7, 30
Anselm, saint 5
Aquinas, saint Thomas; Thomism 12, 192
Archimedes 61
Aristippus of Cyrene 37
Aristotle 3–8 and *passim*
Arnauld, Antoine 38
Arnim, Bettina von 74
Arnold, Matthew 166, 222, 224–5, 236
Ashley, Anthony 74
Auden, W. H. 225
Augustine, saint 5, 93, 149, 155, 192, 203, 225
Austen, Jane 236
Austin, J. L. (20c philosopher) 146, 148–52, 158
Austin, John (19c jurist) 248
Autrecourt, Nicholas of 9
Averroës 15
Ayer, A. J. 16, 62, 91, 120, 137–52, 153, 158, 198

Bacon, Francis 3–16, 33, 35, 154–5, 171, 197, 223
Bacon, Roger 10–11, 13
Balfour, A. J. 84
Balliol, John 21
Baring, Harriet, wife of 2nd baron Ashburton 73
Barnes, W. H. F. (20c philosopher) 143
Barnes, William (19c poet) 256–7
Barts (St Bartholomew's Hospital) 29
Bathurst, Ralph 23
Baur, F. C. 61
Beaufort, Henry, 2nd duke of 27–8
Beerbohm, Max 257–8
Bell, Clive 137
Bentham, Jeremy 10, 82, 146

Bentley, Richard 22
Bergson, Henri 52, 103, 105, 107, 109, 110–11, 118–19, 121, 139, 227
Berkeley, George 16, 44, 54, 82, 89, 91, 145, 153–4, 156
Betterton, Thomas 25
Bewick, Thomas 188
Bingham, Joseph 22, 29–30
Bismarck, Otto, Fürst von 71, 73
Blandford, John, marquess of 27
Blessington, Marguerite, countess of 73–4
Blumberg, Albert 140
Bodin, Jean 13
Boerhaave, Hermann 34
Bogart, Humphrey 34
Bolingbroke, Henry, 1st viscount 30, 155
Bolton, Henrietta, duchess of 28
Bolzano, Bernard 108
Boyle, Robert 24, 33, 149
Bradley, F. H. 82–3, 90, 111, 139, 145, 156
Bradwardine, Thomas 3
Brandt, R. B. 246
Broad, C. D. 138–40, 145, 149, 157
Brontë, Charlotte 78
Brontë, Emily 236
Brown, Charles 72
Browning, Robert & Elizabeth Barrett 76
Buchan, John 80
Buffon, Georges-Louis, comte de 36
Bunsen, Christian, Freiherr von 71
Buridan, Jean 9, 12
Burke, Edmund 107, 246
Burkhardt, Johanna 62
Burns, Robert 78, 225
Burton, Richard 78
Bury, J. B. 13
Butler, Joseph 155, 168, 172, 246
Byron, George, 6th baron 70–1

Caird, Edward 64
Calvin, Jean 215
Cambridge Apostles 70
Cambridge Platonists 5, 82
canon 223–8, 231–9, 244–5
Cardano, Girolamo 7, 13
Carlyle, Thomas 68–9, 73, 78, 81
Carnap, Rudolf 120, 122, 139–45, 147, 150–1, 157
Carritt, E. F. 246
Cassirer, Ernst 139

Castiglioni, Arturo 34
causality, causation 9, 51–3, 57–9, 87, 101, 145, 201, 208–9
Cecil, Hugh, 1st baron Quickswood 103
Chandler, Raymond 139
Charles II, king of England 22, 25
Charlett, Arthur 29
Chaucer, Geoffrey 263
chimpanzees with linguistic ability 36, 196–7
Churchill, Winston 254
Cicero 7, 155, 219
Clark, Kenneth 188
Clarke, Samuel 155
Clifford, W. K. 151
Clough, A. H. 255
Coady, C. A. J. 160
Cobden, Richard 76
Cohen, Hermann 139
Cohen, M. R. 150
Coleridge, George 47
Coleridge, Hartley 40
Coleridge, Samuel Taylor 31, 34, 40–8, 80, 82, 225, 236
Coleridge, Sara, née Fricker 40–2
Colet, Louise 63
Collingwood, R. G. 137, 220
Conan Doyle, Arthur 31
Confucius 223, 244
Cook Wilson, J. 137–8, 140
Coolidge, Calvin 258
Copernicus, Nicolas 8, 14
Copleston, Frederick 7, 60
Cousin, Victor 63
Coverdale, Miles 257
Craven, William, 2nd baron 28
Crewe, Annabelle 68, 75–6
Crewe, Hungerford 68
Croce, Benedetto 139
Cromwell, Oliver 254

Dancy, Jonathan 160
Darwin, Charles 36, 180, 186, 192
Daudet, Alphonse 77
deists 155
Democritus 13, 15
Dennis, Nigel 28
Derby, Edward, 14th earl of 79
Derrida, Jacques 220, 227–8, 230, 232, 240, 242, 244
Derwentwater, earls of 22
Descartes, Cartesianism 5, 16, and *passim*
Dewey, John 5, 91–102, 138–9
Dewhurst, John 30
dialectic 64–6
Dickens, Charles 76, 235, 237, 258
Diderot, Denis 36–7
Didi-Huberman, G. 228

Digby, Everard 7
Disraeli, Benjamin 68–9, 72, 74, 76, 79, 254
Dryden, John 235
dualism 5, 36, 38, 149, 186, 192–4, 197–8
Dummett, Michael 158–9
Duns Scotus 12
Dürer, Albrecht 44, 188
Dworkin, Ronald 247

Edwards, Paul 137
Elgin, Thomas, 7th earl of 71
Eliot, T. S. 103, 105–6, 222, 236
Ellis, John 227
Emerson, Ralph Waldo 68, 76–7
Epicurus 13, 15, 37
Epstein, Jacob 105
Erasmus, Desiderius 3, 10, 156, 171, 225
Euclidean geometry 51
Euripides 222
Ewing, A. C. 157

falsification 12
Fanon, Frantz 226
Feigl, Herbert 140
Feuerbach, Ludwig 259
Feyerabend, Paul 220
Fichte, J. G. 5, 61, 62, 64–5, 86
Fischer, Ludwig 62
Fish, Stanley 229, 242
Fitzgerald, Edward 70, 233
Flaubert, Gustave 63, 77
Florentine Academy 6
Forster, E. M. 236–7
Foucault, Michel 220, 227–9
Fox, Charles James 69
Francis of Assisi, saint 203
Frege, Gottlob 5, 108, 122, 142, 158–9
Freud, Sigmund 37, 173, 228–9
Freudenthal, J. 7
Friedrich II, king in Prussia 36
Friedrich Wilhelm IV, king of Prussia 74
Froude, J. A. 78
funded experience 93

Galen 33
Galileo 111
Gallie, W. B. 91
Galois, Evariste 61
Galsworthy, John 237
Gasking, Douglas 148
Gassendi, Pierre 5, 149
Gaudier-Brzeska, Henri 103
Gemistus Pletho, George 6
George I, king of England 30
George, prince of Denmark 26
Gettier, Edmund 159

Gibbons, William 25
Gibbs, James 31
Gide, André 236
Gilbert, William 6, 8, 14
Gladstone, William Ewart 68, 70, 74, 77, 254
Gloucester, prince William, duke of 26
Godolphin, Sidney, 1st earl of 27
Goethe, J. W. von 74, 78, 233
Goldman, Alvin 159–61
Goncourt, Edmond & Jules de 78
Goya, Francisco de 188
Gray, Thomas 80, 225
Green, T. H. 54, 61, 82–90, 156
Grose, T. H. 83, 156
Grosseteste, Robert 12
Grote, George & Harriet 73
Grotius, Hugo 253
Guizot, F. P. G. 68

Haack, Susan 160
Habermas, Jürgen 220, 227
Hahn, Hans 142
Hallam, Arthur 70
Hamilton, Patrick 265
Hamilton, William 82, 155
Hamlyn, D. W. 155
Hanley, Fred 78
Hannes, Edward 26
Hardy, Thomas 226, 237
Harley, Robert, 1st earl of Oxford 30
Harris, W. T. 91
Hart, H. L. A. 253
Hartley, David 31, 34, 37
Hartmann, Nicolai 139
Harvey, William 8, 14, 35
Harwood, Edward 257
Hawthorne, Nathaniel 76
Hazlitt, William 43
Hearne, Thomas 22–3, 31
Hegel, Christiane 61
Hegel, Georg Wilhelm Friedrich 5, 34, 60–7, 90, 111, 137, 145, 155–6, 227–8, 246–7
Heidegger, Martin 138–9, 145, 220, 227
Helvétius, Claude-Adrien 34, 37
Hempel, C. G. 141
Henry VIII, king of England 3
Heraclitus 110, 114
Heytesbury, William 8–9
Hickes, George 23
high culture 222, 224–5, 231–3, 244–5
Hitler, Adolf 103
Hobbes, Thomas 5, 9–10, 16, 33, 36, 82, 106–7, 155, 192, 212–13, 223, 246–7
Høffding, Harald 7
Holbach, Paul-Henri, baron d' 36–8
Holcot, Roger 8

Hölderlin, Friedrich 62
Homer 97, 222, 235
Hone, Campbell 24
Hood, Thomas 74
Hooke, Robert 24
Hooker, Richard 5
Hopkins, Gerard Manley 225
Horkheimer, Max 227
Hornsby, Thomas 32
Hospers, John 246
Housman, A. E. 225
Hulme, T. E. 103–9
Humboldt, Alexander von 63, 74
Hume, David 4–5 and *passim*
Hunt, Holman 80
Hunt, Leigh 77–8
Husserl, Edmund 103, 107, 139
Hutchinson, Sara 42
Hynes, Samuel 107

idols of the mind 6, 9–10
Isocrates 222

Jackson, Jesse 220
James II, king of England 22–3, 25–6, 34
James, Henry 68, 77, 238
James, William 5, 34, 91–2, 110, 139–40, 147–8, 169
James Stuart, the Old Pretender 26
Joachim, H. H. 137, 139
Joad, C. E. M. 245, 246, 249
Johnson, Samuel 223, 225, 236
Jones, Alun 105
Jones, William 233
Joseph, H. W. B. 137–40

Kamptz, Karl Albert, Freiherr von 64
Kant, Immanuel 4–5 and *passim*
Karl I Ludwig, elector Palatine 19
Keats, John 68, 71–2, 75, 78, 80
Keble, John 21
Kemp Smith, Norman 138
Keppel, Joost van, 1st earl of Albemarle 26
Keynes, J. M. 142
Kierkegaard, Søren 17–18, 66
Kimball, Roger 232
Kinglake, A. W. 69–70, 76
Kipling, Rudyard 186
Kotzebue, August von 64
Krylov, I. A. 186
Kuhn, Thomas 220, 229

La Fontaine, Jean de 186
Laird, John 138, 155
Lamartine, Alphonse de 74–5
Lamb, Charles & Mary 41–3

Lamennais, Félicité de 68, 71
Landor, W. S. 68, 71–2, 80
Landseer, Edwin 188
Lange, F. A. 36
Lankester, Ray 31
Lansdowne, Henry, 3rd marquess of 76
Lawrence, D. H. & Frieda 43
Leavis, F. R. 236
Leavis, Q. D. 237
Leibniz, G. W. 4–5, 54, 154, 198
lekta 123
Leonardo da Vinci 188
Levi, Peter 256–7
Lewis, C. I. 139, 144, 151, 157, 170
Lewis, C. S. 205
Lewis, Wyndham 103, 105, 107
Linacre, Thomas 25
Liszt, Franz 74
Livingstone, David 79
Lloyd, Charles 41
Locke, John 5 and *passim*
Lodge, David 229
London Library 69, 73, 81
Longfellow, H. W. 76
Lorenz, Konrad 187–8
Lotze, Hermann 34
Louis Philippe, king of France 68, 74
Lower, Richard 24

Macaulay, Thomas Babington 76
Mach, Ernst 92, 151, 157
Machiavelli, Niccolò 246, 255
Mackie, J. L. 249
McTaggart, John 84, 138–9, 151
Malcolm, Norman 148
Mallock, W. H. 103
Mannheim, Karl 240
Mansel, H. L. 82, 155
Marcuse, Herbert 227
Marlborough, Sarah, duchess of 30
Marlowe, Christopher 225
Marshall, Thomas 23
Marx, Karl; Marxism 20, 62, 64, 66, 182, 201–2, 215–16, 218, 227–9, 229, 235, 246
Mary II, queen of England 26
Masham, Abigail 30
Mazzini, Giuseppe 80
Mead, Richard 23, 25, 29–30
Mehemet Ali 74
Melbourne, William, 2nd viscount 73
Menander 222
Merivale, Charles 70
Merton, Walter de 21
Merton calculators 3
Metternich, Klemens, Fürst von 75
Mettre, Julien Offray de la 34–9
Michelangelo 188

Midgley, Mary 189, 203
Mill, John Stuart 12, 16, 85, 87, 91, 123, 142–3, 150, 152, 155, 212, 226, 243, 246
Milman, Henry Hart 31
Milnes, Harriet 70
Milnes, Richard Monckton, 1st baron Houghton 68–81
Milnes, Robert Offley Ashburton, 1st marquess of Crewe 68, 76
Milnes, Robert Pemberton 69–70, 74, 78–9
Mirecourt, Jean de 9
Moltke, Helmut, Graf von 79
Monet, Claude 44
Montaigne, Michel de 10, 156, 171, 203
Montalembert, Charles, comte de 68, 71, 74
Moore, G. E. 103, 107–8, 137–9, 141, 143, 145, 148, 150, 153, 156–7, 246
moralistes 171
More, Thomas 3
Morrell, Ottoline 139
Moses 256
Mowat, Farley 187
Mure, G. R. G. 64
Mussolini, Benito 103

Nagel, Ernest 140
Napoleon III, emperor of France 68, 73, 76
Nettleship, R. L. 262
Neurath, Otto 141
Newman, J. H. 124
Newton, Isaac 15, 27, 61, 111, 148
Nias, J. B. 25–6, 31
Nicholls, Arthur 78
Nicod, Jean 140
Niethammer, F. I. 62
Nietzsche, F. W. 5, 66, 106, 110, 121, 161, 228–30, 232
Nifo, Agostino 15
Nightingale, Fanny, née Smith 76
Nightingale, Florence 75
Nizolius, Marius 7
Norton, Caroline & George Chapple 73
Nuffield, 1st viscount (William Morris) 21
Nutley, William 28–9

Ockham, William of 3, 8–12, 16, 54, 84
Ogden, C. K. 143
Oliphant, Laurence 77
Oresme, Nicholas 9
original sin 104, 106
Orsay, Alfred, comte d' 73, 76
Orwell, George 233, 237

Palissy, Bernard 13
Palmerston, Henry, 3rd viscount 68–9, 73, 75, 78–9, 254
Parmenides 156

Pascal, Blaise 13, 225
Passmore, J. A. 107
Paterson, John 26
Patmore, Coventry 68, 74
Pearson, Karl 151
Peel, Robert 68–9, 72–3, 75
Peirce, C. S. 5, 89, 91–2, 94, 148, 150
Pembroke, William Herbert, 3rd Earl of 21
Perry, R. B. 169
Philobiblion Society 77
Picasso, Pablo 188
Pinkard, Terry 63–6
Pittis, William 25–8
Plato 4 and *passim*
pleasure 37, 104, 170–2, 194
Poincaré, Henri 140
Poole, Thomas 40–1, 43–4
Pope, Alexander 27
Popper, K. R. 12, 64, 92, 150–1, 160–1, 176
Potter, Beatrix 186
Potter, John 22
Pound, Ezra 103, 235
Price, H. H. 91, 101, 138–9, 143, 145–6, 149, 153, 157, 160, 195
Prichard, H. A. 137–40, 150, 157
Priestley, Joseph 37
process philosophy 110–21
Proust, Marcel 238

Quiller-Couch, Arthur 69
Quine, W. V. 5, 97, 122–36, 146–7, 150–1, 153

Radcliffe, George 22
Radcliffe, John 21–33
Ramsey, Frank 138–42, 145
Ramus, Petrus 7–8
Raphael (Italian painter) 188
Raphael, D. D. 246, 249
Rawls, John 247
Read, Herbert 105
Reichenbach, Hans 140, 151, 157
Reid, Thomas 155, 157
relations 9, 53–4, 82–90, 156
Rensberger, Boyce 187
Rhys, Ernest 224
Richards, I. A. 107, 143
Roberts, Michael 105
Roget, P. M. 263–4
Rorty, Richard 221, 225, 229–30, 240
Rosenkranz, Karl 60
Ross, W. D. 253
Rossetti, Dante Gabriel 80
Rossi, Paolo 6–7, 11, 13
Rousseau, Jean Jacques 217, 246
Rowney, Thomas 32
Royal Society 24, 27
Royce, Josiah 139

Rudolf, crown prince of Austria-Hungary 79
Russell, Bertrand 5 and *passim*
Rye House plot 25–6
Ryle, Gilbert 120, 122, 138–40, 144, 146, 149, 151, 157

Sacheverell, Henry 27
Sade, marquis de 68
Sand, George 74
Sanderson, Robert 82
Santayana, George 138–9
Sappho 236
Sartre, Jean-Paul 193, 220, 227–8
Scaliger, J. J. 15
Schelling, Friedrich 5, 62–3
Schiller, Ferdinand 92, 110
Schiller, Friedrich 62
Schlegel, August, Karoline, & Karl 62
Schleiermacher, Friedrich 63–4
Schlick, Moritz 120, 122, 141, 145, 147, 157
Schliemann, Heinrich 77
Schopenhauer, Arthur 5, 66, 171, 260
Scott, Gilbert 21
Scott, Walter 237–8
Seton, Ernest Thompson 186
Sextus Empiricus 9, 156
Shaftesbury, Anthony, 1st earl of 25, 34
Shaftesbury, Anthony, 7th earl of 74
Shakespeare, William 226
Sheldon, Gilbert 24
Shelley, Percy Bysshe 70–1, 237
Sherlock, William 30
Sherman, William Tecumseh 77
Shoemaker, Sydney 144
Short, Thomas 26
Sibthorp, John 31
Sidgwick, Henry 246
Singer, Charles 34
Singer, Peter 180
Smart, J. J. C. 151
Smith, Sydney 74
Smythe, George (Lord Strangford) 72, 75
sociobiology 201–2, 209
Sophia, electress of Hanover 30
Sophists 155
Sorel, Georges 103, 105–6
Sorley, W. R. 7
Spedding, James 70, 73
Spencer, Jane, née Gerrard 25
Spinoza, Baruch 17–20, 65, 154, 203
Sprat, Thomas 27
Steele, Richard 28
Stewart, Dugald 155
Stirling, J. H. 82
Stirling-Maxwell, William 77
Stoics 98, 123, 214
Stout, G. F. 156

Strawson, Peter 153, 158
Strickland, Agnes 81
Stubbs, George 188
Suleiman Pasha 76
Swift, Jonathan 27
Swinburne, Algernon 68, 76–8, 80
Sydenham, Thomas 24–5, 33
synthetic *a priori* 51

Tarski, Alfred 229
Telesio, Bernardino 11, 15–16
Temple, William 7
Tennyson, Alfred 68, 70–1, 74, 76–7, 85
testimony 101–2, 147, 154, 160–1, 165–6
Thackeray, William Makepeace 68, 70, 235
Thelwall, John 43
Thiers, Adolphe 68, 74
Thirlwall, Connop 75–6
Thomism *see* Aquinas
Ticknor, George 76
Titian 188
Tocqueville, Alexis de 68, 74
Tolstoy, Leo 226, 237–8
Trilling, Lionel 239
Trollope, Anthony 77
Turgenev, I. S. 77
Twain, Mark 237
Tyndale, William 256–7

Urbach, Peter 8, 14
Urmson, J. O. 157

Vaihinger, Hans 110, 139
Valera, Eamonn de 74
Valla, Laurentius 7
Varnhagen von Ense, K. A. 74
Vaughan, Charles 31
Veronese, Paolo 188
Vico, Giambattista 66
Villon, François 225
Virgil 235
Vives, Ludovicus 11
Voltaire 20, 36, 78, 154, 171, 203

Wadham, Nicholas & Dorothy 21
Waismann, Friedrich 148

Waley, Arthur 233
Walker, Obadiah 22–3, 26
Wallis, John 24
Walpole, Robert, 1st earl of Orford 254
Walton, Izaak 82
Warburton, Elliot 69, 78
Ward, James 111, 156–7
Warnock, Geoffrey 100
Washoe *see* chimpanzees with linguistic ability
Watts, Alaric 81
Waugh, Evelyn 237
Wedgwood family 43
Wellman, Kathleen 34, 37
Wells, H. G. 31
Whewell, William 150
Whitehead, A. N. 45, 110–12, 118, 120, 129, 138
Whitman, Walt 68, 76, 225
Wilkins, John 24
William III, king of England 26–7
Williams, Bernard 144
Williams, Raymond 232
Williamson, Henry 186
Willis, Thomas 24–5, 33
Wilson, E. O. 188, 201, 209
Wilson, Patrick 161
Windelband, Wilhelm 246
Wisdom, John 148
Wise, Francis 32
Wiseman, Nicholas 71
Wittgenstein, Ludwig 5, 122, 138–9, 141–2, 144–5, 148–9, 151–2, 157–9, 161, 193, 201
Wodham, Adam 8
Wolff, Christian, Freiherr von 4, 206
Wolfson, Isaac 21
Woolf, Virginia 236
Wordsworth, Dorothy 41–4
Wordsworth, William 41–4, 46, 64, 71
Wren, Christopher 24, 33
Wright, G. H. von 169
Wyclif, John 3, 82

Yeats, W. B. 103

Zola, Emile 77